# RADIANT

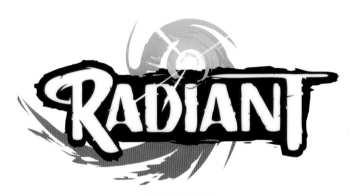

TONY VALENTE

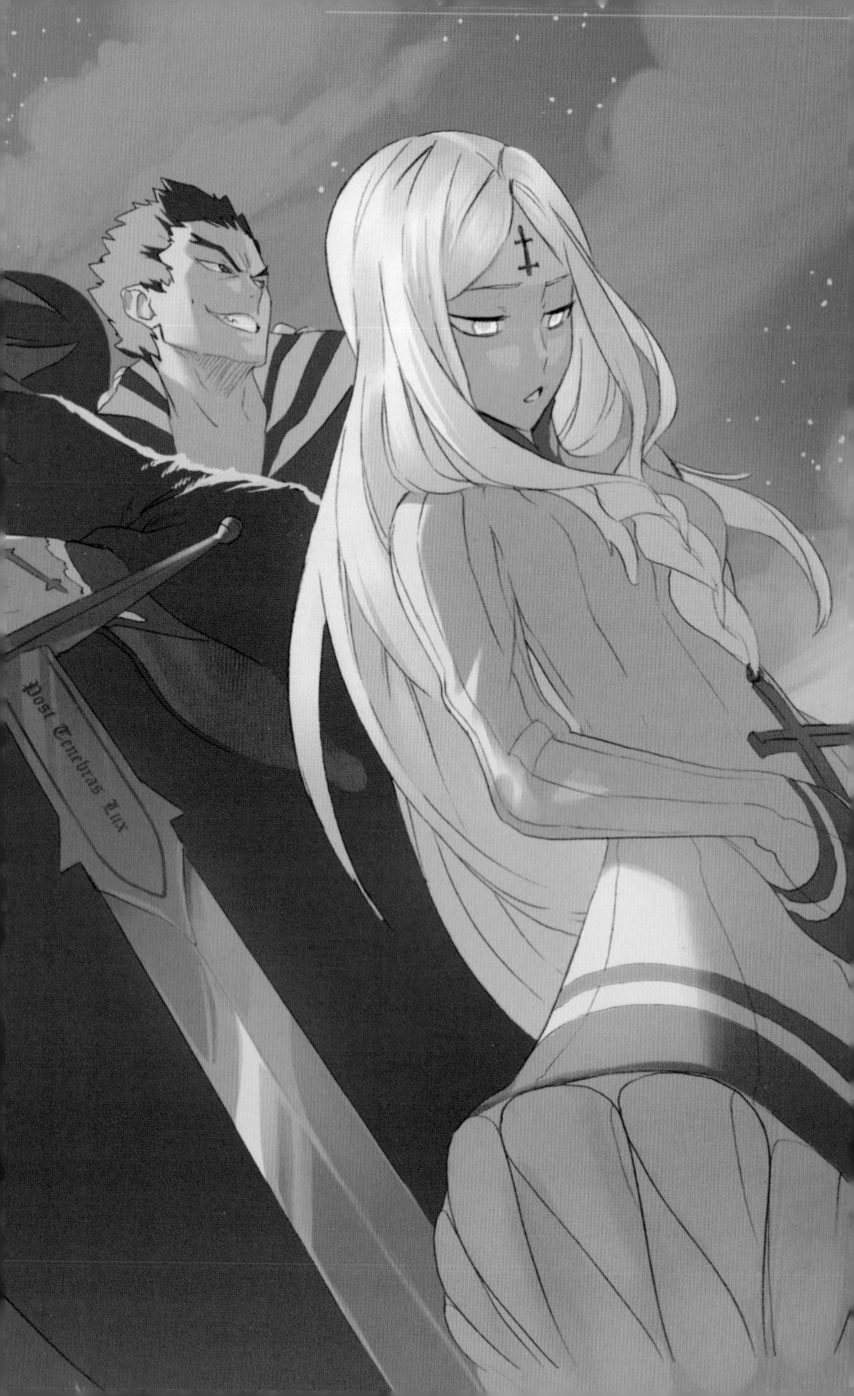
Post Tenebras Lux

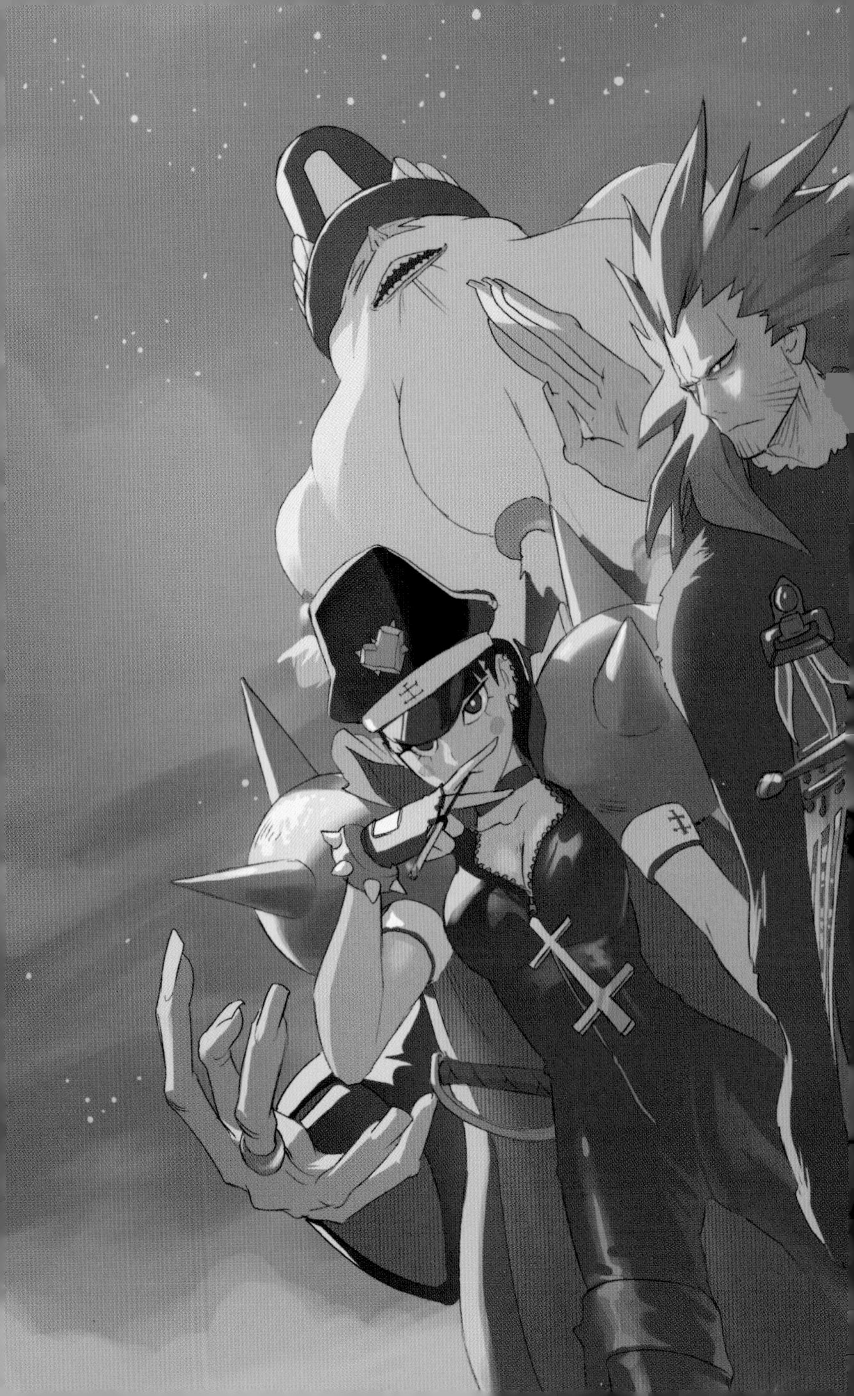

# CONTENTS

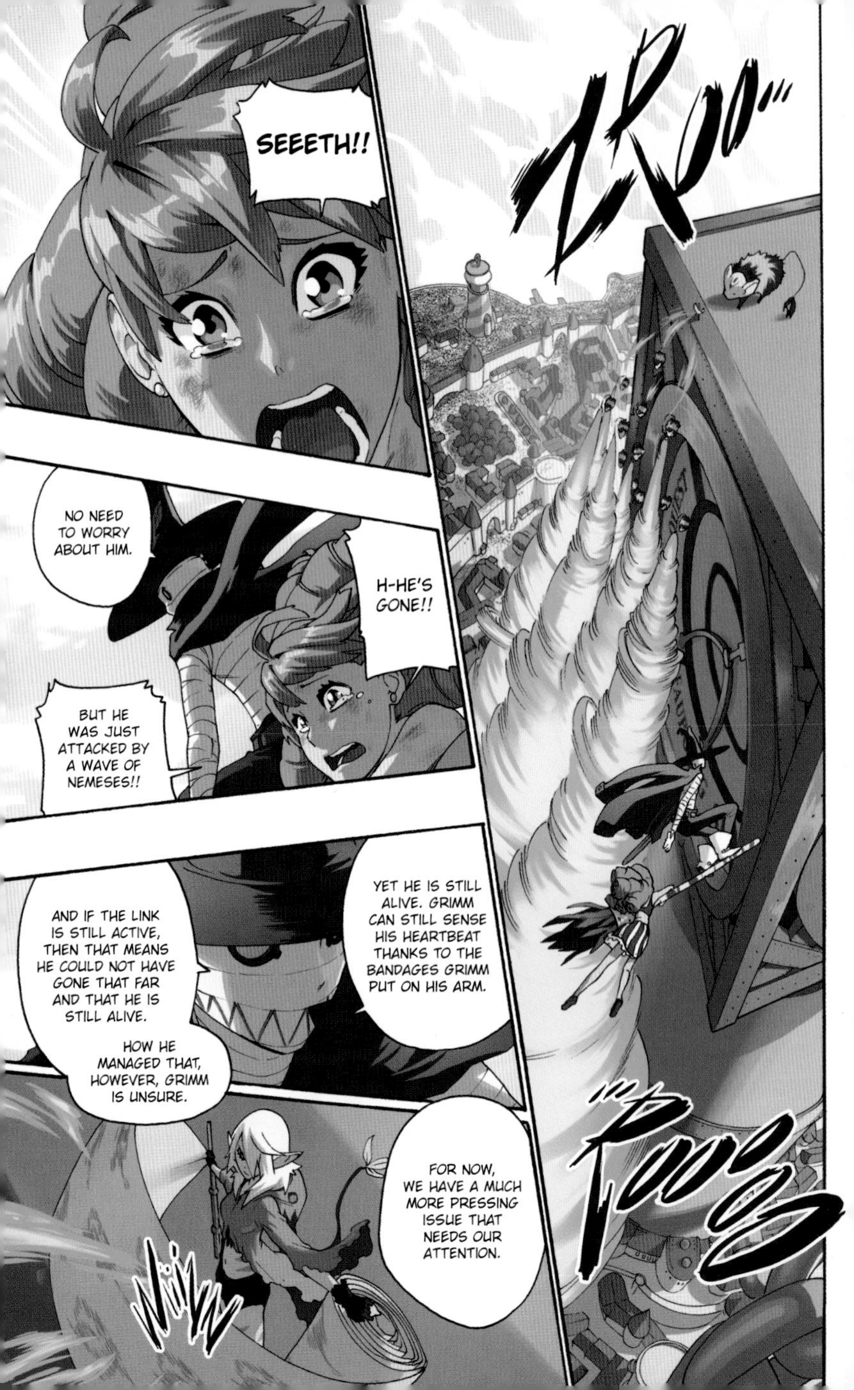
SEEETH!!
H-HE'S GONE!!
NO NEED TO WORRY ABOUT HIM.
BUT HE WAS JUST ATTACKED BY A WAVE OF NEMESES!!
YET HE IS STILL ALIVE. GRIMM CAN STILL SENSE HIS HEARTBEAT THANKS TO THE BANDAGES GRIMM PUT ON HIS ARM.
AND IF THE LINK IS STILL ACTIVE, THEN THAT MEANS HE COULD NOT HAVE GONE THAT FAR AND THAT HE IS STILL ALIVE.
HOW HE MANAGED THAT, HOWEVER, GRIMM IS UNSURE.
FOR NOW, WE HAVE A MUCH MORE PRESSING ISSUE THAT NEEDS OUR ATTENTION.

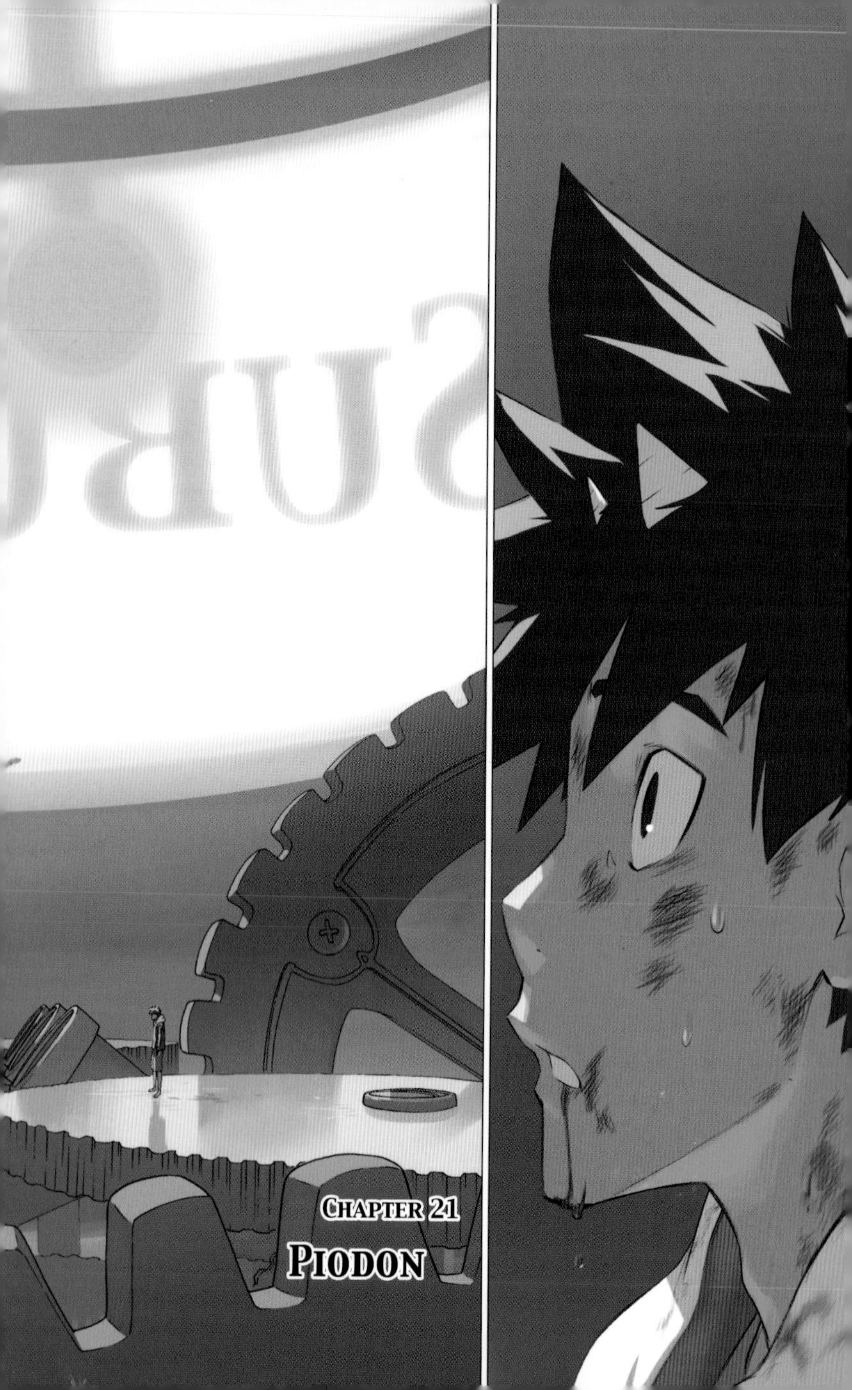
Chapter 21
Piodon

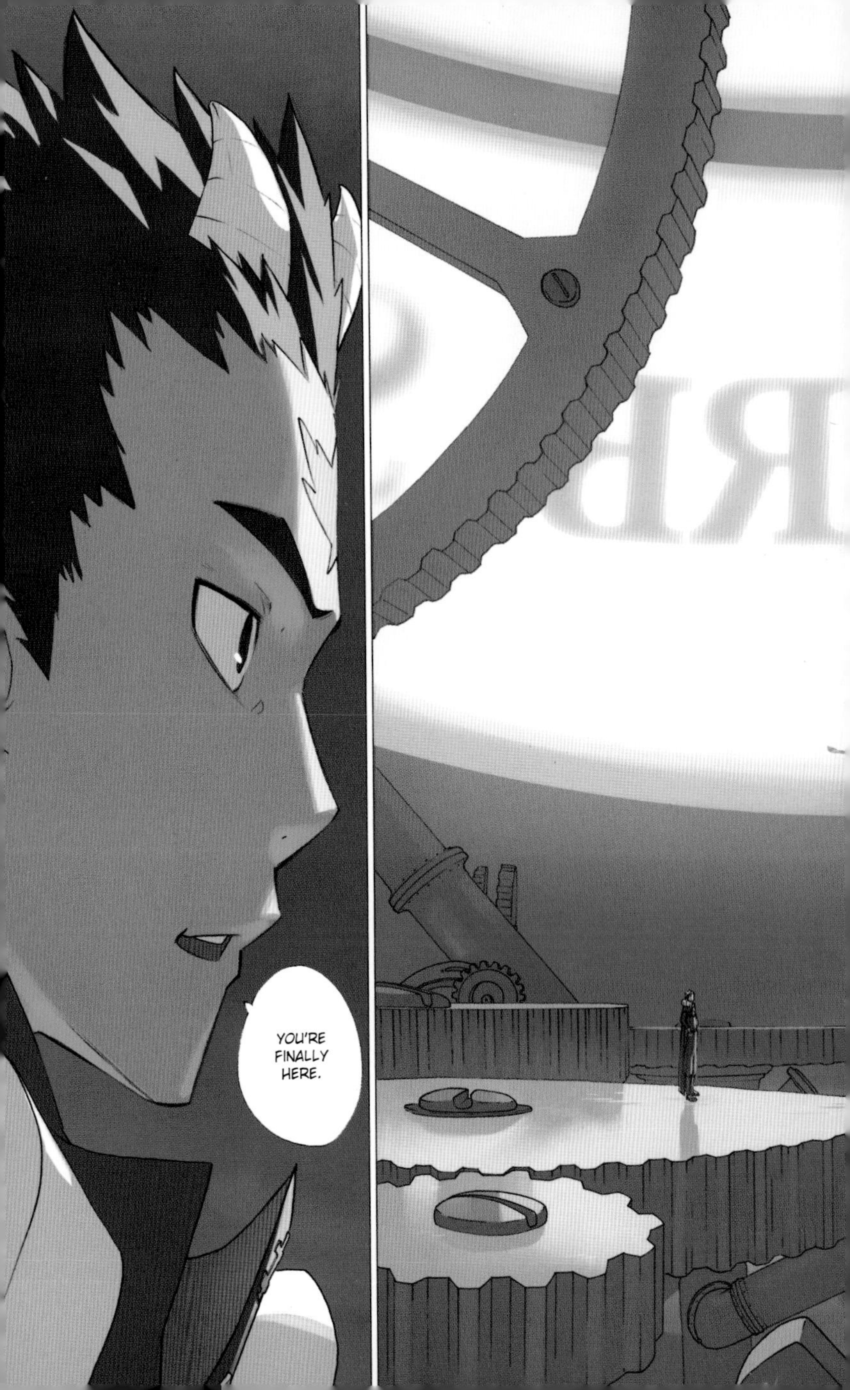
YOU'RE FINALLY HERE.

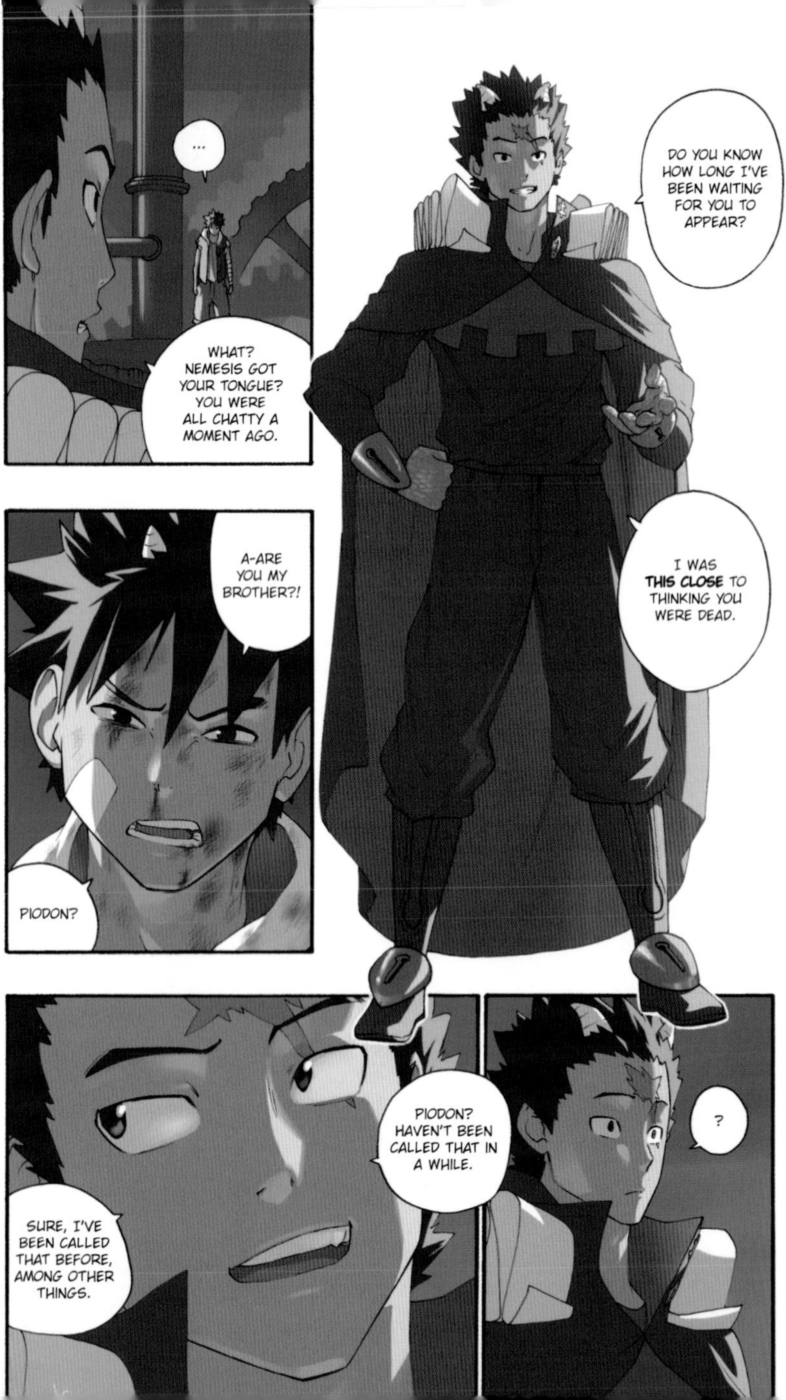
DO YOU KNOW HOW LONG I'VE BEEN WAITING FOR YOU TO APPEAR?
I WAS **THIS CLOSE** TO THINKING YOU WERE DEAD.
...
WHAT? NEMESIS GOT YOUR TONGUE? YOU WERE ALL CHATTY A MOMENT AGO.
A-ARE YOU MY BROTHER?!
PIODON?
?
PIODON? HAVEN'T BEEN CALLED THAT IN A WHILE.
SURE, I'VE BEEN CALLED THAT BEFORE, AMONG OTHER THINGS.

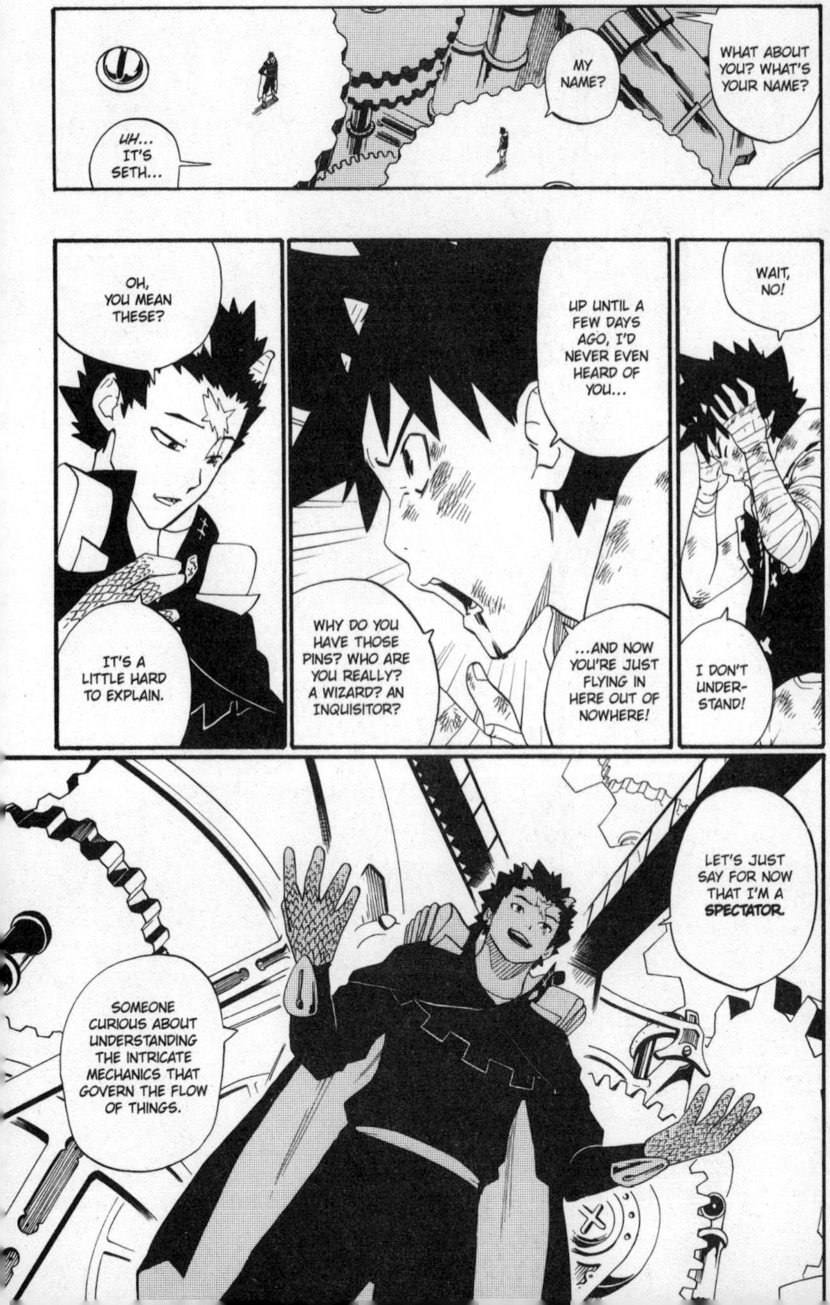
WHAT ABOUT YOU? WHAT'S YOUR NAME?
MY NAME?
UH... IT'S SETH...
WAIT, NO!
I DON'T UNDER-STAND!
UP UNTIL A FEW DAYS AGO, I'D NEVER EVEN HEARD OF YOU...
...AND NOW YOU'RE JUST FLYING IN HERE OUT OF NOWHERE!
WHY DO YOU HAVE THOSE PINS? WHO ARE YOU REALLY? A WIZARD? AN INQUISITOR?
OH, YOU MEAN THESE?
IT'S A LITTLE HARD TO EXPLAIN.
LET'S JUST SAY FOR NOW THAT I'M A **SPECTATOR**.
SOMEONE CURIOUS ABOUT UNDERSTANDING THE INTRICATE MECHANICS THAT GOVERN THE FLOW OF THINGS.

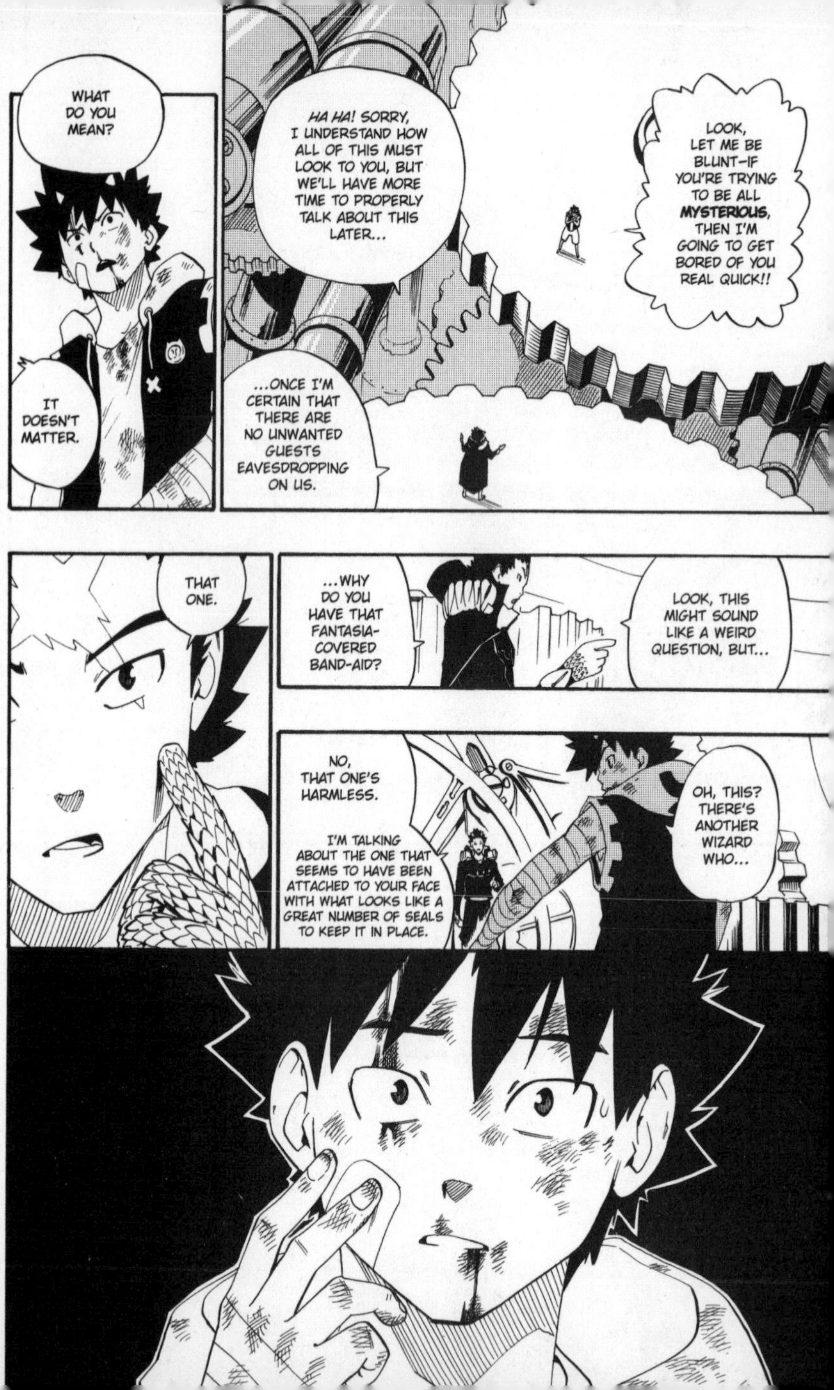
LOOK, LET ME BE BLUNT—IF YOU'RE TRYING TO BE ALL **MYSTERIOUS**, THEN I'M GOING TO GET BORED OF YOU REAL QUICK!!
*HA HA!* SORRY, I UNDERSTAND HOW ALL OF THIS MUST LOOK TO YOU, BUT WE'LL HAVE MORE TIME TO PROPERLY TALK ABOUT THIS LATER...
...ONCE I'M CERTAIN THAT THERE ARE NO UNWANTED GUESTS EAVESDROPPING ON US.
WHAT DO YOU MEAN?
IT DOESN'T MATTER.
LOOK, THIS MIGHT SOUND LIKE A WEIRD QUESTION, BUT...
...WHY DO YOU HAVE THAT FANTASIA-COVERED BAND-AID?
OH, THIS? THERE'S ANOTHER WIZARD WHO...
NO, THAT ONE'S HARMLESS.
I'M TALKING ABOUT THE ONE THAT SEEMS TO HAVE BEEN ATTACHED TO YOUR FACE WITH WHAT LOOKS LIKE A GREAT NUMBER OF SEALS TO KEEP IT IN PLACE.
THAT ONE.

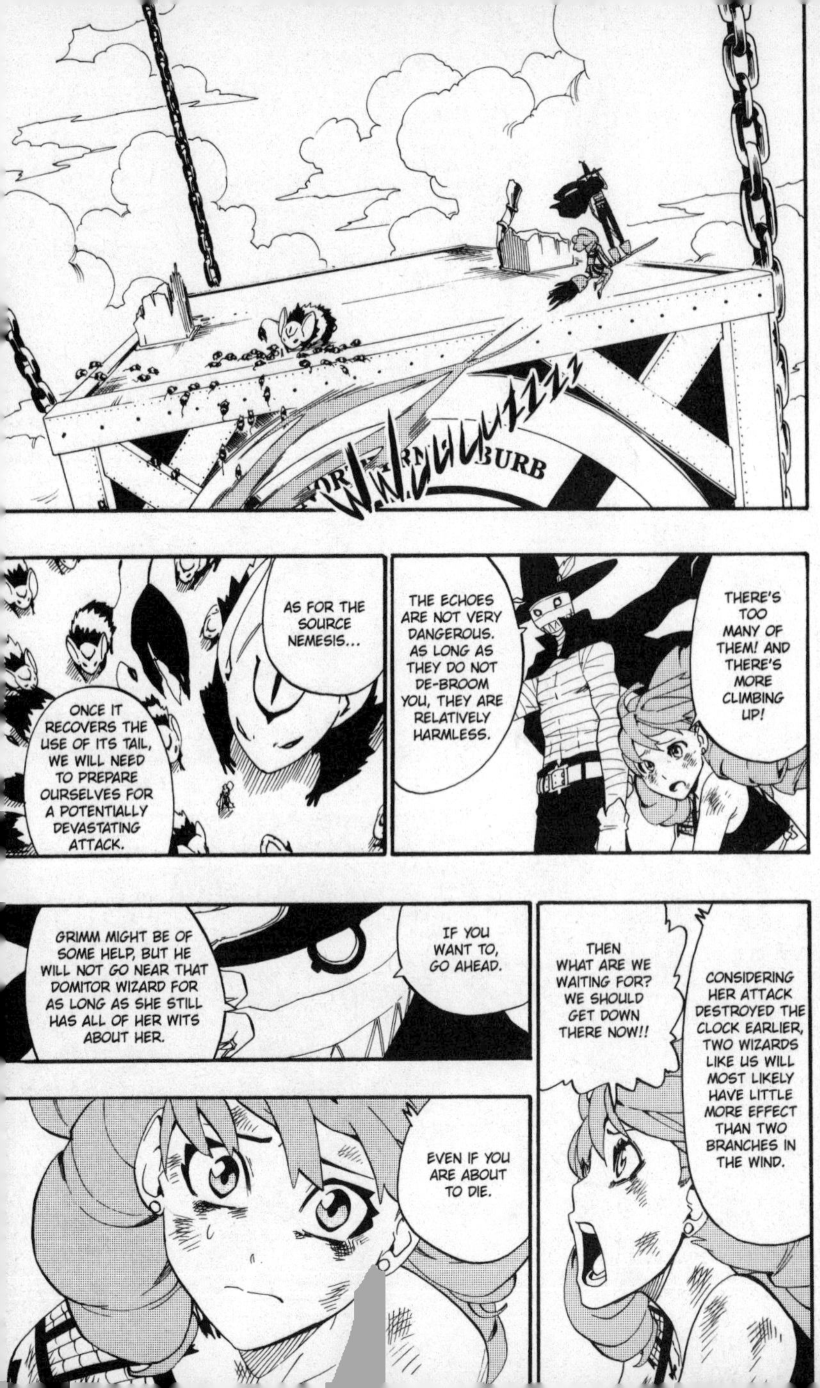
THERE'S TOO MANY OF THEM! AND THERE'S MORE CLIMBING UP!
THE ECHOES ARE NOT VERY DANGEROUS. AS LONG AS THEY DO NOT DE-BROOM YOU, THEY ARE RELATIVELY HARMLESS.
AS FOR THE SOURCE NEMESIS...
ONCE IT RECOVERS THE USE OF ITS TAIL, WE WILL NEED TO PREPARE OURSELVES FOR A POTENTIALLY DEVASTATING ATTACK.
THEN WHAT ARE WE WAITING FOR? WE SHOULD GET DOWN THERE NOW!!
CONSIDERING HER ATTACK DESTROYED THE CLOCK EARLIER, TWO WIZARDS LIKE US WILL MOST LIKELY HAVE LITTLE MORE EFFECT THAN TWO BRANCHES IN THE WIND.
GRIMM MIGHT BE OF SOME HELP, BUT HE WILL NOT GO NEAR THAT DOMITOR WIZARD FOR AS LONG AS SHE STILL HAS ALL OF HER WITS ABOUT HER.
IF YOU WANT TO, GO AHEAD.
EVEN IF YOU ARE ABOUT TO DIE.

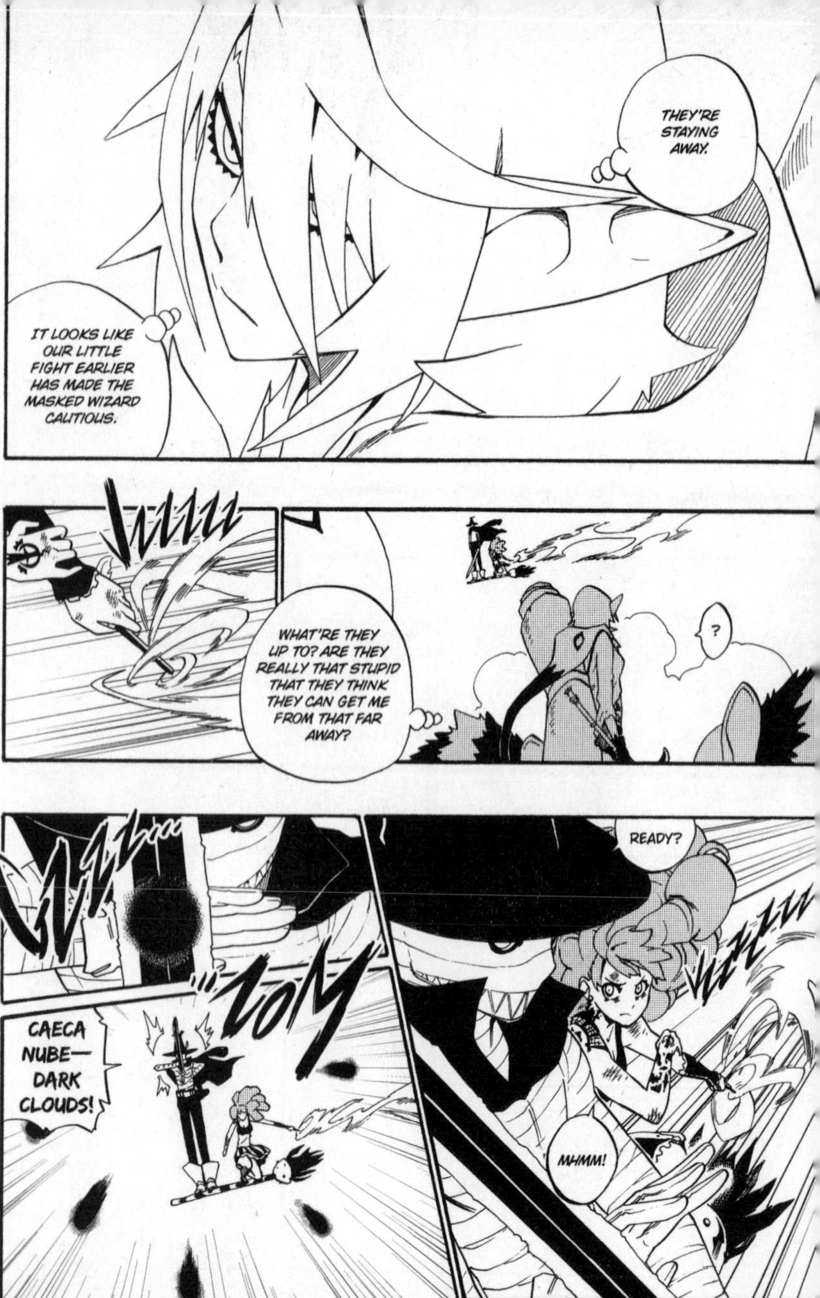
THEY'RE STAYING AWAY.
IT LOOKS LIKE OUR LITTLE FIGHT EARLIER HAS MADE THE MASKED WIZARD CAUTIOUS.
?
WHAT'RE THEY UP TO? ARE THEY REALLY THAT STUPID THAT THEY THINK THEY CAN GET ME FROM THAT FAR AWAY?
READY?
MHMM!
ZOOM
CAECA NUBE— DARK CLOUDS!

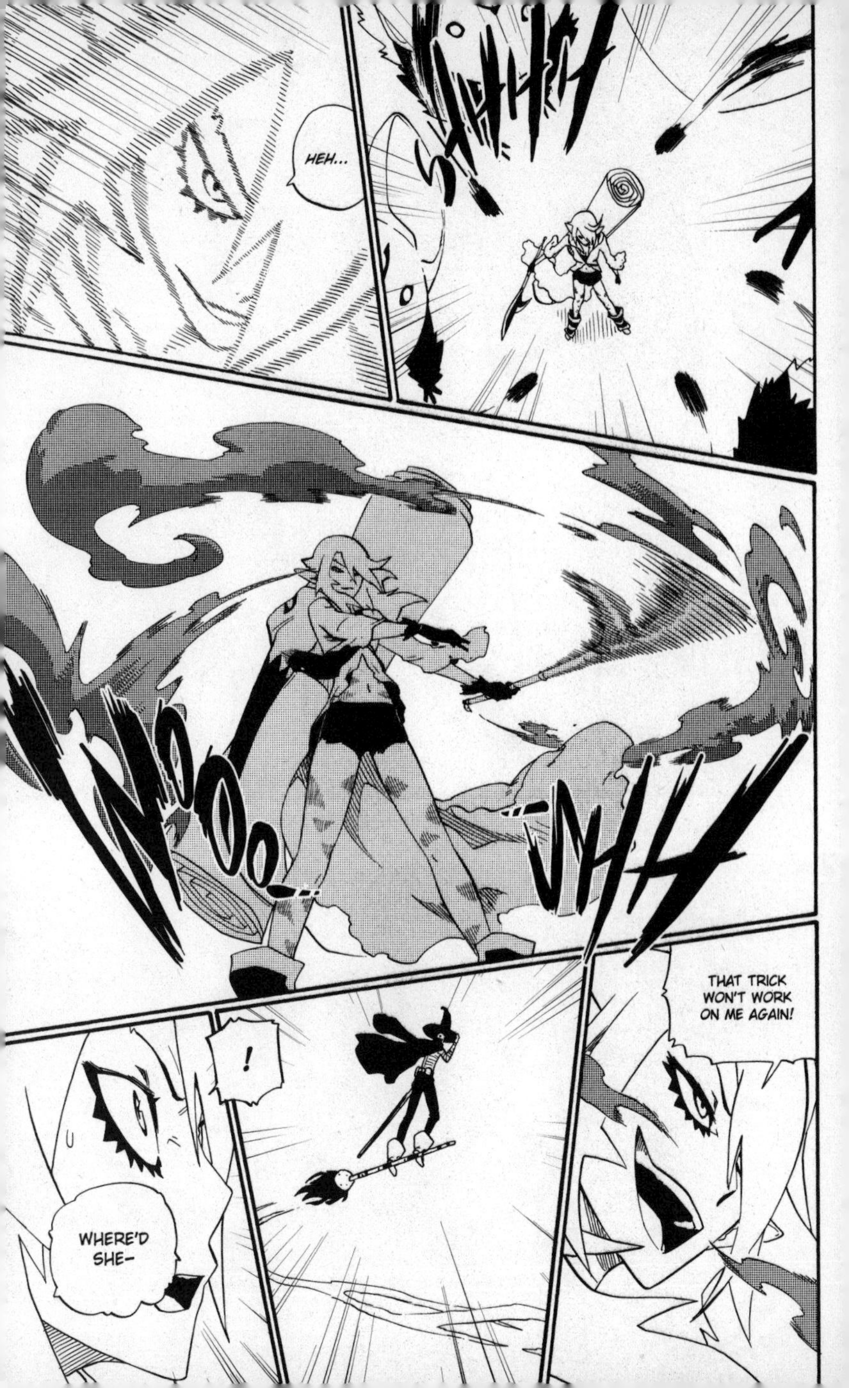

HEH...
THAT TRICK WON'T WORK ON ME AGAIN!
!
WHERE'D SHE-

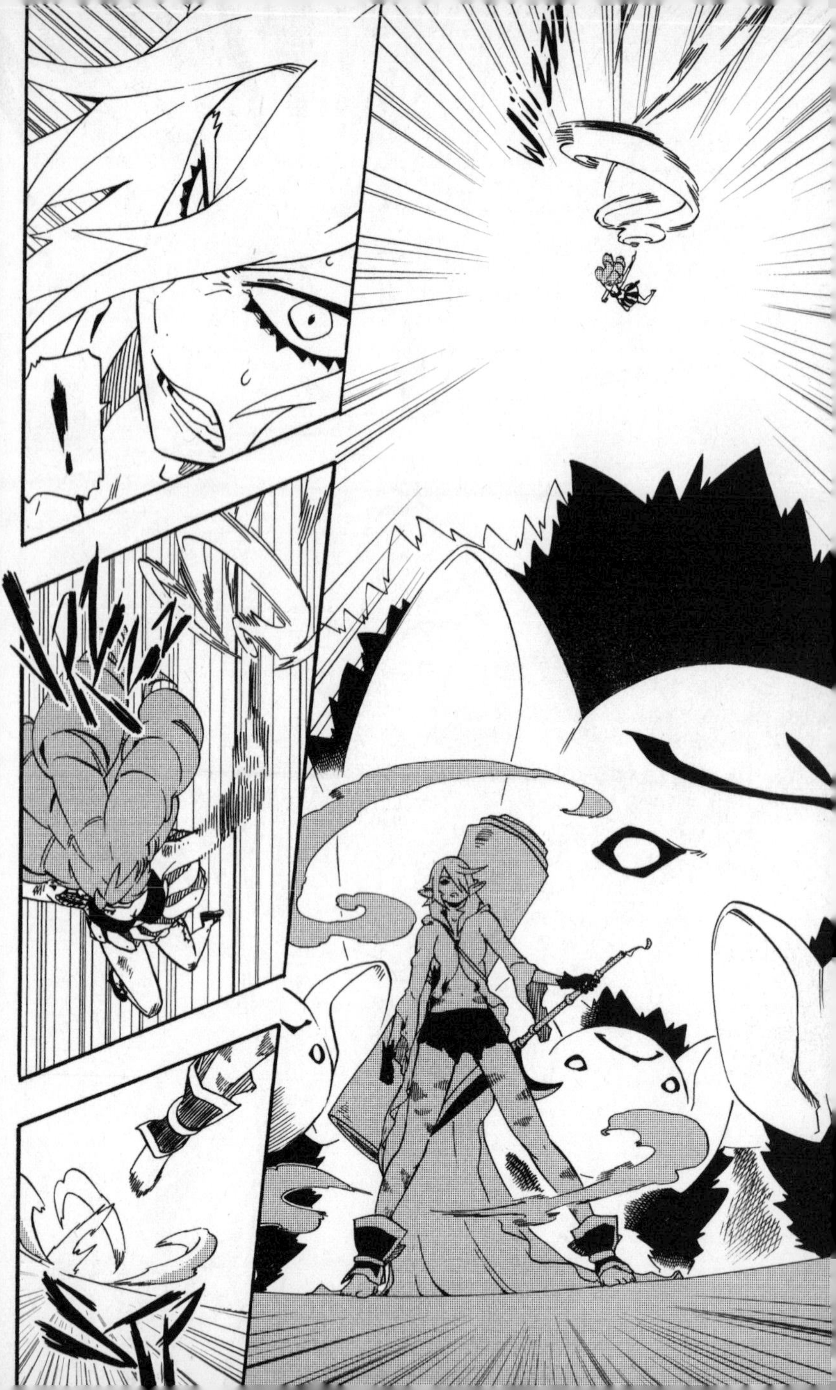
BAM

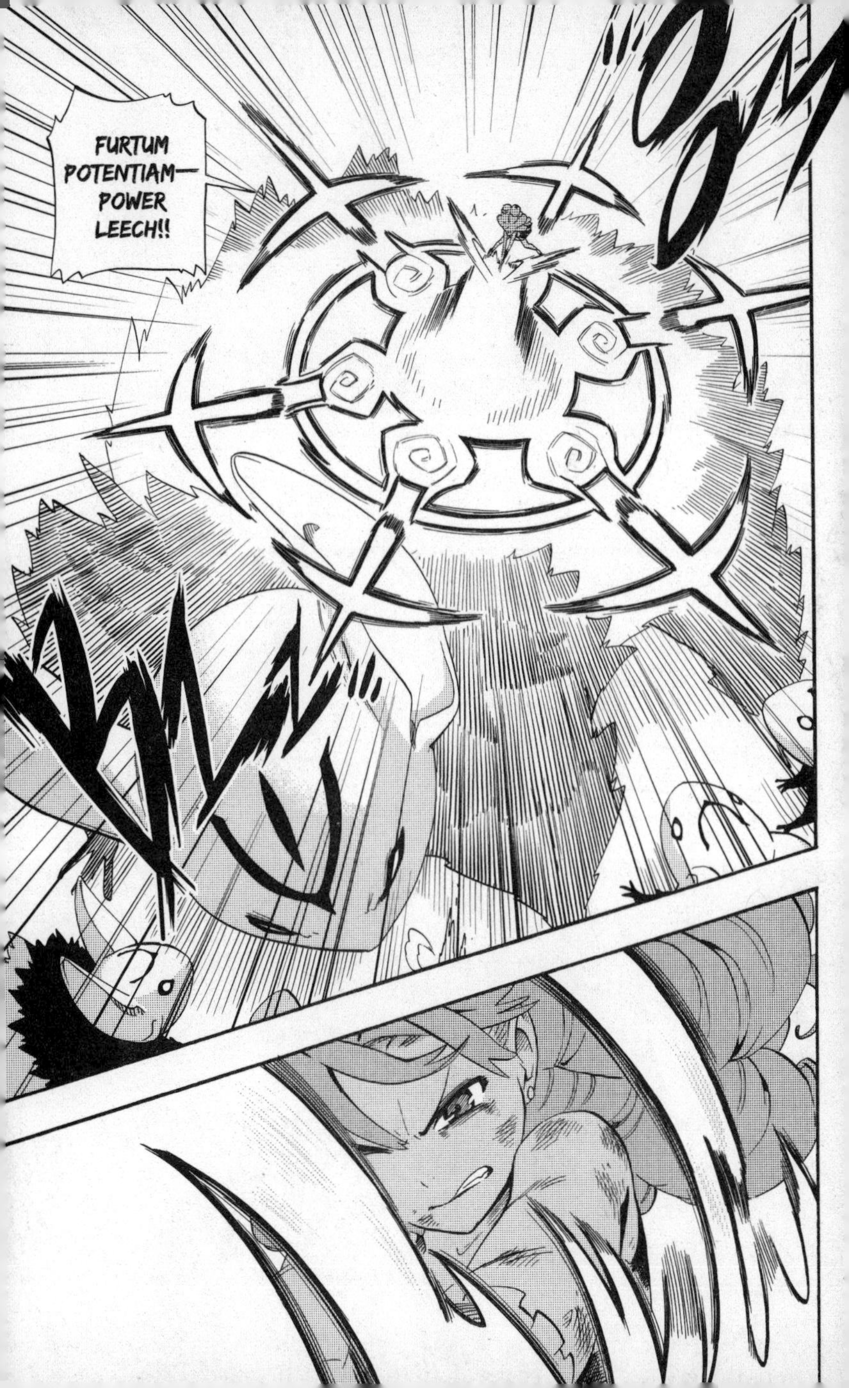
FURTUM POTENTIAM—POWER LEECH!!

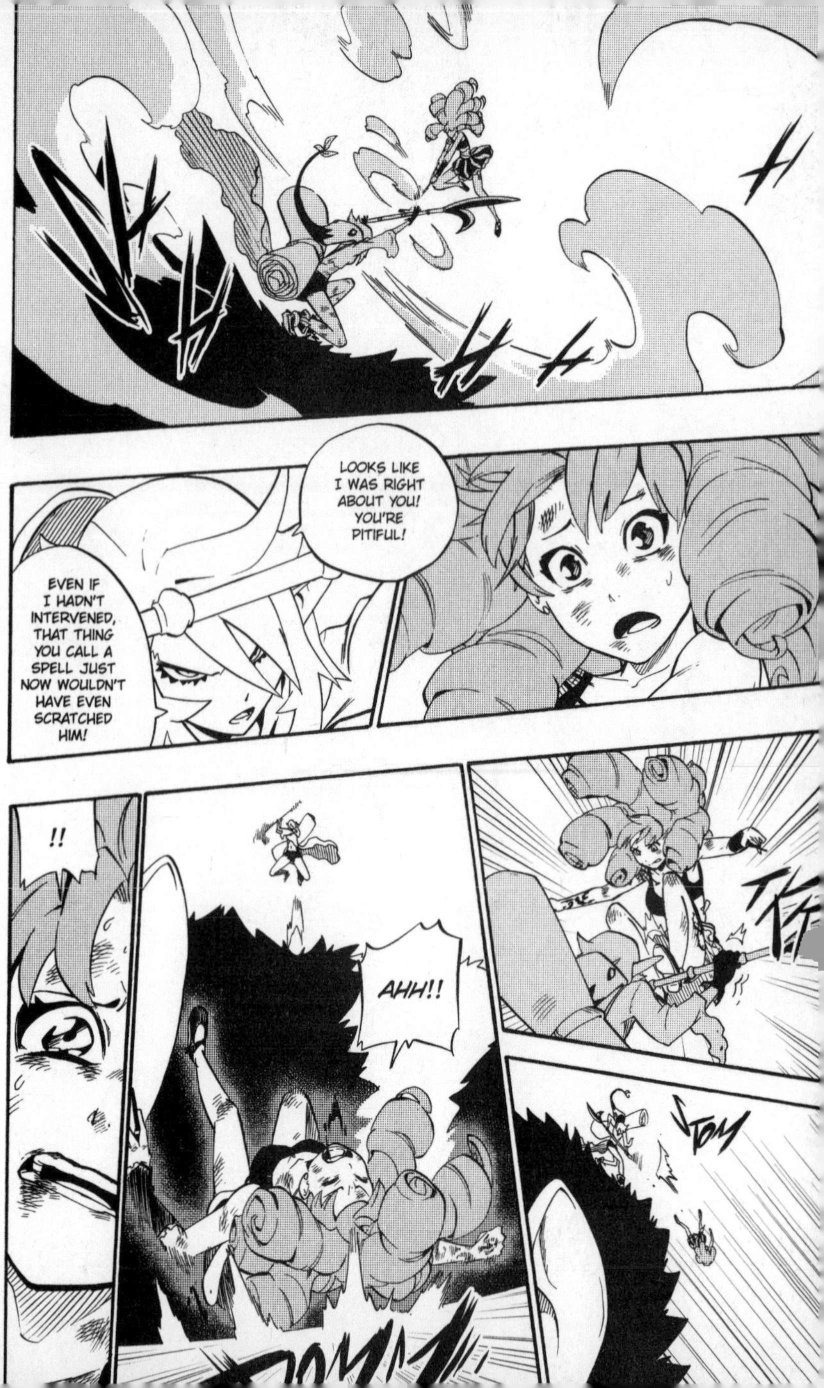
LOOKS LIKE I WAS RIGHT ABOUT YOU! YOU'RE PITIFUL!
EVEN IF I HADN'T INTERVENED, THAT THING YOU CALL A SPELL JUST NOW WOULDN'T HAVE EVEN SCRATCHED HIM!
AHH!!
!!

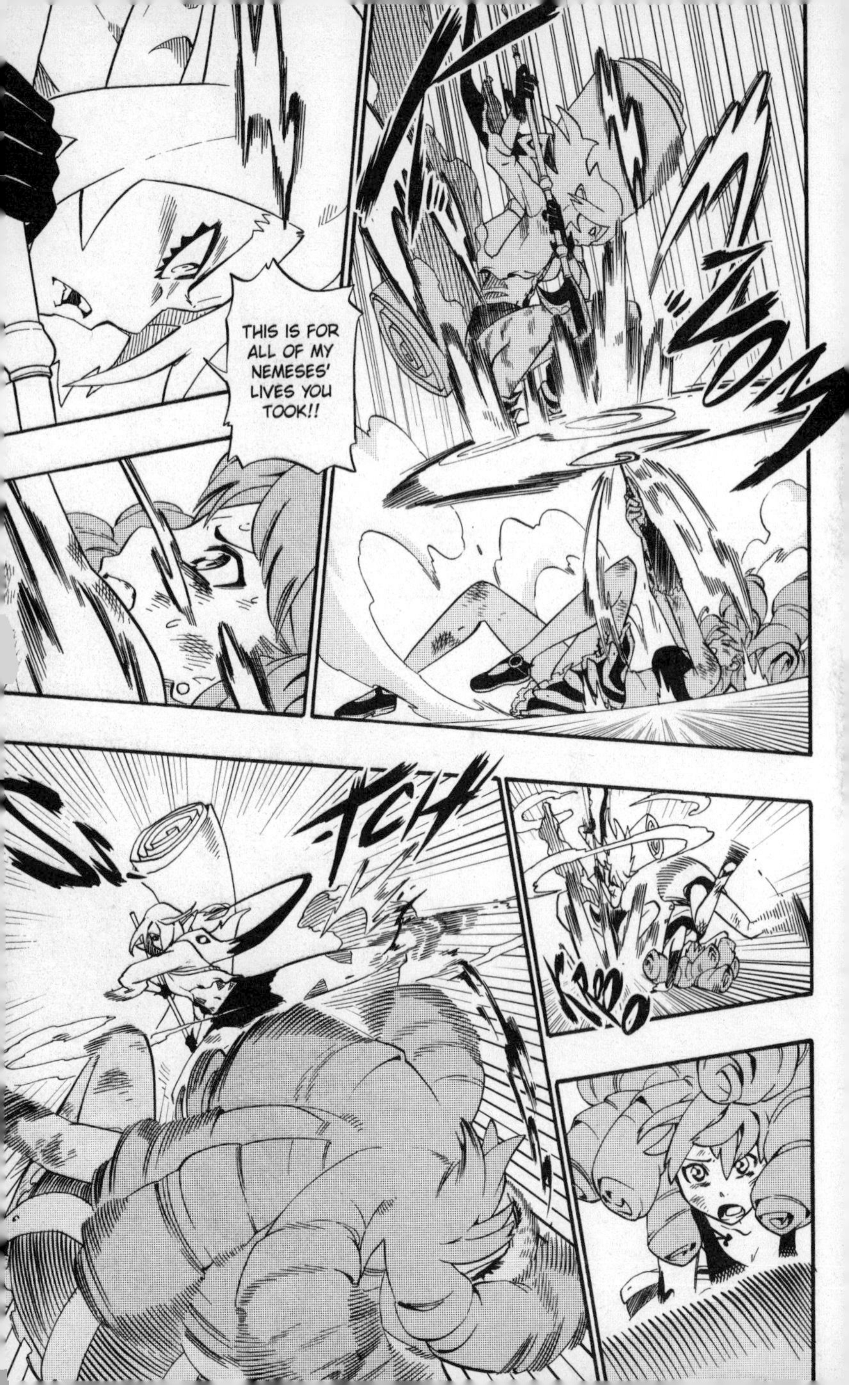
THIS IS FOR ALL OF MY NEMESES' LIVES YOU TOOK!!
KROOO

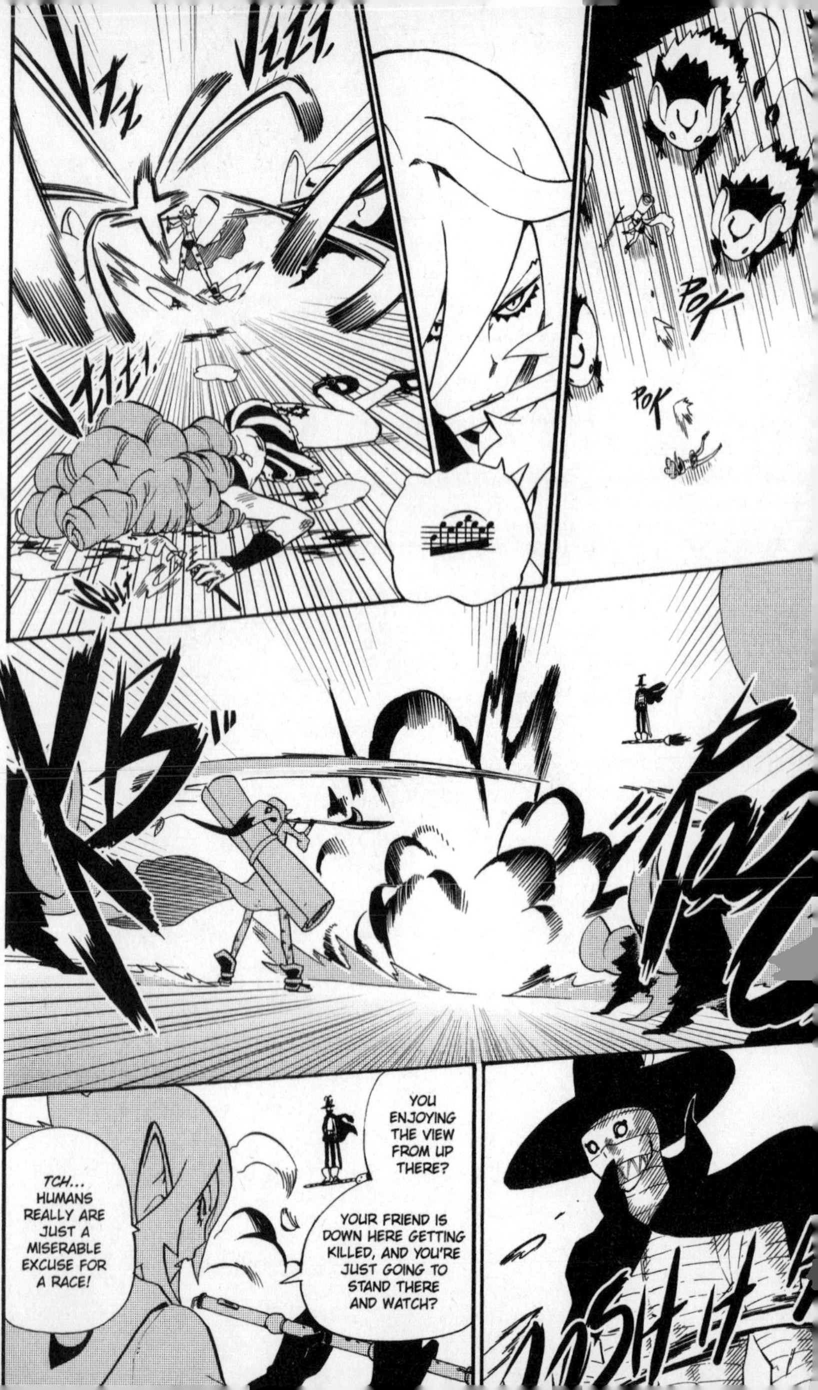
POK
POK
YOU ENJOYING THE VIEW FROM UP THERE?
YOUR FRIEND IS DOWN HERE GETTING KILLED, AND YOU'RE JUST GOING TO STAND THERE AND WATCH?
TCH... HUMANS REALLY ARE JUST A MISERABLE EXCUSE FOR A RACE!

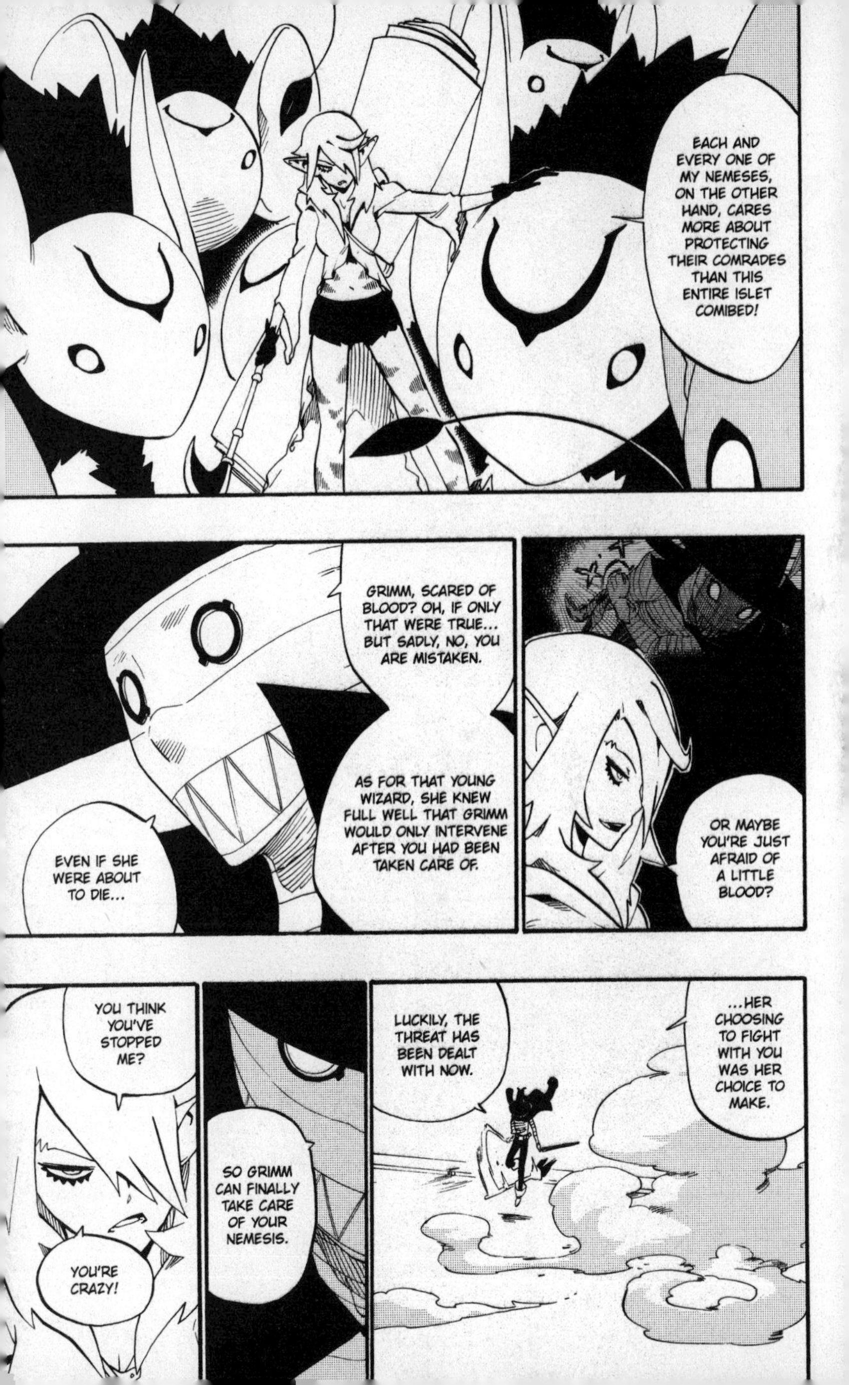
EACH AND EVERY ONE OF MY NEMESES, ON THE OTHER HAND, CARES MORE ABOUT PROTECTING THEIR COMRADES THAN THIS ENTIRE ISLET COMIBED!
OR MAYBE YOU'RE JUST AFRAID OF A LITTLE BLOOD?
GRIMM, SCARED OF BLOOD? OH, IF ONLY THAT WERE TRUE... BUT SADLY, NO, YOU ARE MISTAKEN.
AS FOR THAT YOUNG WIZARD, SHE KNEW FULL WELL THAT GRIMM WOULD ONLY INTERVENE AFTER YOU HAD BEEN TAKEN CARE OF.
EVEN IF SHE WERE ABOUT TO DIE...
...HER CHOOSING TO FIGHT WITH YOU WAS HER CHOICE TO MAKE.
LUCKILY, THE THREAT HAS BEEN DEALT WITH NOW.
SO GRIMM CAN FINALLY TAKE CARE OF YOUR NEMESIS.
YOU THINK YOU'VE STOPPED ME?
YOU'RE CRAZY!

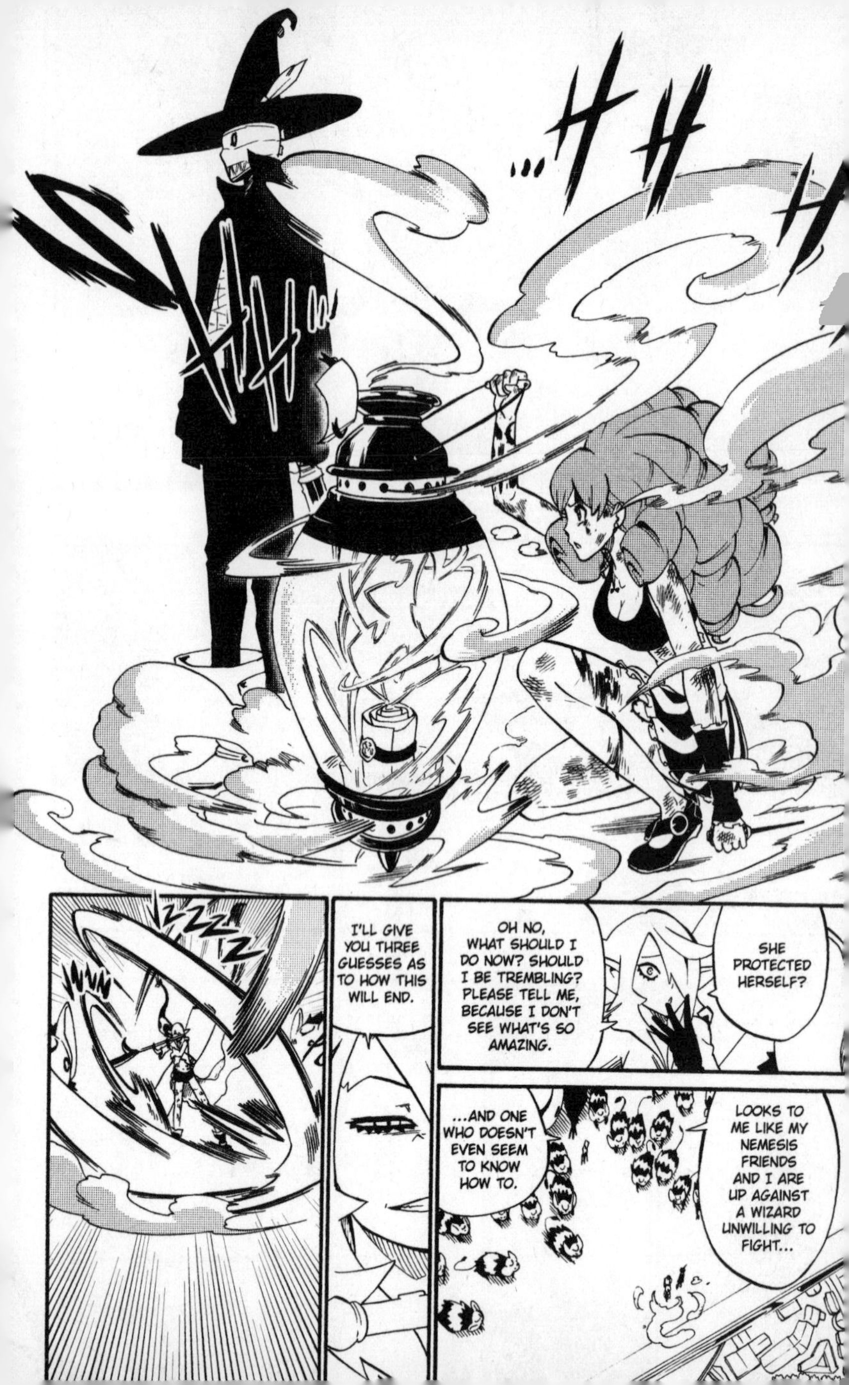
SHH...
...HHHH
SHE PROTECTED HERSELF?
OH NO, WHAT SHOULD I DO NOW? SHOULD I BE TREMBLING? PLEASE TELL ME, BECAUSE I DON'T SEE WHAT'S SO AMAZING.
LOOKS TO ME LIKE MY NEMESIS FRIENDS AND I ARE UP AGAINST A WIZARD UNWILLING TO FIGHT...
...AND ONE WHO DOESN'T EVEN SEEM TO KNOW HOW TO.
I'LL GIVE YOU THREE GUESSES AS TO HOW THIS WILL END.

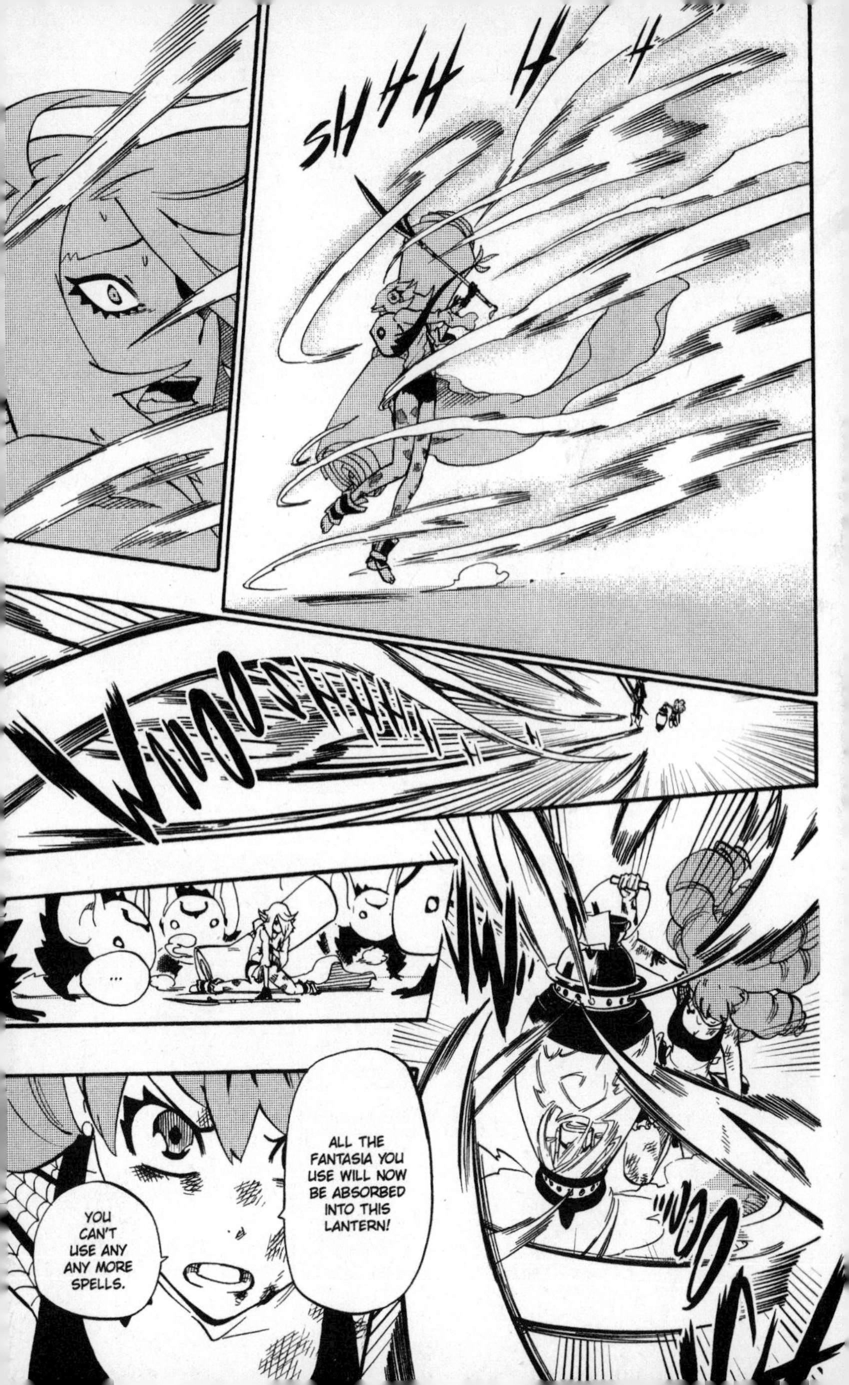
SHHHHH
WHOOSHHH
...
ALL THE FANTASIA YOU USE WILL NOW BE ABSORBED INTO THIS LANTERN!
YOU CAN'T USE ANY ANY MORE SPELLS.

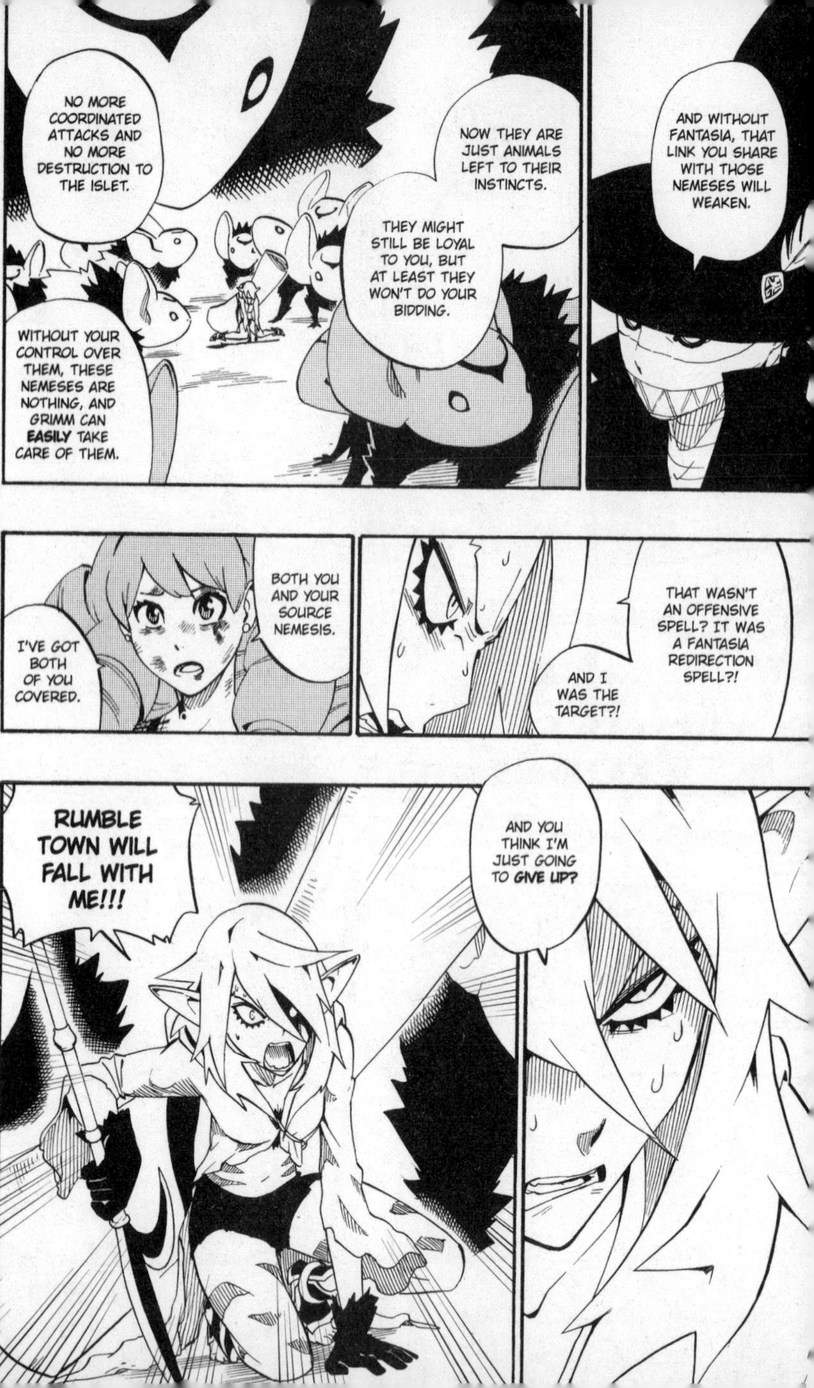
AND WITHOUT FANTASIA, THAT LINK YOU SHARE WITH THOSE NEMESES WILL WEAKEN.
NOW THEY ARE JUST ANIMALS LEFT TO THEIR INSTINCTS.
NO MORE COORDINATED ATTACKS AND NO MORE DESTRUCTION TO THE ISLET.
THEY MIGHT STILL BE LOYAL TO YOU, BUT AT LEAST THEY WON'T DO YOUR BIDDING.
WITHOUT YOUR CONTROL OVER THEM, THESE NEMESES ARE NOTHING, AND GRIMM CAN **EASILY** TAKE CARE OF THEM.
THAT WASN'T AN OFFENSIVE SPELL? IT WAS A FANTASIA REDIRECTION SPELL?!
AND I WAS THE TARGET?!
BOTH YOU AND YOUR SOURCE NEMESIS.
I'VE GOT BOTH OF YOU COVERED.
AND YOU THINK I'M JUST GOING TO **GIVE UP?**
**RUMBLE TOWN WILL FALL WITH ME!!!**

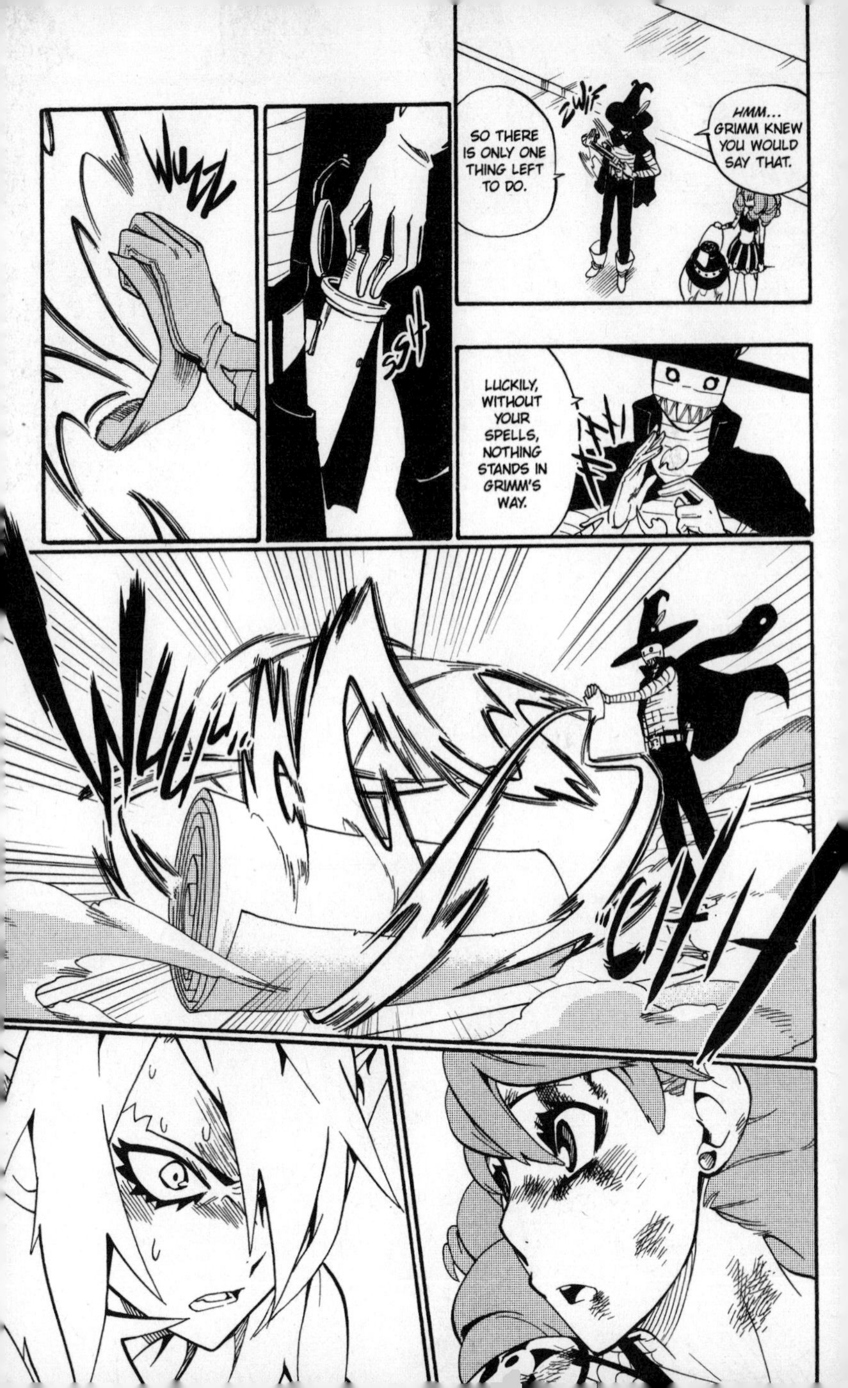
HMM... GRIMM KNEW YOU WOULD SAY THAT.
SWIF
SO THERE IS ONLY ONE THING LEFT TO DO.
LUCKILY, WITHOUT YOUR SPELLS, NOTHING STANDS IN GRIMM'S WAY.
WUZZ

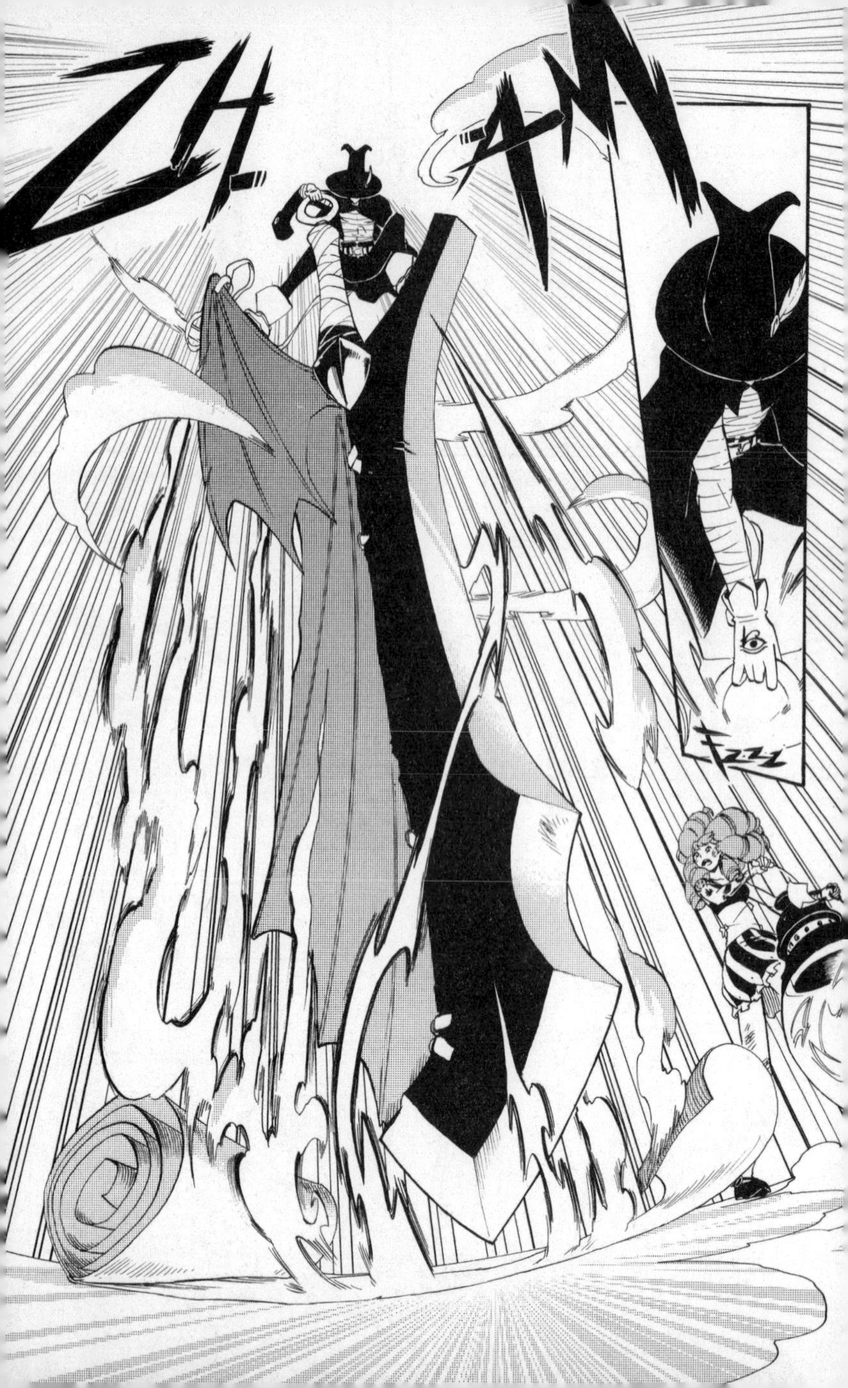
FZZZ
ZHAM

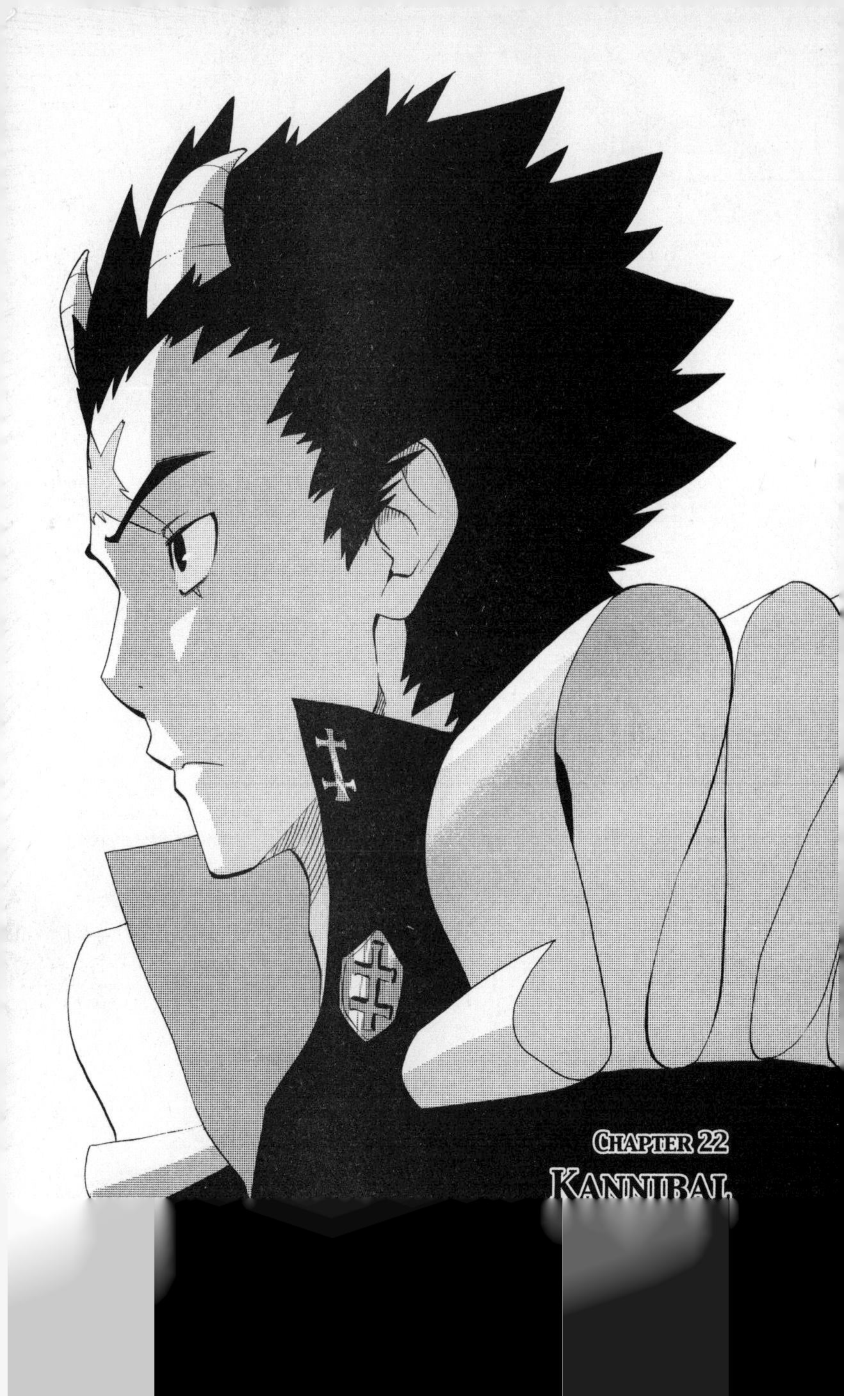
CHAPTER 22
KANNIBAL

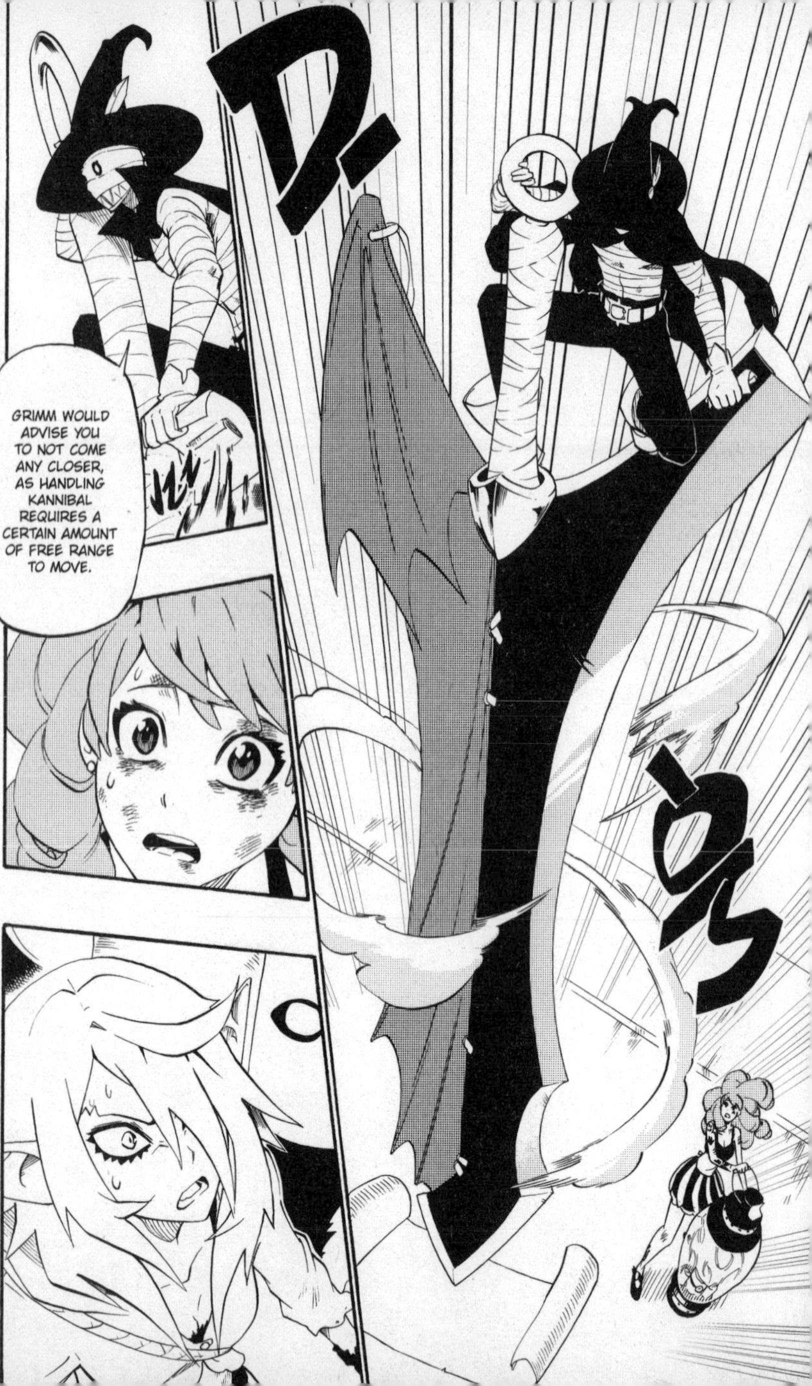
GRIMM WOULD ADVISE YOU TO NOT COME ANY CLOSER, AS HANDLING KANNIBAL REQUIRES A CERTAIN AMOUNT OF FREE RANGE TO MOVE.

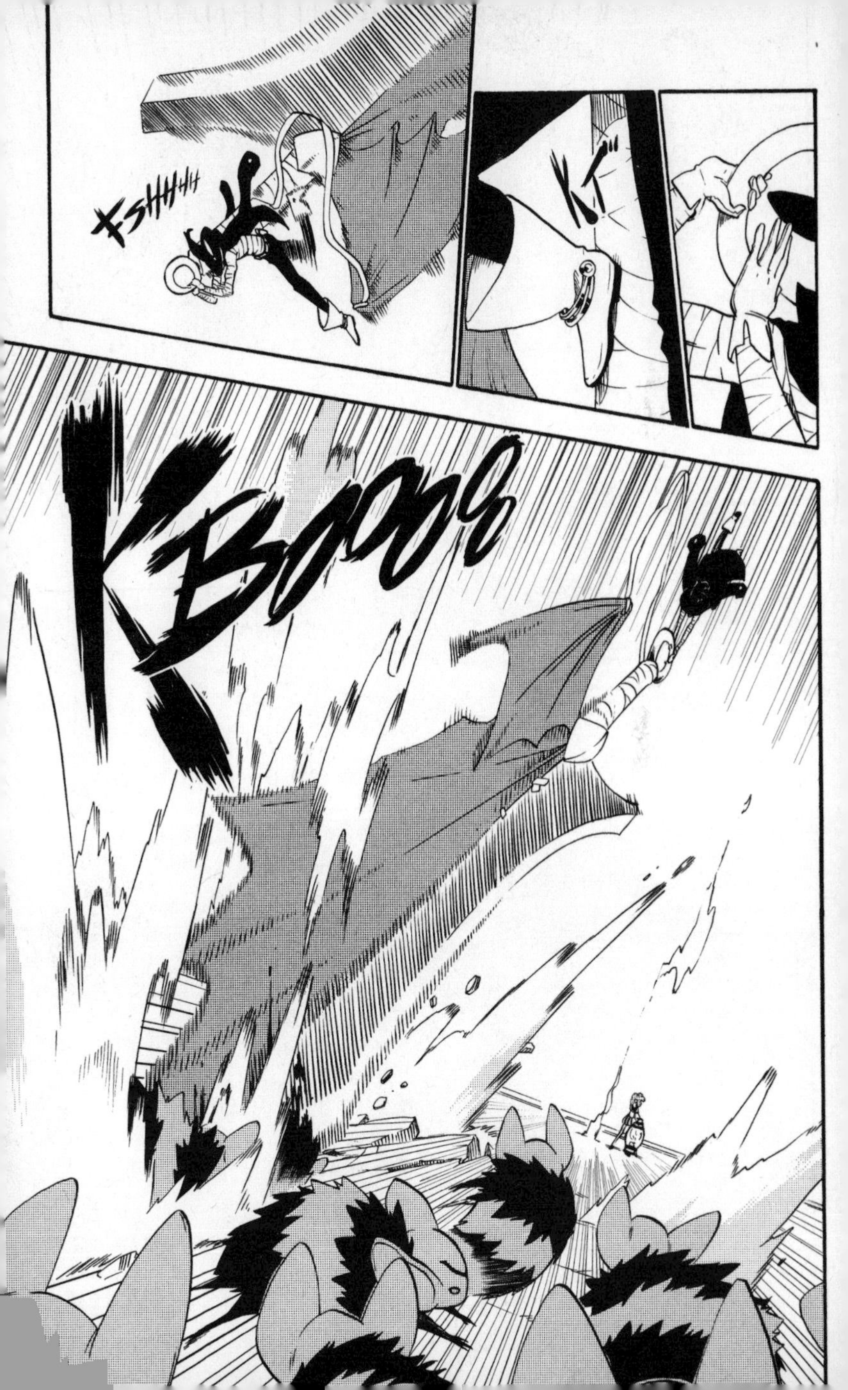
FSHHHH
KBOOOM

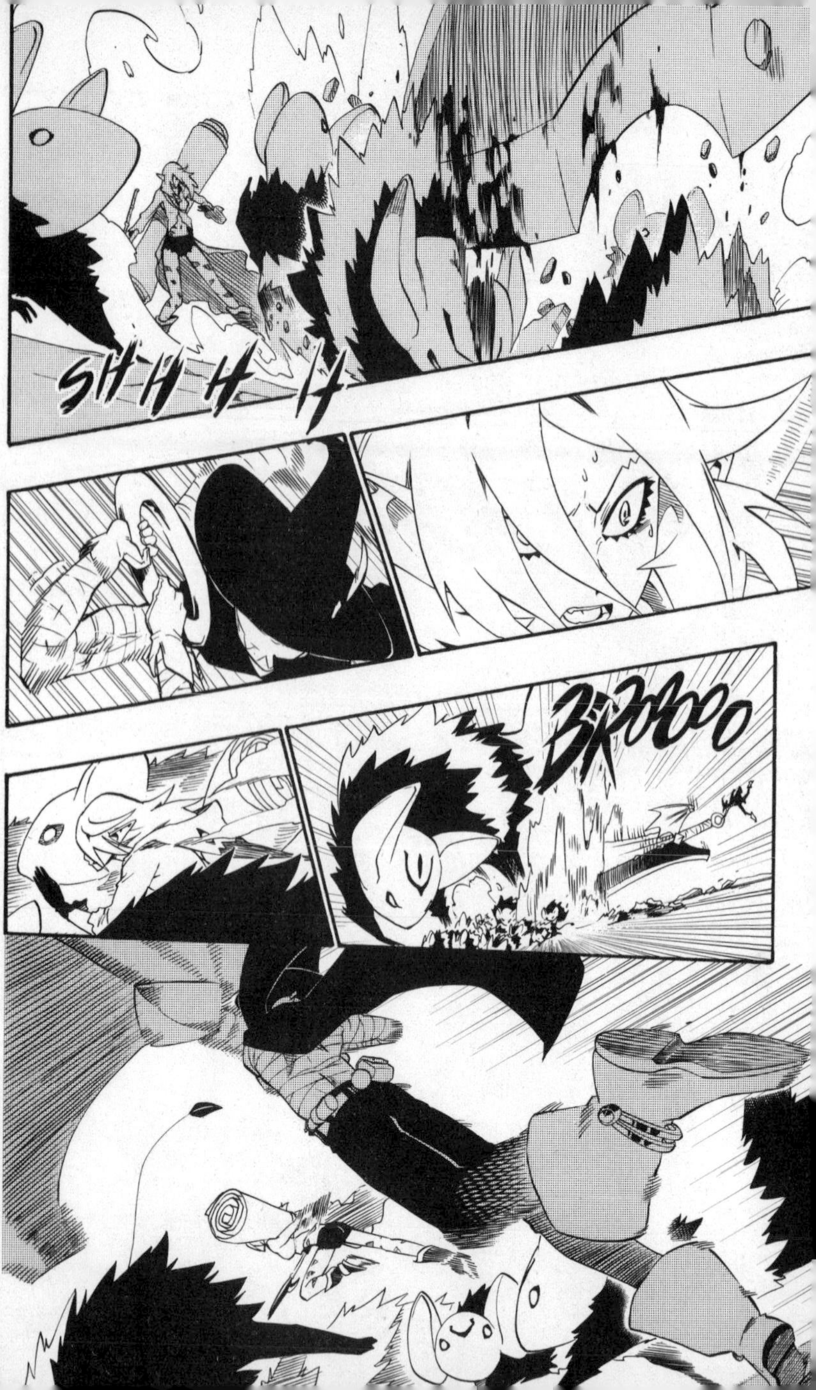
SHHHH
BRZOOOO

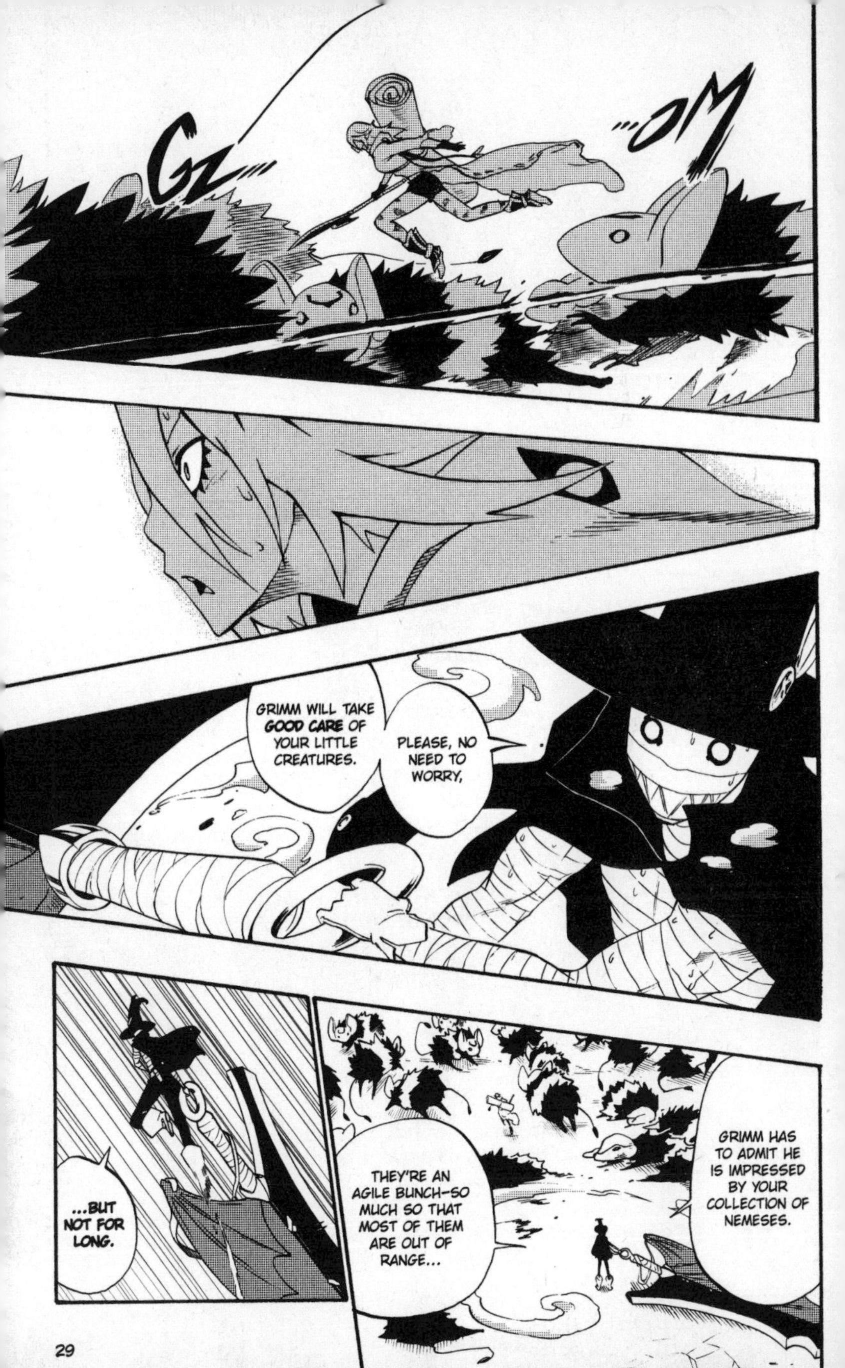
GZ...
...OM
PLEASE, NO NEED TO WORRY,
GRIMM WILL TAKE **GOOD CARE** OF YOUR LITTLE CREATURES.
GRIMM HAS TO ADMIT HE IS IMPRESSED BY YOUR COLLECTION OF NEMESES.
THEY'RE AN AGILE BUNCH—SO MUCH SO THAT MOST OF THEM ARE OUT OF RANGE...
...BUT NOT FOR LONG.

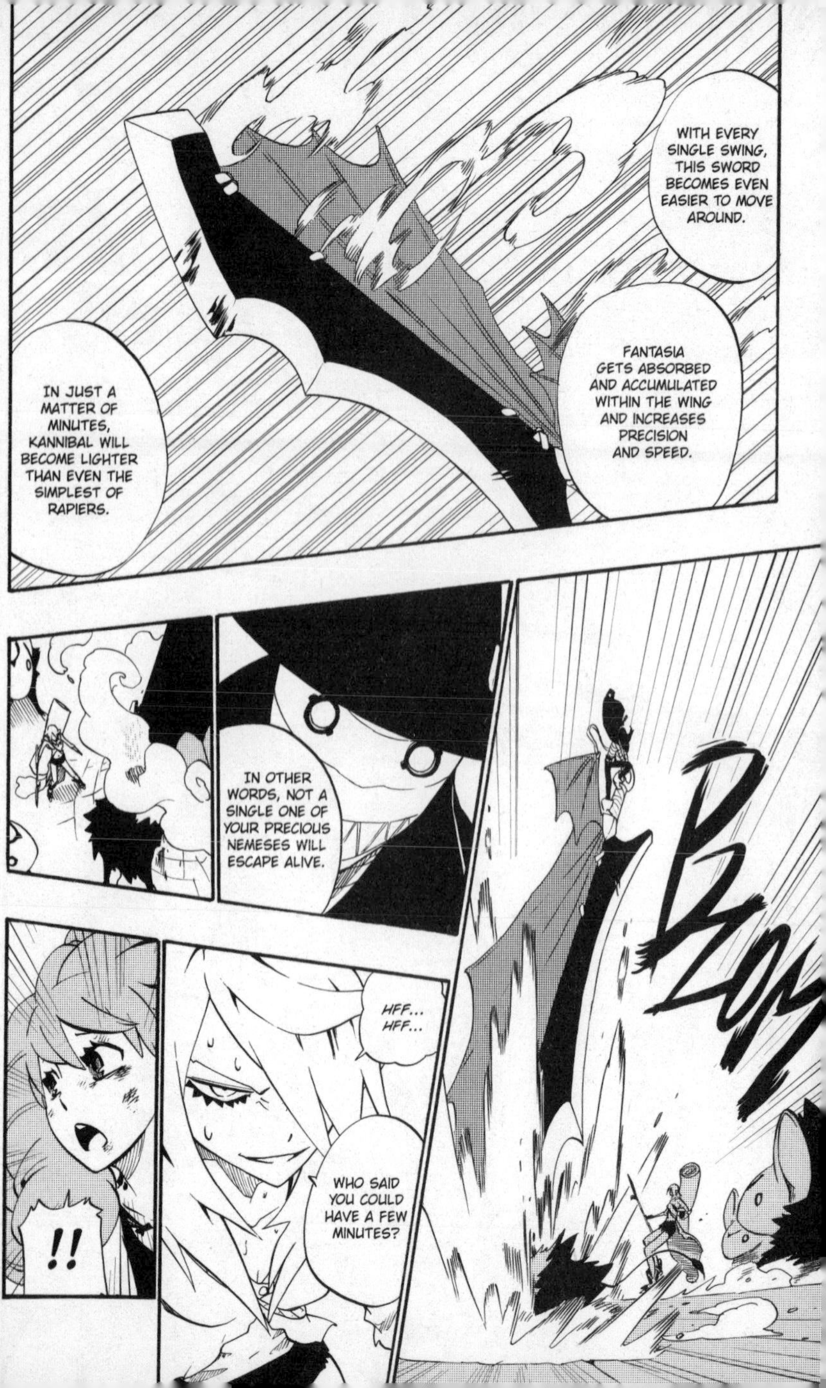
WITH EVERY SINGLE SWING, THIS SWORD BECOMES EVEN EASIER TO MOVE AROUND.
FANTASIA GETS ABSORBED AND ACCUMULATED WITHIN THE WING AND INCREASES PRECISION AND SPEED.
IN JUST A MATTER OF MINUTES, KANNIBAL WILL BECOME LIGHTER THAN EVEN THE SIMPLEST OF RAPIERS.
BOOM
IN OTHER WORDS, NOT A SINGLE ONE OF YOUR PRECIOUS NEMESES WILL ESCAPE ALIVE.
HFF... HFF...
WHO SAID YOU COULD HAVE A FEW MINUTES?
!!

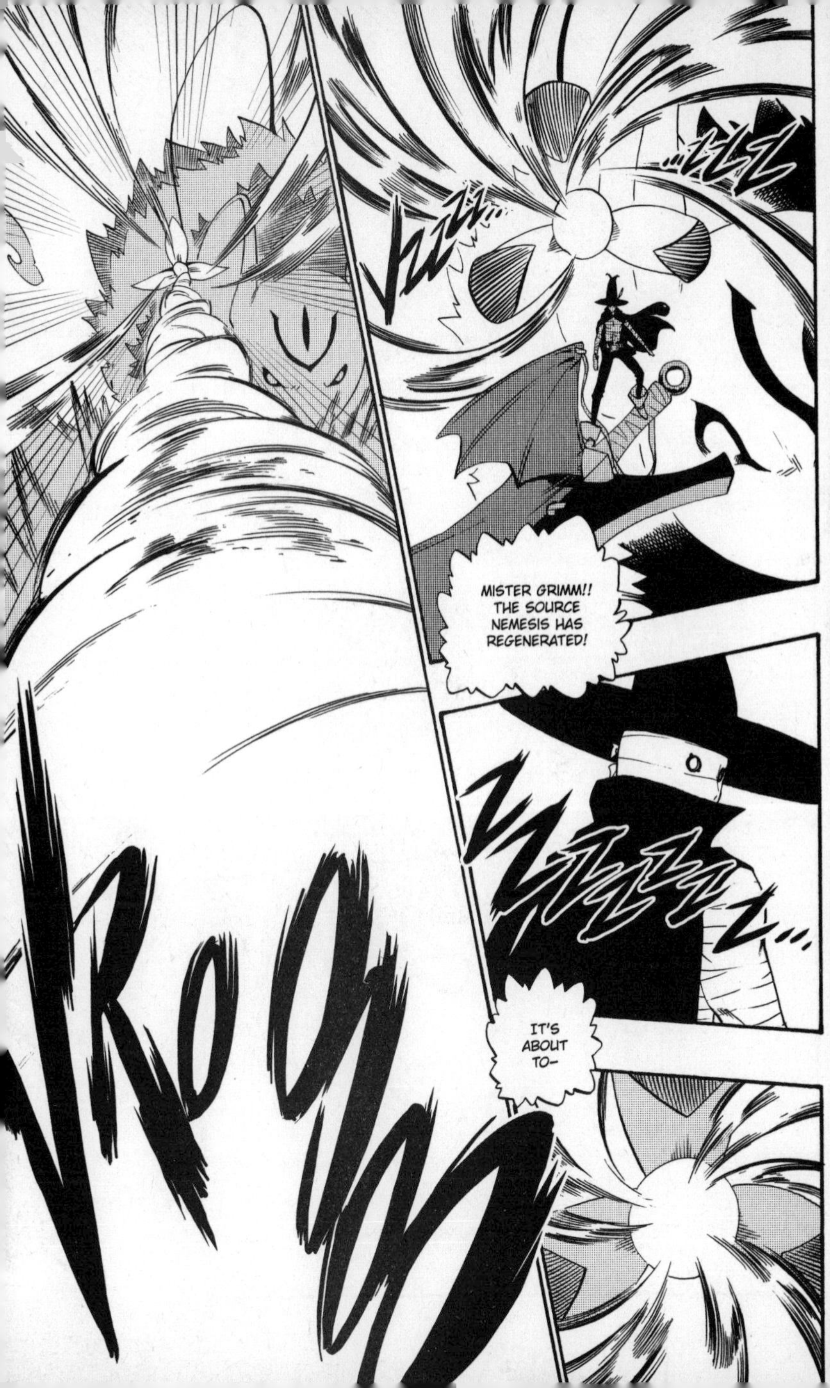
MISTER GRIMM!! THE SOURCE NEMESIS HAS REGENERATED!
IT'S ABOUT TO-

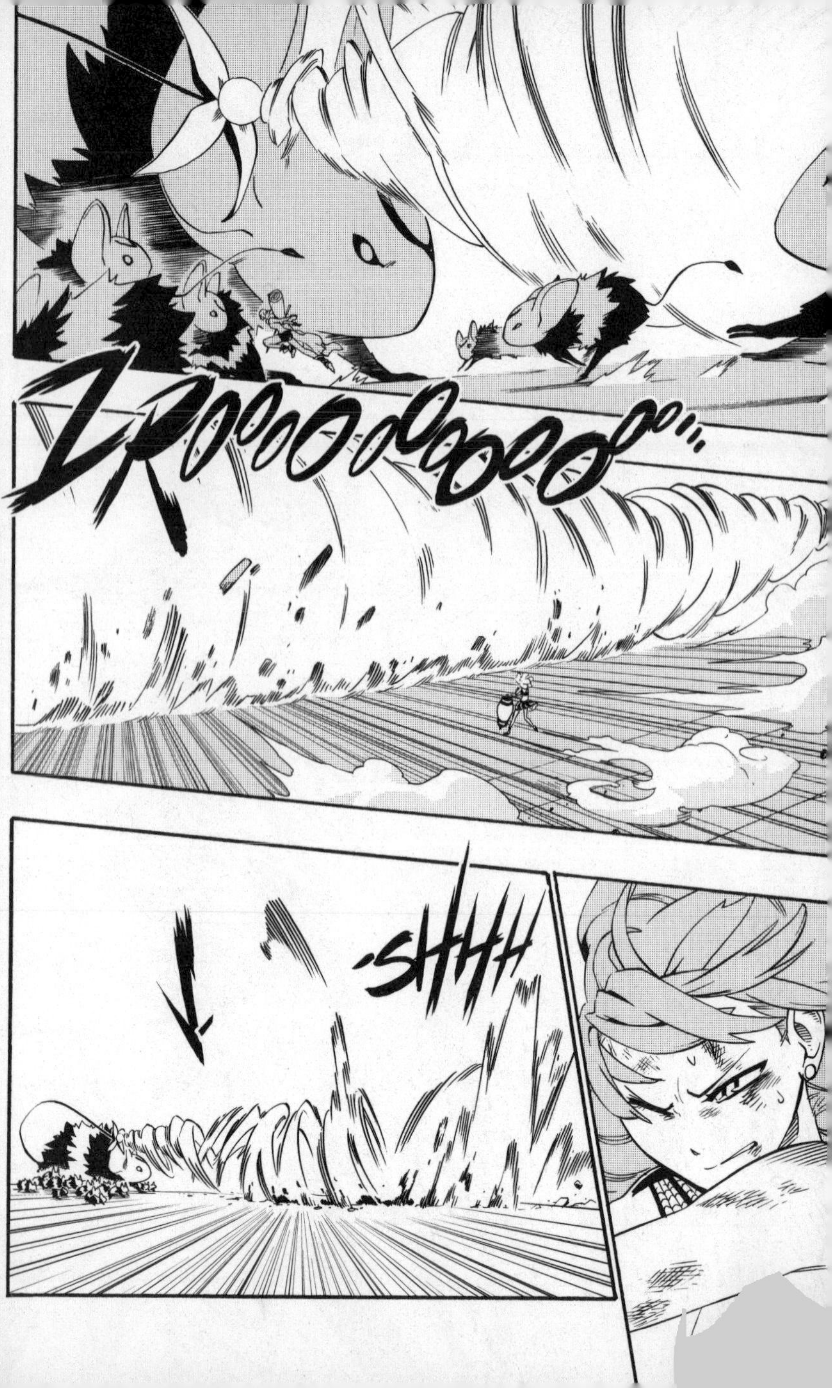
ZROOOOOOOOO...
SHHH

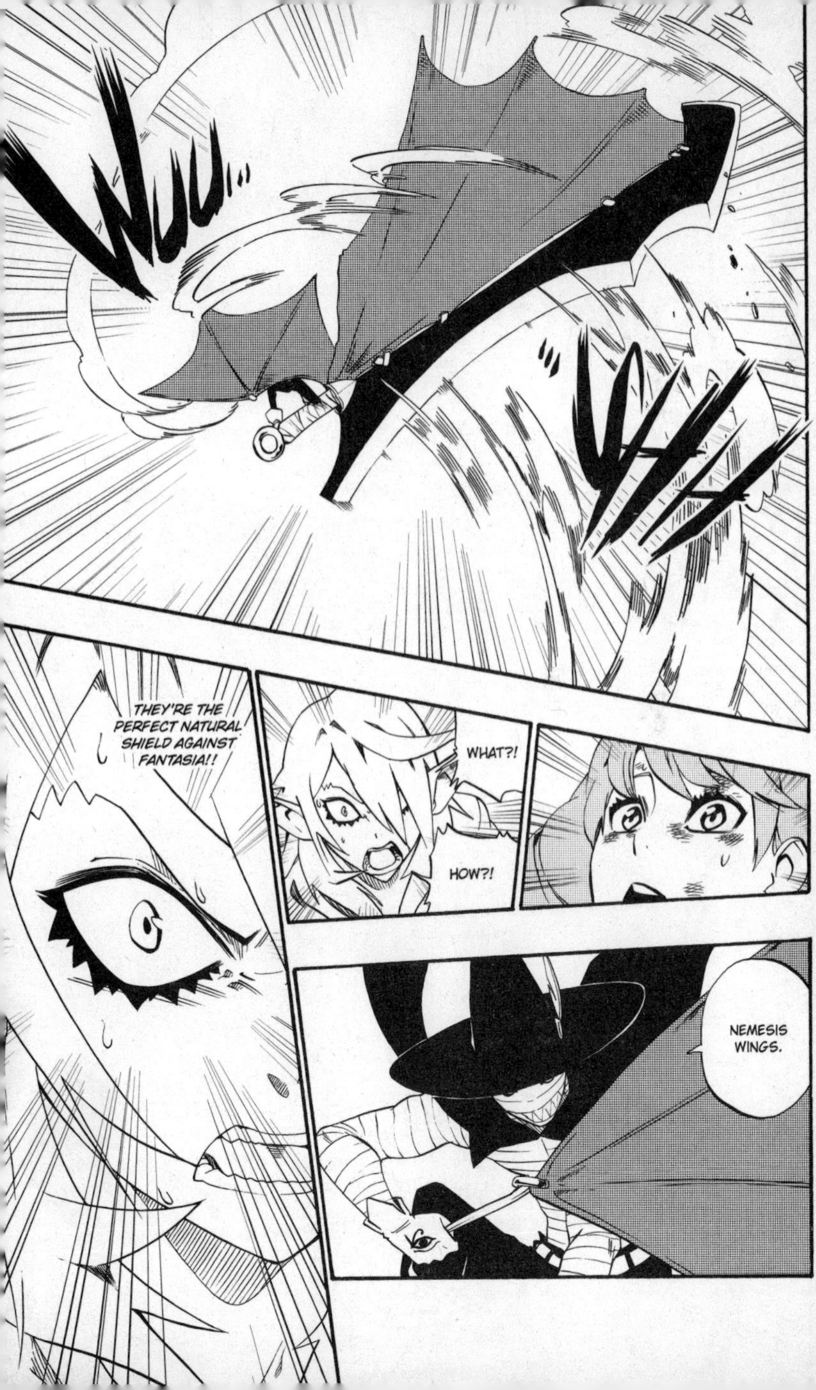
WUU..
WHAT?!
HOW?!
NEMESIS WINGS.
THEY'RE THE PERFECT NATURAL SHIELD AGAINST FANTASIA!!

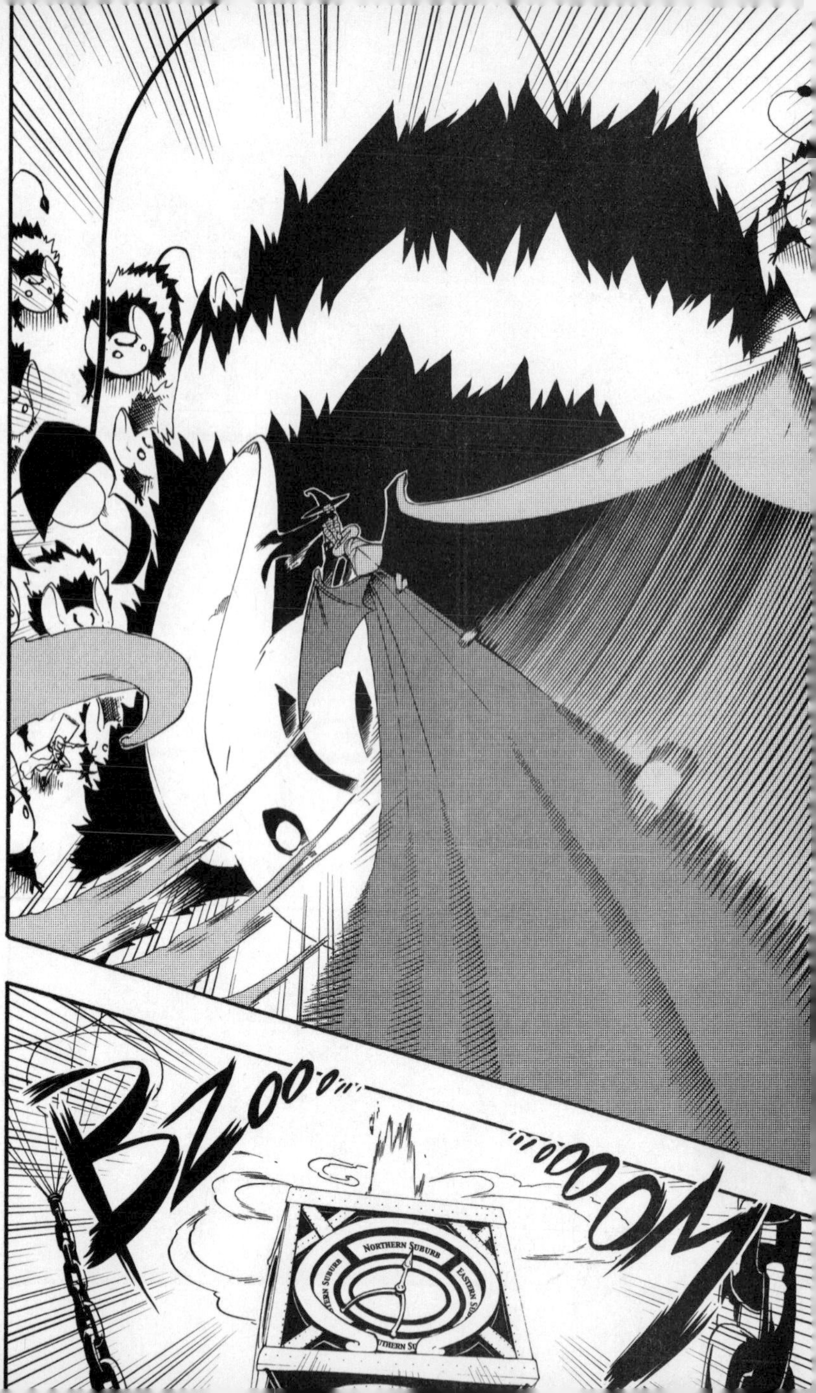
BZOOooo...
...ooOOOM
NORTHERN SUBURB

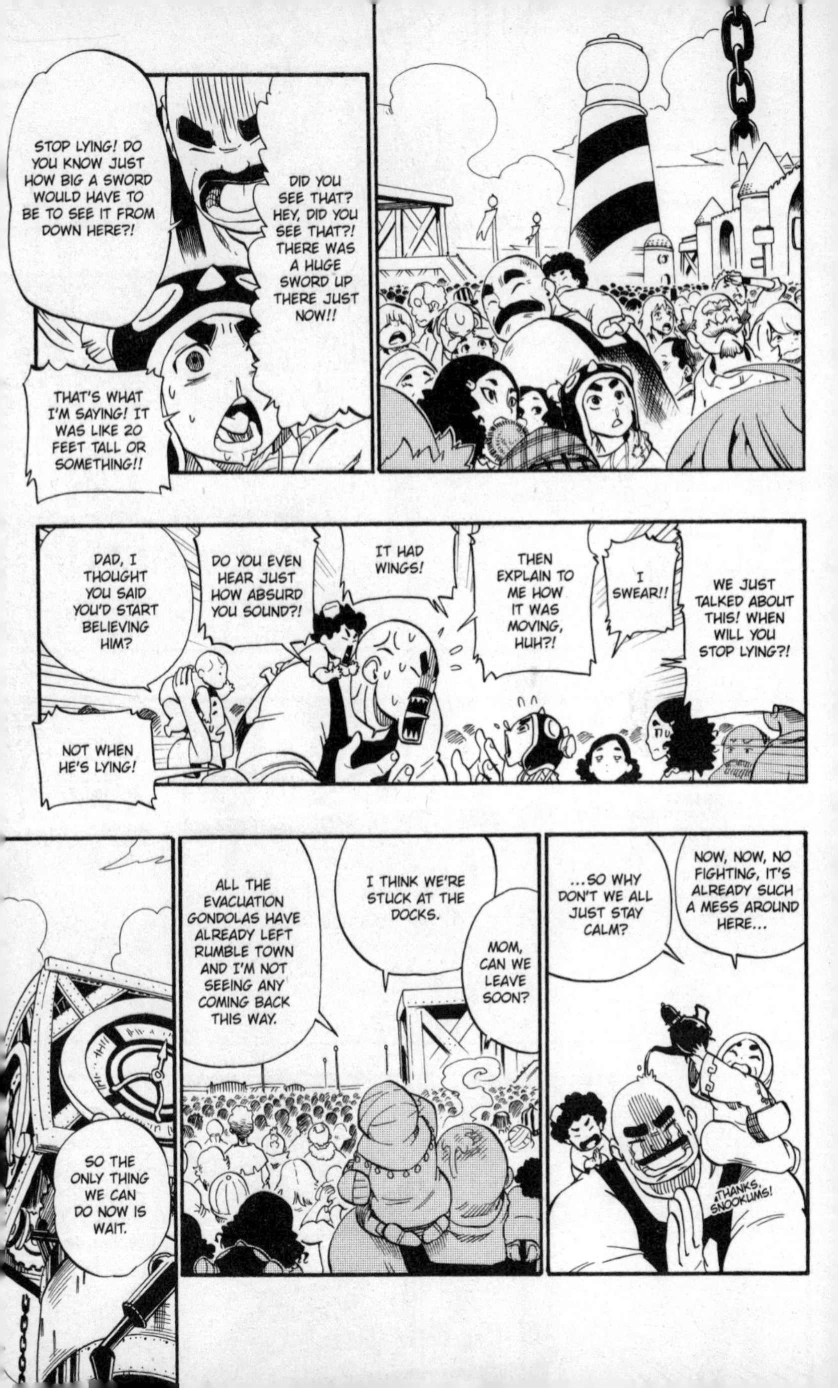
DID YOU SEE THAT? HEY, DID YOU SEE THAT?! THERE WAS A HUGE SWORD UP THERE JUST NOW!!
STOP LYING! DO YOU KNOW JUST HOW BIG A SWORD WOULD HAVE TO BE TO SEE IT FROM DOWN HERE?!
THAT'S WHAT I'M SAYING! IT WAS LIKE 20 FEET TALL OR SOMETHING!!
WE JUST TALKED ABOUT THIS! WHEN WILL YOU STOP LYING?!
I SWEAR!!
THEN EXPLAIN TO ME HOW IT WAS MOVING, HUH?!
IT HAD WINGS!
DO YOU EVEN HEAR JUST HOW ABSURD YOU SOUND?!
DAD, I THOUGHT YOU SAID YOU'D START BELIEVING HIM?
NOT WHEN HE'S LYING!
NOW, NOW, NO FIGHTING, IT'S ALREADY SUCH A MESS AROUND HERE...
...SO WHY DON'T WE ALL JUST STAY CALM?
THANKS, SNOOKUMS!
I THINK WE'RE STUCK AT THE DOCKS.
ALL THE EVACUATION GONDOLAS HAVE ALREADY LEFT RUMBLE TOWN AND I'M NOT SEEING ANY COMING BACK THIS WAY.
MOM, CAN WE LEAVE SOON?
SO THE ONLY THING WE CAN DO NOW IS WAIT.

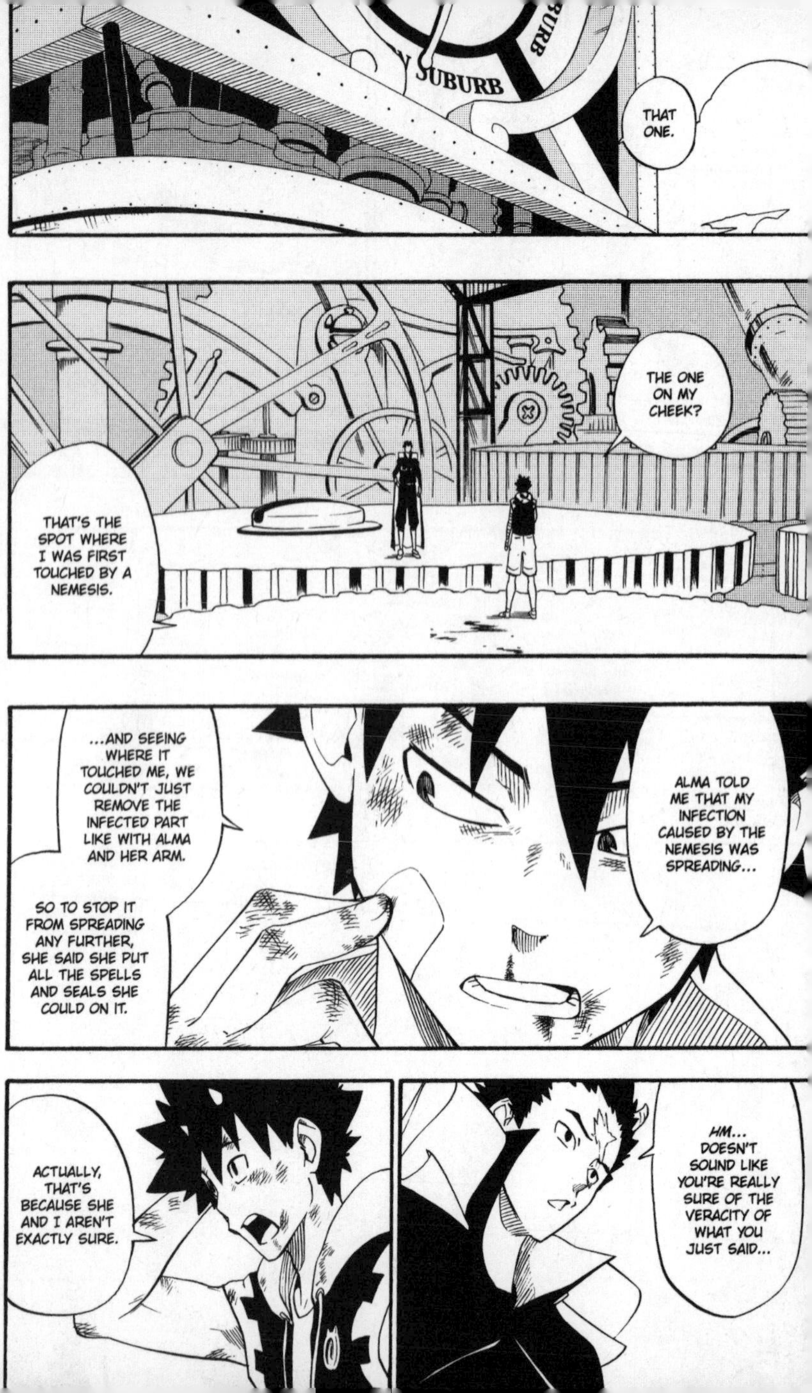
SUBURB
THAT ONE.
THE ONE ON MY CHEEK?
THAT'S THE SPOT WHERE I WAS FIRST TOUCHED BY A NEMESIS.
ALMA TOLD ME THAT MY INFECTION CAUSED BY THE NEMESIS WAS SPREADING...
...AND SEEING WHERE IT TOUCHED ME, WE COULDN'T JUST REMOVE THE INFECTED PART LIKE WITH ALMA AND HER ARM.
SO TO STOP IT FROM SPREADING ANY FURTHER, SHE SAID SHE PUT ALL THE SPELLS AND SEALS SHE COULD ON IT.
HM... DOESN'T SOUND LIKE YOU'RE REALLY SURE OF THE VERACITY OF WHAT YOU JUST SAID...
ACTUALLY, THAT'S BECAUSE SHE AND I AREN'T EXACTLY SURE.

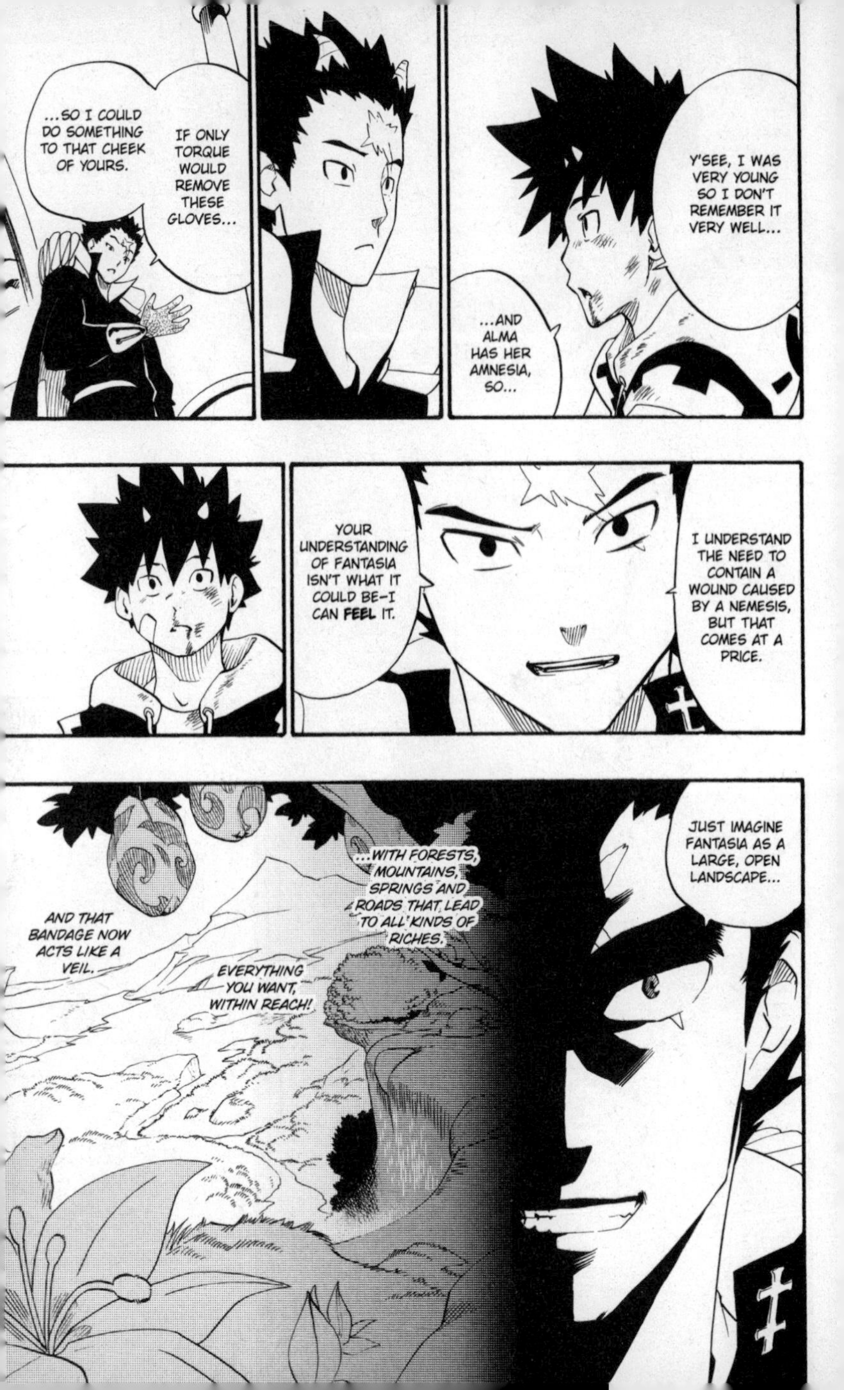
Y'SEE, I WAS VERY YOUNG SO I DON'T REMEMBER IT VERY WELL...
...AND ALMA HAS HER AMNESIA, SO...
IF ONLY TORQUE WOULD REMOVE THESE GLOVES...
...SO I COULD DO SOMETHING TO THAT CHEEK OF YOURS.
I UNDERSTAND THE NEED TO CONTAIN A WOUND CAUSED BY A NEMESIS, BUT THAT COMES AT A PRICE.
YOUR UNDERSTANDING OF FANTASIA ISN'T WHAT IT COULD BE—I CAN **FEEL** IT.
JUST IMAGINE FANTASIA AS A LARGE, OPEN LANDSCAPE...
...WITH FORESTS, MOUNTAINS, SPRINGS AND ROADS THAT LEAD TO ALL KINDS OF RICHES.
EVERYTHING YOU WANT, WITHIN REACH!
AND THAT BANDAGE NOW ACTS LIKE A VEIL.

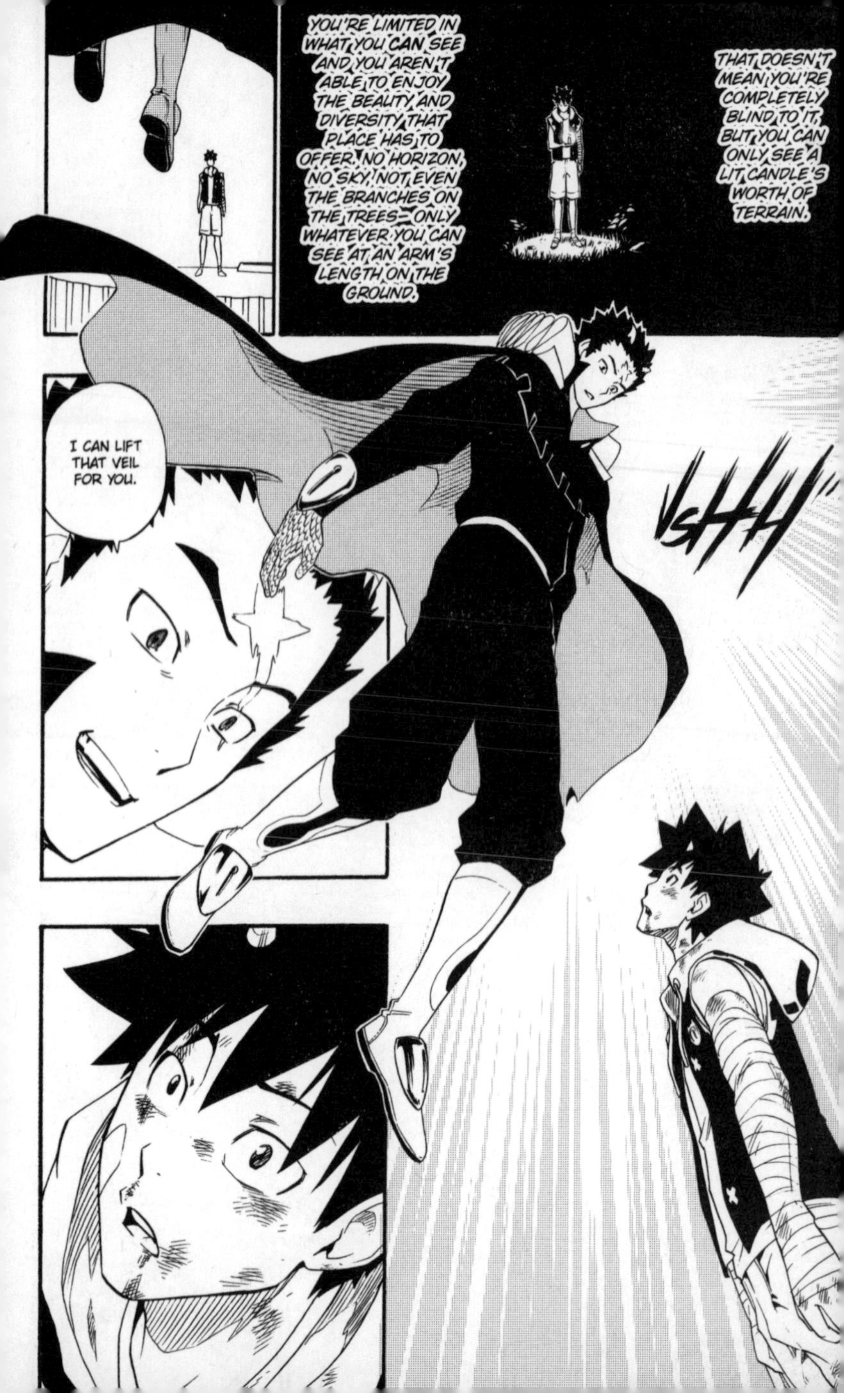
THAT DOESN'T MEAN YOU'RE COMPLETELY BLIND TO IT, BUT YOU CAN ONLY SEE A LIT CANDLE'S WORTH OF TERRAIN.
YOU'RE LIMITED IN WHAT YOU CAN SEE AND YOU AREN'T ABLE TO ENJOY THE BEAUTY AND DIVERSITY THAT PLACE HAS TO OFFER. NO HORIZON, NO SKY, NOT EVEN THE BRANCHES ON THE TREES—ONLY WHATEVER YOU CAN SEE AT AN ARM'S LENGTH ON THE GROUND.
VSHH
I CAN LIFT THAT VEIL FOR YOU.

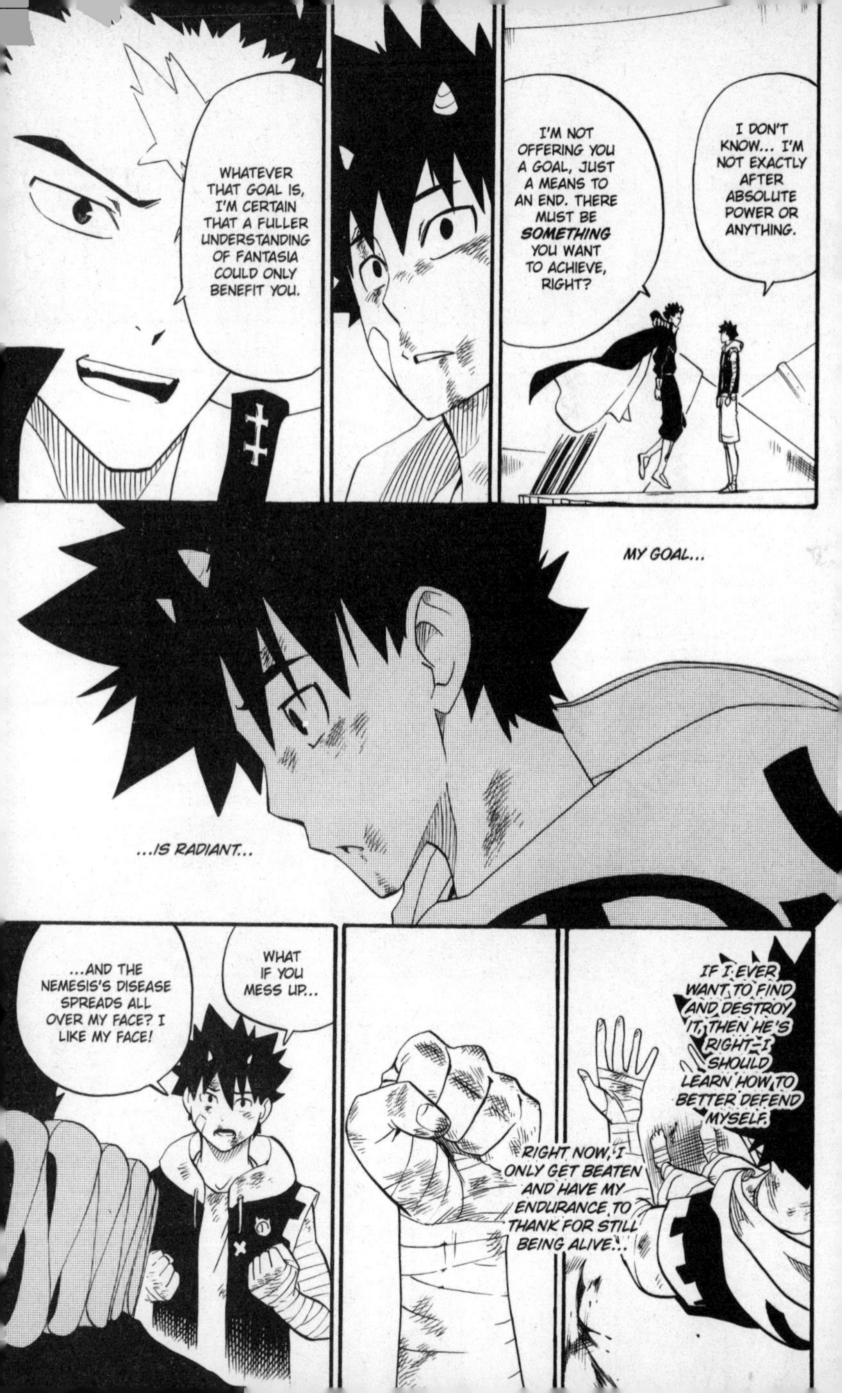
I DON'T KNOW... I'M NOT EXACTLY AFTER ABSOLUTE POWER OR ANYTHING.
I'M NOT OFFERING YOU A GOAL, JUST A MEANS TO AN END. THERE MUST BE SOMETHING YOU WANT TO ACHIEVE, RIGHT?
WHATEVER THAT GOAL IS, I'M CERTAIN THAT A FULLER UNDERSTANDING OF FANTASIA COULD ONLY BENEFIT YOU.
MY GOAL...
...IS RADIANT...
IF I EVER WANT TO FIND AND DESTROY IT, THEN HE'S RIGHT—I SHOULD LEARN HOW TO BETTER DEFEND MYSELF.
RIGHT NOW, I ONLY GET BEATEN AND HAVE MY ENDURANCE TO THANK FOR STILL BEING ALIVE...
WHAT IF YOU MESS UP...
...AND THE NEMESIS'S DISEASE SPREADS ALL OVER MY FACE? I LIKE MY FACE!

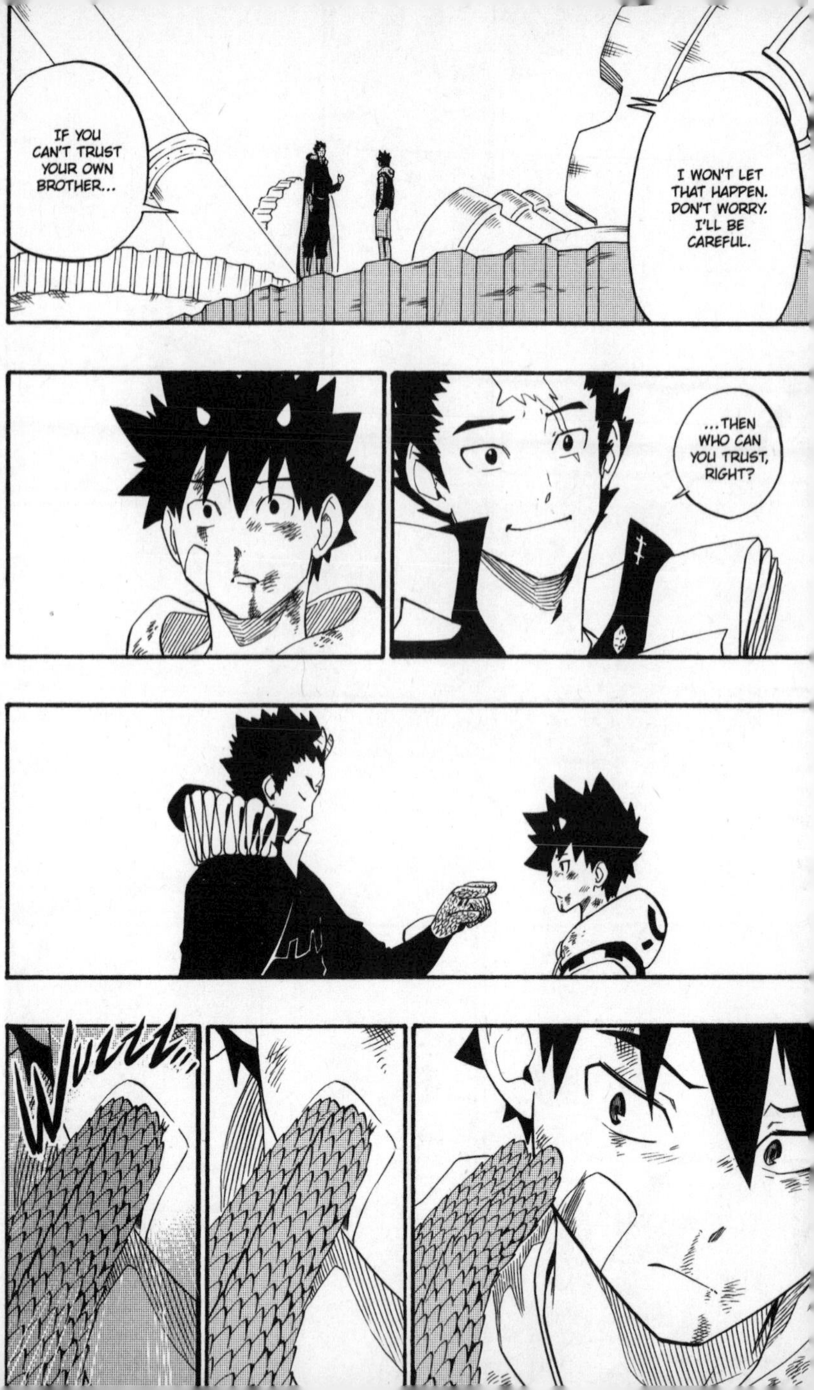
I WON'T LET THAT HAPPEN. DON'T WORRY. I'LL BE CAREFUL.
IF YOU CAN'T TRUST YOUR OWN BROTHER...
...THEN WHO CAN YOU TRUST, RIGHT?

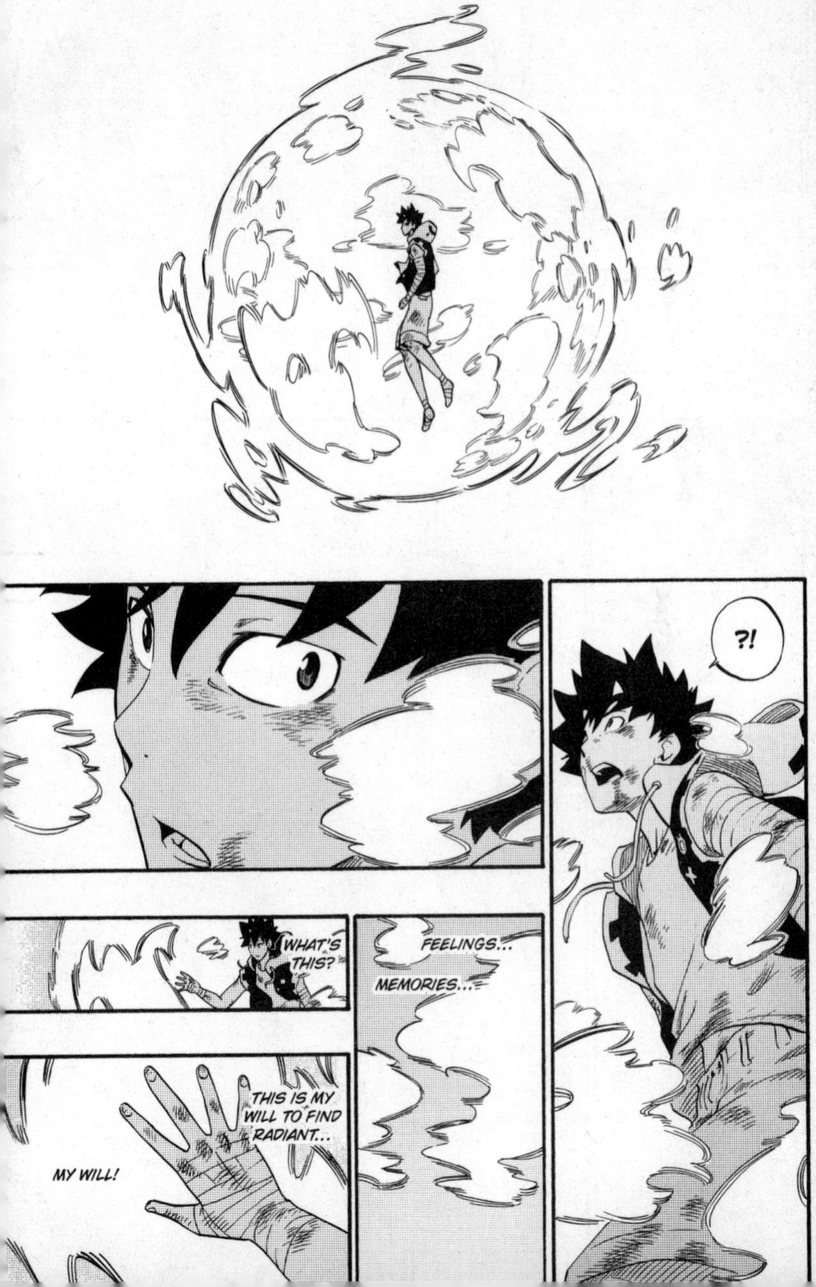
?!
WHAT'S THIS?
FEELINGS...
MEMORIES...
THIS IS MY WILL TO FIND RADIANT...
MY WILL!

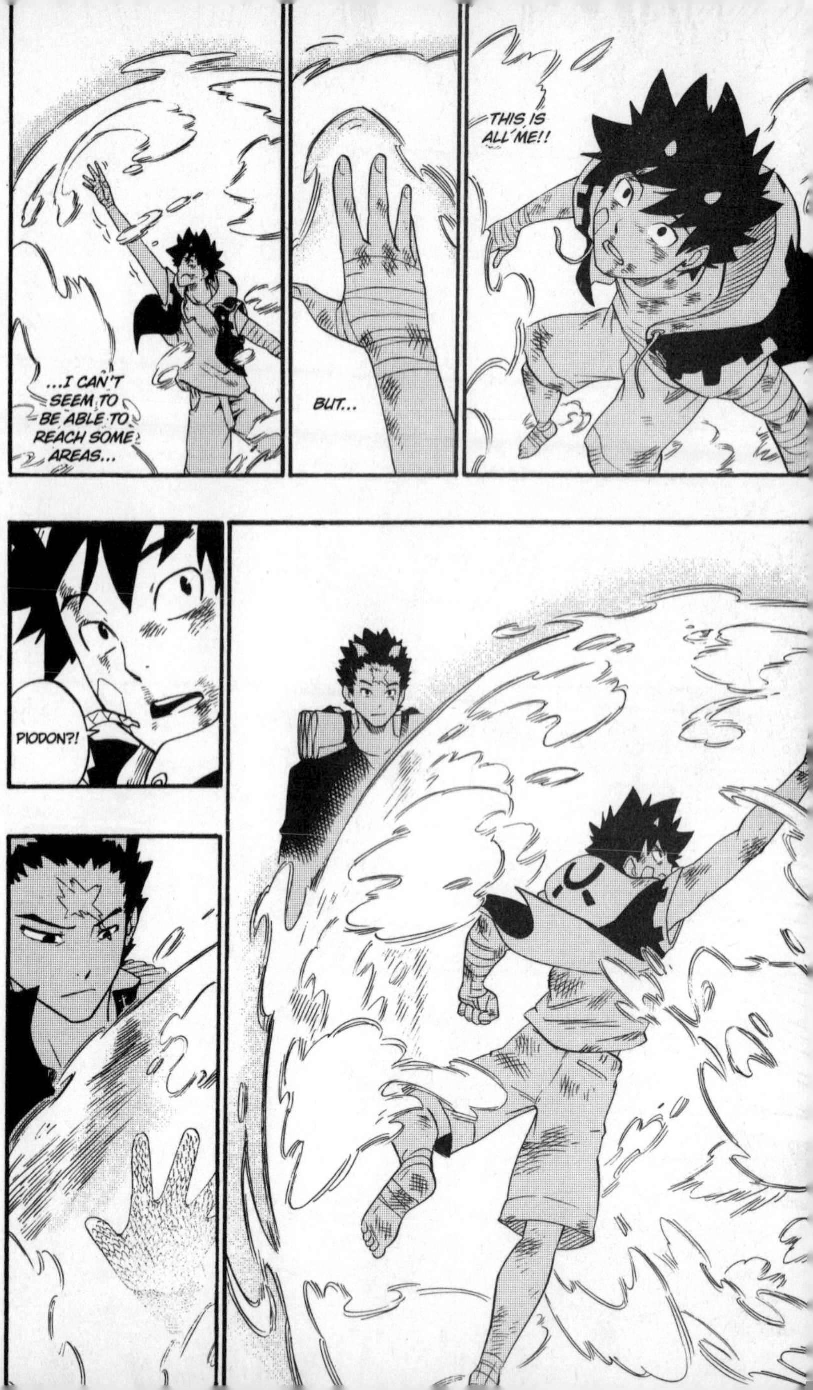
THIS IS ALL ME!!
BUT...
...I CAN'T SEEM TO BE ABLE TO REACH SOME AREAS...
PIODON?!

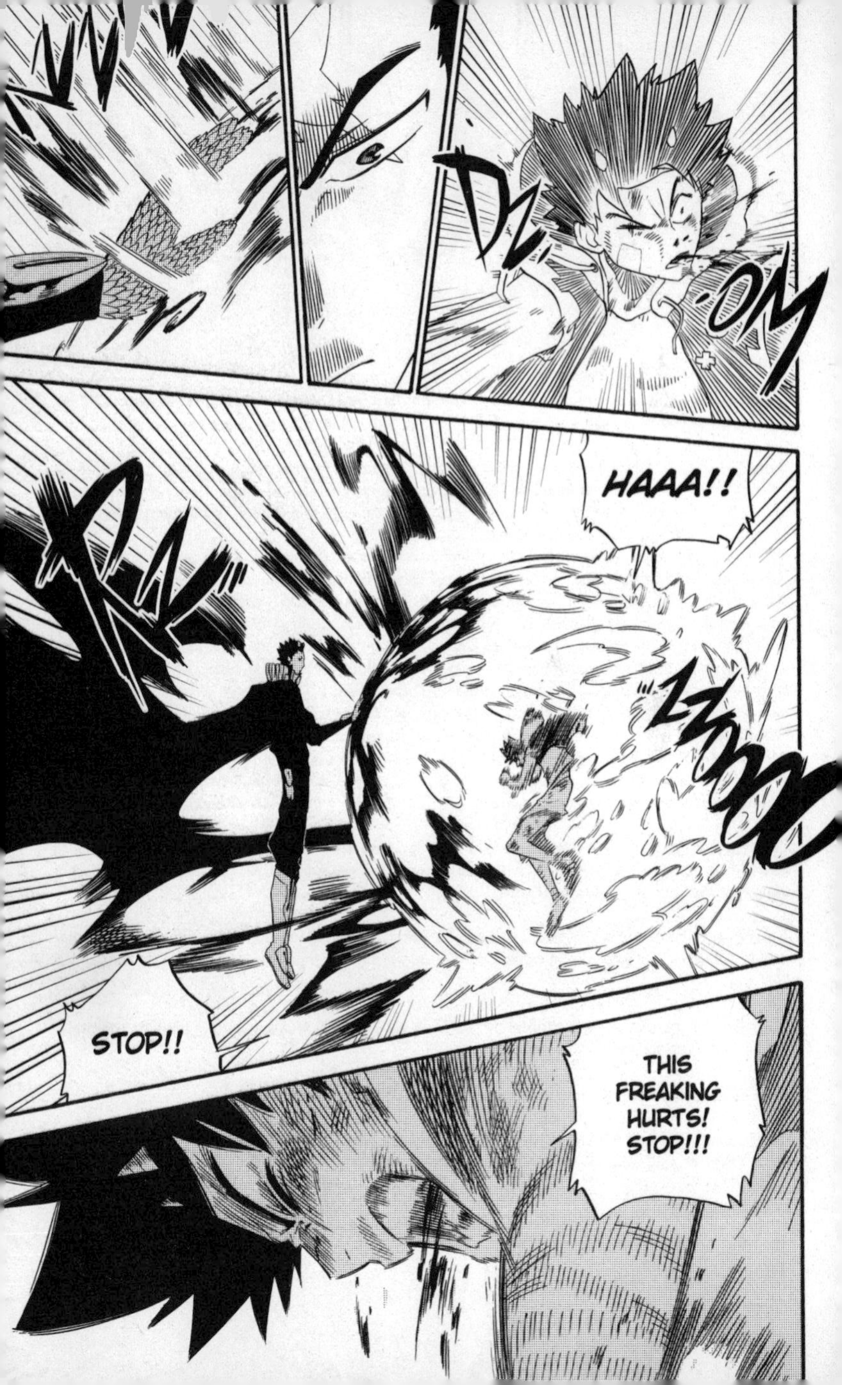
HAAA!!
STOP!!
THIS FREAKING HURTS! STOP!!!

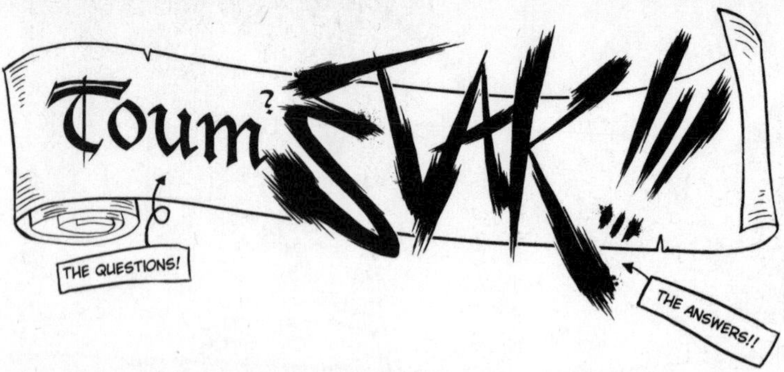
Toum?
STAK!!!
THE QUESTIONS!
THE ANSWERS!!

**<u>Guerriero Thomas</u>: Are the characters in *Radiant* inspired by real or fictional characters? If so, could you tell us who they were based on?**

<u>**Tony Valente:**</u> Some of them are, yes! In terms of historical figures, Torque comes from Tomás de Torquemada, the first Grand Inquisitor in the 15th century Spanish Inquisition. Same for Konrad von Marburg, who was the first German Inquisitor (in the 13th century), and Santori, whose name comes from Giulio Antonio Santorio, an Italian inquisitor.

In terms of folklore, I borrowed the Slavic legend of the witch, Baba Yaga, for Yaga (though in *Radiant* he's a man, not a woman). Hameline is the female version of the main character in the story of *The Pied Piper of Hamelin*. As for Boobrie, he's actually a mythological creature in Scottish folklore—a bird capable of roaring that haunts the Scottish lochs. I'm probably forgetting a few others, but those are the main ones. Since we're talking about references anyway, let me just add this about the Inquisition. In volume 3, chapter 18, Ullmina recites a passage from a book about witches who manipulate men. "Witches sometimes collect virile people in great numbers (20 or 30) and then drop them off in bird nests or trap them in boxes where they'll be kept alive, eating oats and other things." That line came straight out of the French translated version of a book called the *Malleus Maleficarum*, a book written by two inquisitors in 1486 and which served as a reference for quite a few inquisitors back then to help detect witches. Yup, nests of men who eat oats. I mean...seriously, guys? Can you believe that?! Why not oats and ravioli too while you're at it? And what about drinks, huh? What'd they drink?? At least be complete about it.

---

**<u>Bodevin Pierrick</u>: The world of *Radiant* is very focused on what's up in the sky right now, with basically only islets and airships. I wanted to know if are we going to get any information on what happens underneath all those clouds?**

<u>**Tony Valente:**</u> Yes, that will be talked about in the future! I also promised a map of the world and other related elements, but I decided it would be more relevant to put that in volume 5 with the start of the next arc.

**<u>Bodevin Pierrick</u>: I'm really intrigued by the flask we see Seth wearing on the back of volume 1, is that just a normal magic potion?**

<u>**Tony Valente:**</u> It's pee. Pee from the infamous nest of oats-eating men.

---

**<u>Camarahmad0</u>: Could a human or even a wizard touch Radiant? If so, then could he possibly level up to a higher rank (like, Sorcerers and Demons)?**

<u>**Tony Valente:**</u> No.

Send your questions to: <u>radiant@ankama.com</u>

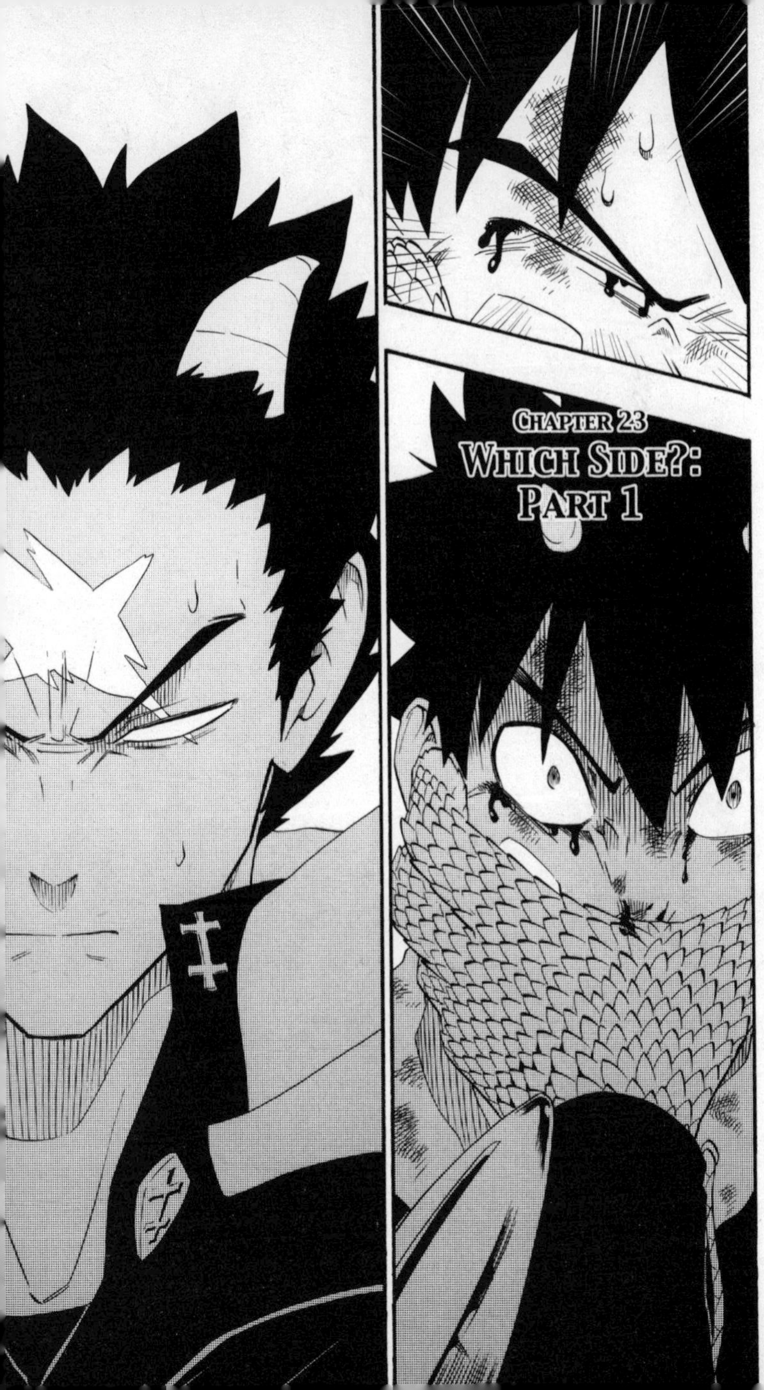
Chapter 23
Which Side?:
Part 1

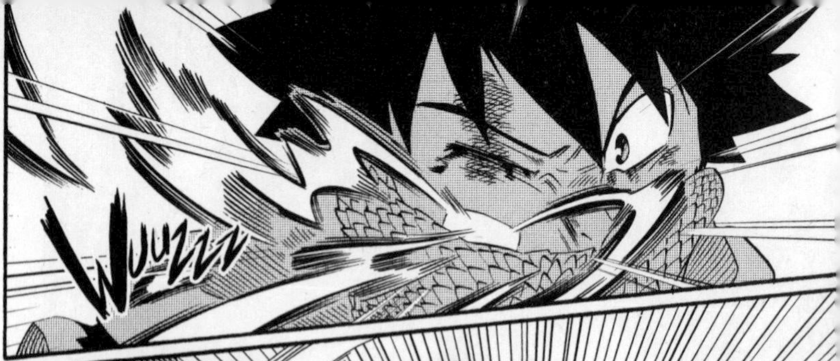
WUUZZZ
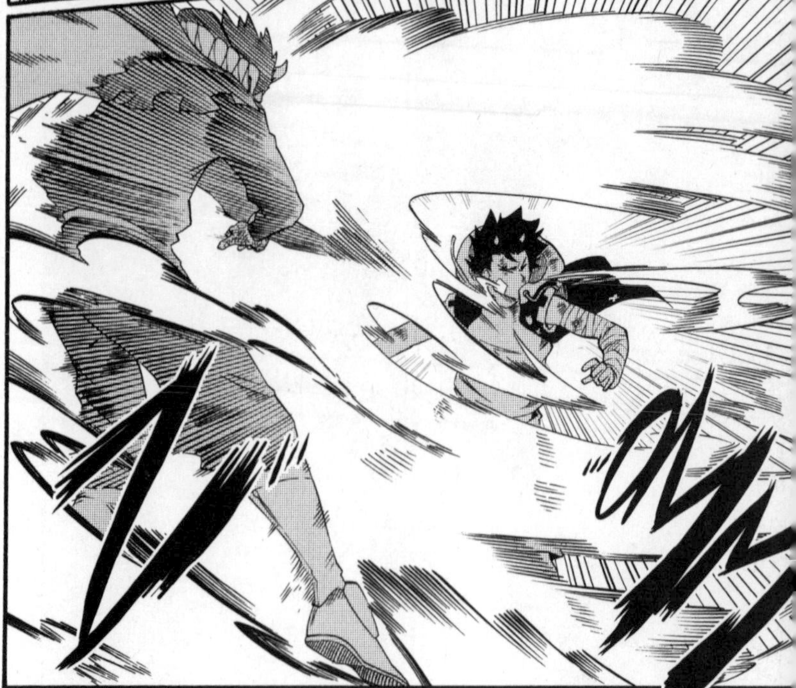
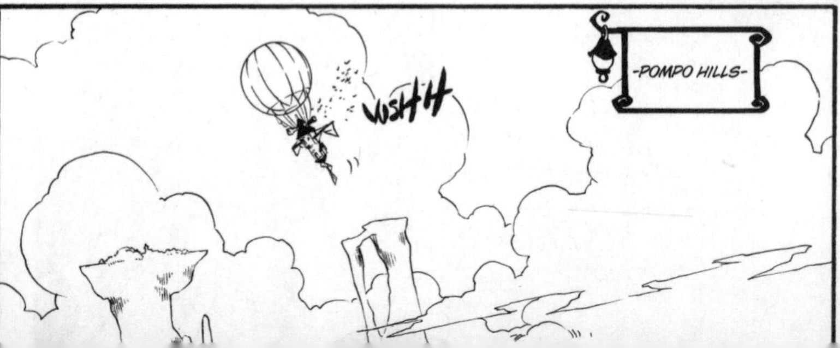
-POMPO HILLS-
WSHH

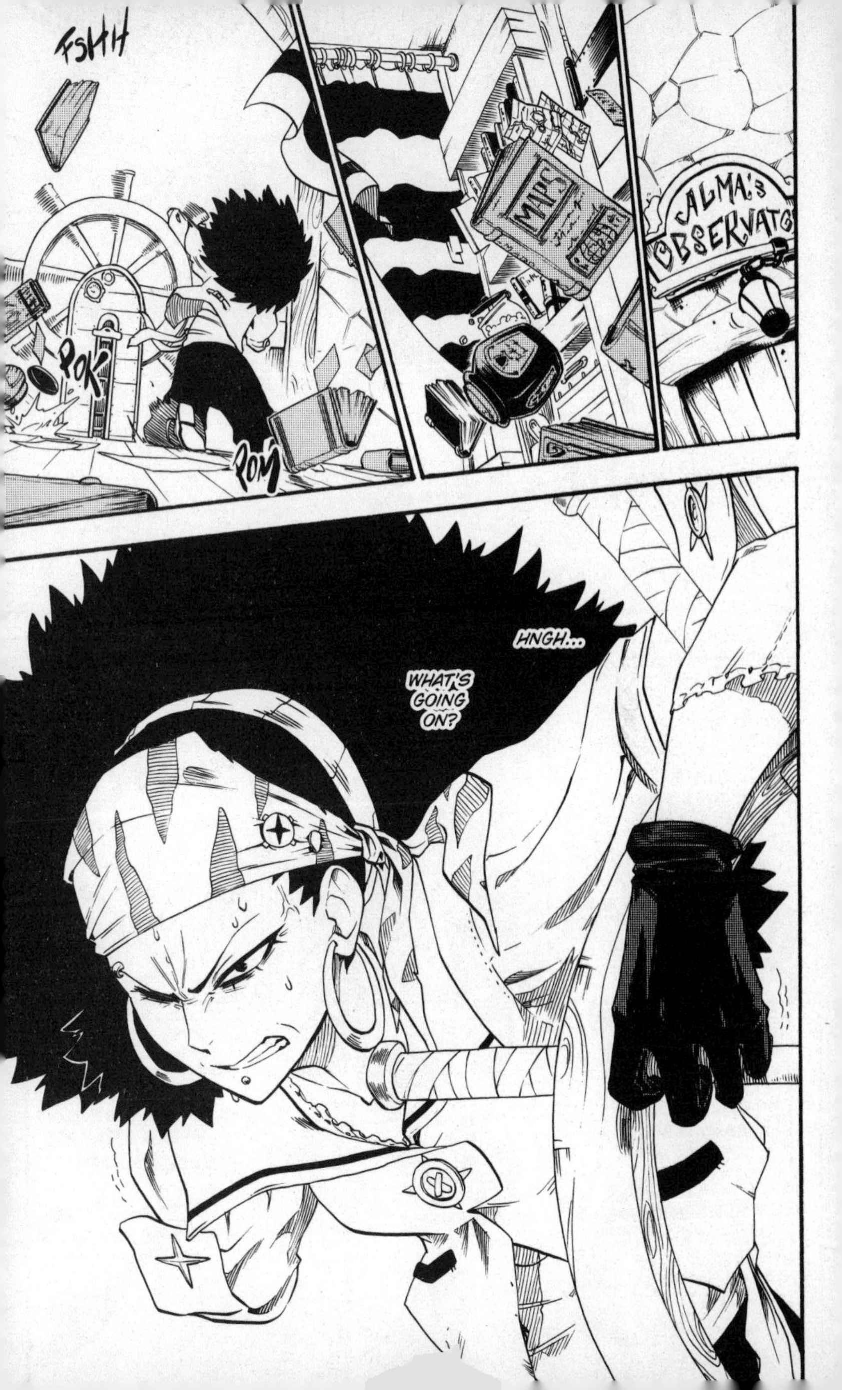
ALMA's
OBSERVATO
POM
POK
FSHH
HNGH...
WHAT'S GOING ON?

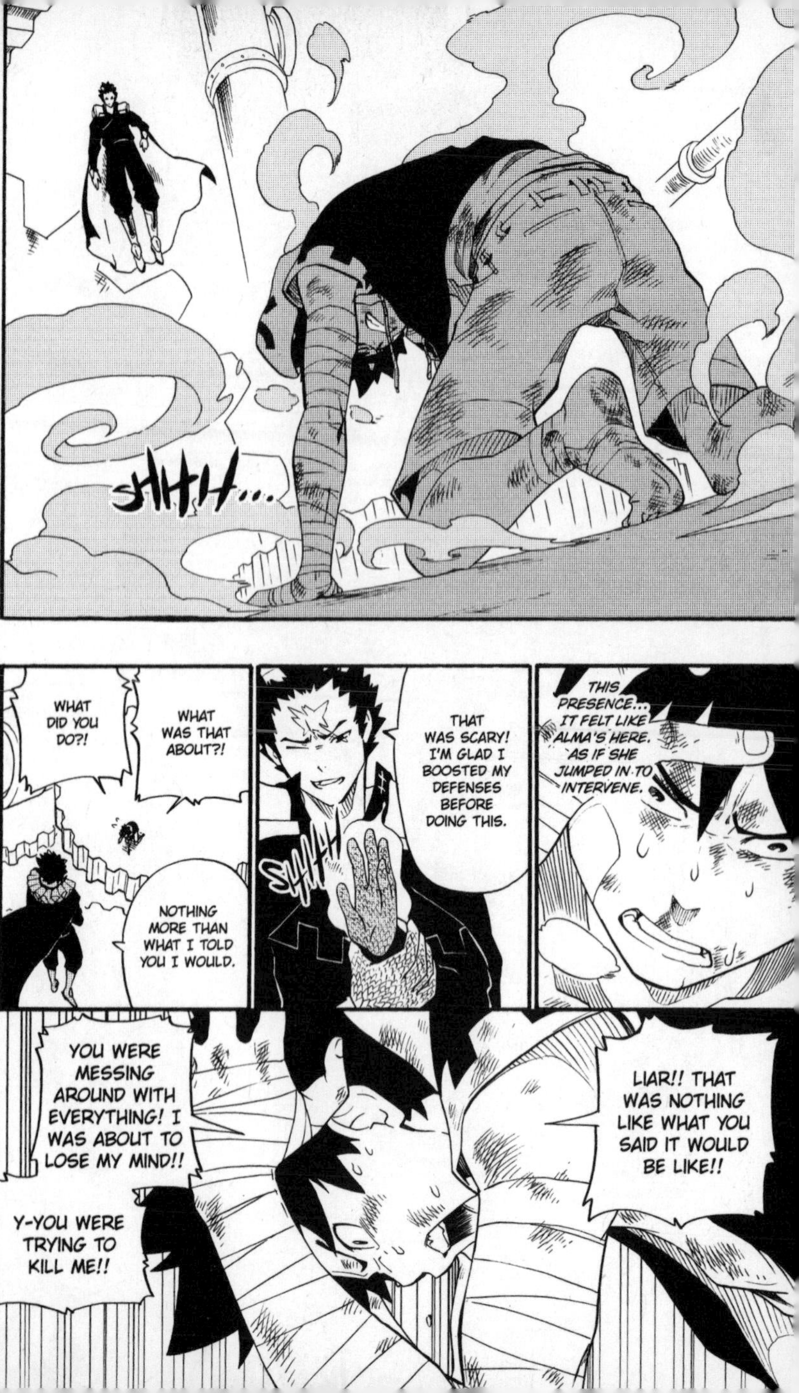
SHHH...
THIS PRESENCE... IT FELT LIKE ALMA'S HERE. AS IF SHE JUMPED IN TO INTERVENE.
THAT WAS SCARY! I'M GLAD I BOOSTED MY DEFENSES BEFORE DOING THIS.
WHAT WAS THAT ABOUT?!
WHAT DID YOU DO?!
NOTHING MORE THAN WHAT I TOLD YOU I WOULD.
LIAR!! THAT WAS NOTHING LIKE WHAT YOU SAID IT WOULD BE LIKE!!
YOU WERE MESSING AROUND WITH EVERYTHING! I WAS ABOUT TO LOSE MY MIND!!
Y-YOU WERE TRYING TO KILL ME!!

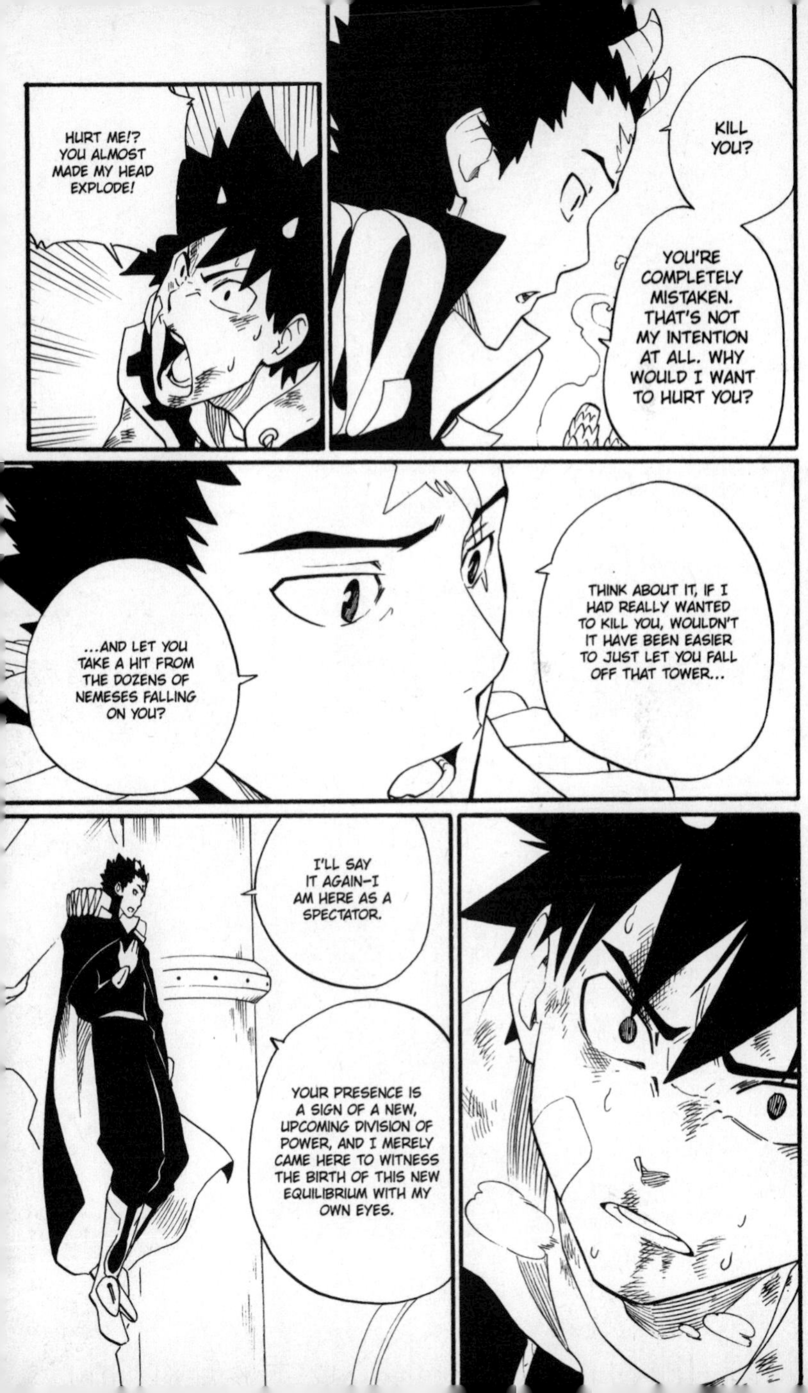
KILL YOU?
YOU'RE COMPLETELY MISTAKEN. THAT'S NOT MY INTENTION AT ALL. WHY WOULD I WANT TO HURT YOU?
HURT ME!? YOU ALMOST MADE MY HEAD EXPLODE!
THINK ABOUT IT, IF I HAD REALLY WANTED TO KILL YOU, WOULDN'T IT HAVE BEEN EASIER TO JUST LET YOU FALL OFF THAT TOWER...
...AND LET YOU TAKE A HIT FROM THE DOZENS OF NEMESES FALLING ON YOU?
I'LL SAY IT AGAIN—I AM HERE AS A SPECTATOR.
YOUR PRESENCE IS A SIGN OF A NEW, UPCOMING DIVISION OF POWER, AND I MERELY CAME HERE TO WITNESS THE BIRTH OF THIS NEW EQUILIBRIUM WITH MY OWN EYES.

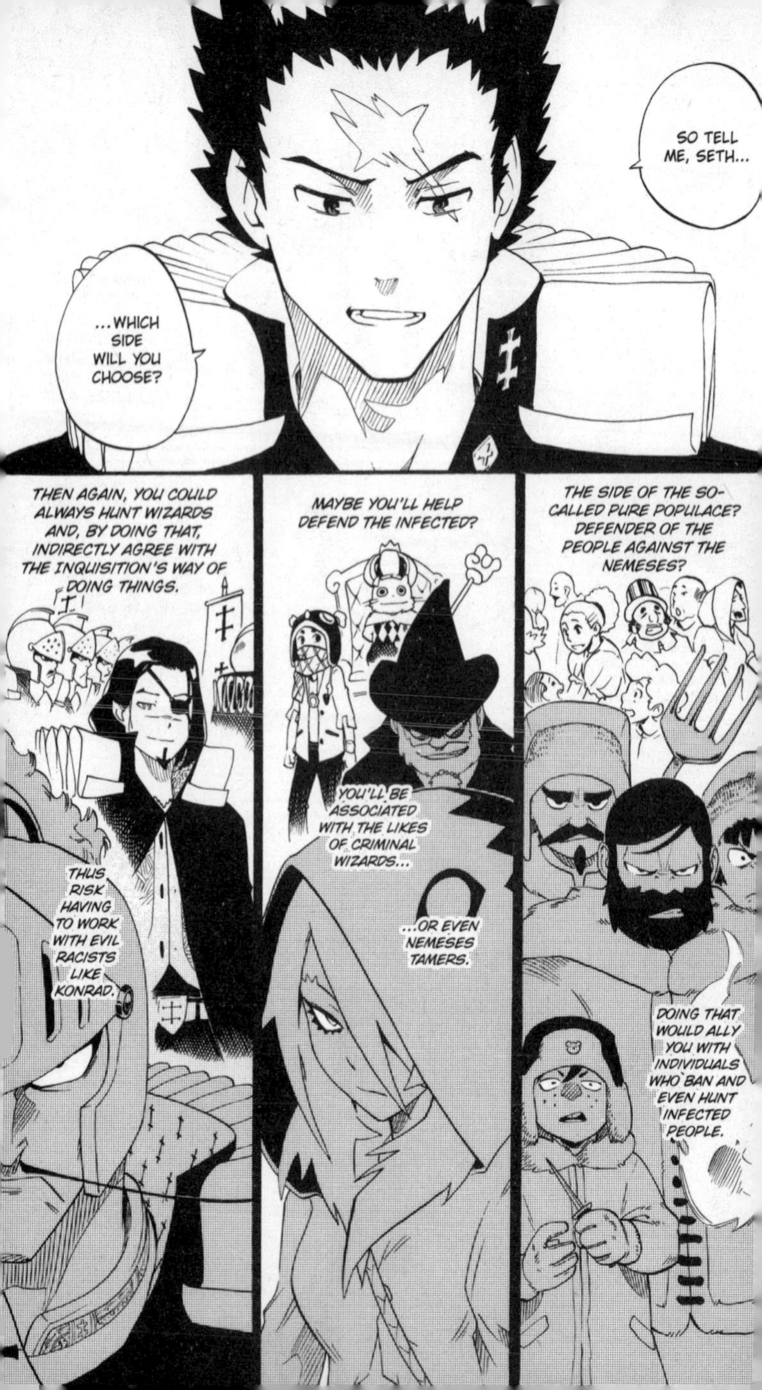
SO TELL ME, SETH...
...WHICH SIDE WILL YOU CHOOSE?
THE SIDE OF THE SO-CALLED PURE POPULACE? DEFENDER OF THE PEOPLE AGAINST THE NEMESES?
DOING THAT WOULD ALLY YOU WITH INDIVIDUALS WHO BAN AND EVEN HUNT INFECTED PEOPLE.
MAYBE YOU'LL HELP DEFEND THE INFECTED?
YOU'LL BE ASSOCIATED WITH THE LIKES OF CRIMINAL WIZARDS...
...OR EVEN NEMESES TAMERS.
THEN AGAIN, YOU COULD ALWAYS HUNT WIZARDS AND, BY DOING THAT, INDIRECTLY AGREE WITH THE INQUISITION'S WAY OF DOING THINGS.
THUS RISK HAVING TO WORK WITH EVIL RACISTS LIKE KONRAD.

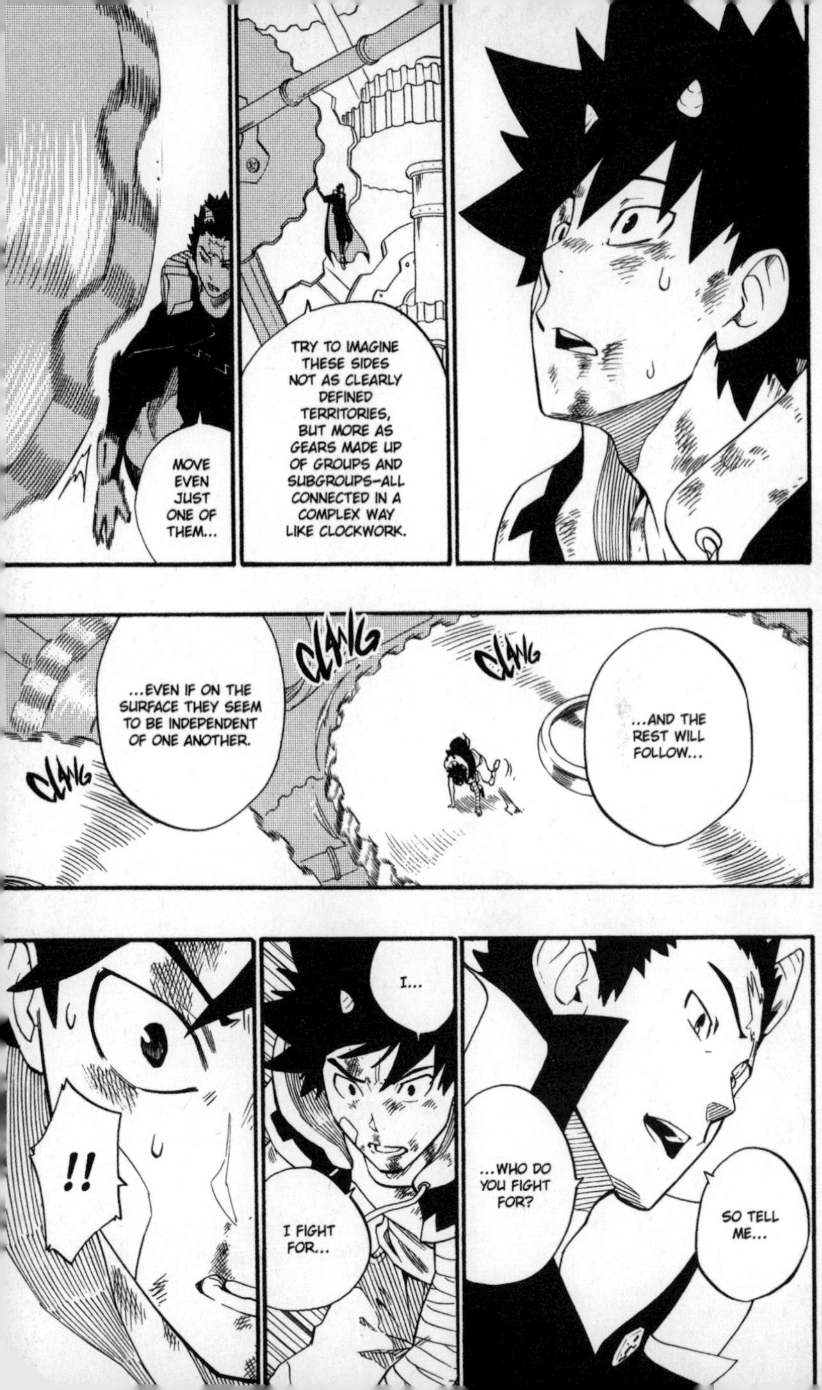
TRY TO IMAGINE THESE SIDES NOT AS CLEARLY DEFINED TERRITORIES, BUT MORE AS GEARS MADE UP OF GROUPS AND SUBGROUPS—ALL CONNECTED IN A COMPLEX WAY LIKE CLOCKWORK.
MOVE EVEN JUST ONE OF THEM...
...AND THE REST WILL FOLLOW...
CLANG
CLANG
...EVEN IF ON THE SURFACE THEY SEEM TO BE INDEPENDENT OF ONE ANOTHER.
CLANG
SO TELL ME...
...WHO DO YOU FIGHT FOR?
I...
I FIGHT FOR...
!!

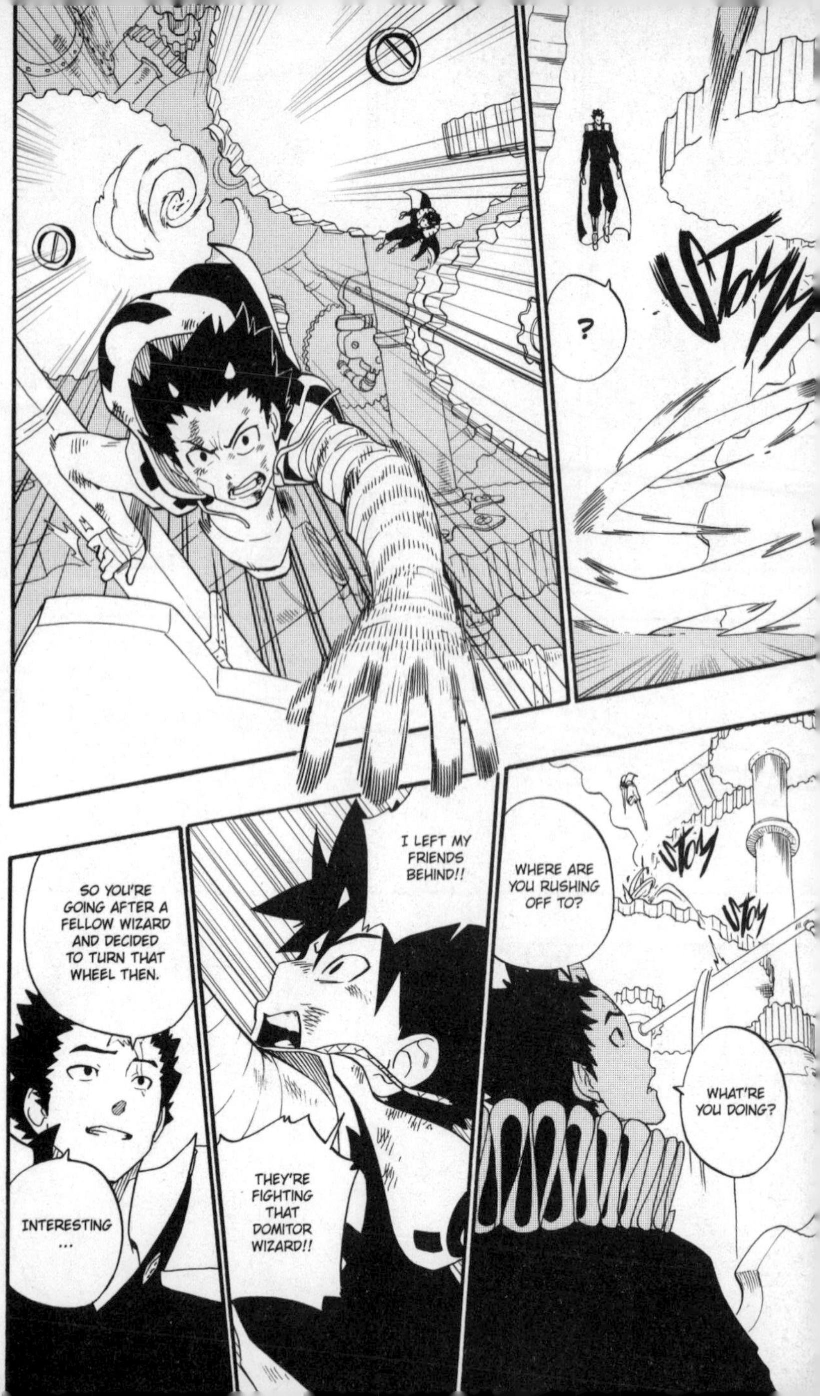

?
STOM
WHERE ARE YOU RUSHING OFF TO?
STOM
STOM
WHAT'RE YOU DOING?
I LEFT MY FRIENDS BEHIND!!
THEY'RE FIGHTING THAT DOMITOR WIZARD!!
SO YOU'RE GOING AFTER A FELLOW WIZARD AND DECIDED TO TURN THAT WHEEL THEN.
INTERESTING ...

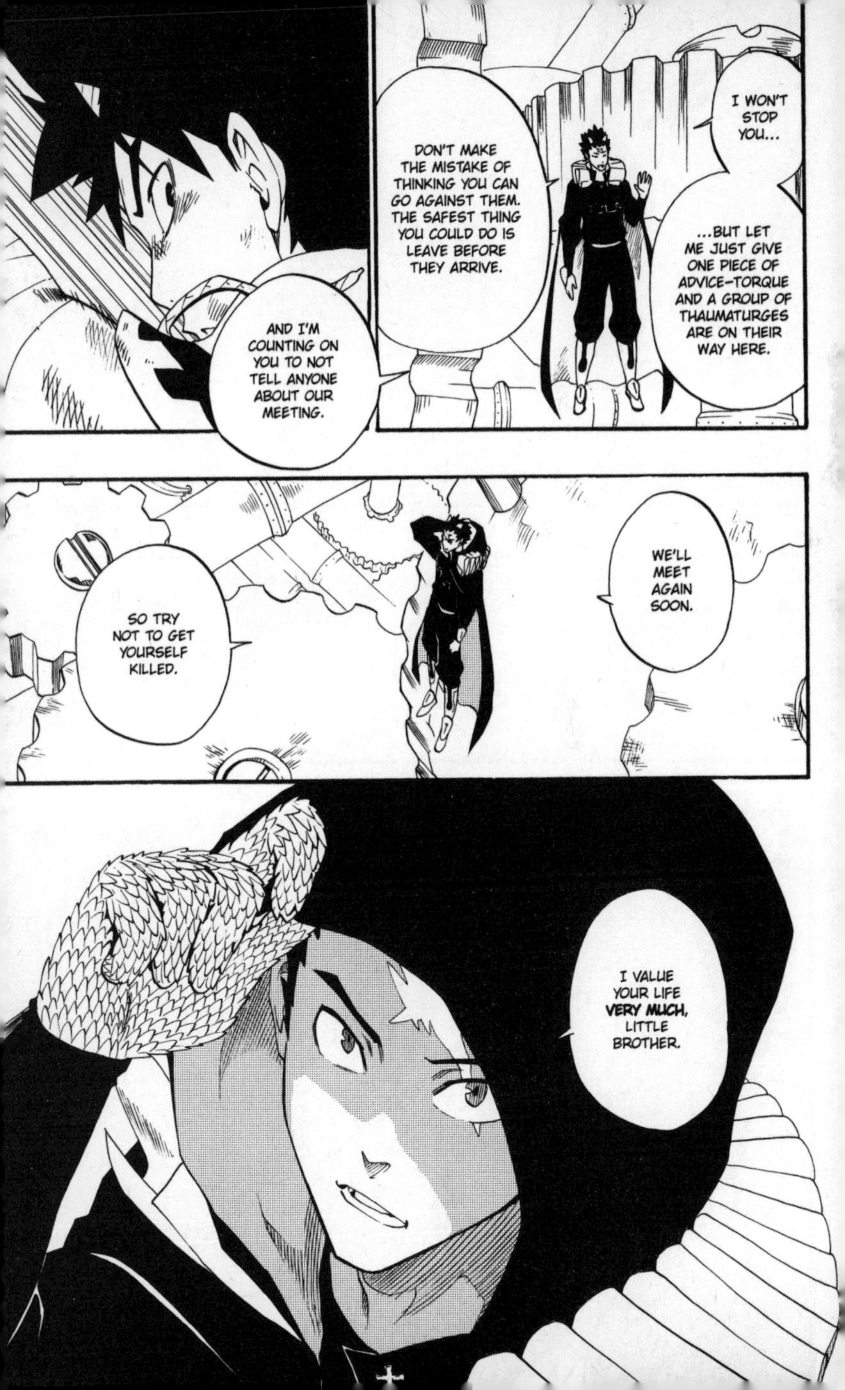
I WON'T STOP YOU...
...BUT LET ME JUST GIVE ONE PIECE OF ADVICE–TORQUE AND A GROUP OF THAUMATURGES ARE ON THEIR WAY HERE.
DON'T MAKE THE MISTAKE OF THINKING YOU CAN GO AGAINST THEM. THE SAFEST THING YOU COULD DO IS LEAVE BEFORE THEY ARRIVE.
AND I'M COUNTING ON YOU TO NOT TELL ANYONE ABOUT OUR MEETING.
WE'LL MEET AGAIN SOON.
SO TRY NOT TO GET YOURSELF KILLED.
I VALUE YOUR LIFE **VERY MUCH,** LITTLE BROTHER.

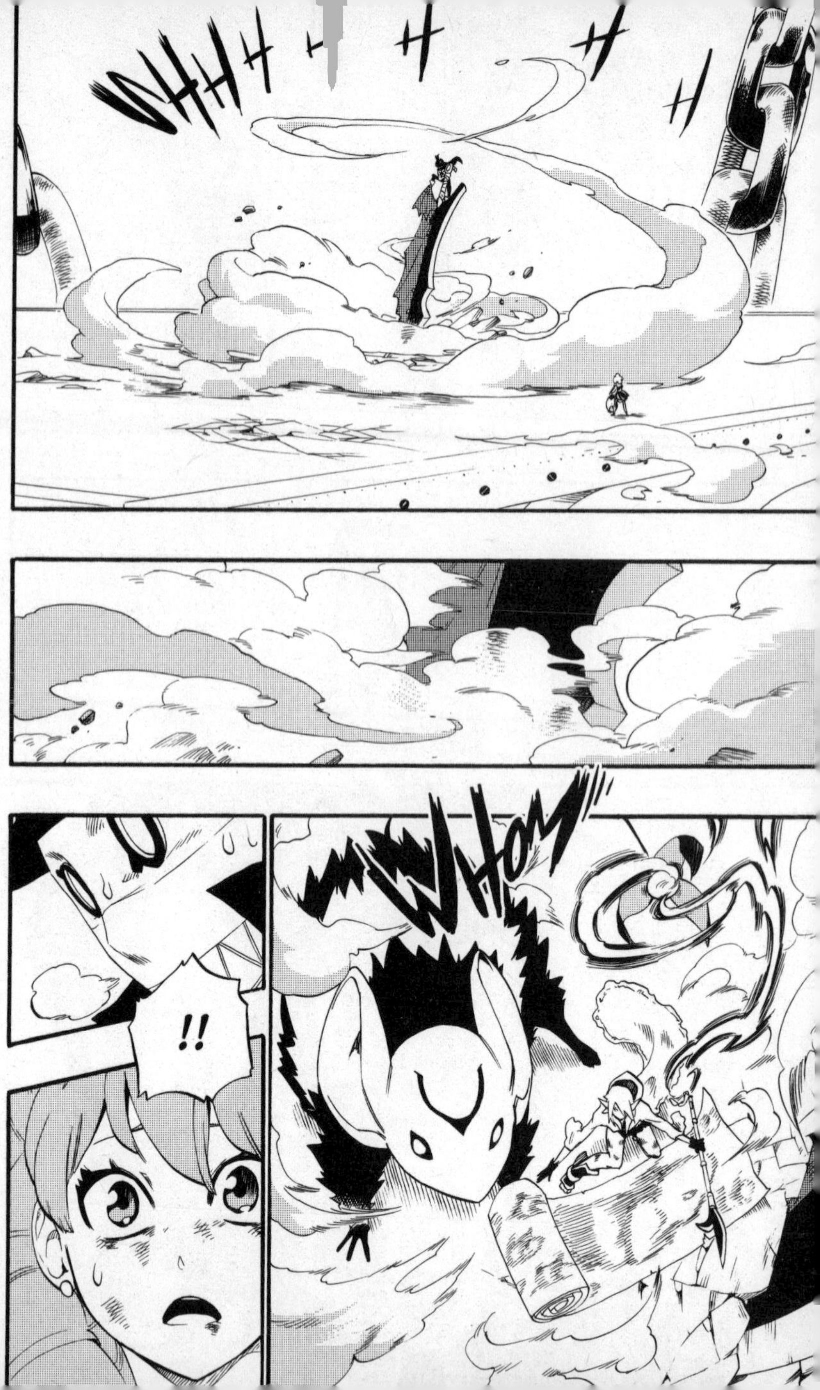

OHHHH
WHOM
!!

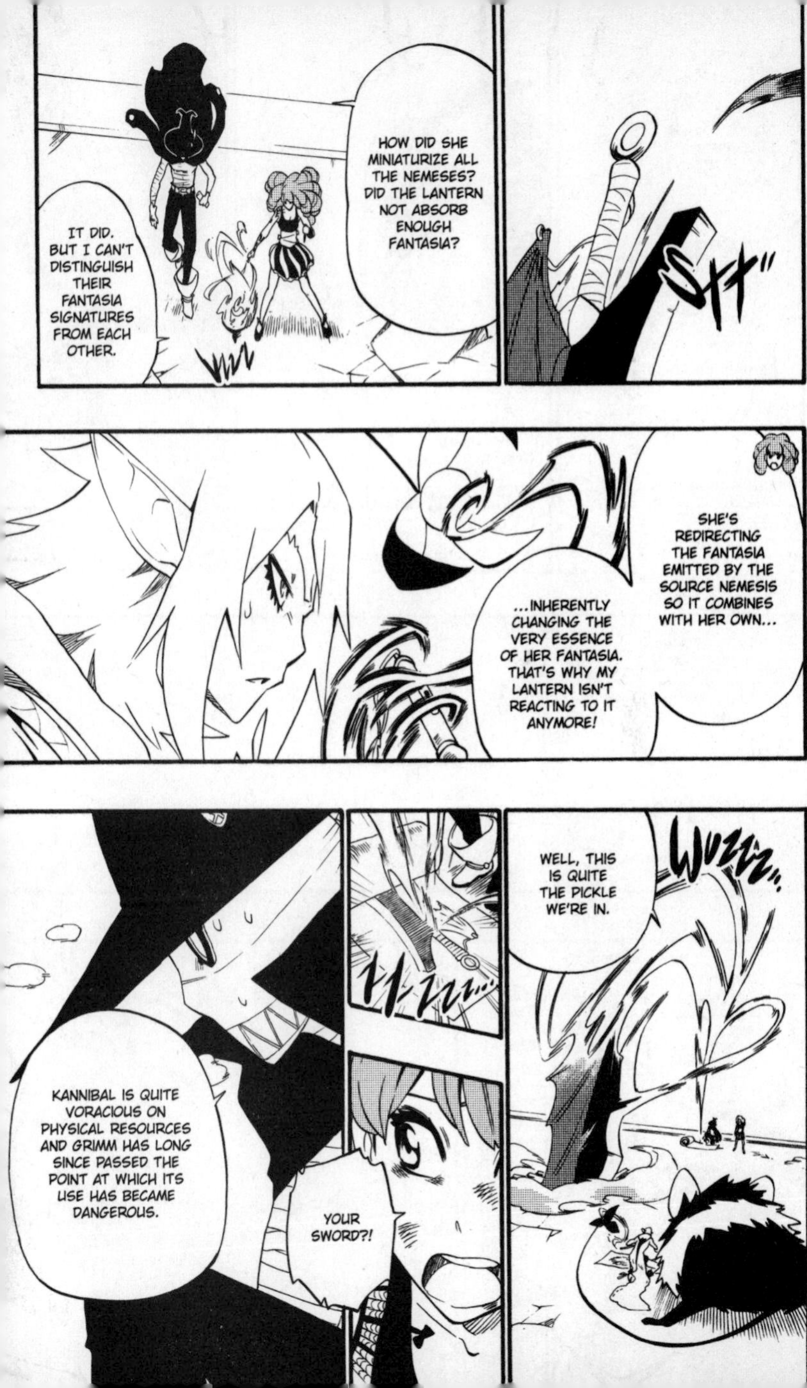
HOW DID SHE MINIATURIZE ALL THE NEMESES? DID THE LANTERN NOT ABSORB ENOUGH FANTASIA?
IT DID. BUT I CAN'T DISTINGUISH THEIR FANTASIA SIGNATURES FROM EACH OTHER.
SHE'S REDIRECTING THE FANTASIA EMITTED BY THE SOURCE NEMESIS SO IT COMBINES WITH HER OWN...
...INHERENTLY CHANGING THE VERY ESSENCE OF HER FANTASIA. THAT'S WHY MY LANTERN ISN'T REACTING TO IT ANYMORE!
WELL, THIS IS QUITE THE PICKLE WE'RE IN.
YOUR SWORD?!
KANNIBAL IS QUITE VORACIOUS ON PHYSICAL RESOURCES AND GRIMM HAS LONG SINCE PASSED THE POINT AT WHICH ITS USE HAS BECAME DANGEROUS.

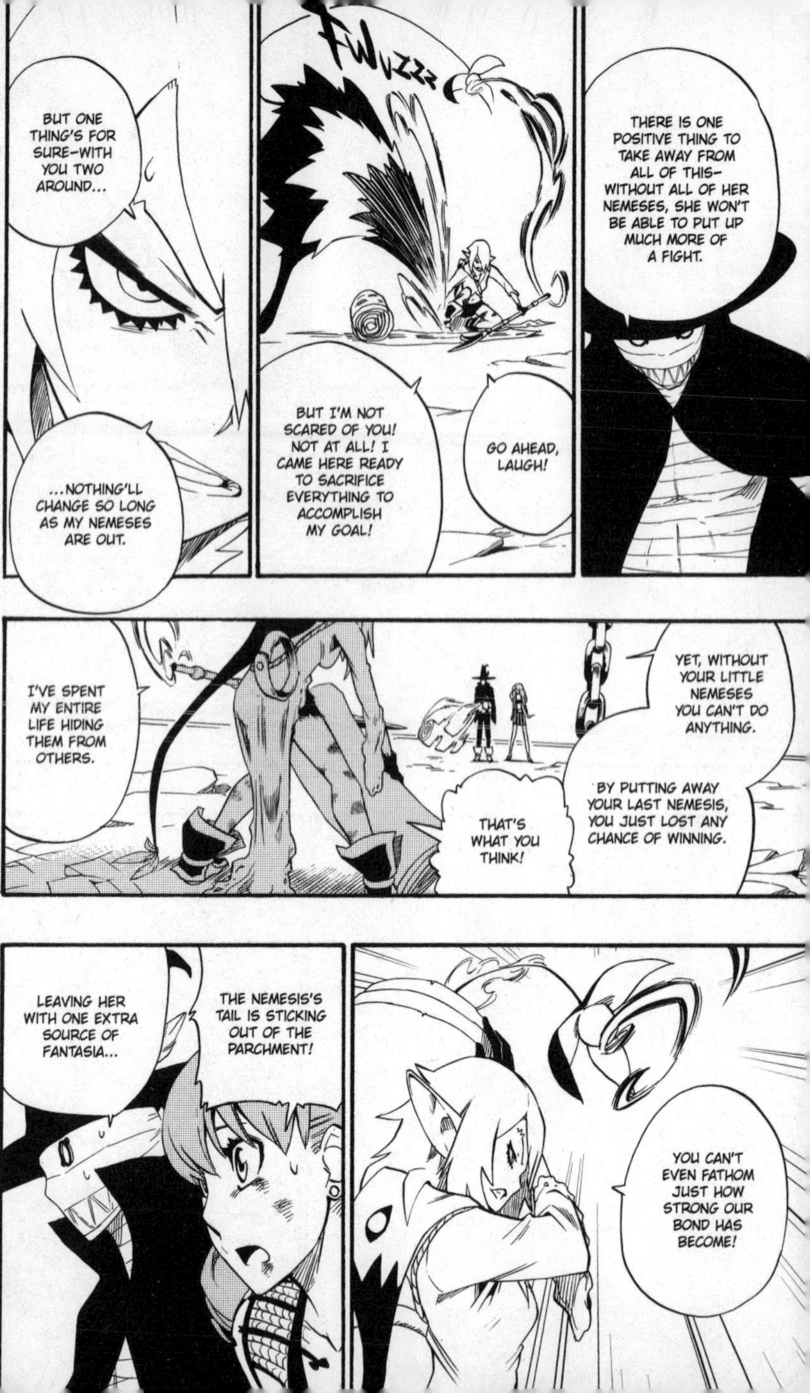
THERE IS ONE POSITIVE THING TO TAKE AWAY FROM ALL OF THIS—WITHOUT ALL OF HER NEMESES, SHE WON'T BE ABLE TO PUT UP MUCH MORE OF A FIGHT.
FWUZZZ
GO AHEAD, LAUGH!
BUT I'M NOT SCARED OF YOU! NOT AT ALL! I CAME HERE READY TO SACRIFICE EVERYTHING TO ACCOMPLISH MY GOAL!
BUT ONE THING'S FOR SURE—WITH YOU TWO AROUND...
...NOTHING'LL CHANGE SO LONG AS MY NEMESES ARE OUT.
YET, WITHOUT YOUR LITTLE NEMESES YOU CAN'T DO ANYTHING.
BY PUTTING AWAY YOUR LAST NEMESIS, YOU JUST LOST ANY CHANCE OF WINNING.
THAT'S WHAT YOU THINK!
I'VE SPENT MY ENTIRE LIFE HIDING THEM FROM OTHERS.
YOU CAN'T EVEN FATHOM JUST HOW STRONG OUR BOND HAS BECOME!
THE NEMESIS'S TAIL IS STICKING OUT OF THE PARCHMENT!
LEAVING HER WITH ONE EXTRA SOURCE OF FANTASIA...

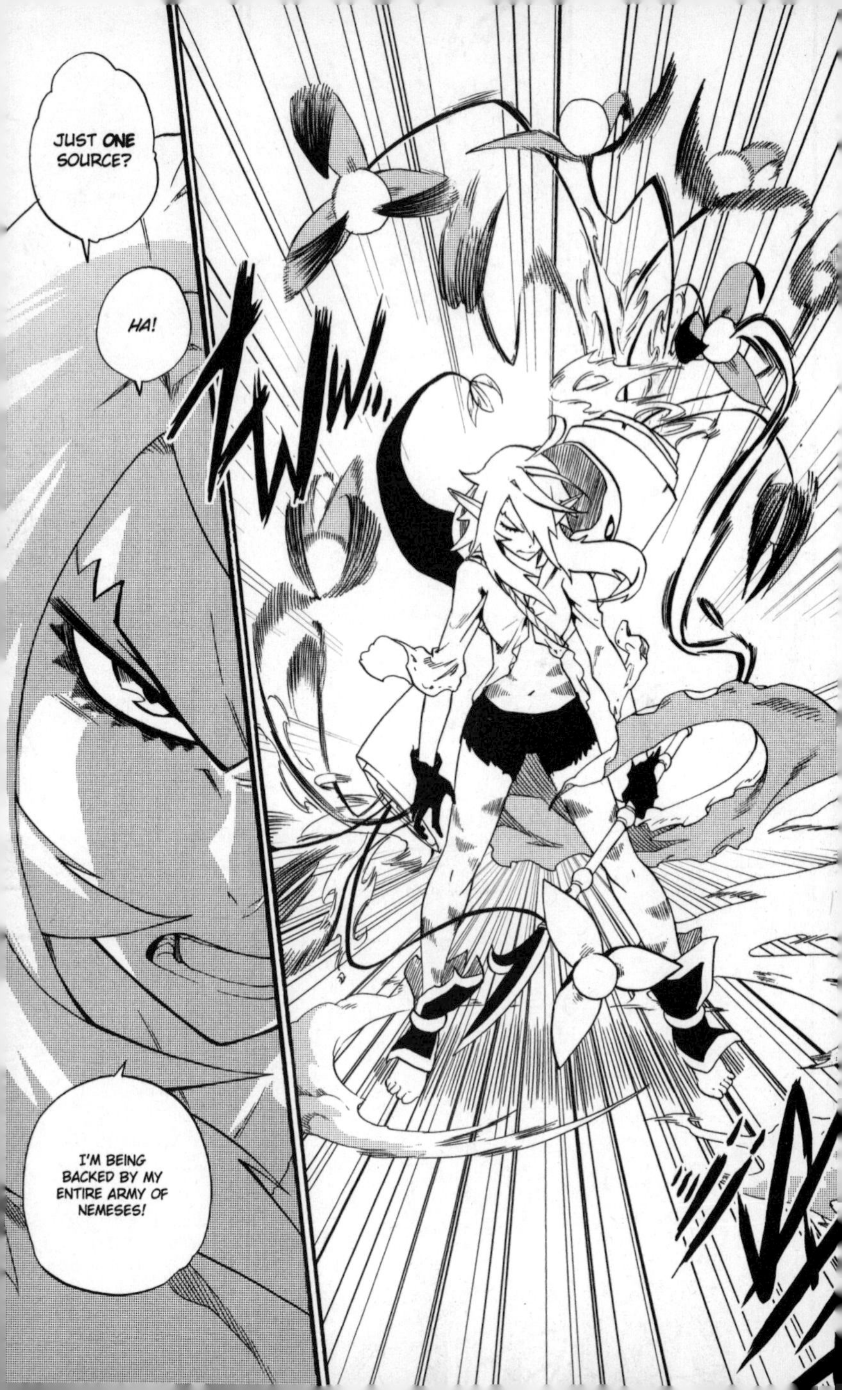
JUST ONE SOURCE?
HA!
I'M BEING BACKED BY MY ENTIRE ARMY OF NEMESES!

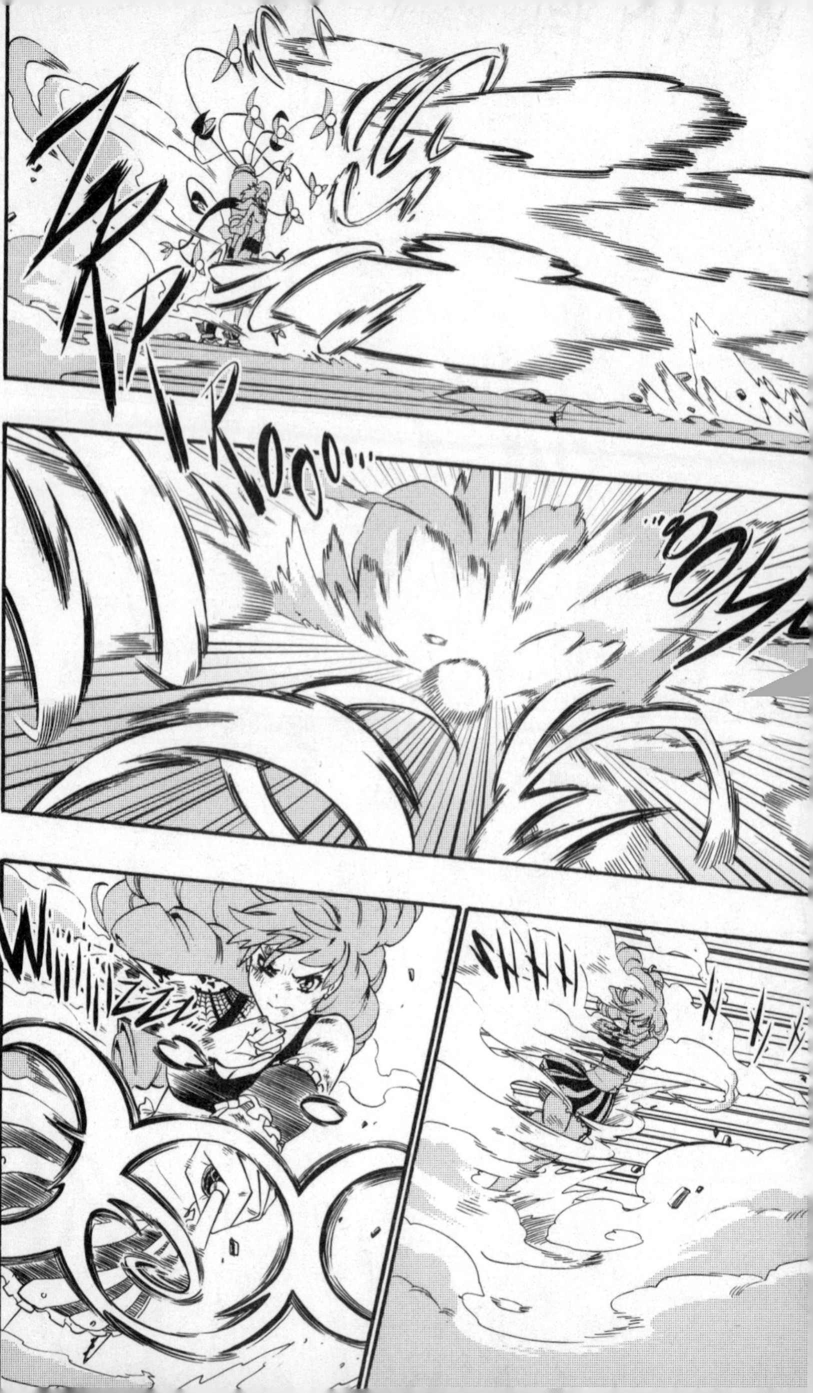
KRRRROOO...
...OOM
SHHHH
WHIIIIIZZZZ

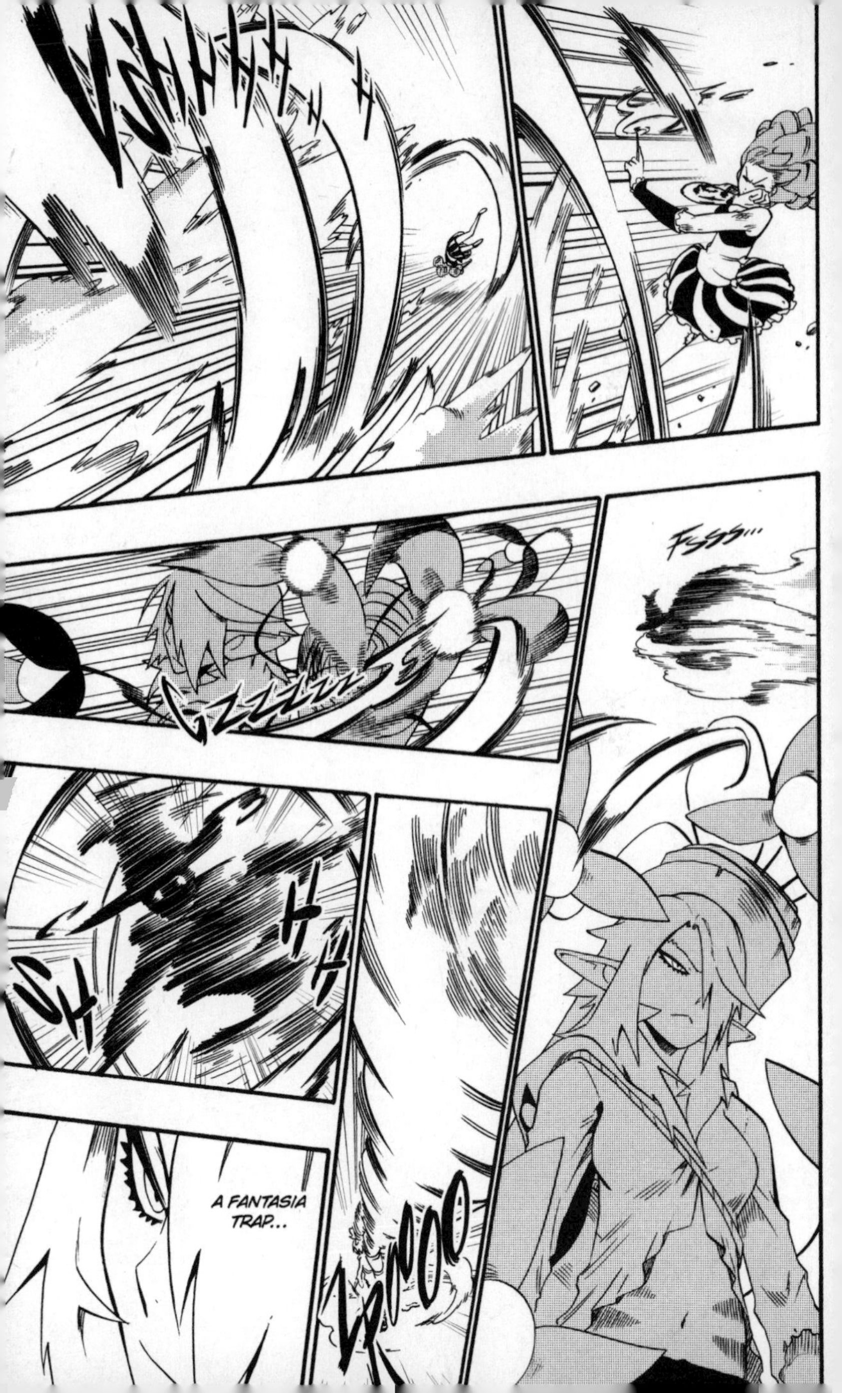
FSSS...
GZZZZZZZ
A FANTASIA TRAP...

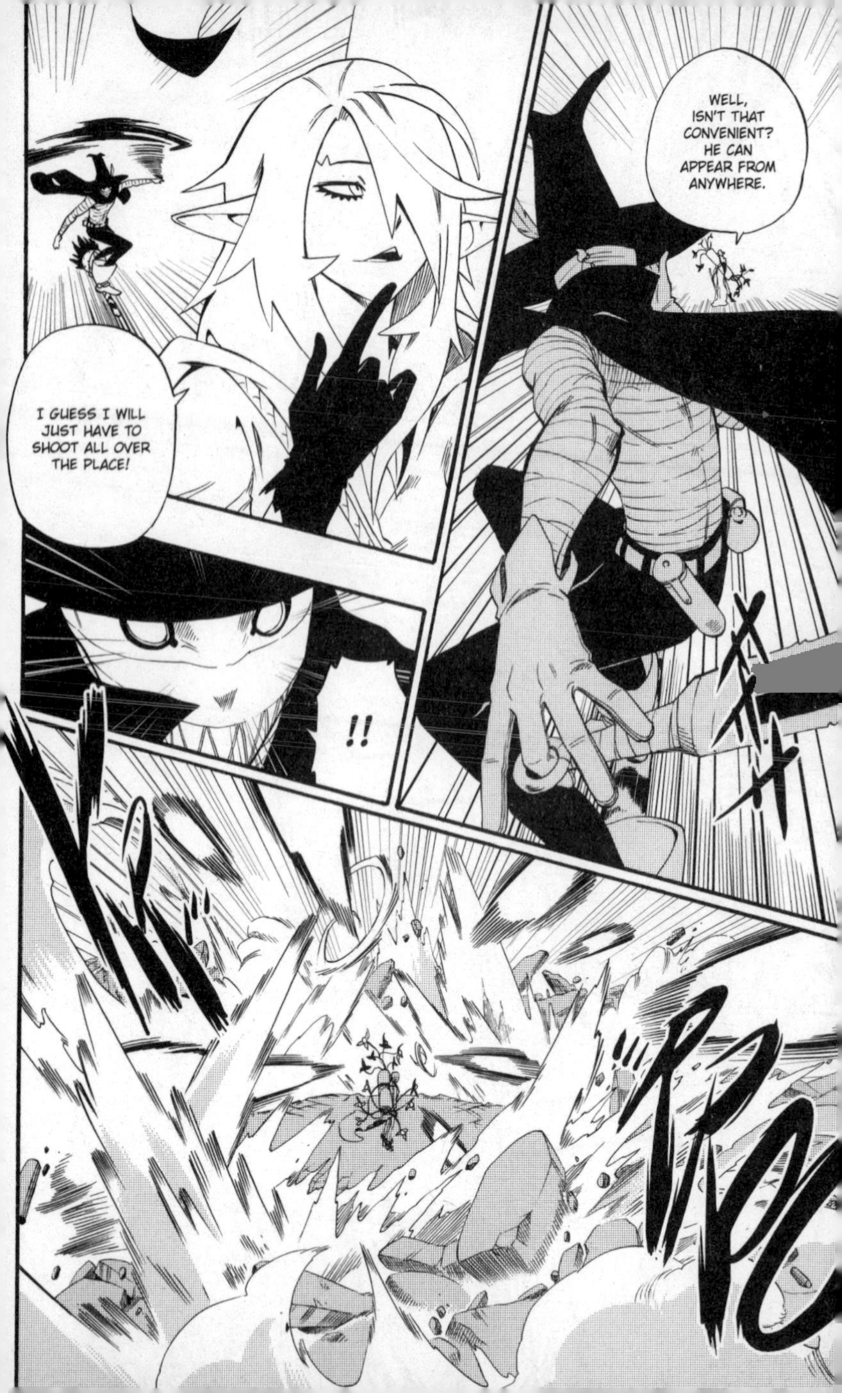
WELL, ISN'T THAT CONVENIENT? HE CAN APPEAR FROM ANYWHERE.
I GUESS I WILL JUST HAVE TO SHOOT ALL OVER THE PLACE!
!!

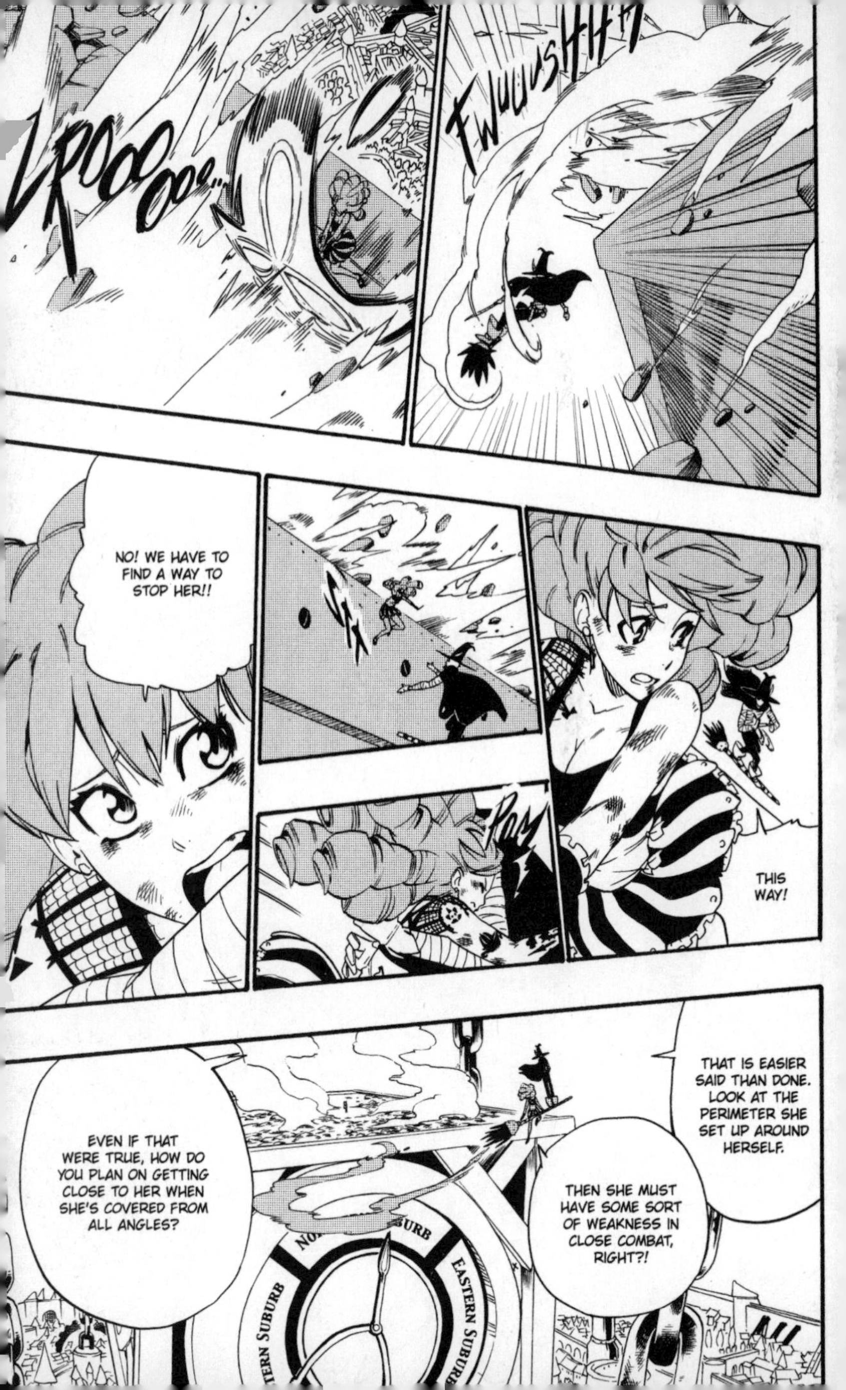
THIS WAY!
NO! WE HAVE TO FIND A WAY TO STOP HER!!
THAT IS EASIER SAID THAN DONE. LOOK AT THE PERIMETER SHE SET UP AROUND HERSELF.
THEN SHE MUST HAVE SOME SORT OF WEAKNESS IN CLOSE COMBAT, RIGHT?!
EVEN IF THAT WERE TRUE, HOW DO YOU PLAN ON GETTING CLOSE TO HER WHEN SHE'S COVERED FROM ALL ANGLES?
EASTERN SUBURB

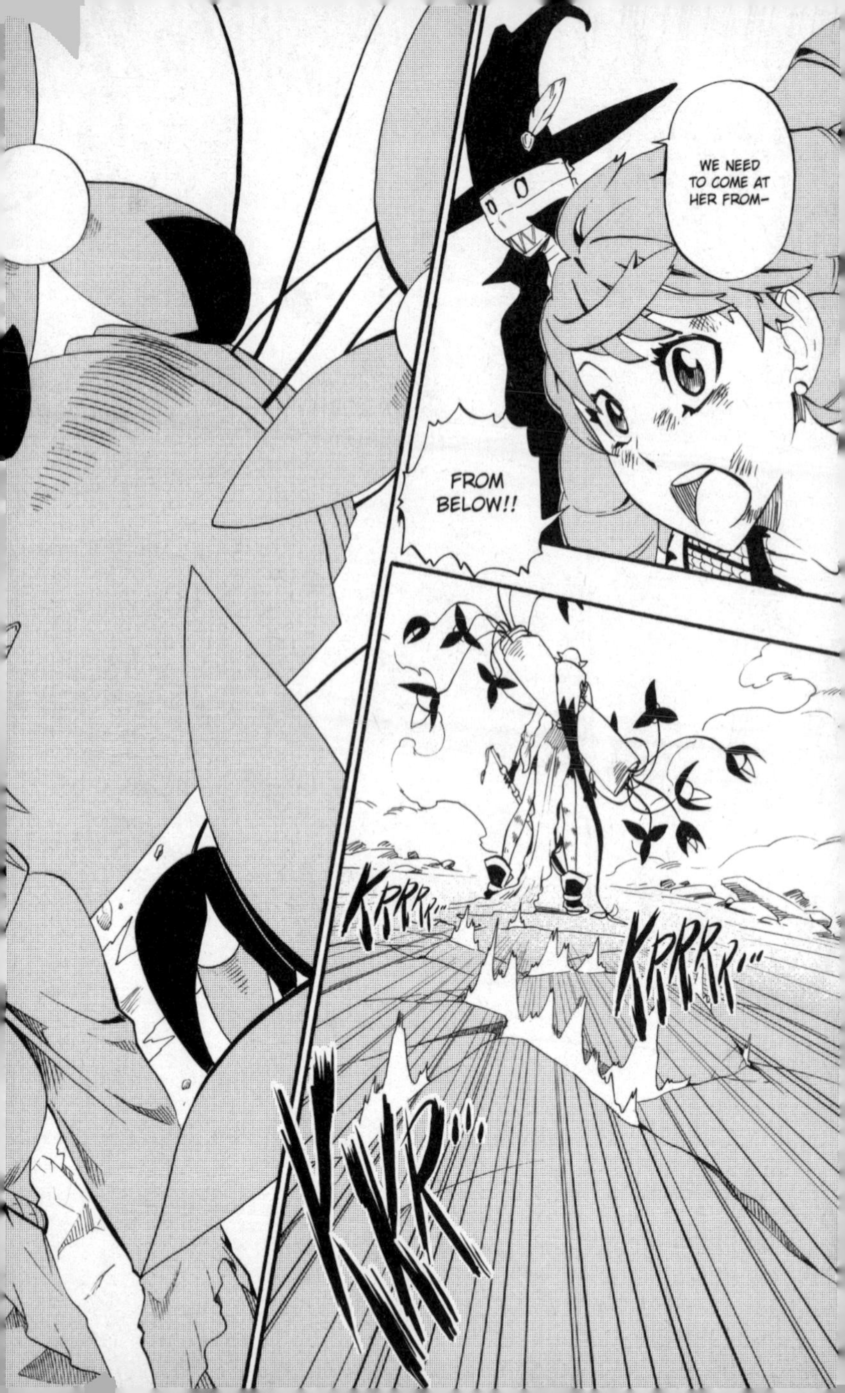
WE NEED TO COME AT HER FROM-
FROM BELOW!!
KRRRR''
KRRRR''
KKR''

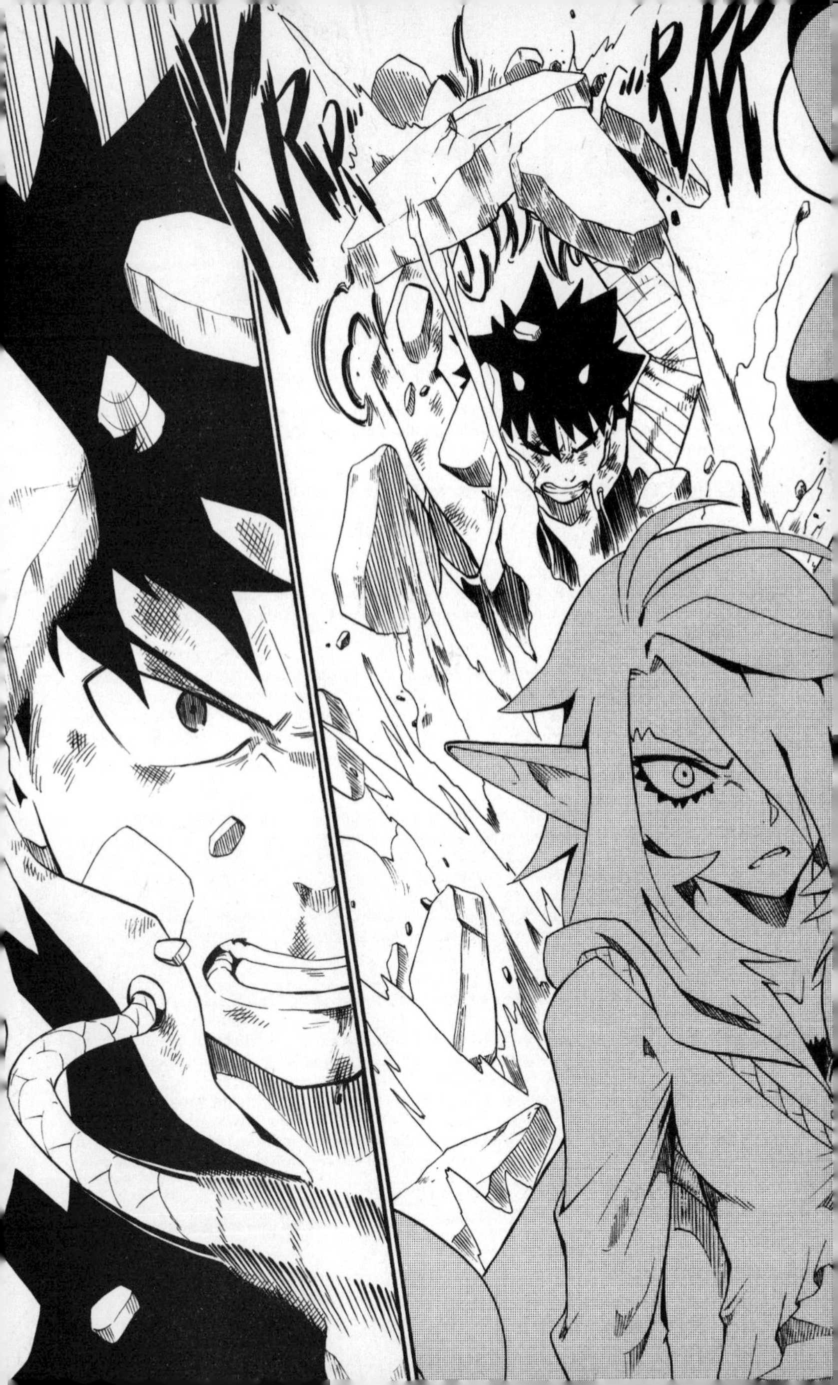
KRR...
...RKK

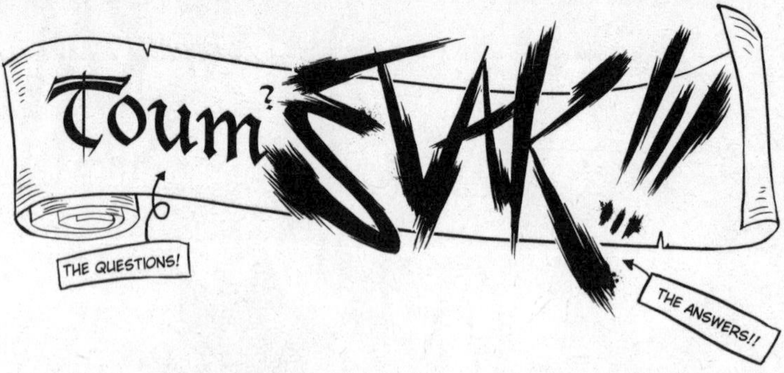
Toum? STAK!!!
THE QUESTIONS!
THE ANSWERS!!

**<u>Steph' Draw</u> Why does doc wear two ties? And why does Dragunov hold his arrow in a strange way when he's about to shoot? Is he just being extra or is there a specific reason for it? Either way I love it!!**

<u>**DOC's Answer:**</u> Serious people put on one tie. Me? I am super serious!

<u>**Tony Valente:**</u> ... As for Dragunov, he holds his arrows like that because he's got a special ace up his sleeve...

---

**<u>Lorienn Catala</u>: Was it hard to start in the manga business? What did you have to study in school? I wish I could become a mangaka but I don't know how to prepare for that. P.S. I love your manga!!!!!!!!!**

<u>**Tony Valente:**</u> Whoa, there! You completely destroyed our exclamation mark budget with that! °_° I would say that starting in the manga business wasn't the hard part. Not quitting it was. It's really physically taxing! And to answer your other question—to be honest, there's nothing you can really study in school for this. You don't need a specific diploma or have to take a certain class, the most important part is to follow the road that makes you progress in your own way. For some, that means going to school with drawing classes, scenario classes, etc. For others (like me) it's more of an autodidact thing. It takes a lot of personal effort, a lot of reading, a lot of practice and a lot of mistakes you need to correct yourself! But little by little, you'll hone your skills. I spend most of my resources in bookstores, I learn to draw new things when I need them for the story, etc. Basically, *Radiant* gradually helps me improve my art. This way worked very well for me because of my personality, but I also know artists who had the opportunity of getting an education in animation school or comics school that helped fill up their technical toolbox! It all depends on what you need to improve on. Some need to be surrounded by a group of other people competing with each other, but others will need something more personal. But in both cases I would say that practice makes perfect! And sending projects you're working on to your editor also helps.

---

**<u>Pauline Petit</u>: Do you draw by hand on paper or do you use some kind of software tool?**

<u>**Tony Valente:**</u> By hand—a pen and Chinese ink. I also use markers for backgrounds, but for this volume I used a pen! I then switch to the computer for rasterization, speed lines and text. I did speed lines by hand on the first two volumes as well, but the time lost on that was just crazy and I wasn't exactly satisfied either. Let's just say that software substitutes a part of the job that assistants would do for me. I have a bedtime assistant though. Since I don't sleep all that much anymore, and since there's no software for me to do that, I just have someone else sleep for me. Right now, I'm not really feeling the effect of it just yet... Actually, I'm really not feeling it at all. But it'll happen... I just need to continue trying.

Send your questions to: <u>radiant@ankama.com</u>

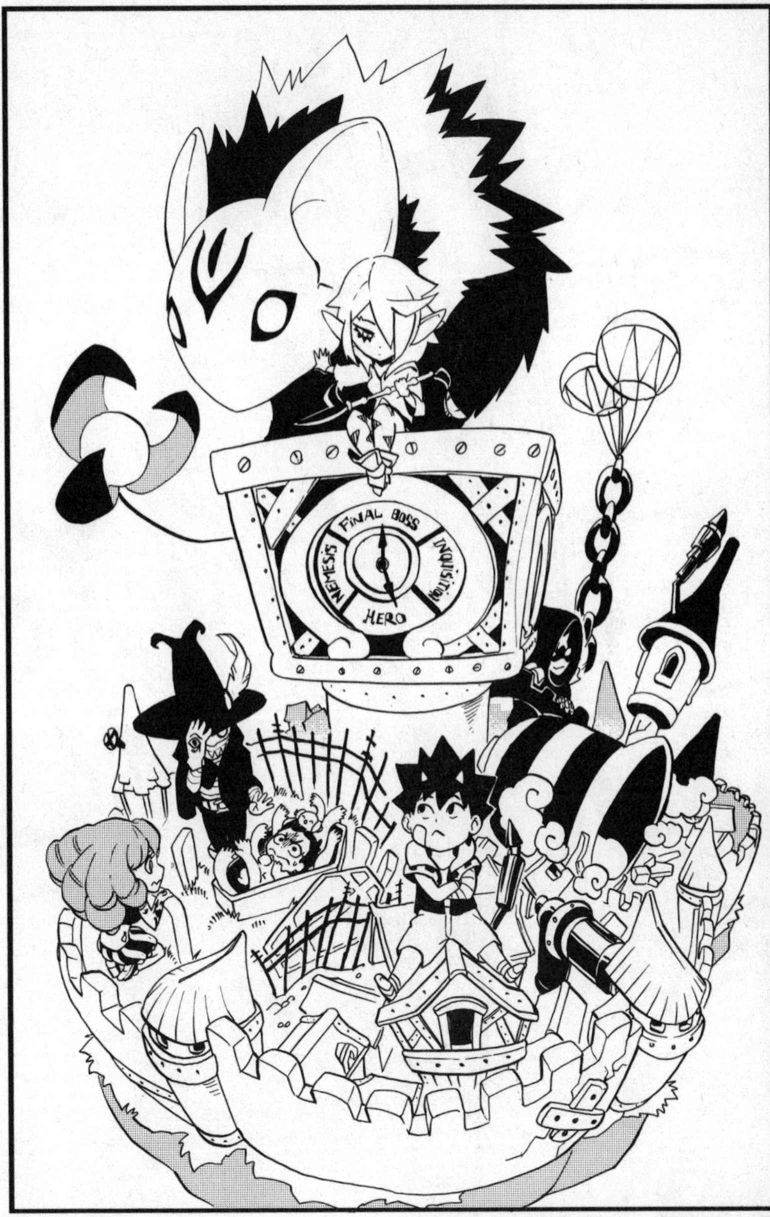
FINAL BOSS
INQUISITION
HERO
NEMESIS

**Chapter 24**

# Which Side?: Part 2

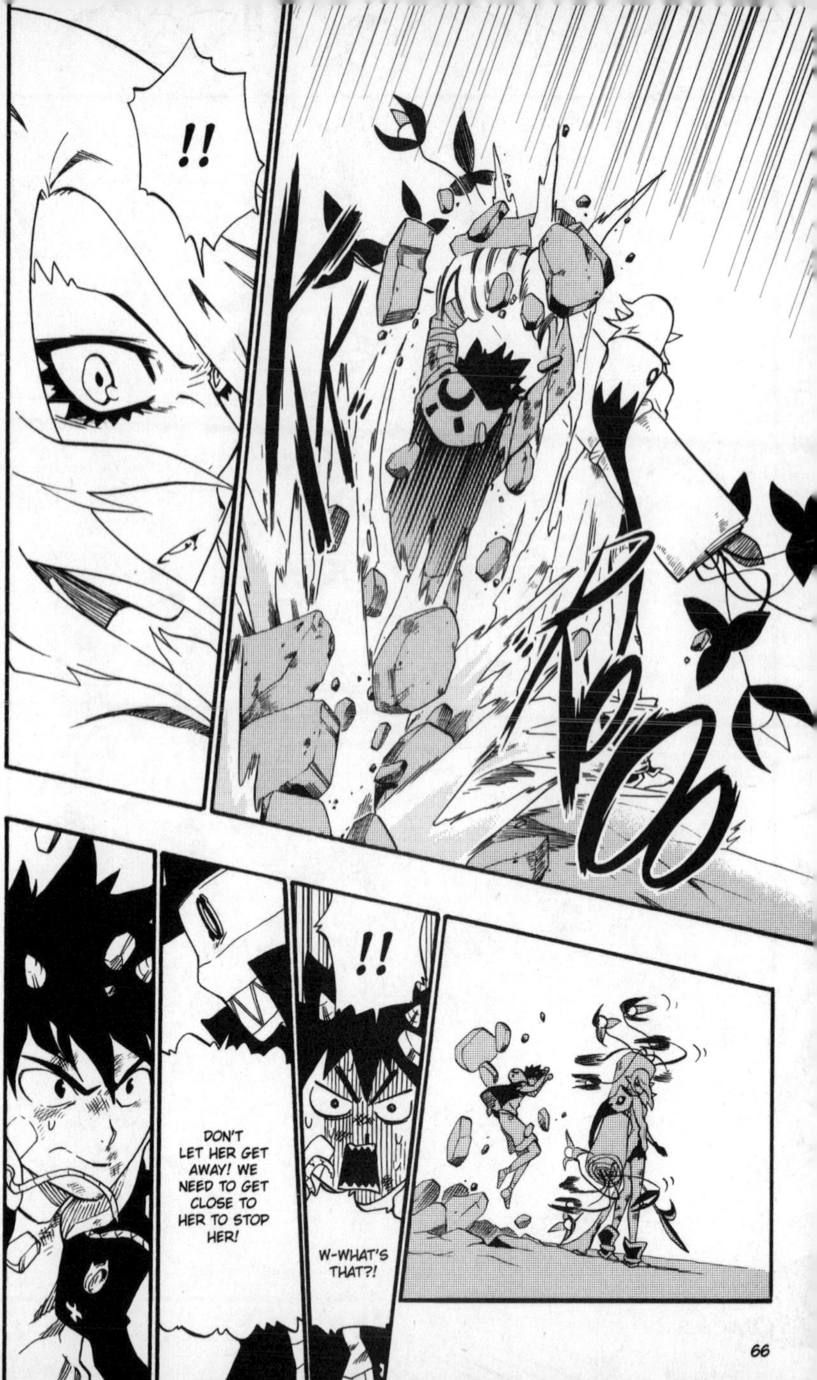
!!
!!
W-WHAT'S THAT?!
DON'T LET HER GET AWAY! WE NEED TO GET CLOSE TO HER TO STOP HER!

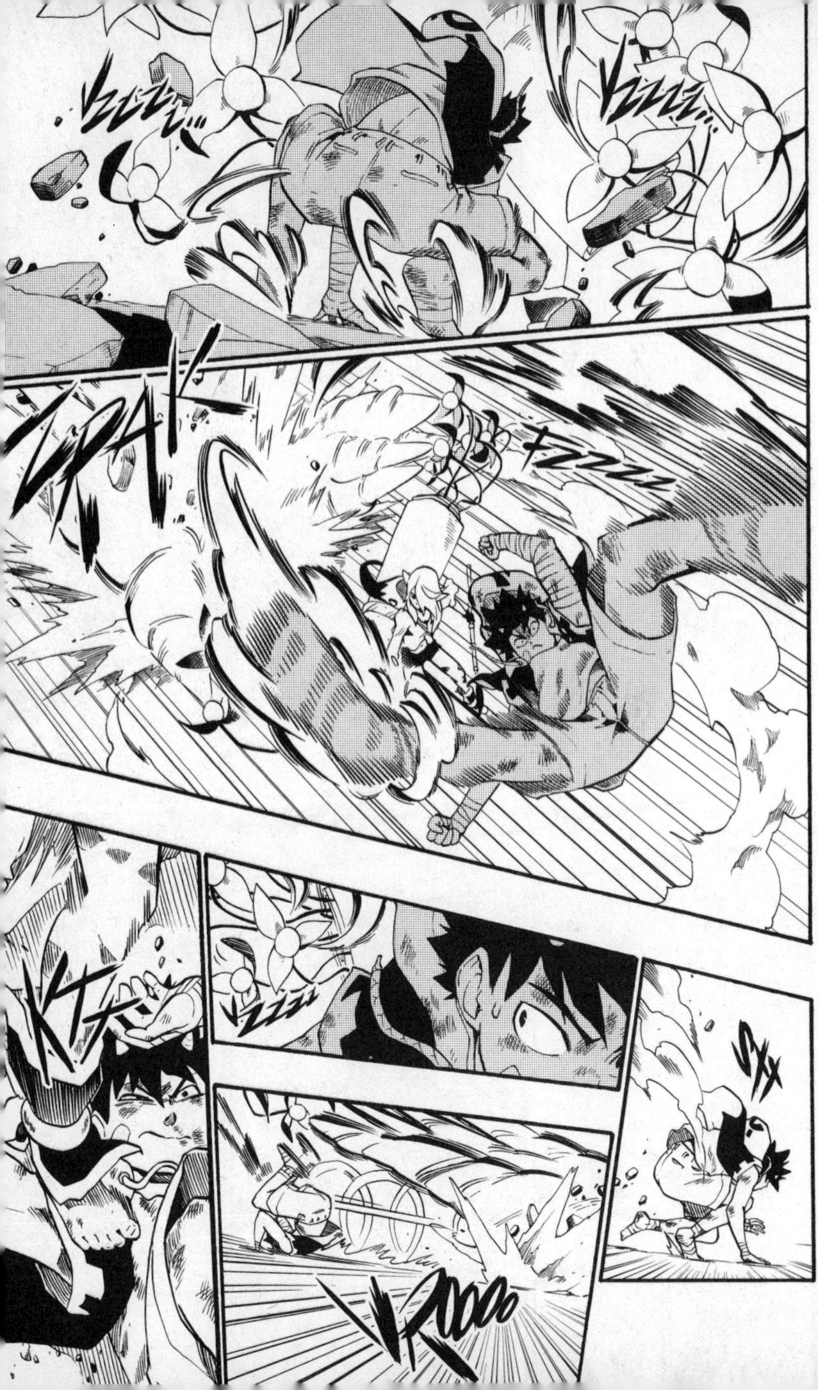
BZZZZZ...
BZZZZZ...
FZZZZZ
ZPAK
BZZZZ
VROOOO

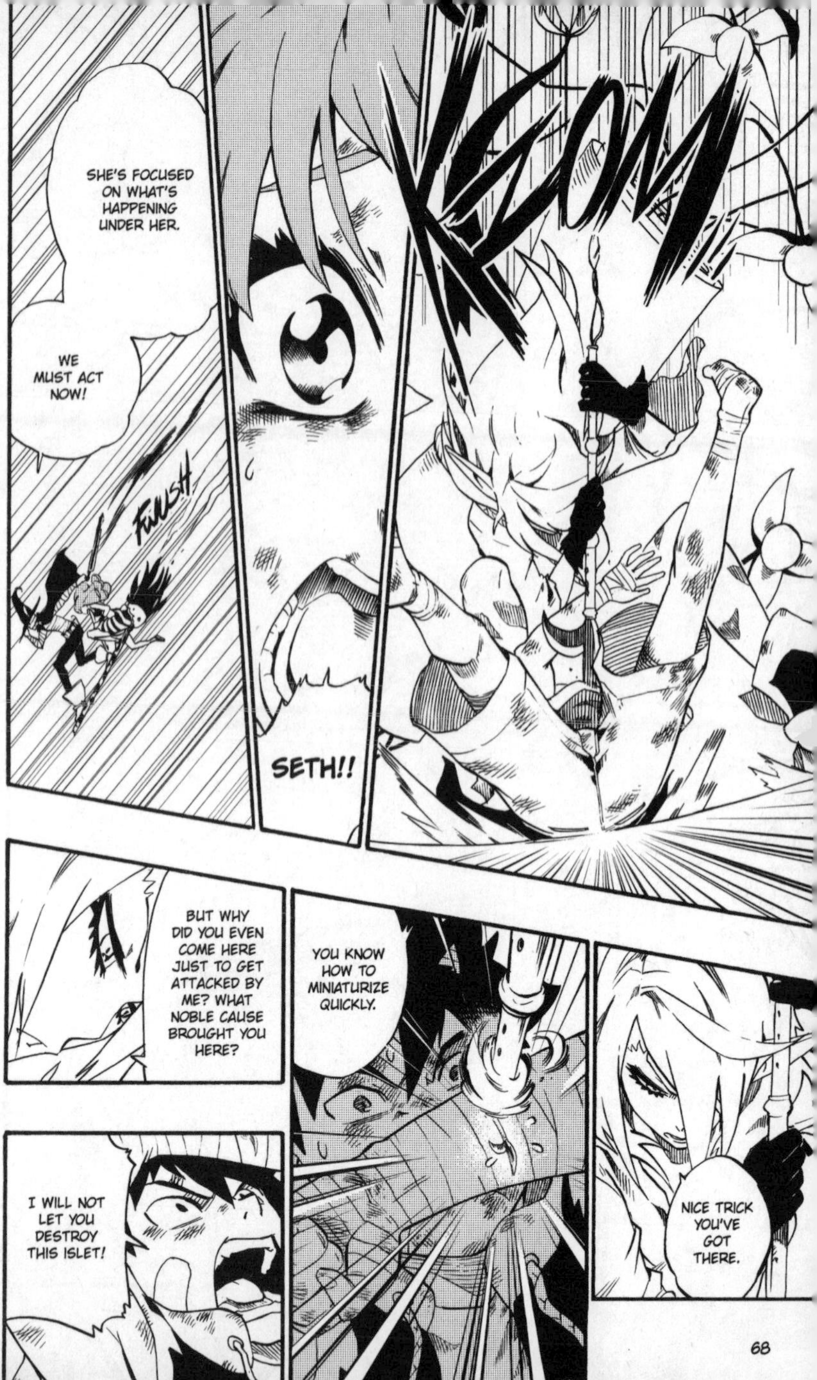
KBOOM
SETH!!
SHE'S FOCUSED ON WHAT'S HAPPENING UNDER HER.
WE MUST ACT NOW!
FWUSH
NICE TRICK YOU'VE GOT THERE.
YOU KNOW HOW TO MINIATURIZE QUICKLY.
BUT WHY DID YOU EVEN COME HERE JUST TO GET ATTACKED BY ME? WHAT NOBLE CAUSE BROUGHT YOU HERE?
I WILL NOT LET YOU DESTROY THIS ISLET!

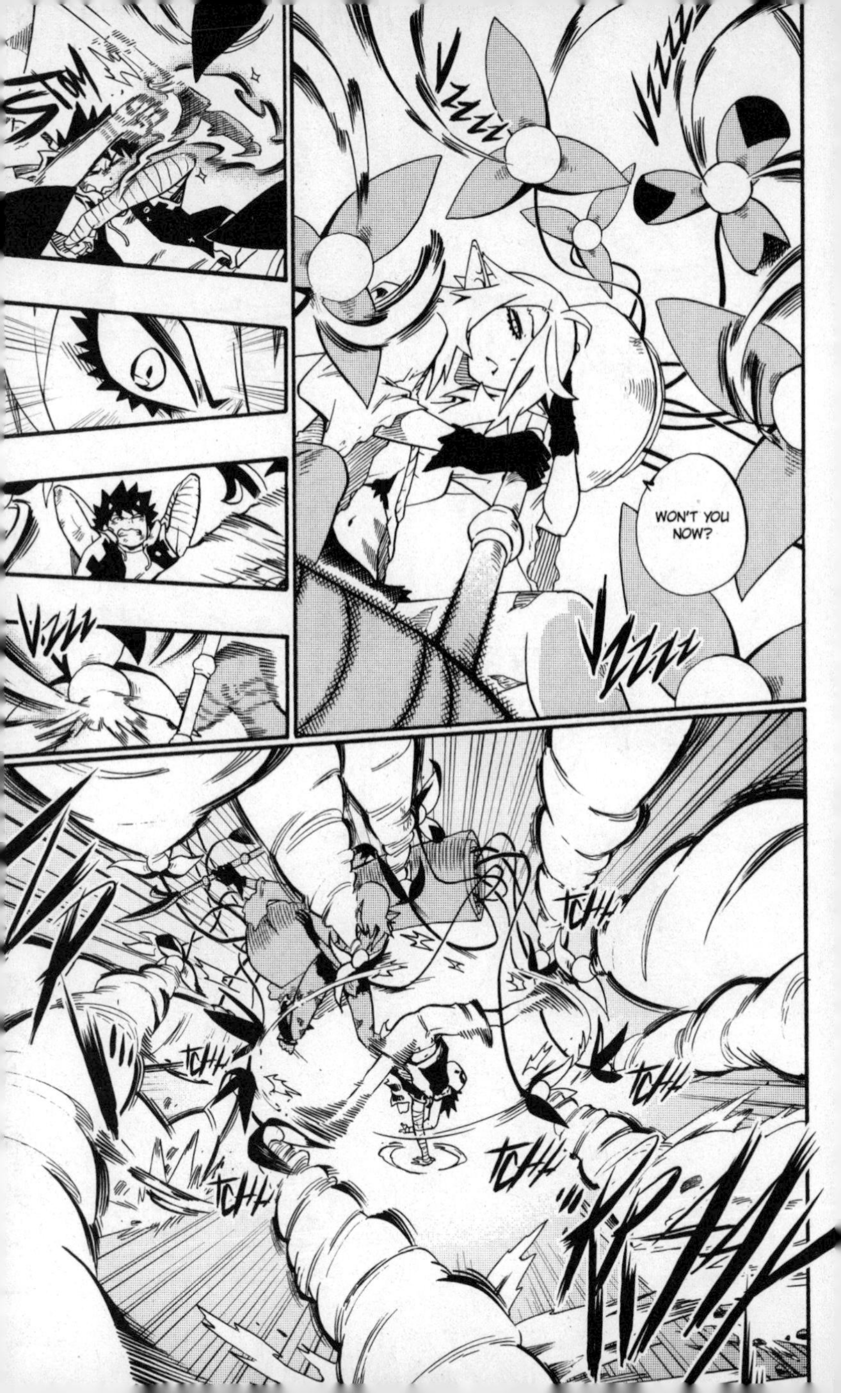
VZZZZ
VZZZZ
WON'T YOU NOW?
VZZZZZ
V-ZZZ
TCHH
TCHH
TCHH
TCHH
TCHH

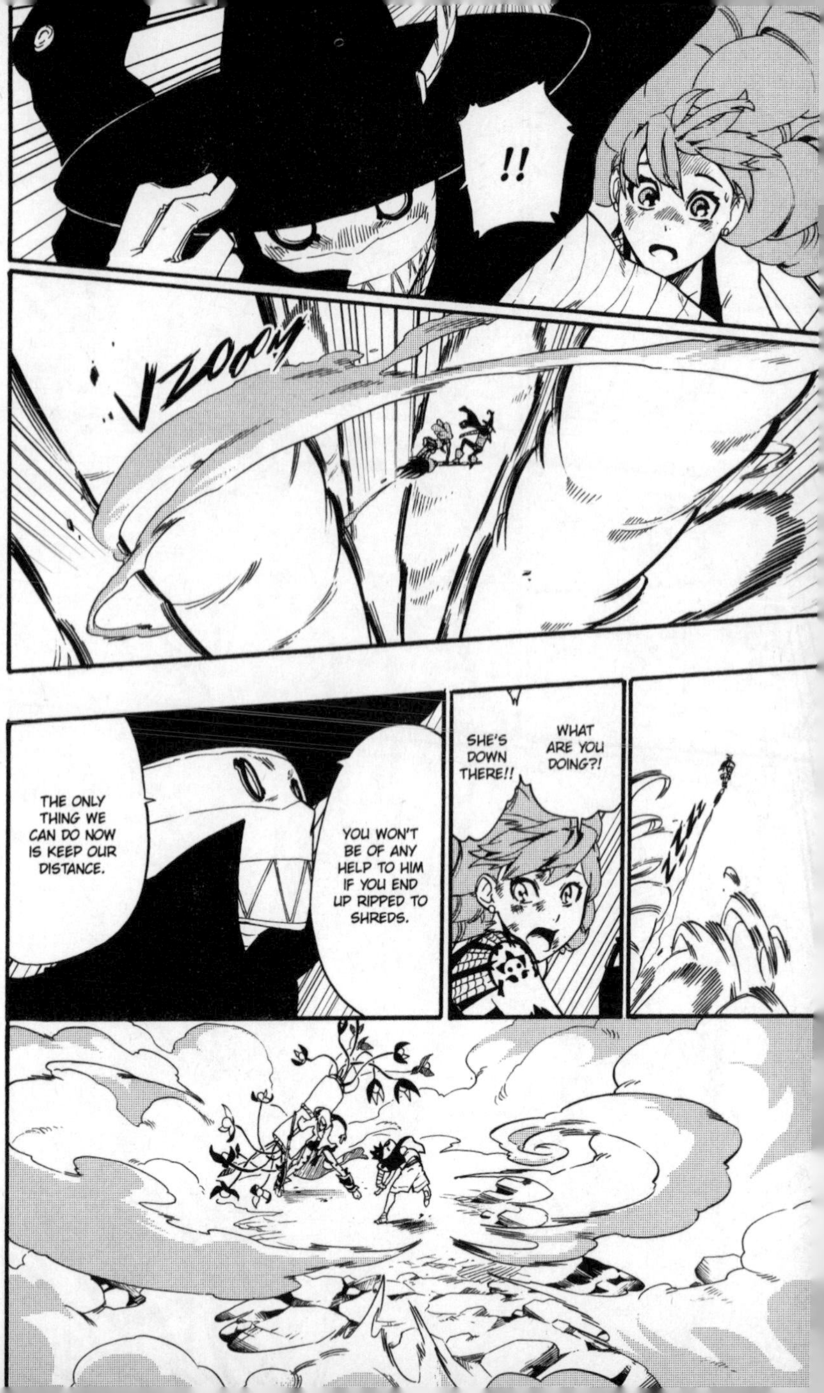
!!
VZOOOM
WHAT ARE YOU DOING?!
SHE'S DOWN THERE!!
YOU WON'T BE OF ANY HELP TO HIM IF YOU END UP RIPPED TO SHREDS.
THE ONLY THING WE CAN DO NOW IS KEEP OUR DISTANCE.

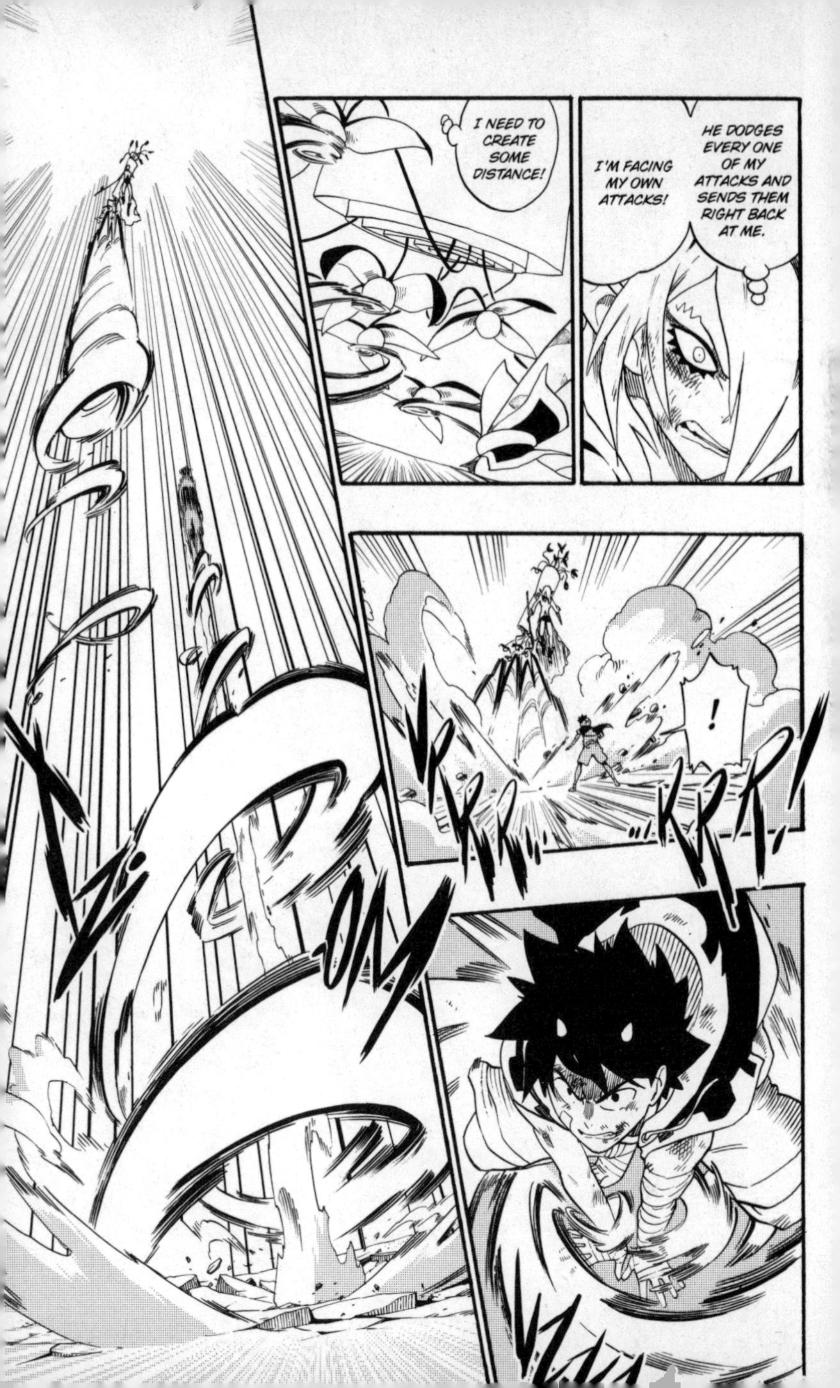
HE DODGES EVERY ONE OF MY ATTACKS AND SENDS THEM RIGHT BACK AT ME.
I'M FACING MY OWN ATTACKS!
I NEED TO CREATE SOME DISTANCE!
!
...KRRR!

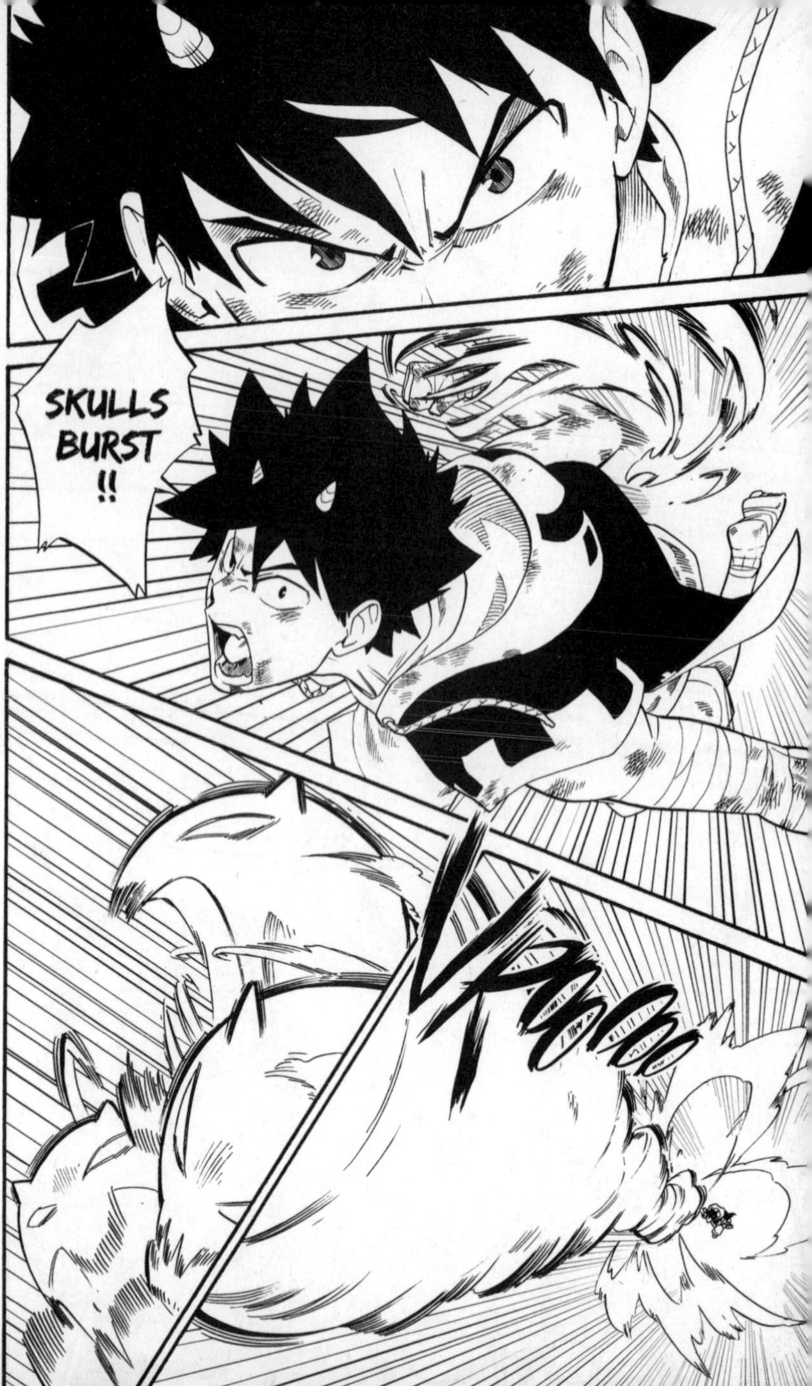
SKULLS BURST !!

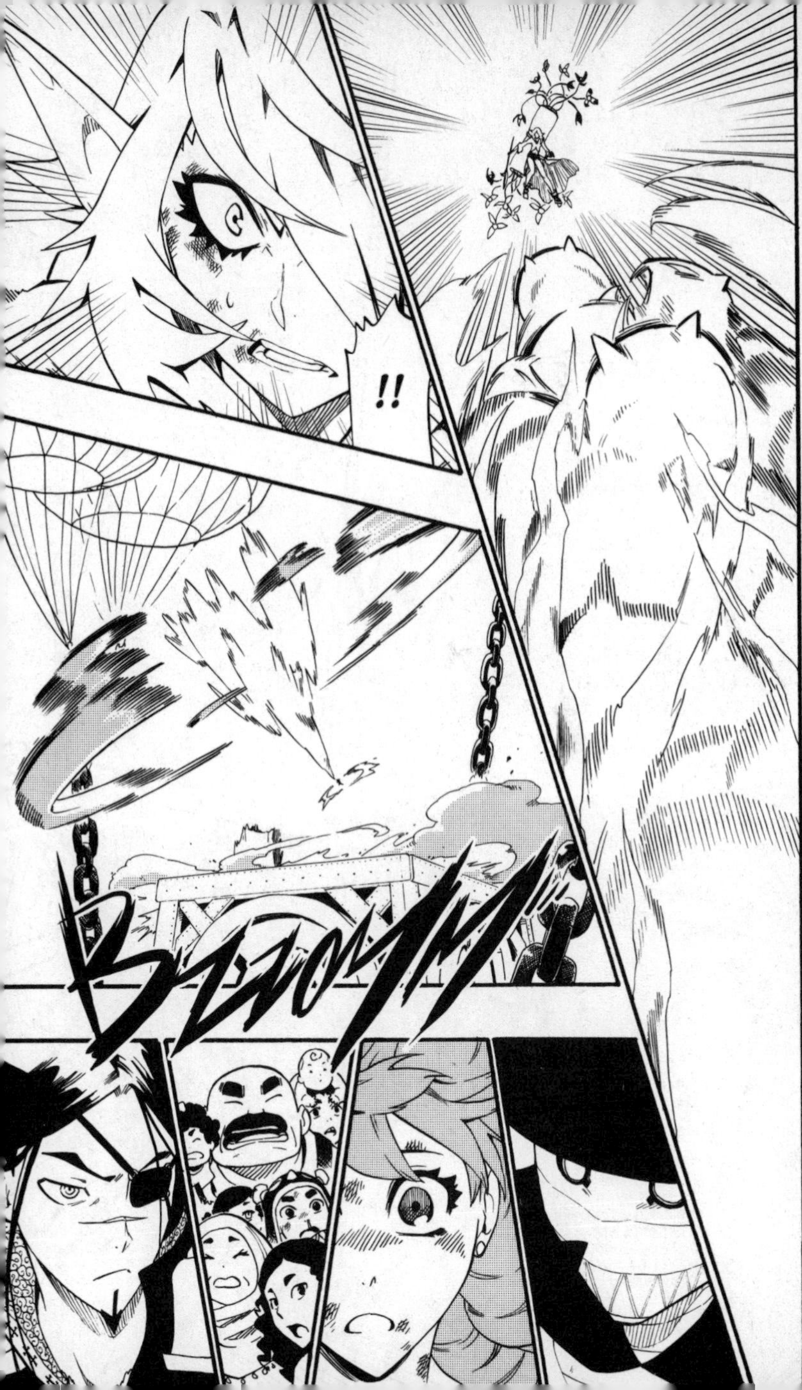
!!
BZZOOM

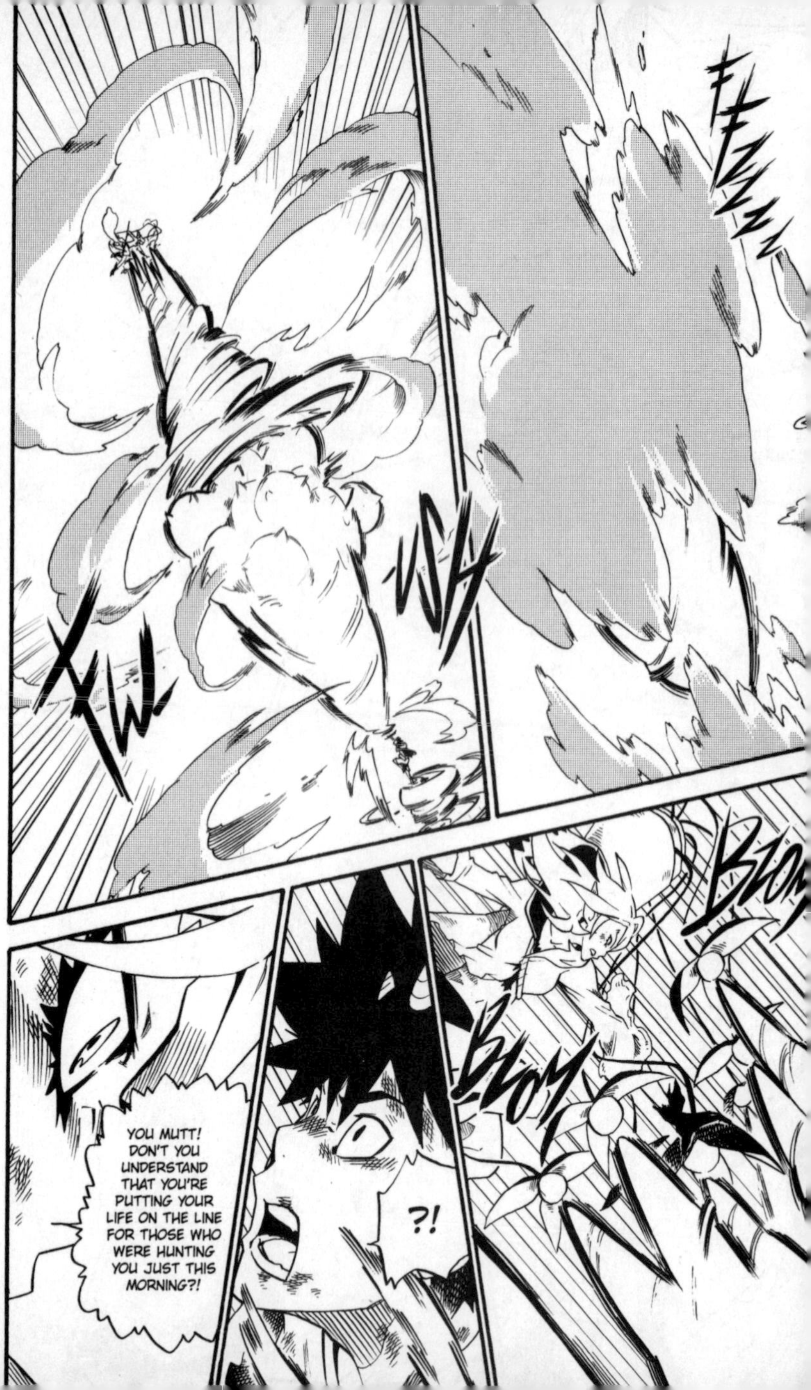
?!
YOU MUTT! DON'T YOU UNDERSTAND THAT YOU'RE PUTTING YOUR LIFE ON THE LINE FOR THOSE WHO WERE HUNTING YOU JUST THIS MORNING?!

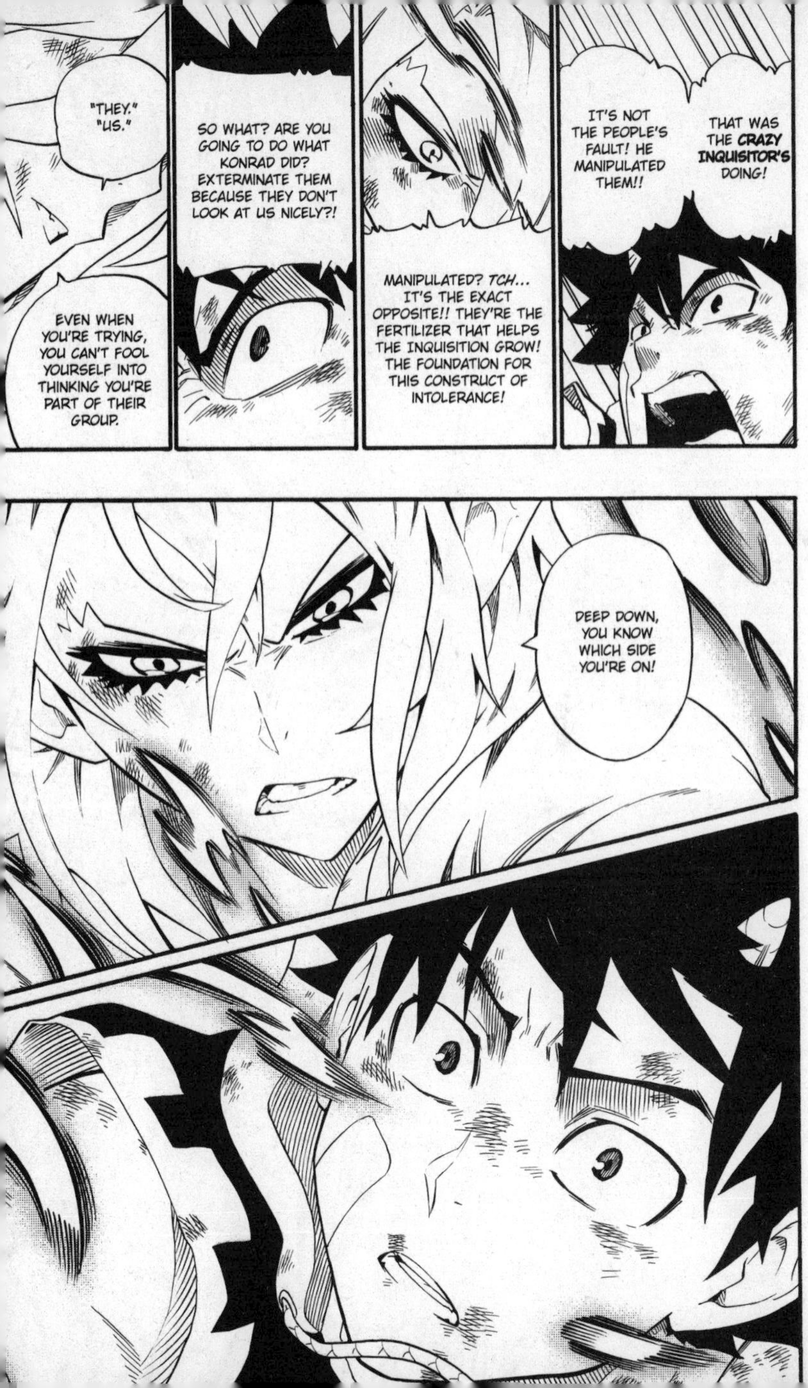
THAT WAS THE **CRAZY INQUISITOR'S** DOING!
IT'S NOT THE PEOPLE'S FAULT! HE MANIPULATED THEM!!
MANIPULATED? *TCH*... IT'S THE EXACT OPPOSITE!! THEY'RE THE FERTILIZER THAT HELPS THE INQUISITION GROW! THE FOUNDATION FOR THIS CONSTRUCT OF INTOLERANCE!
SO WHAT? ARE YOU GOING TO DO WHAT KONRAD DID? EXTERMINATE THEM BECAUSE THEY DON'T LOOK AT US NICELY?!
"THEY." "US."
EVEN WHEN YOU'RE TRYING, YOU CAN'T FOOL YOURSELF INTO THINKING YOU'RE PART OF THEIR GROUP.
DEEP DOWN, YOU KNOW WHICH SIDE YOU'RE ON!

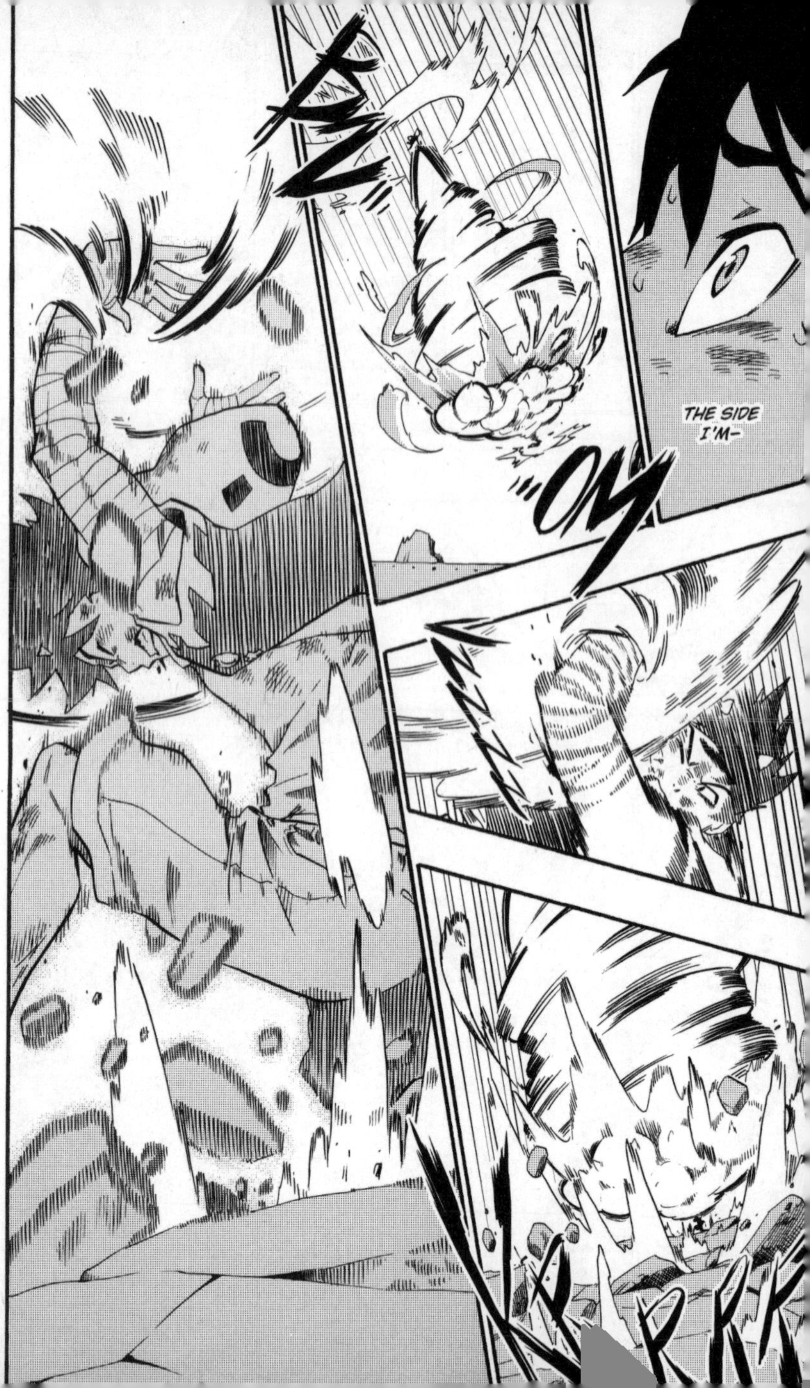
THE SIDE I'M–

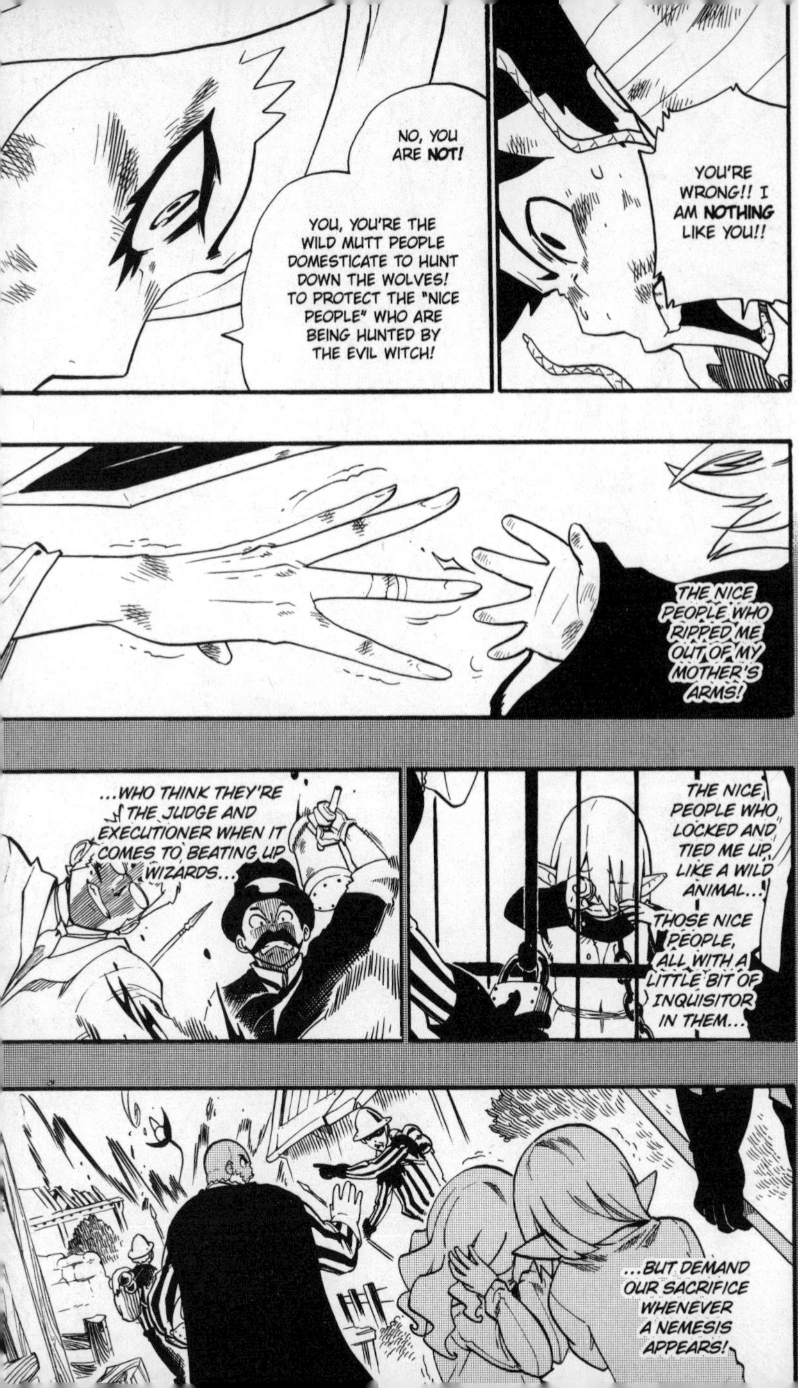
YOU'RE WRONG!! I AM **NOTHING** LIKE YOU!!
NO, YOU ARE **NOT!**
YOU, YOU'RE THE WILD MUTT PEOPLE DOMESTICATE TO HUNT DOWN THE WOLVES! TO PROTECT THE "NICE PEOPLE" WHO ARE BEING HUNTED BY THE EVIL WITCH!
THE NICE PEOPLE WHO RIPPED ME OUT OF MY MOTHER'S ARMS!
THE NICE PEOPLE WHO LOCKED AND TIED ME UP LIKE A WILD ANIMAL...
THOSE NICE PEOPLE, ALL WITH A LITTLE BIT OF INQUISITOR IN THEM...
...WHO THINK THEY'RE THE JUDGE AND EXECUTIONER WHEN IT COMES TO BEATING UP WIZARDS...
...BUT DEMAND OUR SACRIFICE WHENEVER A NEMESIS APPEARS!

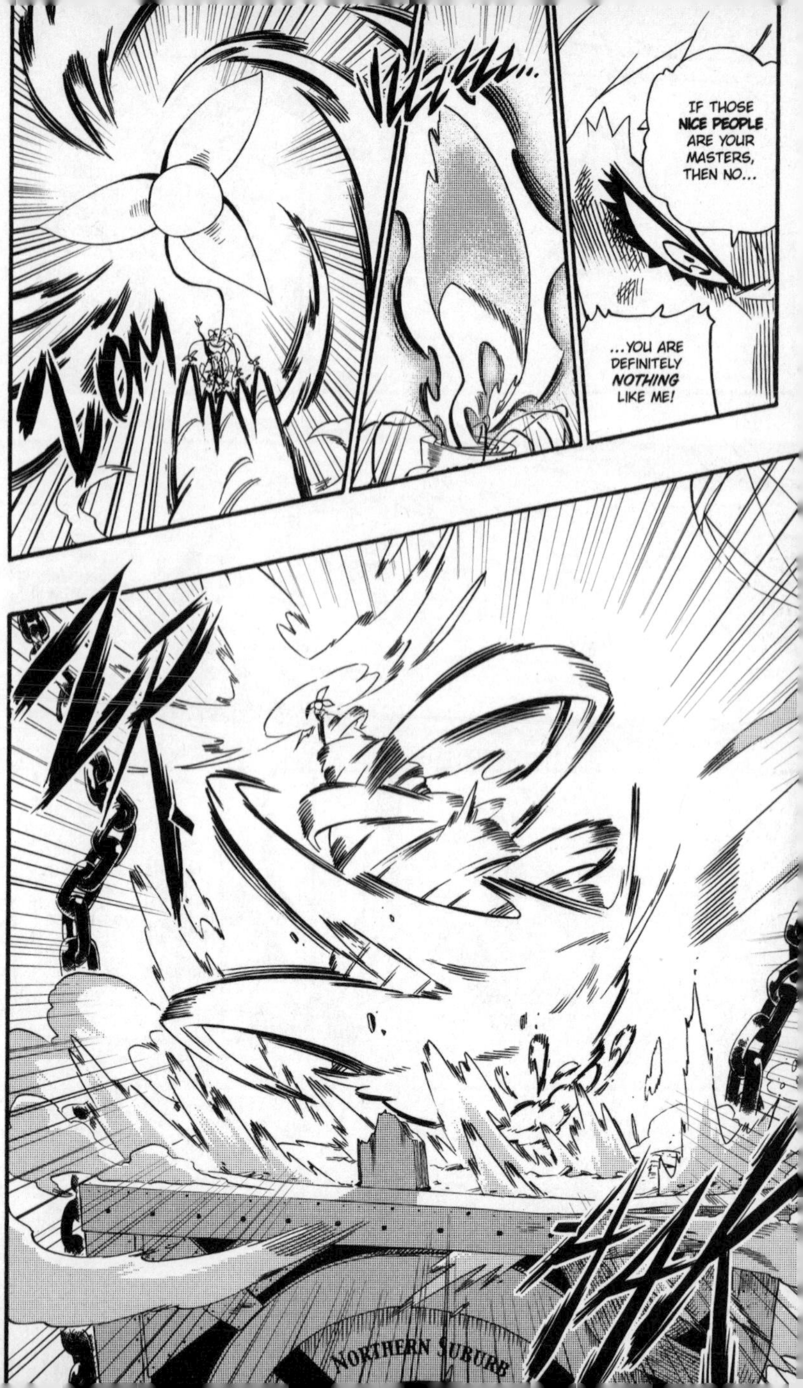
IF THOSE **NICE PEOPLE** ARE YOUR MASTERS, THEN NO...
...YOU ARE DEFINITELY ***NOTHING*** LIKE ME!
VZZZZ...
ZOOM
NORTHERN SUBURB

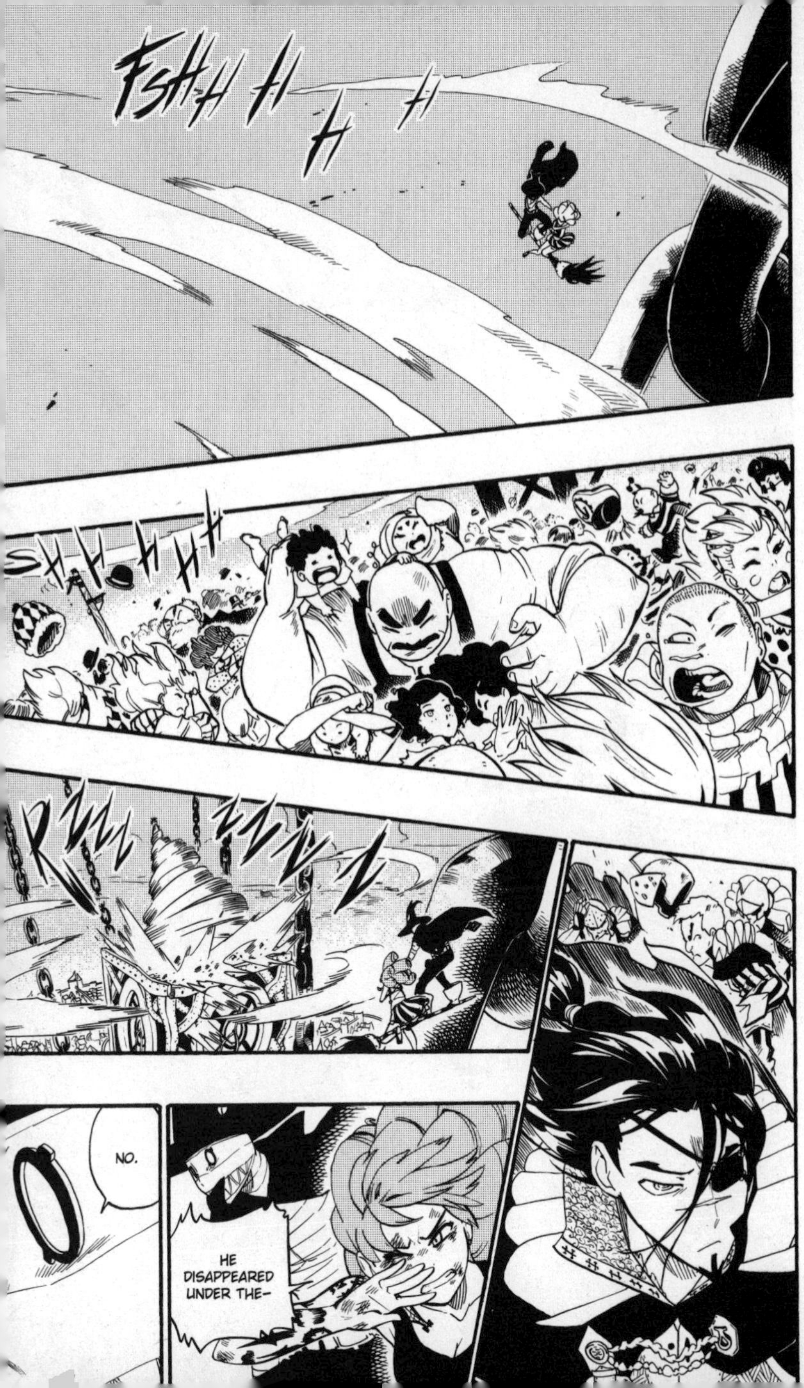
FSHHHHH
SHHHHH
RZZZZZZZ
HE DISAPPEARED UNDER THE-
NO.

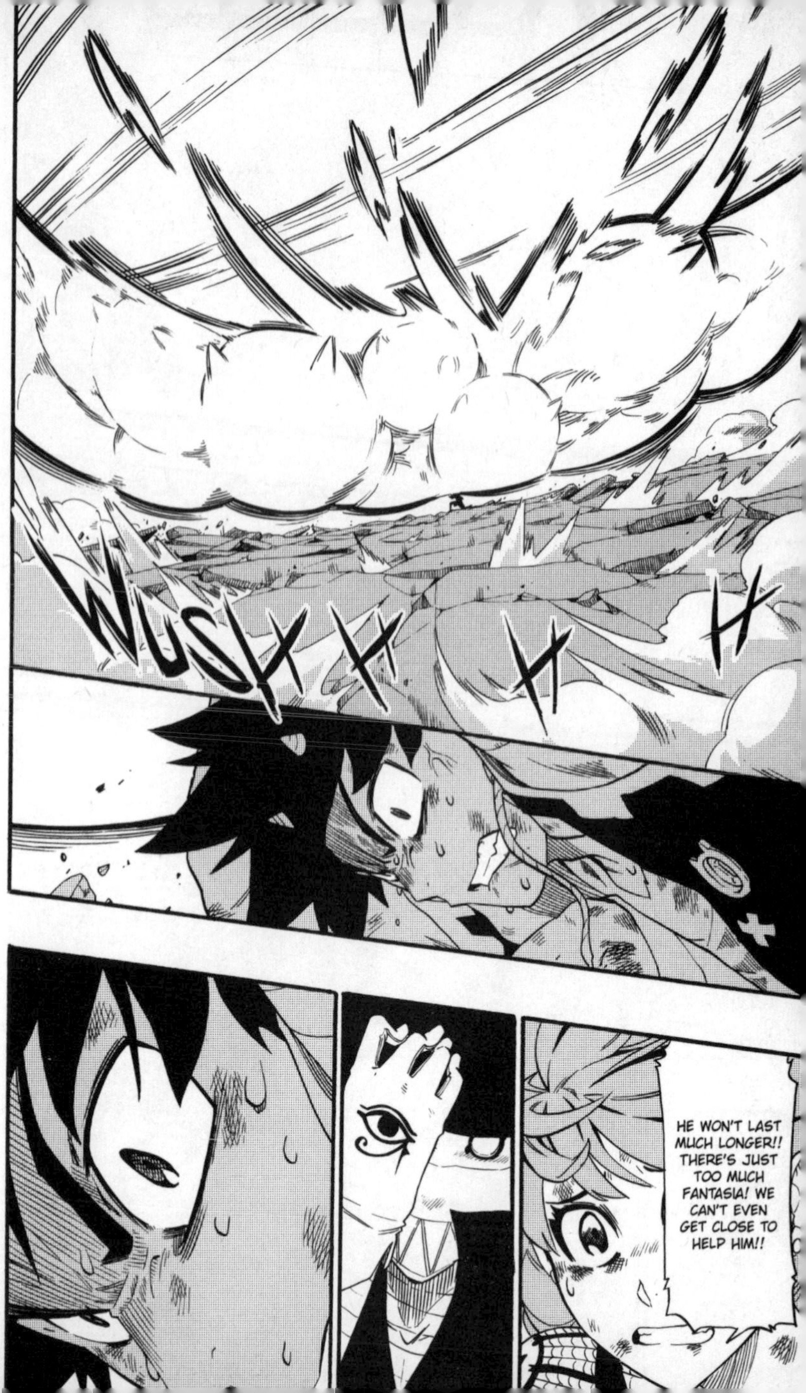
WUSHHHH
HE WON'T LAST MUCH LONGER!! THERE'S JUST TOO MUCH FANTASIA! WE CAN'T EVEN GET CLOSE TO HELP HIM!!

YOU'RE ...

YOU'RE WRONG !!

"LOCKED UP, LIKE AN ANIMAL..."

"...WHO THINK THEY'RE THE JUDGE AND EXECUTIONER WHEN IT COMES TO BEATING UP WIZARDS..."

"THOSE NICE PEOPLE, ALL WITH A LITTLE BIT OF INQUISITOR IN THEM..."

"TIED UP...!"

"...BUT DEMAND OUR SACRIFICE WHENEVER A NEMESIS APPEARS!"

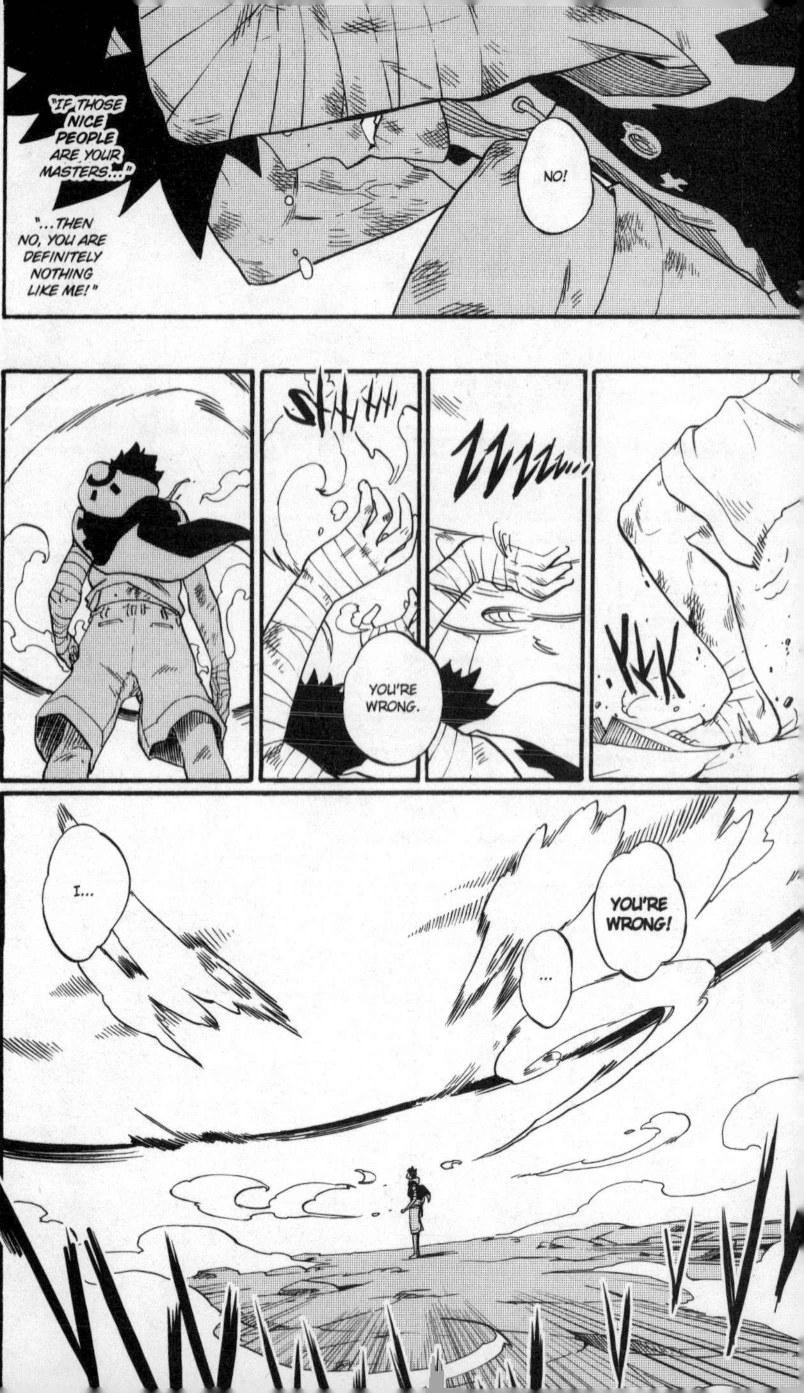
NO!
"IF THOSE NICE PEOPLE ARE YOUR MASTERS..."
"...THEN NO, YOU ARE DEFINITELY NOTHING LIKE ME!"
YOU'RE WRONG.
YOU'RE WRONG!
...
I...

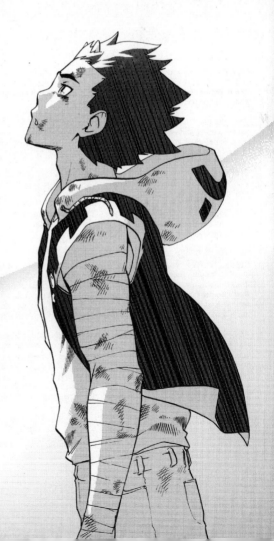

*I AM
LIKE
YOU.*

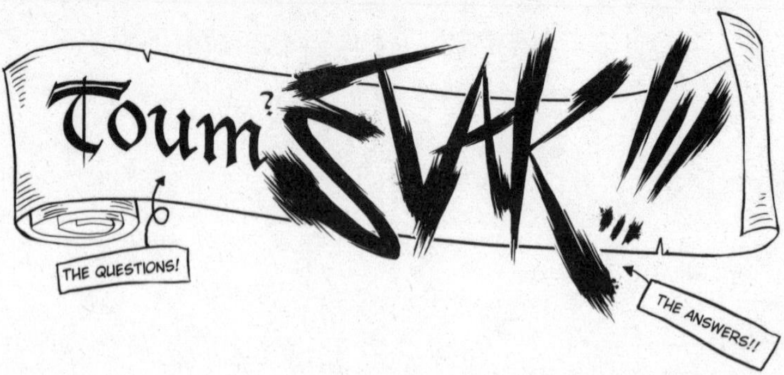
Toum?
STAK!!
THE QUESTIONS!
THE ANSWERS!!

**Cléa Bodart: I was looking at Mélie's pretty dark tattoos and was thinking "Hot dang! How'd a shy girl that cute even think of getting a tattoo like that? Even if they're pretty cool!" Is there any particular reason for the tattoos? Did she have them done during one of her fits? Do they each hold a specific meaning?**

**Tony Valente:** They all correspond to a certain chapter in her life. For example, the tattoo with the woven pattern and skull on her right shoulder refers to a scene in her life shown in a flashback in volume 3 (chapter 20). Then on her right ankle, we see her clan's emblem… Actually, maybe I'll just give some more details when the time is right!

**Cléa Bodart: In volume 3, we see an engraving in Latin on General Torque's sword, what is that? The sword's name? Or is it a sentence related to maintaining justice? An inscription that works like a wizard's scroll?**

**Tony Valente:** *Post Tenebras Lux*, meaning "Light After Darkness," is Torque's motto. The shortened version of his life's philosophy that he sees the Inquisiton as the bringer of light in a world obscured by the practice of witchcraft.

---

**Cassou 12: Were you inspired by the Ankama universe, and more specifically their game *DOFUS*, for your story? I'm wondering, because I thought I noticed a few references to *DOFUS* like Alma's name, or even Seth's horns that made me think of the Osamodas class in the game! And also the floating islands in the sky, just like the Incarnam region in the game! Master Lord Majesty's staff reminded me of the Cawwot armor set xD :) Anyway, it was only a little theory of mine, and I might be completely off about this, so if I am, sorry !! x)**

**Tony Valente**: Well… Yes and no! Actually those worlds don't inspire me directly, but I believe me and Tot, the father of the *DOFUS* universe, share a few similar influences actually. The examples you mentioned however were pure coincidences that I actually didn't know about, but the very well-developed fantasy side of *DOFUS* and *WAKFU's* art has definitely partly been a source of inspiration for my own style. As for the islets in *Radiant*, those aren't actually floating pieces of land! You're not the only person who thought they were, but you can always see a base underneath the islets, so they're not actually flying. I'll go into more detail about them soon...

Send your questions to: radiant@ankama.com

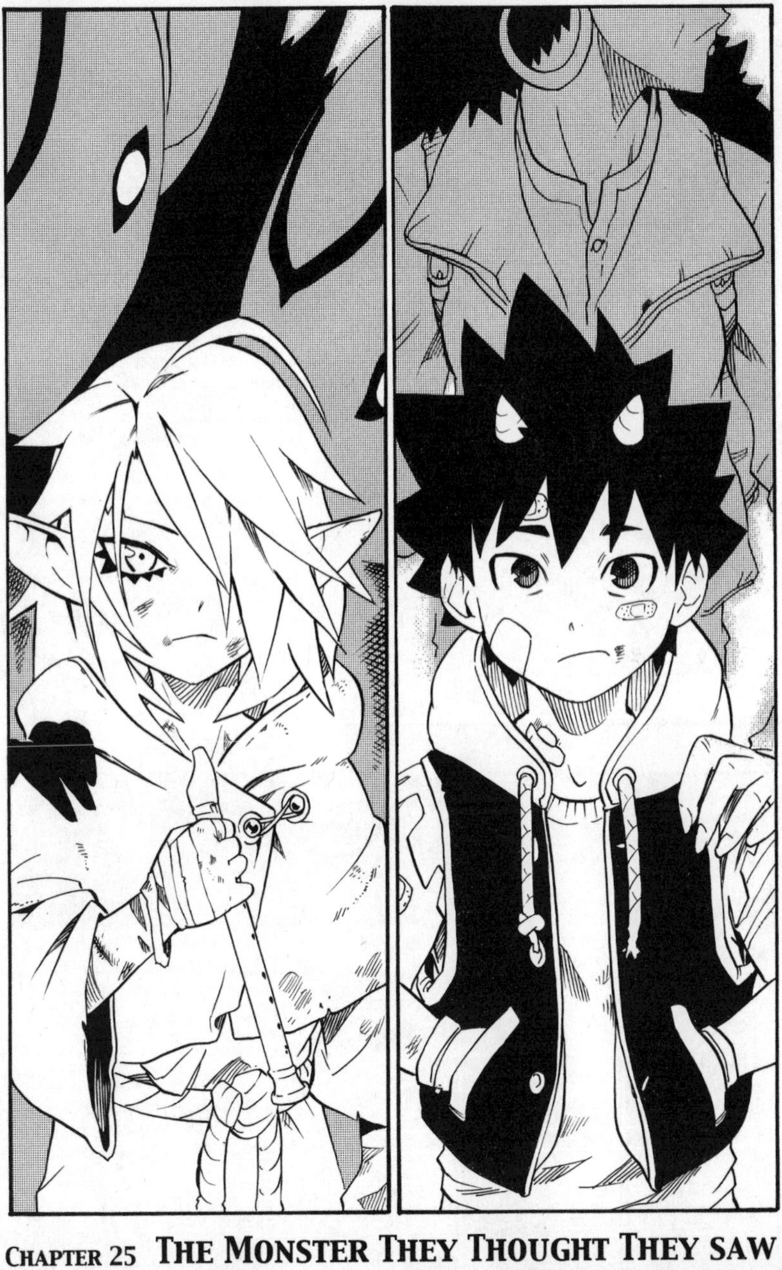

## Chapter 25 The Monster They Thought They saw

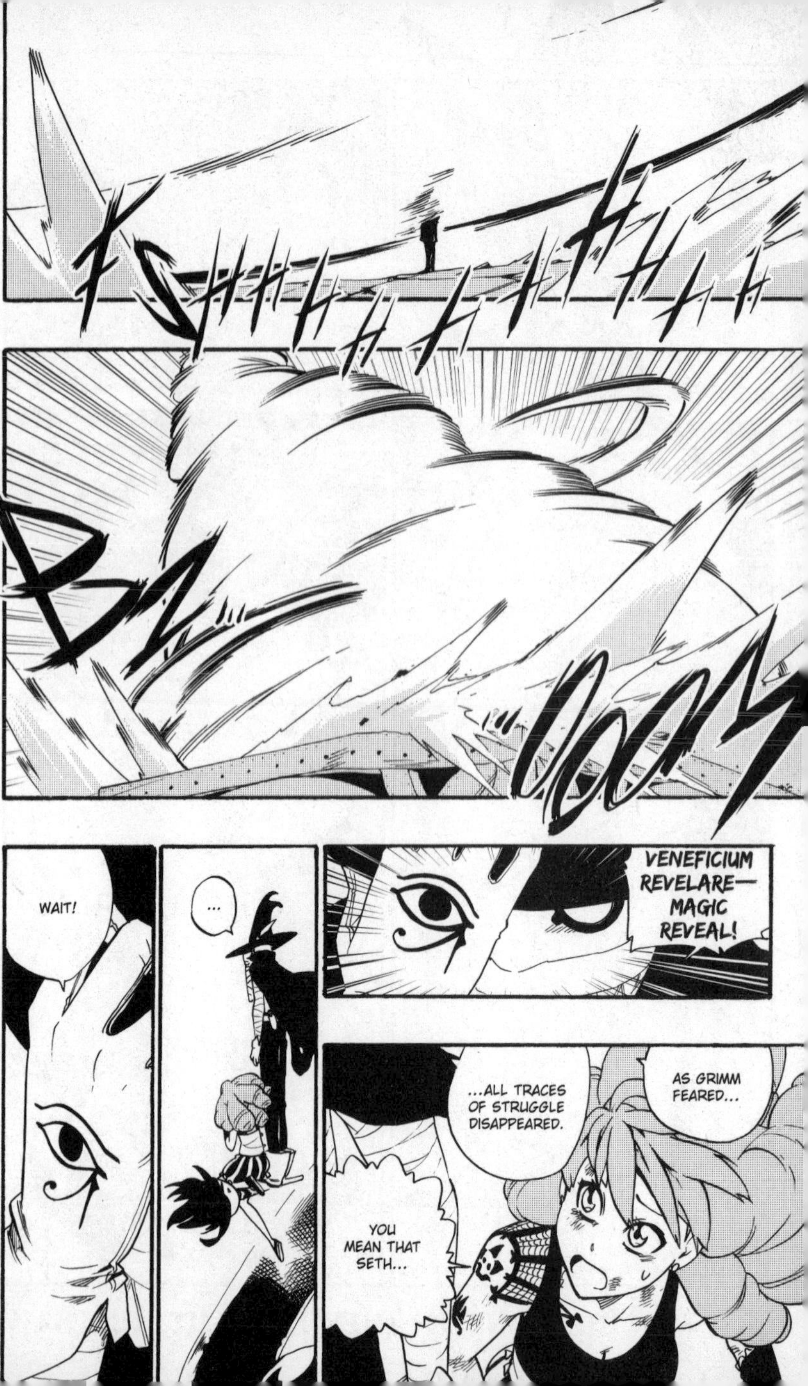
FSHHHHHHHHHHH
BADOOM
VENEFICIUM REVELARE— MAGIC REVEAL!
AS GRIMM FEARED...
...ALL TRACES OF STRUGGLE DISAPPEARED.
YOU MEAN THAT SETH...
...
WAIT!

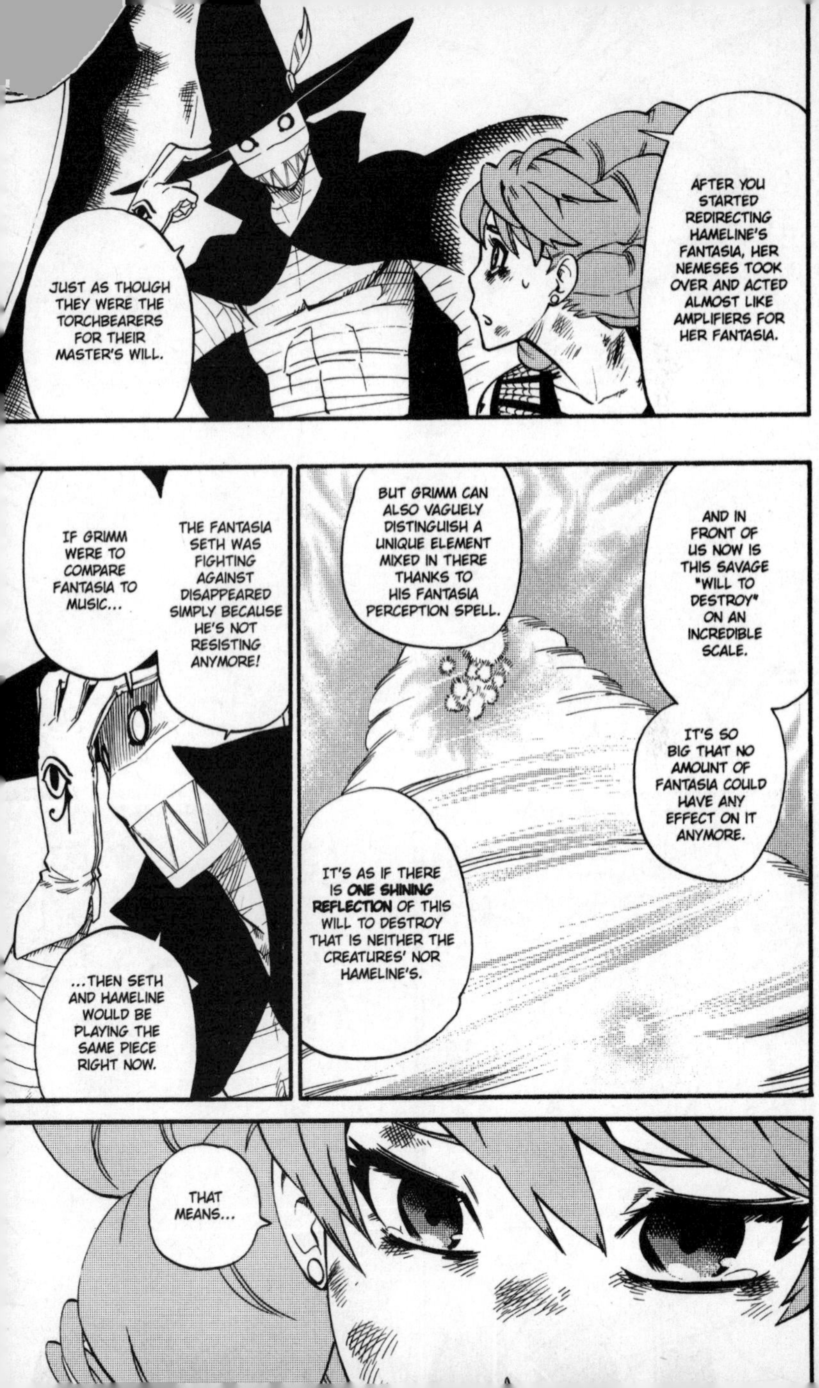
AFTER YOU STARTED REDIRECTING HAMELINE'S FANTASIA, HER NEMESES TOOK OVER AND ACTED ALMOST LIKE AMPLIFIERS FOR HER FANTASIA.
JUST AS THOUGH THEY WERE THE TORCHBEARERS FOR THEIR MASTER'S WILL.
AND IN FRONT OF US NOW IS THIS SAVAGE "WILL TO DESTROY" ON AN INCREDIBLE SCALE.
BUT GRIMM CAN ALSO VAGUELY DISTINGUISH A UNIQUE ELEMENT MIXED IN THERE THANKS TO HIS FANTASIA PERCEPTION SPELL.
IT'S SO BIG THAT NO AMOUNT OF FANTASIA COULD HAVE ANY EFFECT ON IT ANYMORE.
IT'S AS IF THERE IS ONE SHINING REFLECTION OF THIS WILL TO DESTROY THAT IS NEITHER THE CREATURES' NOR HAMELINE'S.
THE FANTASIA SETH WAS FIGHTING AGAINST DISAPPEARED SIMPLY BECAUSE HE'S NOT RESISTING ANYMORE!
IF GRIMM WERE TO COMPARE FANTASIA TO MUSIC...
...THEN SETH AND HAMELINE WOULD BE PLAYING THE SAME PIECE RIGHT NOW.
THAT MEANS...

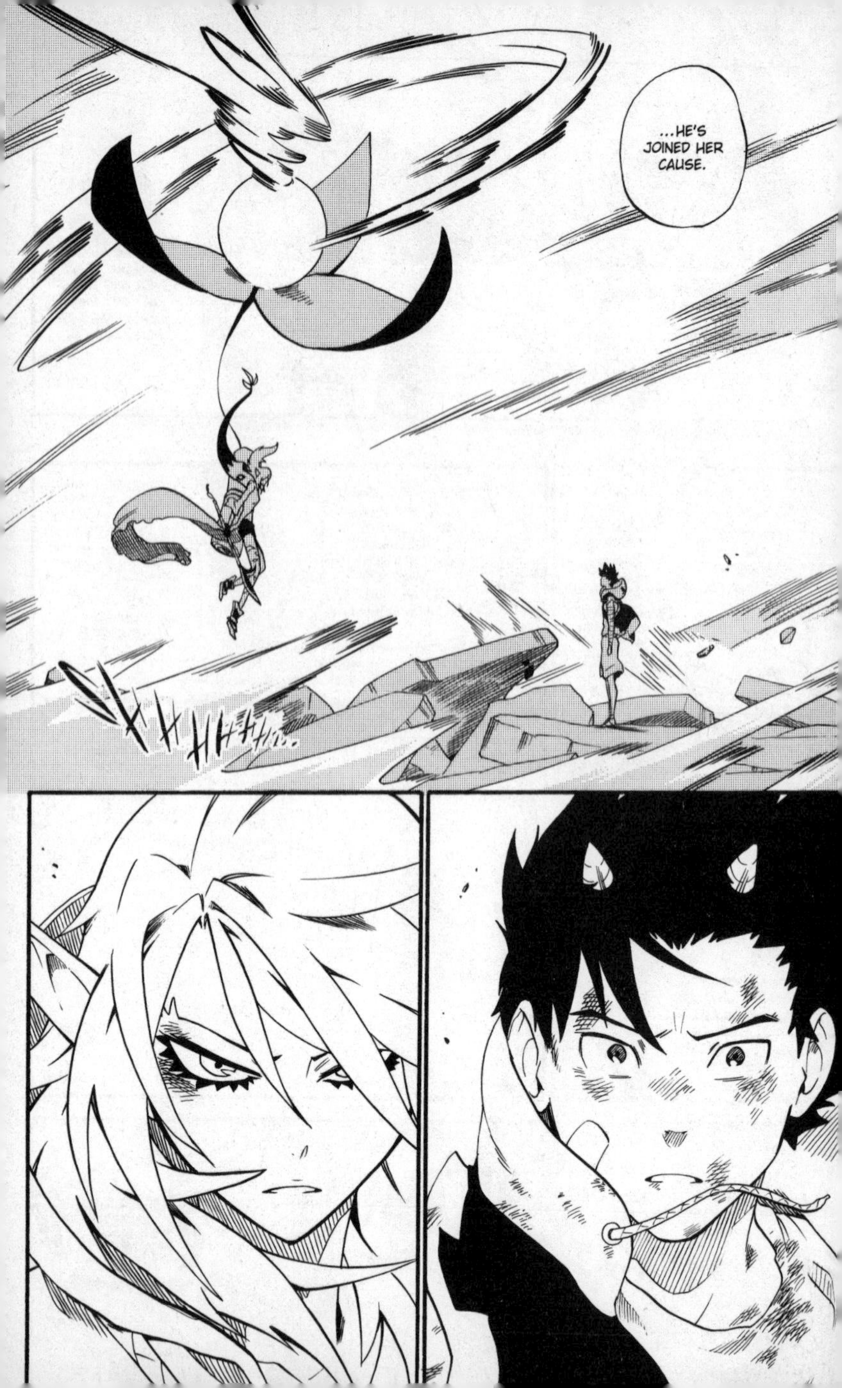
...HE'S JOINED HER CAUSE.

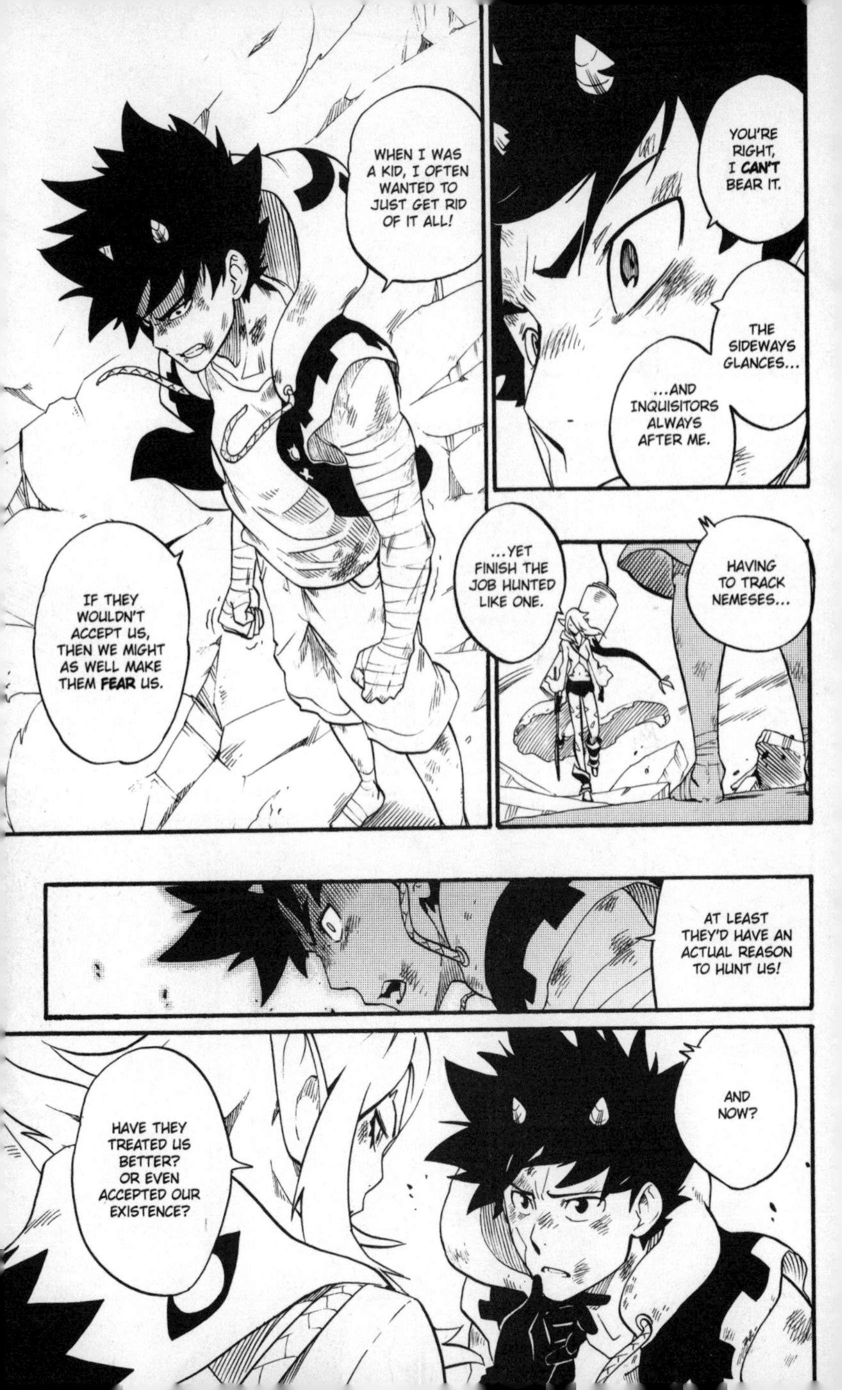
YOU'RE RIGHT, I **CAN'T** BEAR IT.
THE SIDEWAYS GLANCES...
...AND INQUISITORS ALWAYS AFTER ME.
HAVING TO TRACK NEMESES...
...YET FINISH THE JOB HUNTED LIKE ONE.
WHEN I WAS A KID, I OFTEN WANTED TO JUST GET RID OF IT ALL!
IF THEY WOULDN'T ACCEPT US, THEN WE MIGHT AS WELL MAKE THEM **FEAR** US.
AT LEAST THEY'D HAVE AN ACTUAL REASON TO HUNT US!
AND NOW?
HAVE THEY TREATED US BETTER? OR EVEN ACCEPTED OUR EXISTENCE?

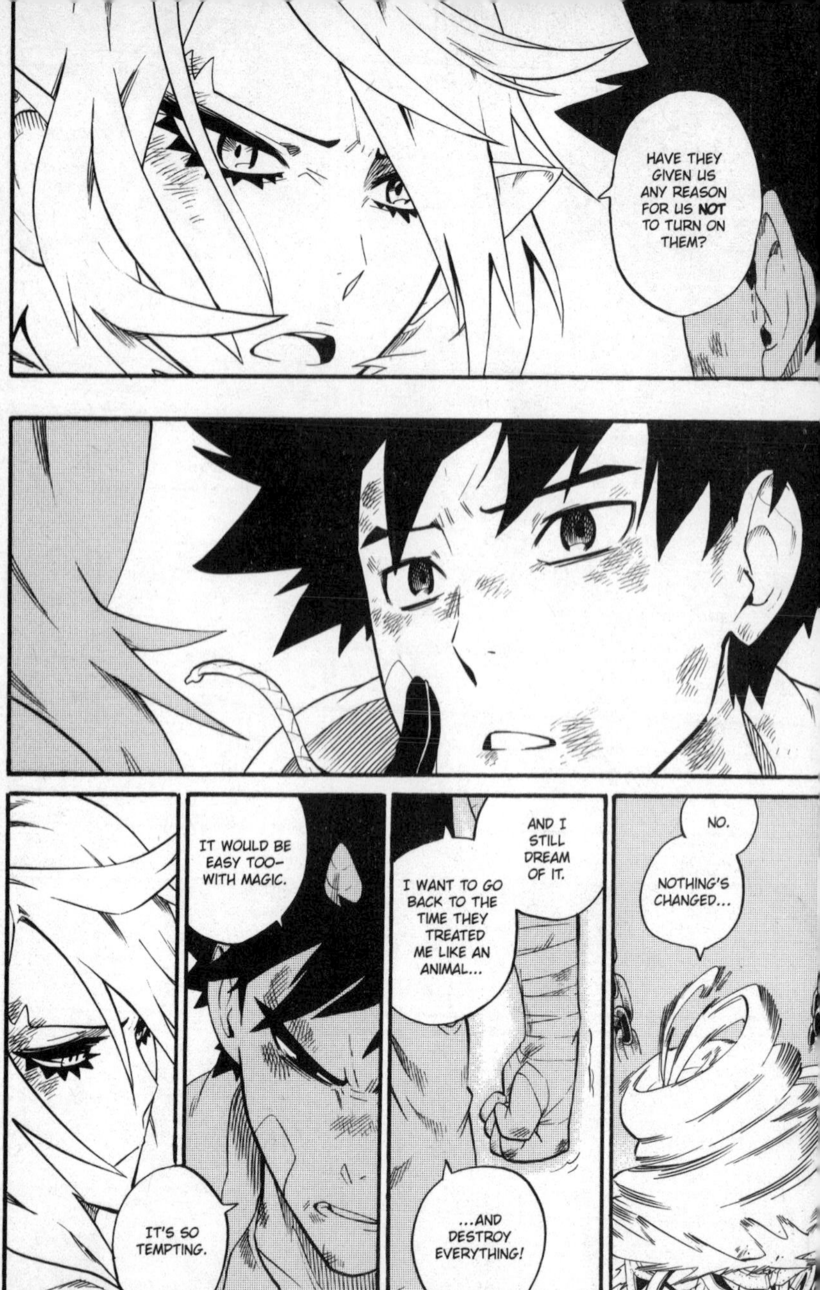
HAVE THEY GIVEN US ANY REASON FOR US **NOT** TO TURN ON THEM?
NO.
NOTHING'S CHANGED...
AND I STILL DREAM OF IT.
I WANT TO GO BACK TO THE TIME THEY TREATED ME LIKE AN ANIMAL...
...AND DESTROY EVERYTHING!
IT WOULD BE EASY TOO—WITH MAGIC.
IT'S SO TEMPTING.

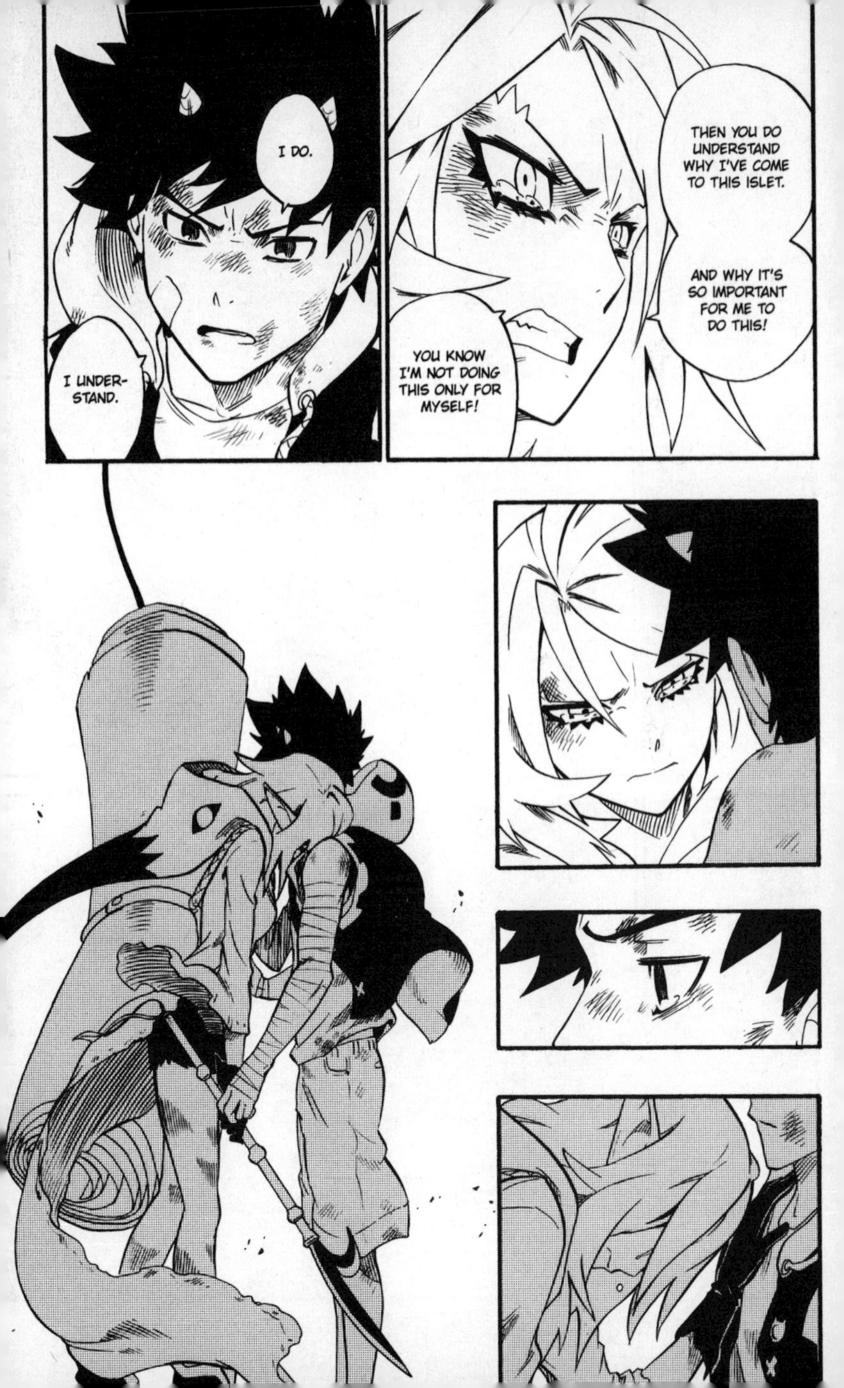
THEN YOU DO UNDERSTAND WHY I'VE COME TO THIS ISLET.
AND WHY IT'S SO IMPORTANT FOR ME TO DO THIS!
YOU KNOW I'M NOT DOING THIS ONLY FOR MYSELF!
I DO.
I UNDER-STAND.

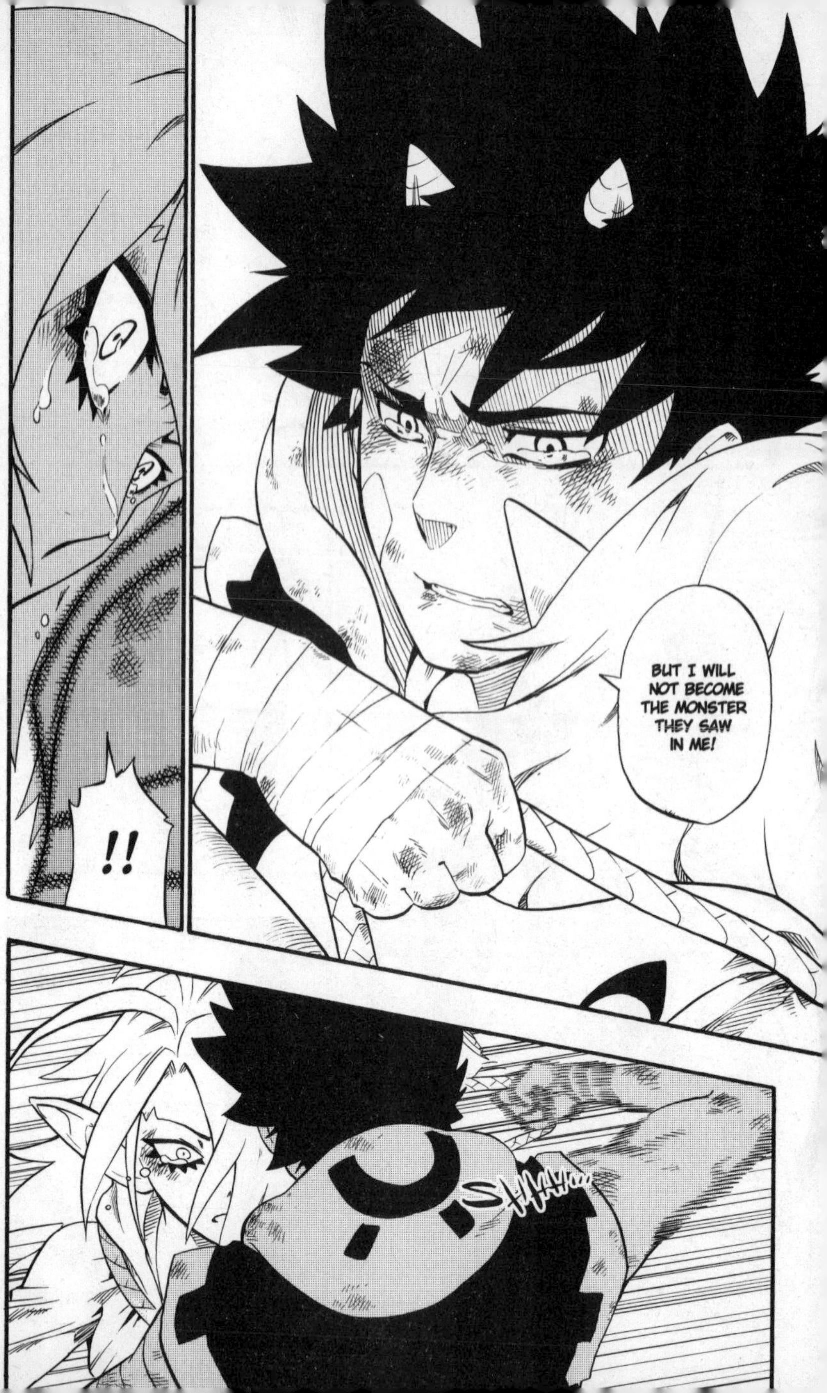
BUT I WILL NOT BECOME THE MONSTER THEY SAW IN ME!
!!

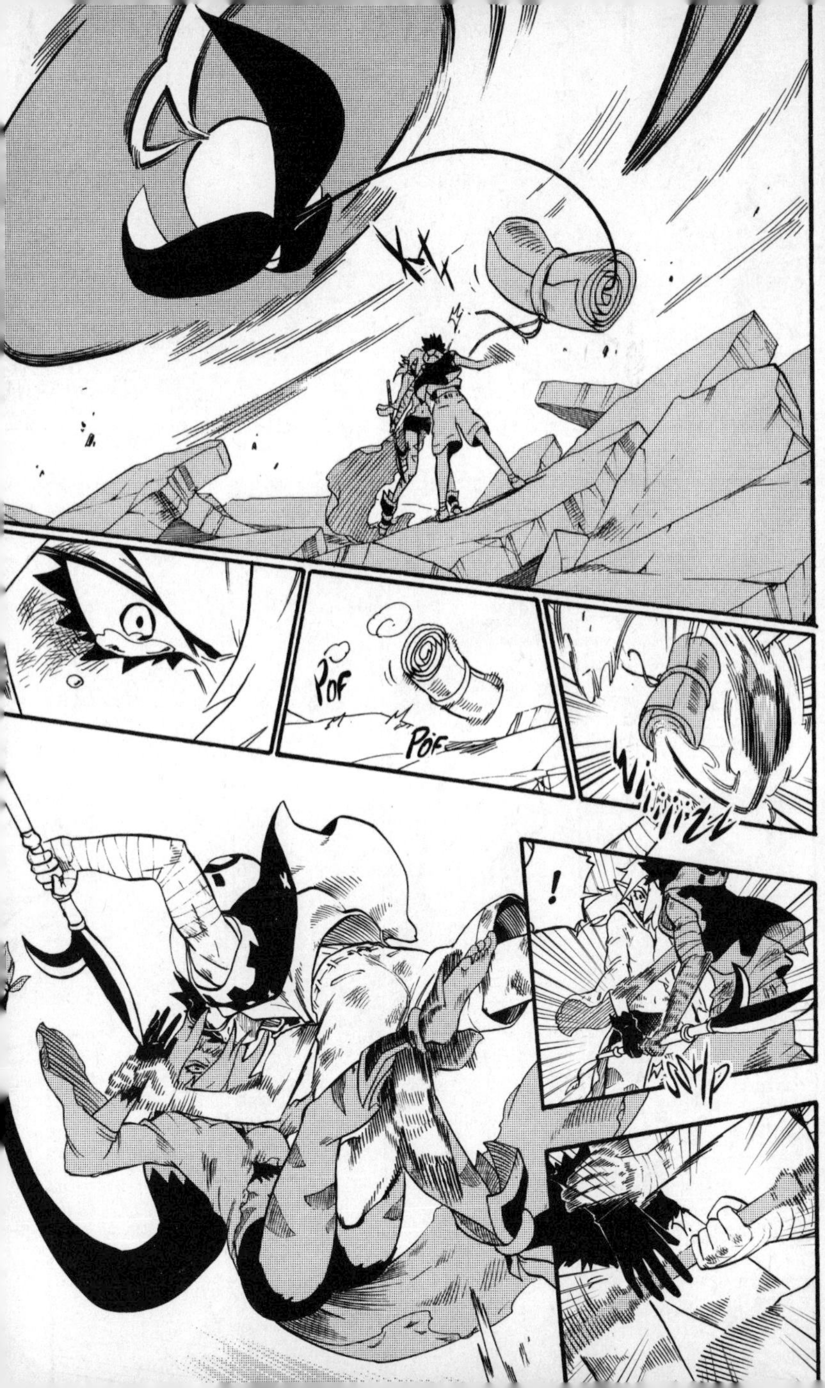
POF
POF
!
SCHP

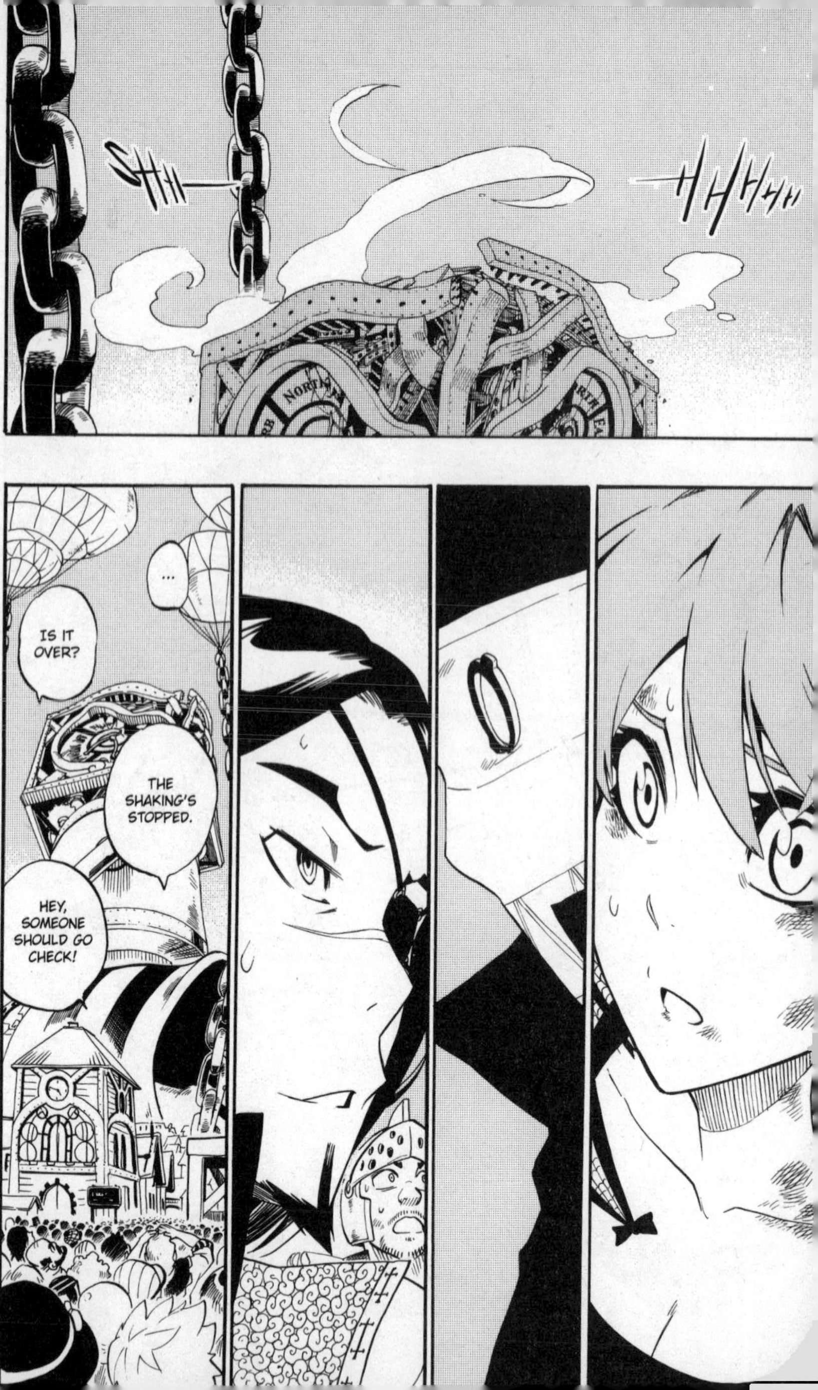
...
IS IT OVER?
THE SHAKING'S STOPPED.
HEY, SOMEONE SHOULD GO CHECK!

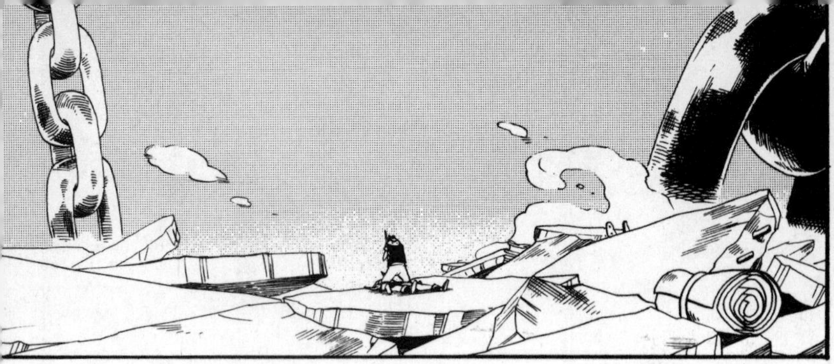

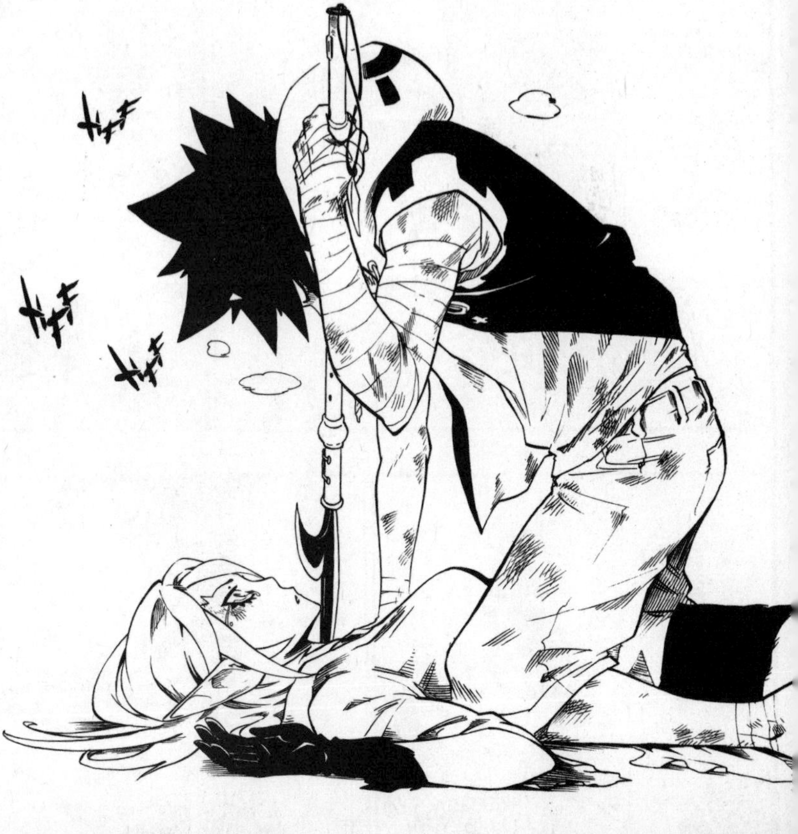
HUFF
HUFF
HUFF

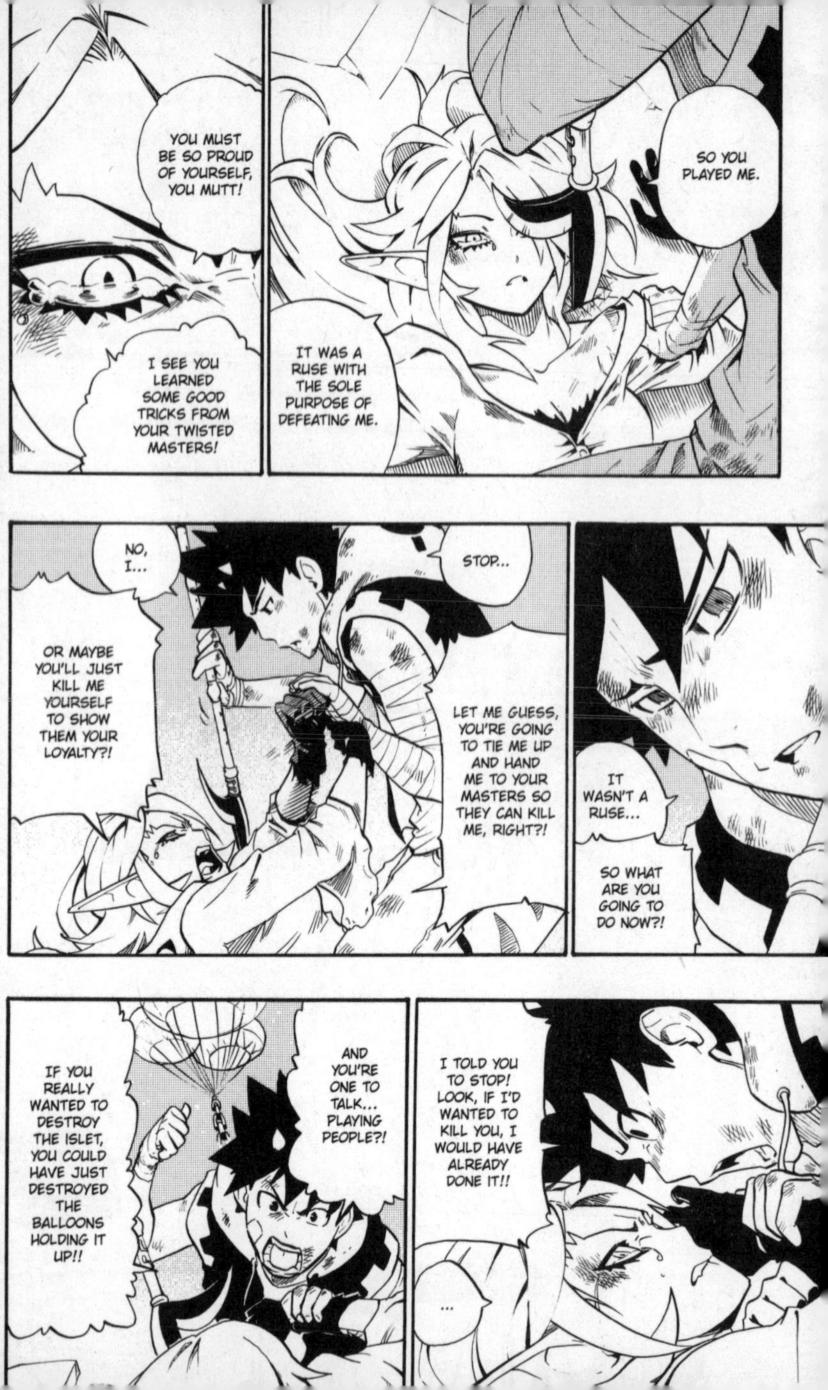
SO YOU PLAYED ME.
IT WAS A RUSE WITH THE SOLE PURPOSE OF DEFEATING ME.
YOU MUST BE SO PROUD OF YOURSELF, YOU MUTT!
I SEE YOU LEARNED SOME GOOD TRICKS FROM YOUR TWISTED MASTERS!
IT WASN'T A RUSE...
SO WHAT ARE YOU GOING TO DO NOW?!
LET ME GUESS, YOU'RE GOING TO TIE ME UP AND HAND ME TO YOUR MASTERS SO THEY CAN KILL ME, RIGHT?!
OR MAYBE YOU'LL JUST KILL ME YOURSELF TO SHOW THEM YOUR LOYALTY?!
NO, I...
STOP...
I TOLD YOU TO STOP! LOOK, IF I'D WANTED TO KILL YOU, I WOULD HAVE ALREADY DONE IT!!
...
AND YOU'RE ONE TO TALK... PLAYING PEOPLE?!
IF YOU REALLY WANTED TO DESTROY THE ISLET, YOU COULD HAVE JUST DESTROYED THE BALLOONS HOLDING IT UP!!

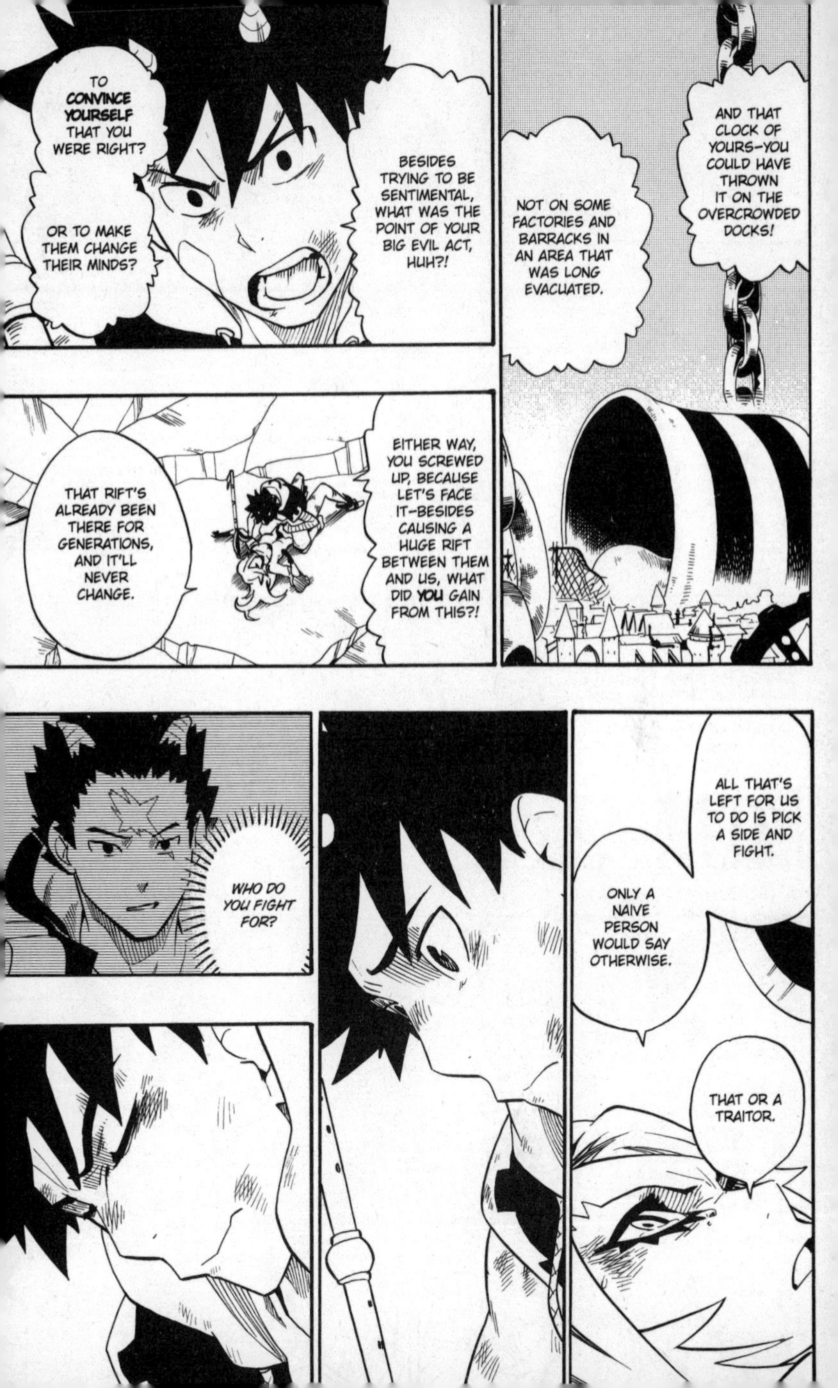
AND THAT CLOCK OF YOURS—YOU COULD HAVE THROWN IT ON THE OVERCROWDED DOCKS!
NOT ON SOME FACTORIES AND BARRACKS IN AN AREA THAT WAS LONG EVACUATED.
BESIDES TRYING TO BE SENTIMENTAL, WHAT WAS THE POINT OF YOUR BIG EVIL ACT, HUH?!
TO **CONVINCE YOURSELF** THAT YOU WERE RIGHT?
OR TO MAKE THEM CHANGE THEIR MINDS?
EITHER WAY, YOU SCREWED UP, BECAUSE LET'S FACE IT—BESIDES CAUSING A HUGE RIFT BETWEEN THEM AND US, WHAT DID **YOU** GAIN FROM THIS?!
THAT RIFT'S ALREADY BEEN THERE FOR GENERATIONS, AND IT'LL NEVER CHANGE.
ALL THAT'S LEFT FOR US TO DO IS PICK A SIDE AND FIGHT.
ONLY A NAIVE PERSON WOULD SAY OTHERWISE.
THAT OR A TRAITOR.
*WHO DO YOU FIGHT FOR?*

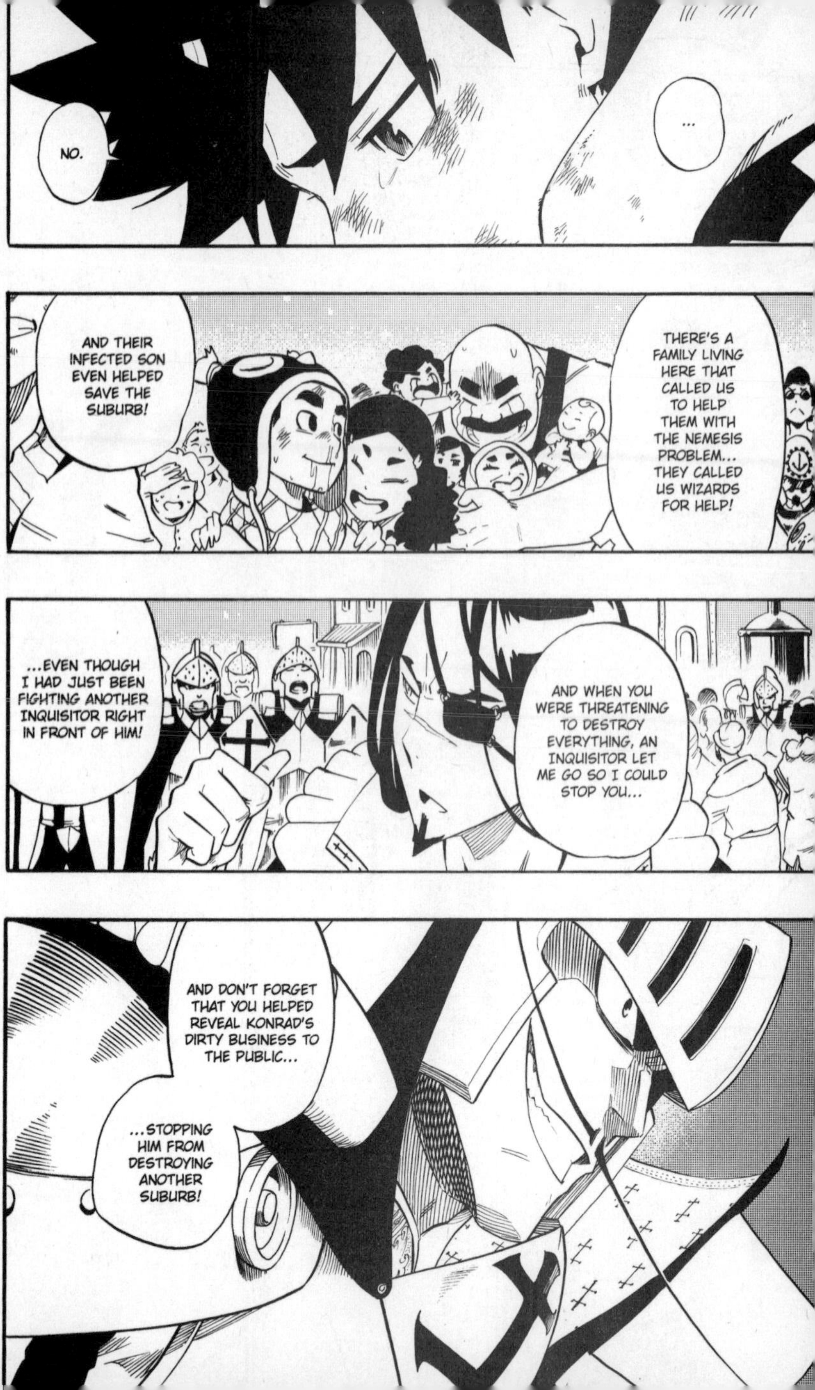
...
NO.
THERE'S A FAMILY LIVING HERE THAT CALLED US TO HELP THEM WITH THE NEMESIS PROBLEM... THEY CALLED US WIZARDS FOR HELP!
AND THEIR INFECTED SON EVEN HELPED SAVE THE SUBURB!
AND WHEN YOU WERE THREATENING TO DESTROY EVERYTHING, AN INQUISITOR LET ME GO SO I COULD STOP YOU...
...EVEN THOUGH I HAD JUST BEEN FIGHTING ANOTHER INQUISITOR RIGHT IN FRONT OF HIM!
AND DON'T FORGET THAT YOU HELPED REVEAL KONRAD'S DIRTY BUSINESS TO THE PUBLIC...
...STOPPING HIM FROM DESTROYING ANOTHER SUBURB!

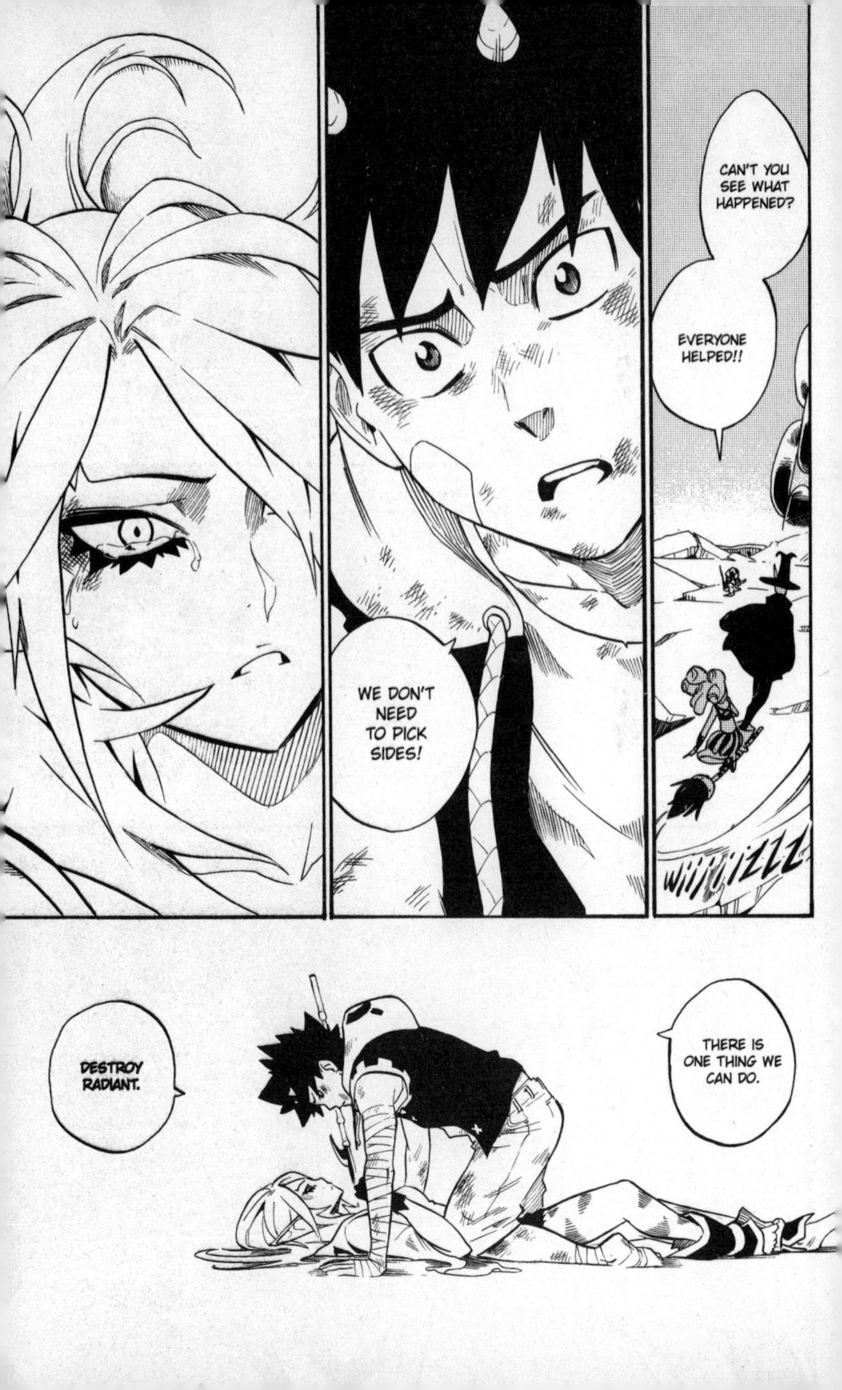
CAN'T YOU SEE WHAT HAPPENED?
EVERYONE HELPED!!
WIIIIIZZZ
WE DON'T NEED TO PICK SIDES!
THERE IS ONE THING WE CAN DO.
DESTROY RADIANT.

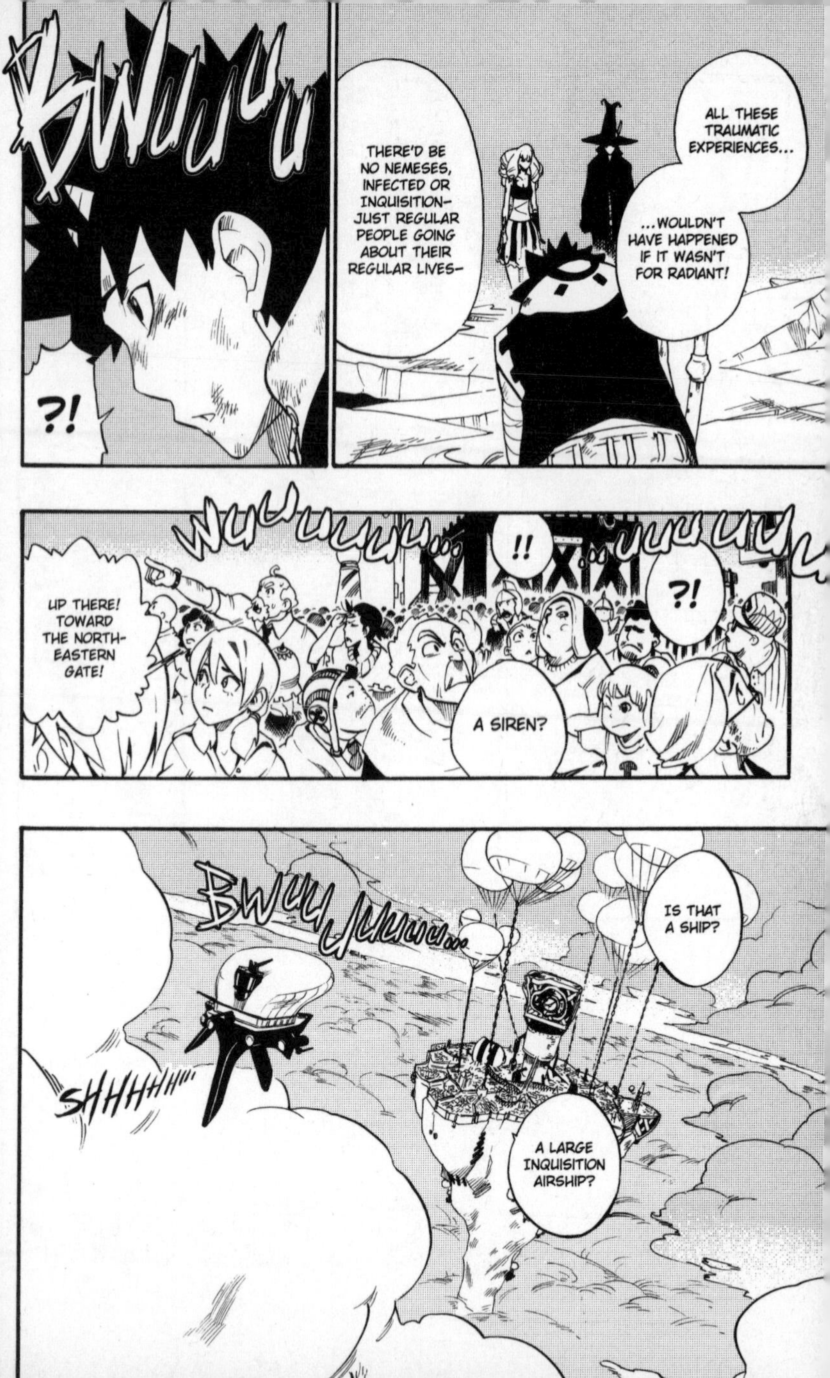
ALL THESE TRAUMATIC EXPERIENCES...
...WOULDN'T HAVE HAPPENED IF IT WASN'T FOR RADIANT!
THERE'D BE NO NEMESES, INFECTED OR INQUISITION- JUST REGULAR PEOPLE GOING ABOUT THEIR REGULAR LIVES-
BWUUUU
?!
WUUUUUU... ...UUUUUU
?!
!!
A SIREN?
UP THERE! TOWARD THE NORTH-EASTERN GATE!
IS THAT A SHIP?
BWUUUUUU...
A LARGE INQUISITION AIRSHIP?
SHHHH

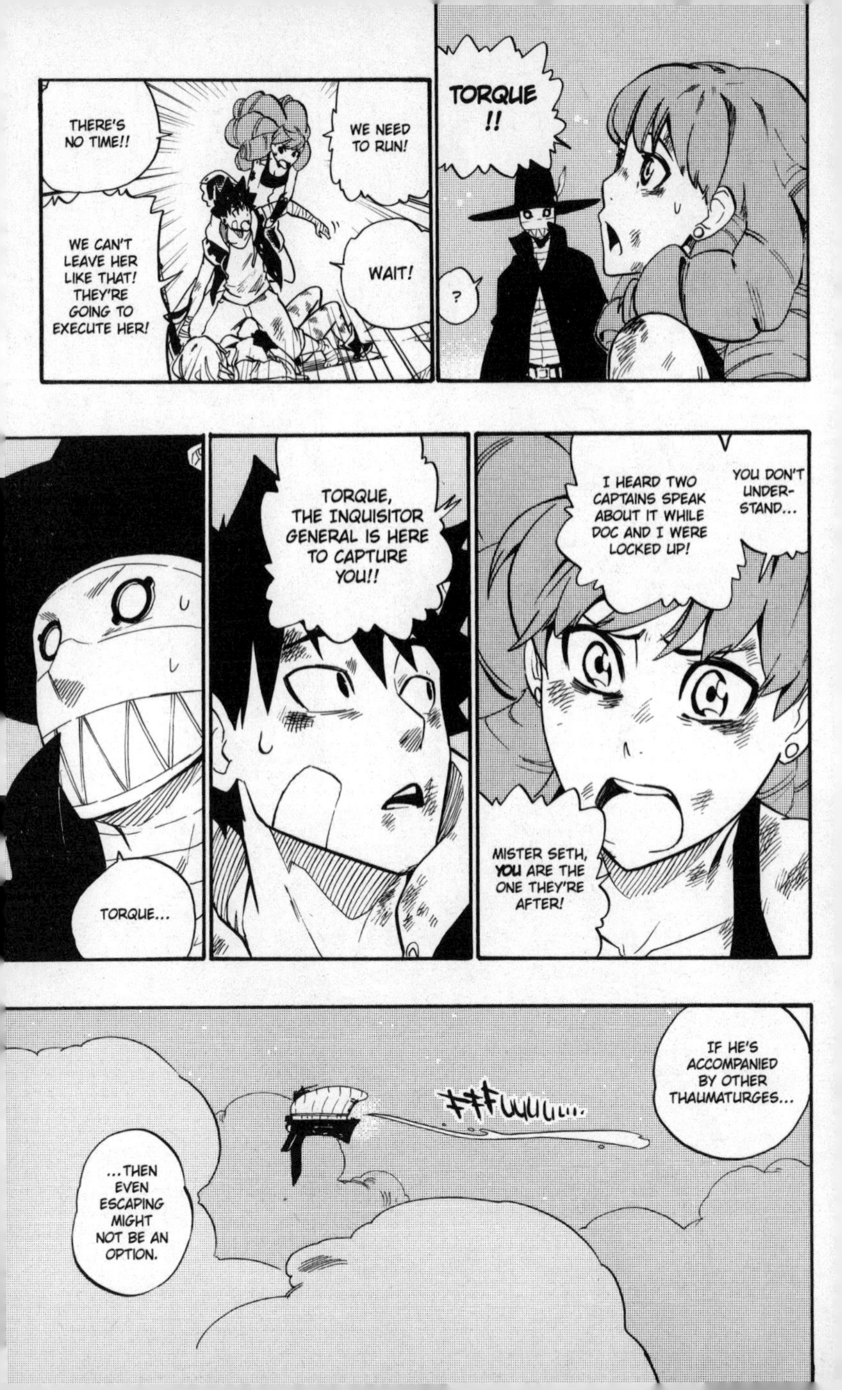
TORQUE!!
?
WE NEED TO RUN!
THERE'S NO TIME!!
WAIT!
WE CAN'T LEAVE HER LIKE THAT! THEY'RE GOING TO EXECUTE HER!
YOU DON'T UNDER-STAND...
I HEARD TWO CAPTAINS SPEAK ABOUT IT WHILE DOC AND I WERE LOCKED UP!
MISTER SETH, YOU ARE THE ONE THEY'RE AFTER!
TORQUE, THE INQUISITOR GENERAL IS HERE TO CAPTURE YOU!!
TORQUE...
IF HE'S ACCOMPANIED BY OTHER THAUMATURGES...
FFFUUUU...
...THEN EVEN ESCAPING MIGHT NOT BE AN OPTION.

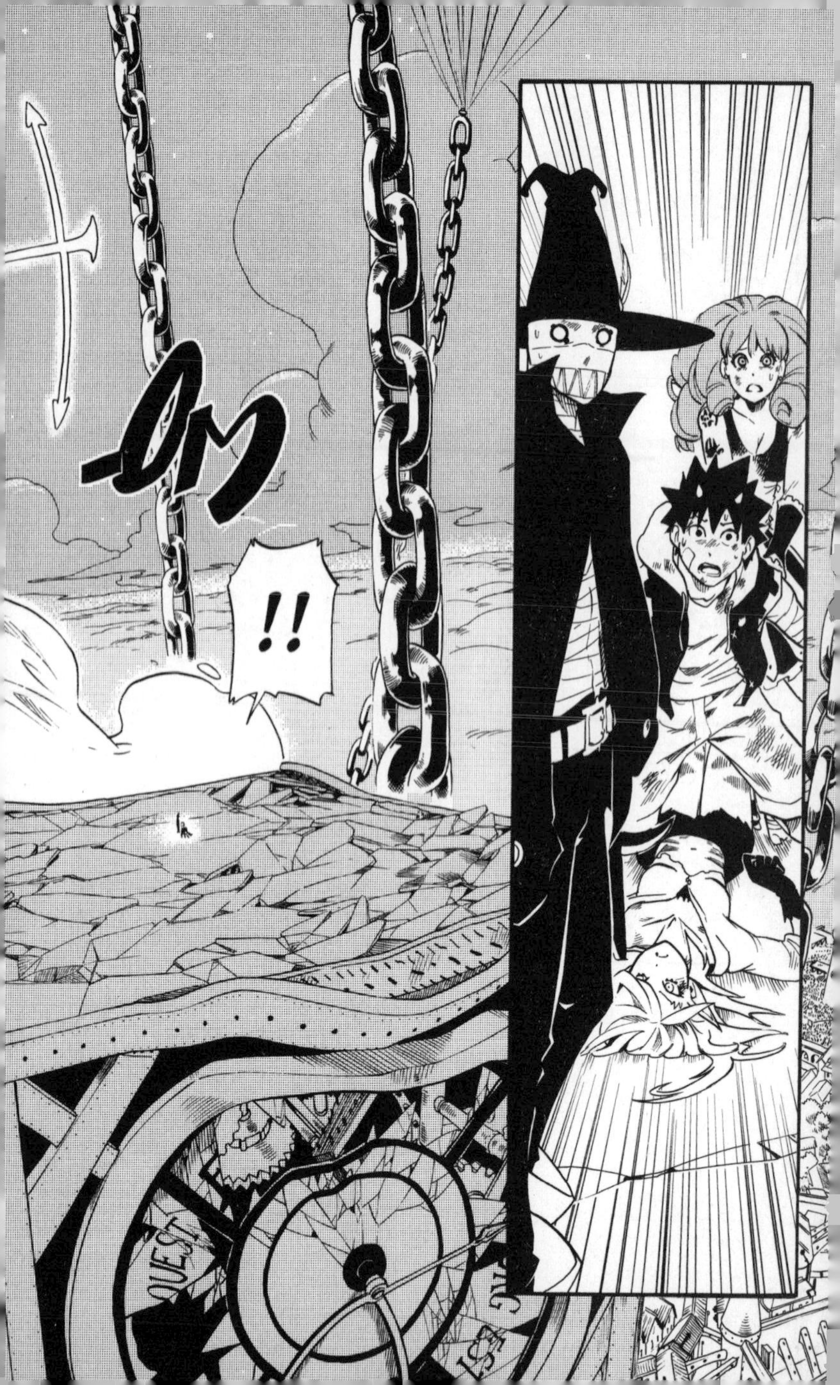
!!

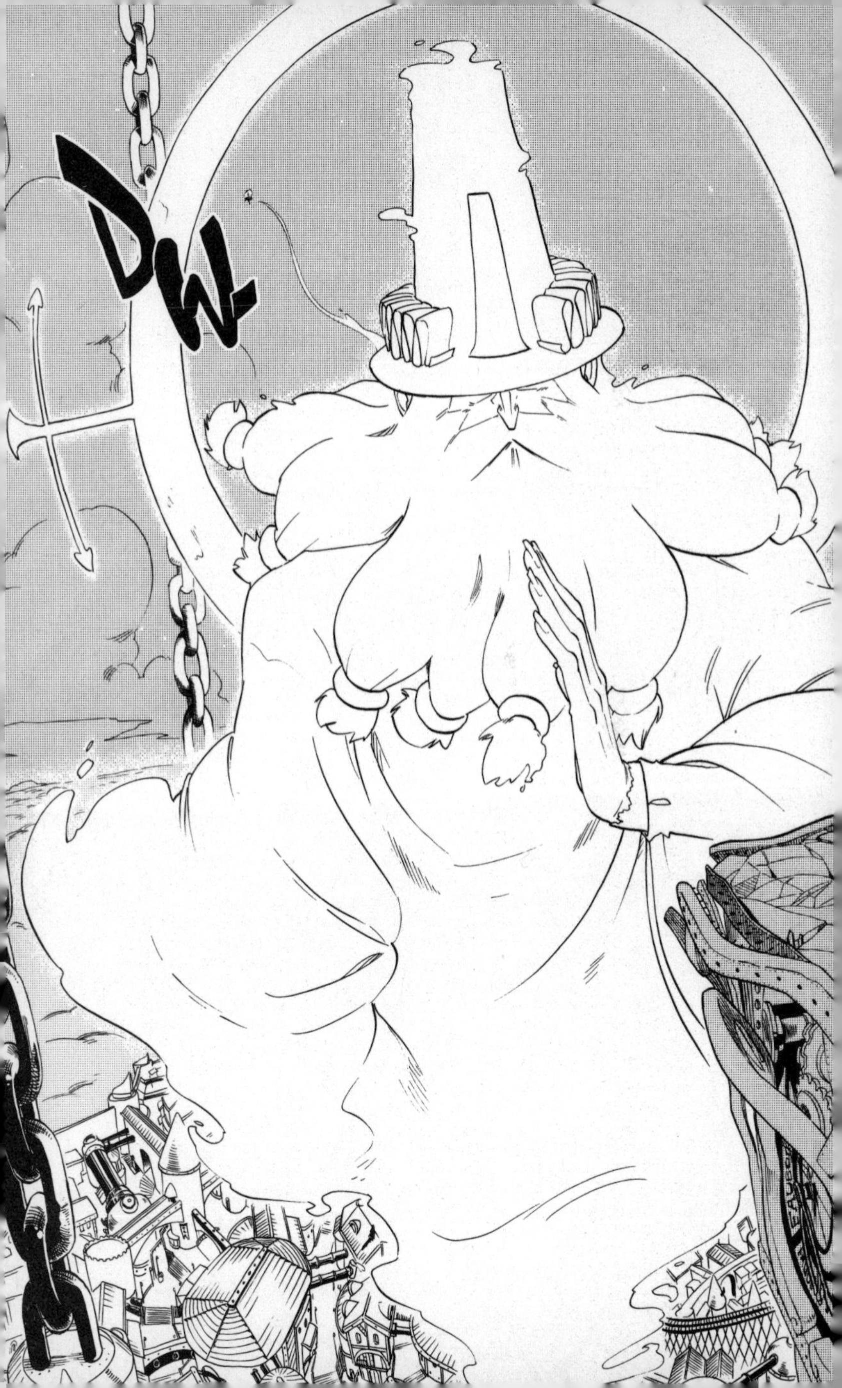
DW

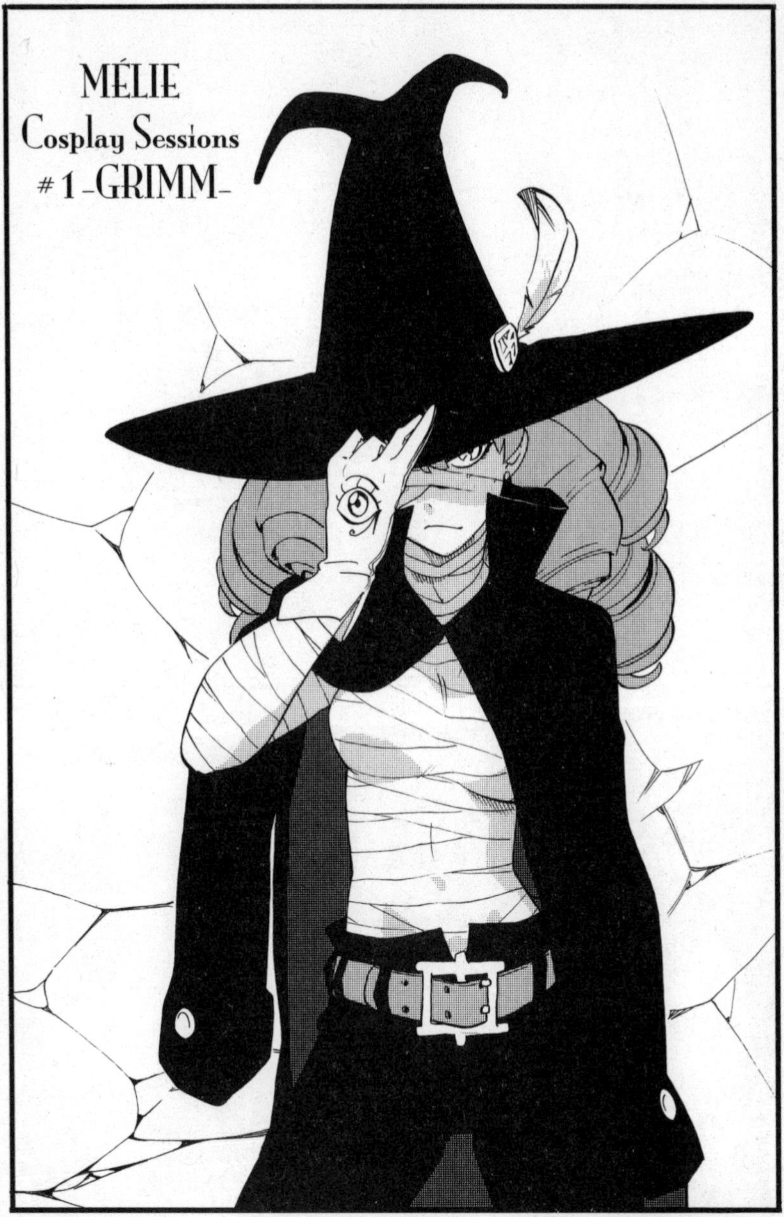
MÉLIE
Cosplay Sessions
#1 -GRIMM-

**CHAPTER 26**

# THE MIRACLE

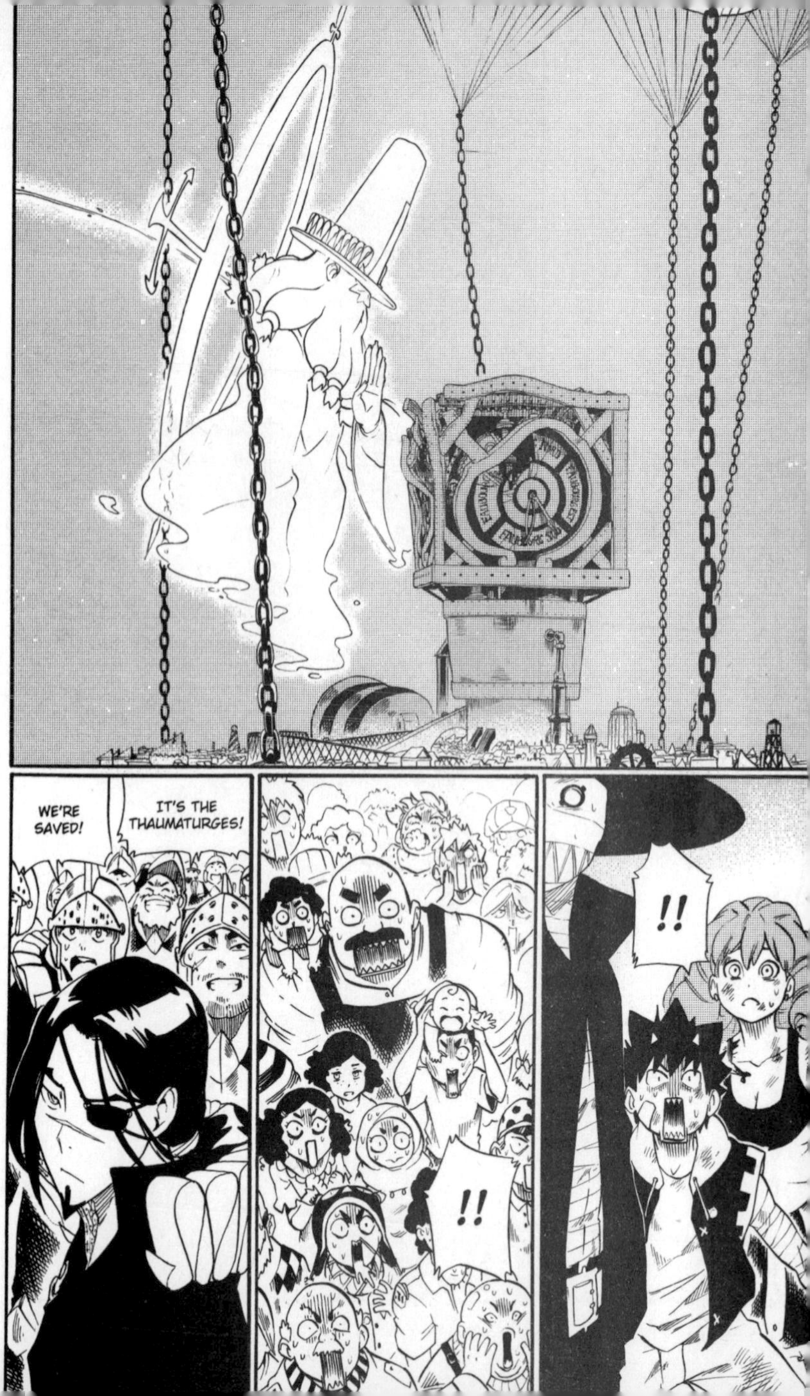
!!
!!
IT'S THE THAUMATURGES!
WE'RE SAVED!

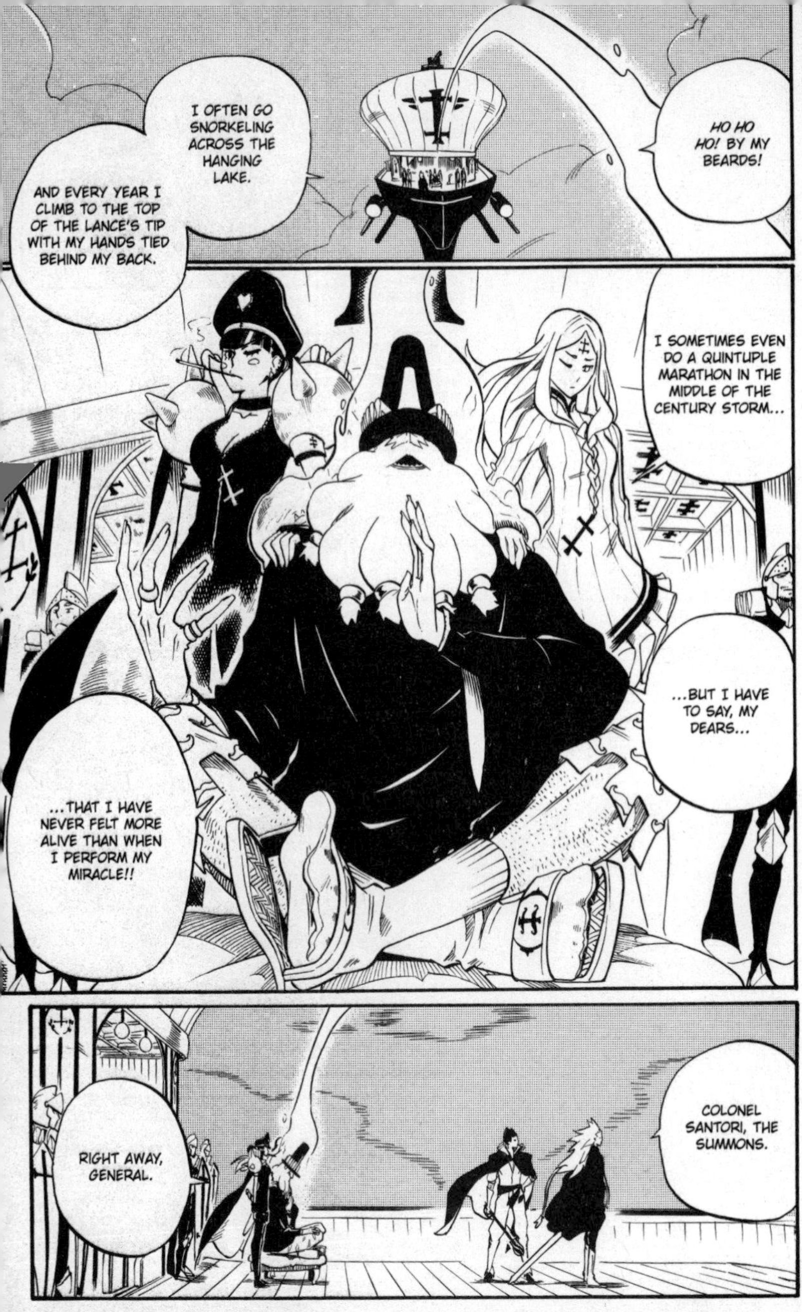
HO HO HO! BY MY BEARDS!
I OFTEN GO SNORKELING ACROSS THE HANGING LAKE.
AND EVERY YEAR I CLIMB TO THE TOP OF THE LANCE'S TIP WITH MY HANDS TIED BEHIND MY BACK.
I SOMETIMES EVEN DO A QUINTUPLE MARATHON IN THE MIDDLE OF THE CENTURY STORM...
...BUT I HAVE TO SAY, MY DEARS...
...THAT I HAVE NEVER FELT MORE ALIVE THAN WHEN I PERFORM MY MIRACLE!!
COLONEL SANTORI, THE SUMMONS.
RIGHT AWAY, GENERAL.

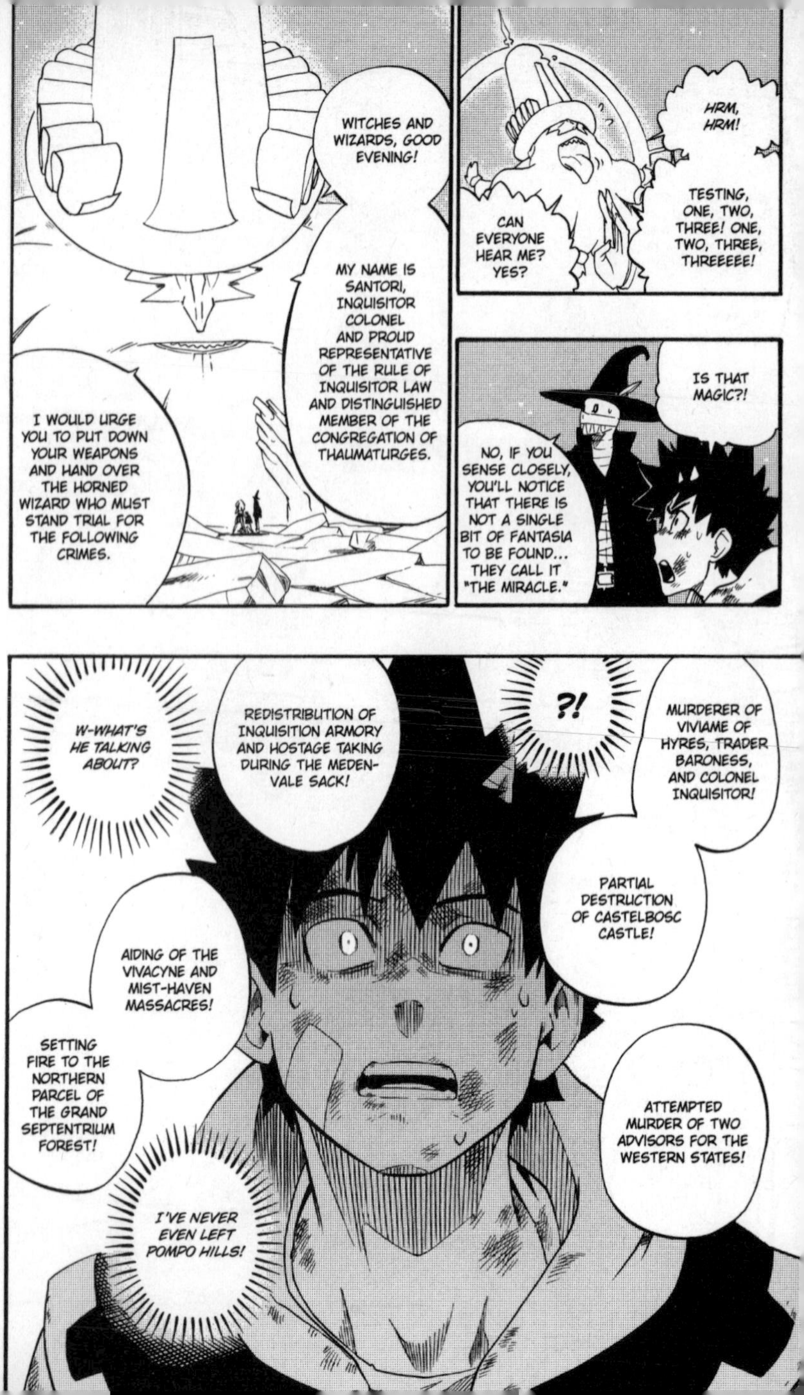
HRM, HRM!
TESTING, ONE, TWO, THREE! ONE, TWO, THREEEEE!
CAN EVERYONE HEAR ME? YES?
IS THAT MAGIC?!
NO, IF YOU SENSE CLOSELY, YOU'LL NOTICE THAT THERE IS NOT A SINGLE BIT OF FANTASIA TO BE FOUND... THEY CALL IT "THE MIRACLE."
WITCHES AND WIZARDS, GOOD EVENING!
MY NAME IS SANTORI, INQUISITOR COLONEL AND PROUD REPRESENTATIVE OF THE RULE OF INQUISITOR LAW AND DISTINGUISHED MEMBER OF THE CONGREGATION OF THAUMATURGES.
I WOULD URGE YOU TO PUT DOWN YOUR WEAPONS AND HAND OVER THE HORNED WIZARD WHO MUST STAND TRIAL FOR THE FOLLOWING CRIMES.
MURDERER OF VIVIAME OF HYRES, TRADER BARONESS, AND COLONEL INQUISITOR!
REDISTRIBUTION OF INQUISITION ARMORY AND HOSTAGE TAKING DURING THE MEDEN-VALE SACK!
?!
W-WHAT'S HE TALKING ABOUT?
PARTIAL DESTRUCTION OF CASTELBOSC CASTLE!
AIDING OF THE VIVACYNE AND MIST-HAVEN MASSACRES!
ATTEMPTED MURDER OF TWO ADVISORS FOR THE WESTERN STATES!
SETTING FIRE TO THE NORTHERN PARCEL OF THE GRAND SEPTENTRIUM FOREST!
I'VE NEVER EVEN LEFT POMPO HILLS!

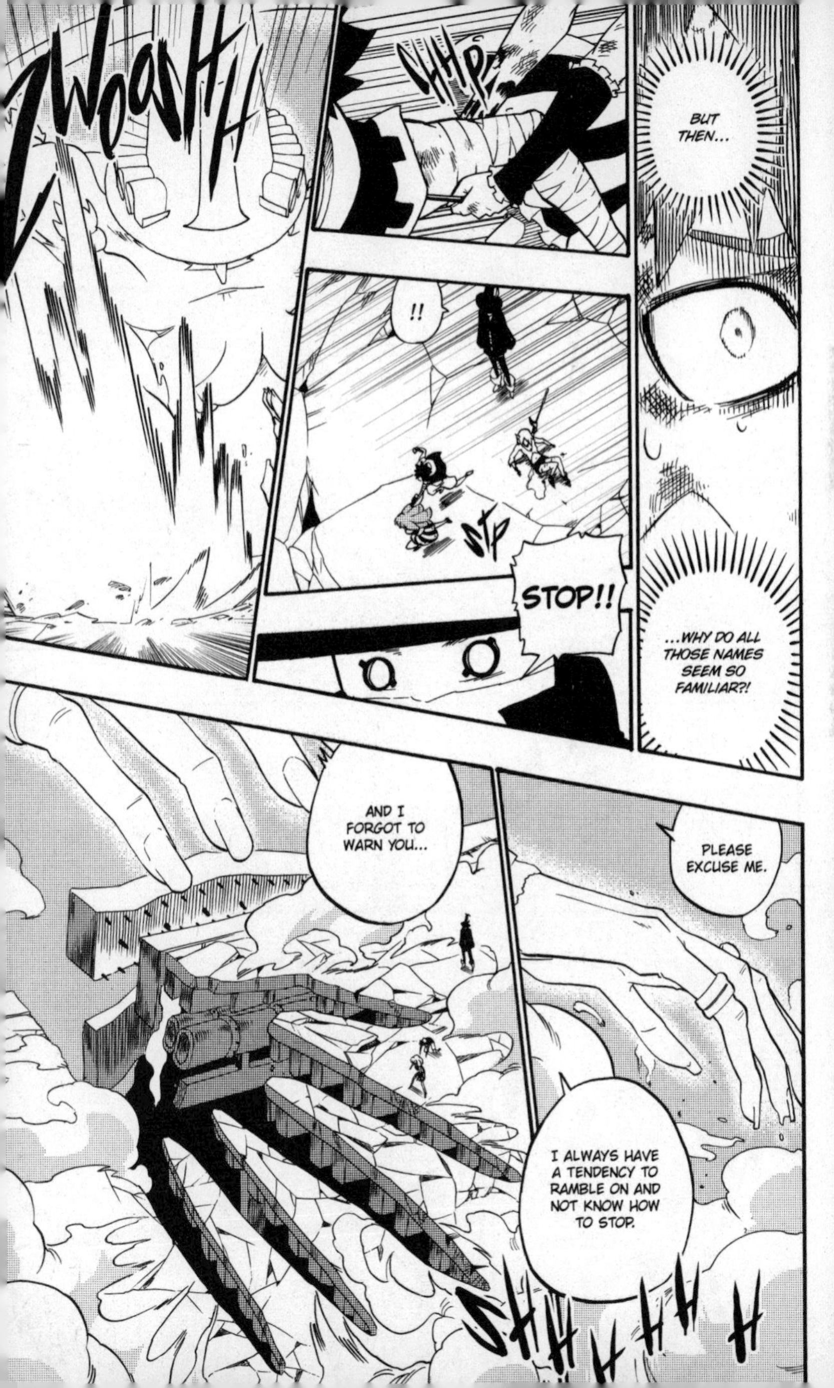
BUT THEN...
...WHY DO ALL THOSE NAMES SEEM SO FAMILIAR?!
CHHP
!!
STP
STOP!!
ZWOOSHH
PLEASE EXCUSE ME.
I ALWAYS HAVE A TENDENCY TO RAMBLE ON AND NOT KNOW HOW TO STOP.
AND I FORGOT TO WARN YOU...
SHHHHHH

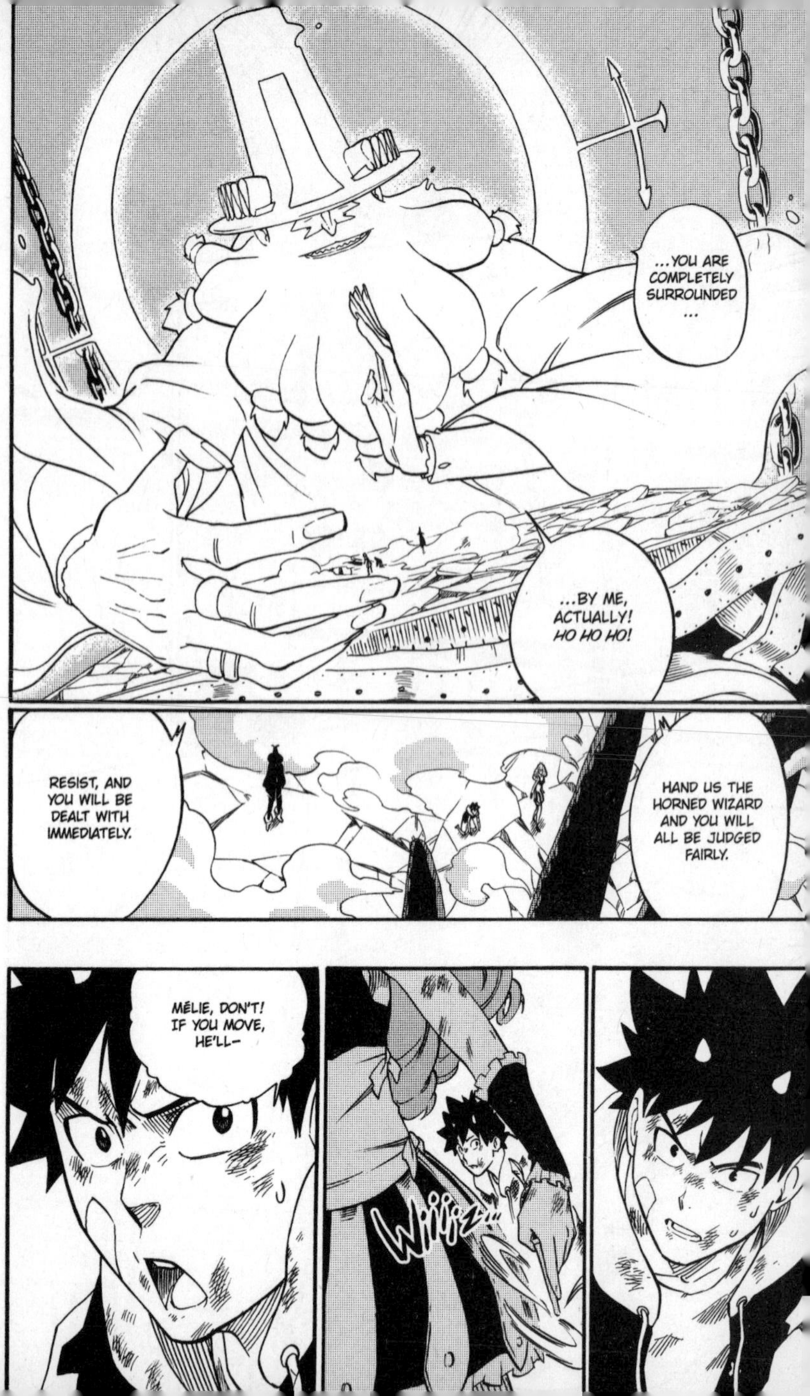

...YOU ARE COMPLETELY SURROUNDED ...
...BY ME, ACTUALLY! *HO HO HO!*
HAND US THE HORNED WIZARD AND YOU WILL ALL BE JUDGED FAIRLY.
RESIST, AND YOU WILL BE DEALT WITH IMMEDIATELY.
WIIIZ...
MÉLIE, DON'T! IF YOU MOVE, HE'LL-

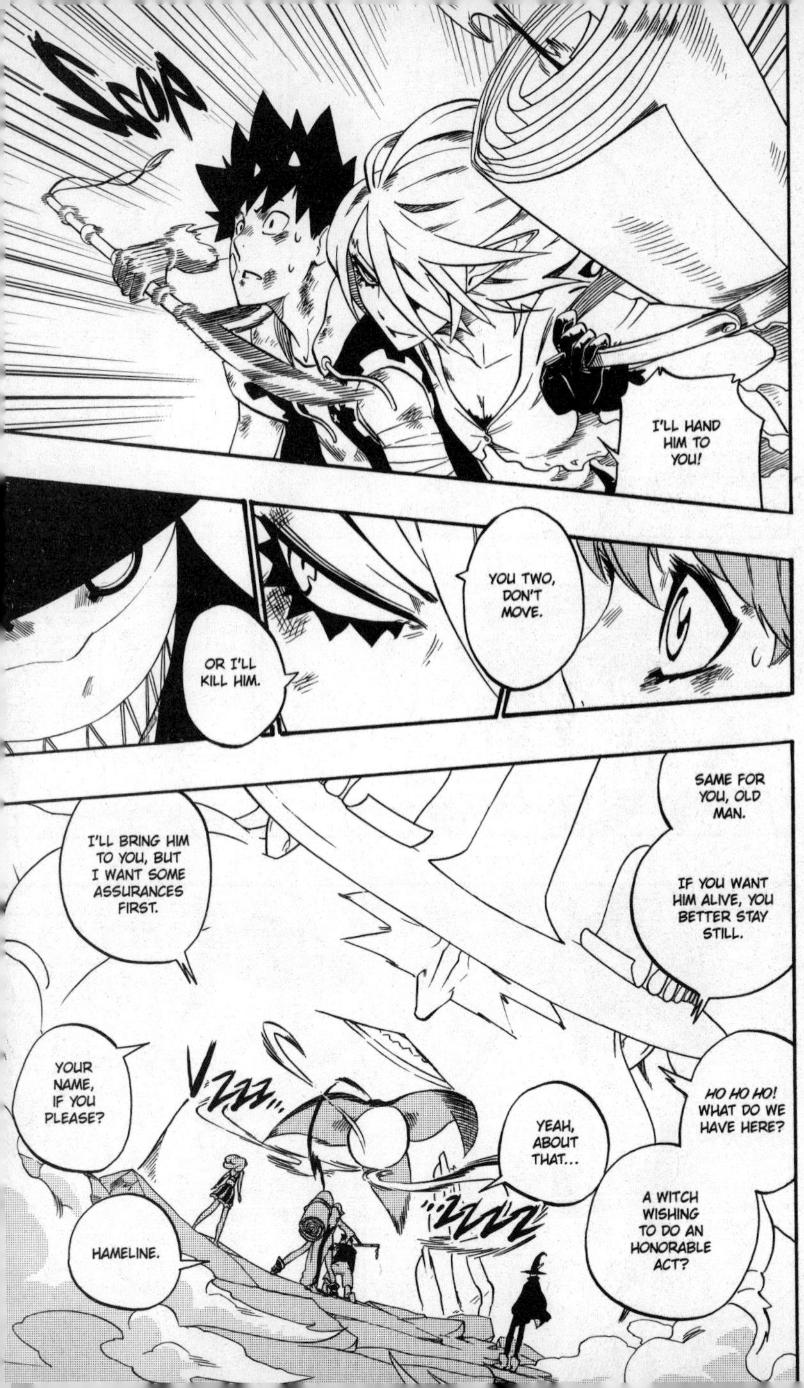
SCOP
I'LL HAND HIM TO YOU!
YOU TWO, DON'T MOVE.
OR I'LL KILL HIM.
SAME FOR YOU, OLD MAN.
IF YOU WANT HIM ALIVE, YOU BETTER STAY STILL.
I'LL BRING HIM TO YOU, BUT I WANT SOME ASSURANCES FIRST.
HO HO HO! WHAT DO WE HAVE HERE?
A WITCH WISHING TO DO AN HONORABLE ACT?
YEAH, ABOUT THAT...
VZZZ
ZZZZZ
YOUR NAME, IF YOU PLEASE?
HAMELINE.

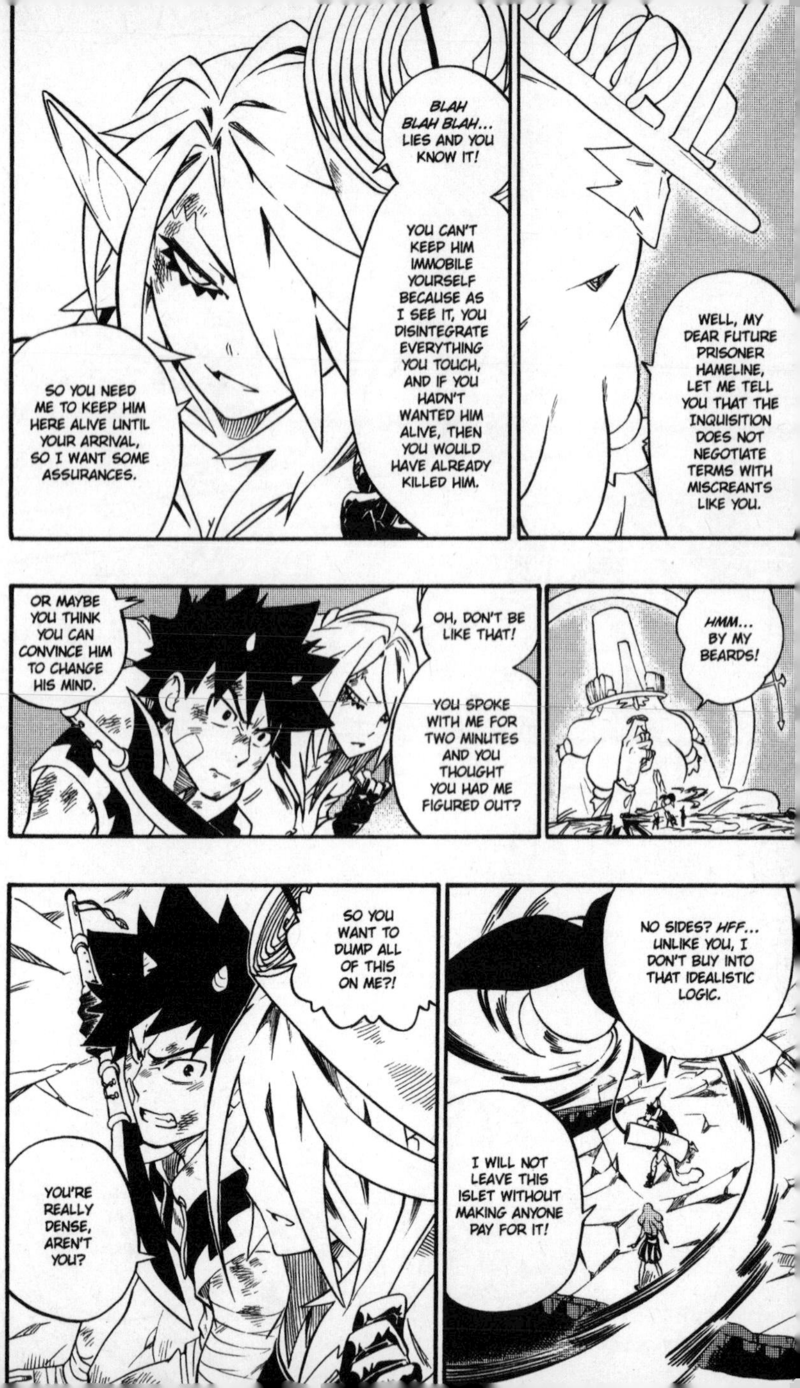
WELL, MY DEAR FUTURE PRISONER HAMELINE, LET ME TELL YOU THAT THE INQUISITION DOES NOT NEGOTIATE TERMS WITH MISCREANTS LIKE YOU.
*BLAH BLAH BLAH*... LIES AND YOU KNOW IT!
YOU CAN'T KEEP HIM IMMOBILE YOURSELF BECAUSE AS I SEE IT, YOU DISINTEGRATE EVERYTHING YOU TOUCH, AND IF YOU HADN'T WANTED HIM ALIVE, THEN YOU WOULD HAVE ALREADY KILLED HIM.
SO YOU NEED ME TO KEEP HIM HERE ALIVE UNTIL YOUR ARRIVAL, SO I WANT SOME ASSURANCES.
*HMM*... BY MY BEARDS!
OH, DON'T BE LIKE THAT!
YOU SPOKE WITH ME FOR TWO MINUTES AND YOU THOUGHT YOU HAD ME FIGURED OUT?
OR MAYBE YOU THINK YOU CAN CONVINCE HIM TO CHANGE HIS MIND.
NO SIDES? *HFF*... UNLIKE YOU, I DON'T BUY INTO THAT IDEALISTIC LOGIC.
I WILL NOT LEAVE THIS ISLET WITHOUT MAKING ANYONE PAY FOR IT!
SO YOU WANT TO DUMP ALL OF THIS ON ME?!
YOU'RE REALLY DENSE, AREN'T YOU?

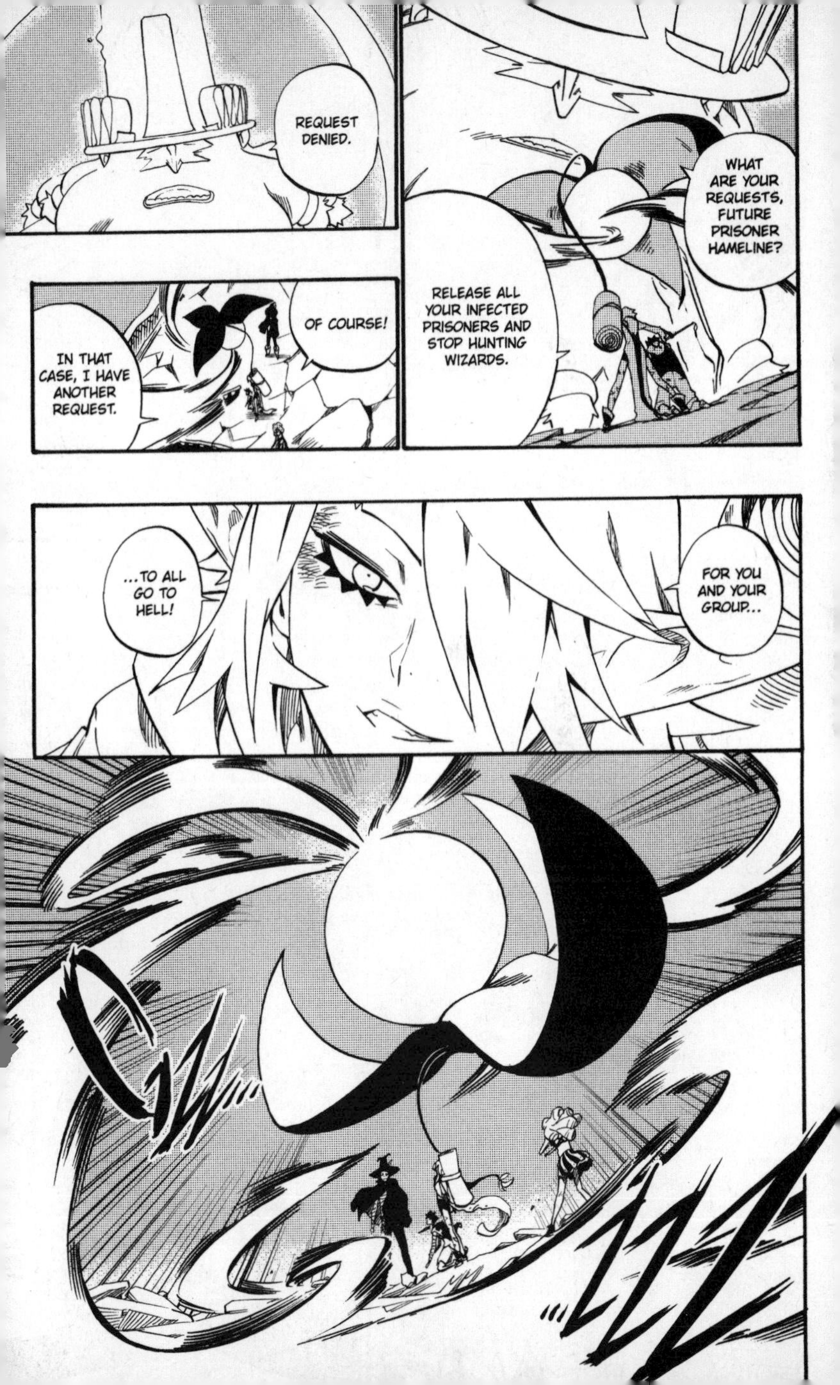
WHAT ARE YOUR REQUESTS, FUTURE PRISONER HAMELINE?
RELEASE ALL YOUR INFECTED PRISONERS AND STOP HUNTING WIZARDS.
REQUEST DENIED.
OF COURSE!
IN THAT CASE, I HAVE ANOTHER REQUEST.
FOR YOU AND YOUR GROUP...
...TO ALL GO TO HELL!

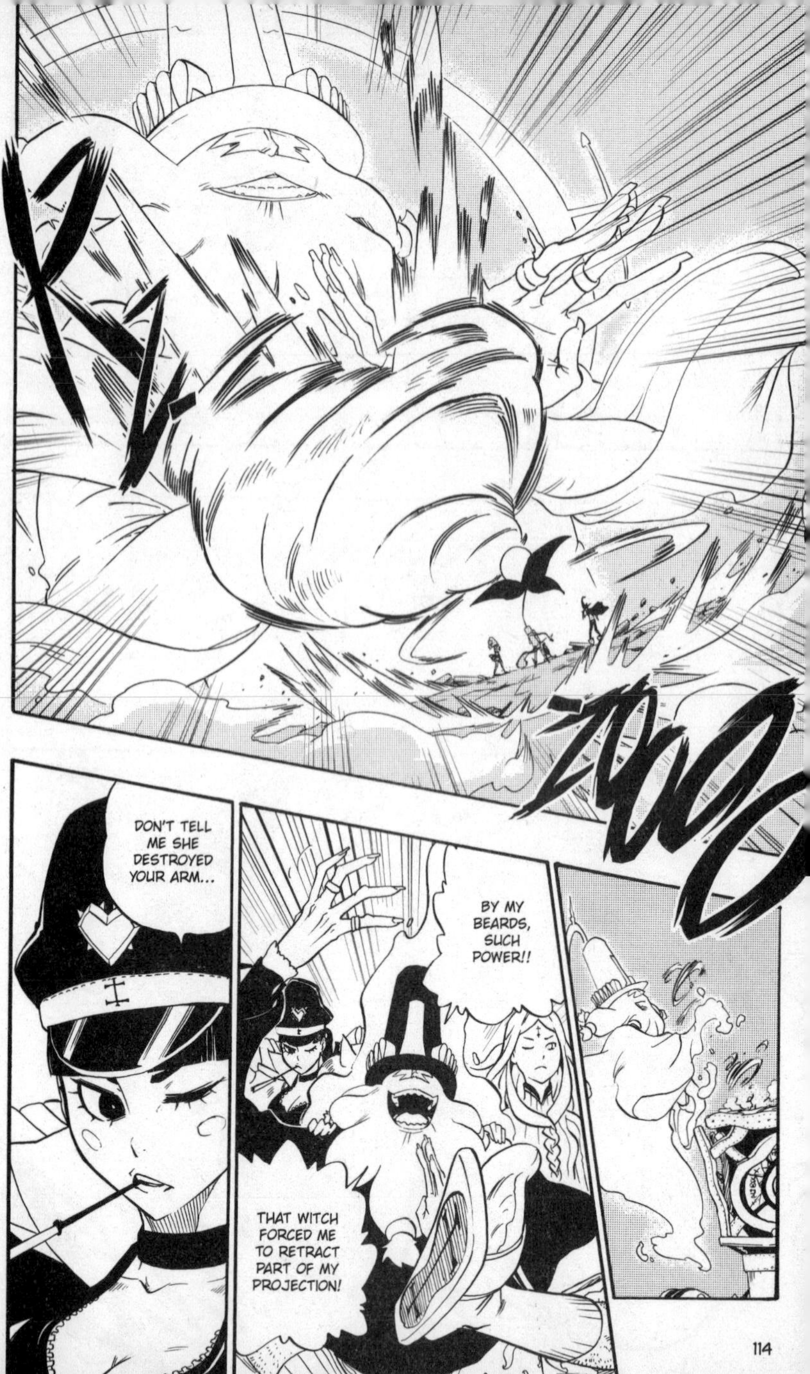
BY MY BEARDS, SUCH POWER!!
THAT WITCH FORCED ME TO RETRACT PART OF MY PROJECTION!
DON'T TELL ME SHE DESTROYED YOUR ARM...

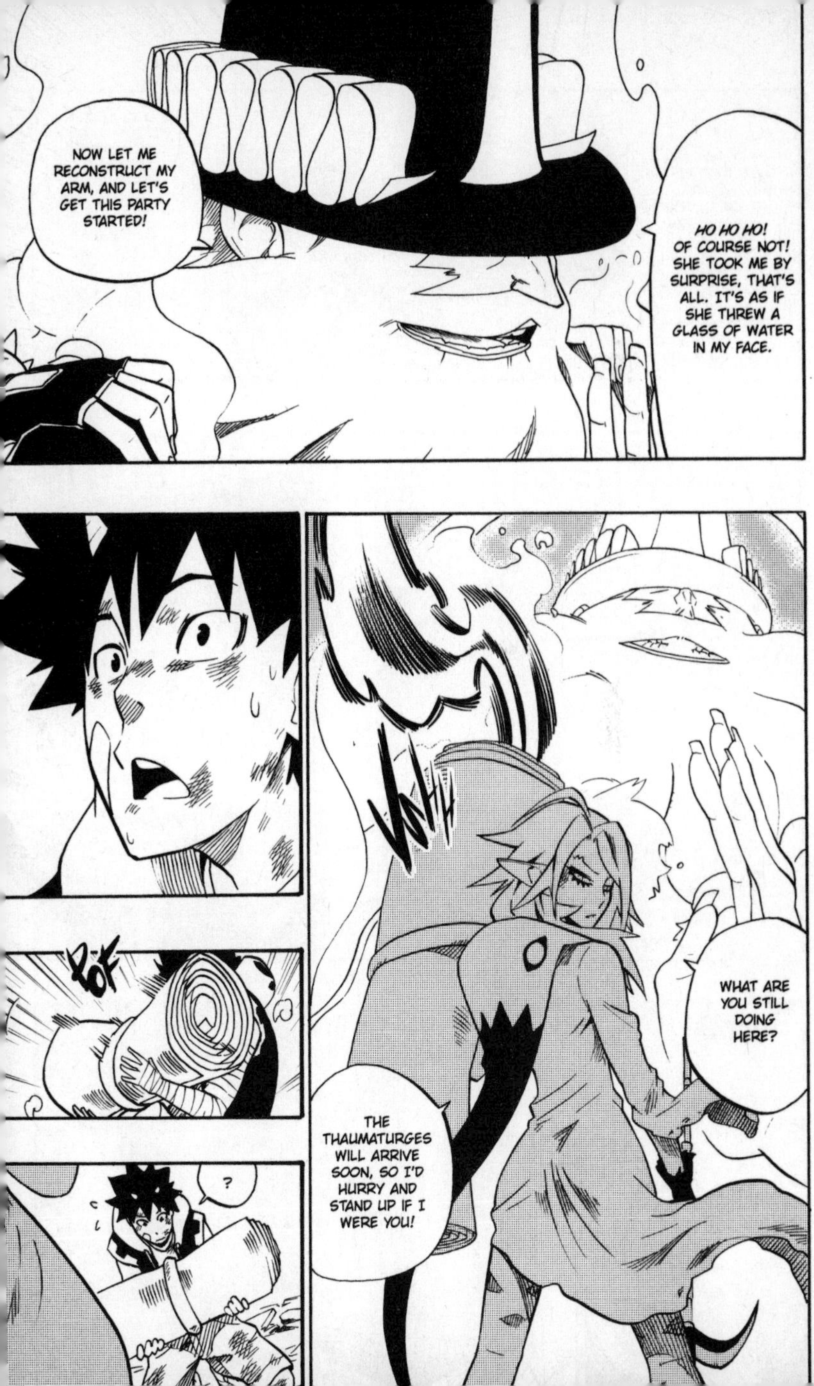
HO HO HO! OF COURSE NOT! SHE TOOK ME BY SURPRISE, THAT'S ALL. IT'S AS IF SHE THREW A GLASS OF WATER IN MY FACE.
NOW LET ME RECONSTRUCT MY ARM, AND LET'S GET THIS PARTY STARTED!
WHAT ARE YOU STILL DOING HERE?
THE THAUMATURGES WILL ARRIVE SOON, SO I'D HURRY AND STAND UP IF I WERE YOU!
POF
?

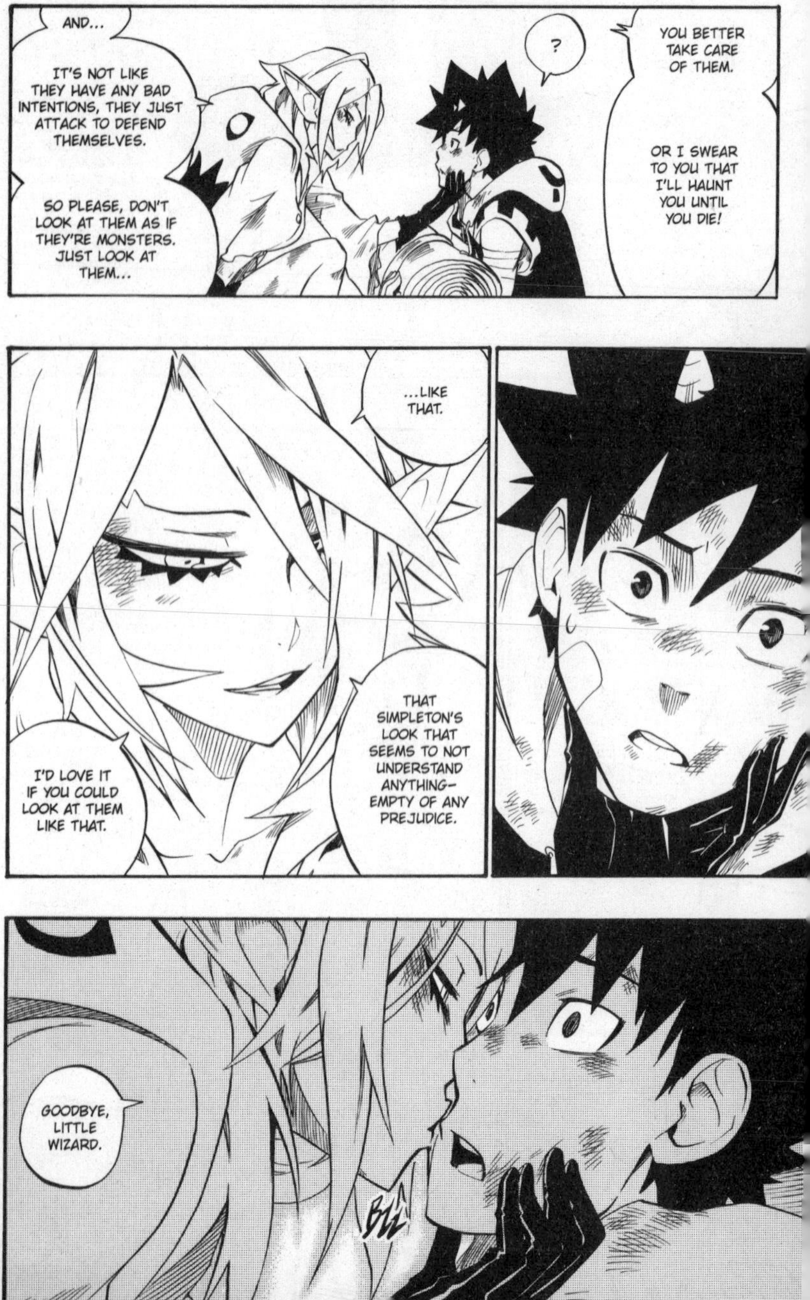
YOU BETTER TAKE CARE OF THEM.
OR I SWEAR TO YOU THAT I'LL HAUNT YOU UNTIL YOU DIE!
?
AND...
IT'S NOT LIKE THEY HAVE ANY BAD INTENTIONS, THEY JUST ATTACK TO DEFEND THEMSELVES.
SO PLEASE, DON'T LOOK AT THEM AS IF THEY'RE MONSTERS. JUST LOOK AT THEM...
...LIKE THAT.
THAT SIMPLETON'S LOOK THAT SEEMS TO NOT UNDERSTAND ANYTHING-EMPTY OF ANY PREJUDICE.
I'D LOVE IT IF YOU COULD LOOK AT THEM LIKE THAT.
GOODBYE, LITTLE WIZARD.
BZZ

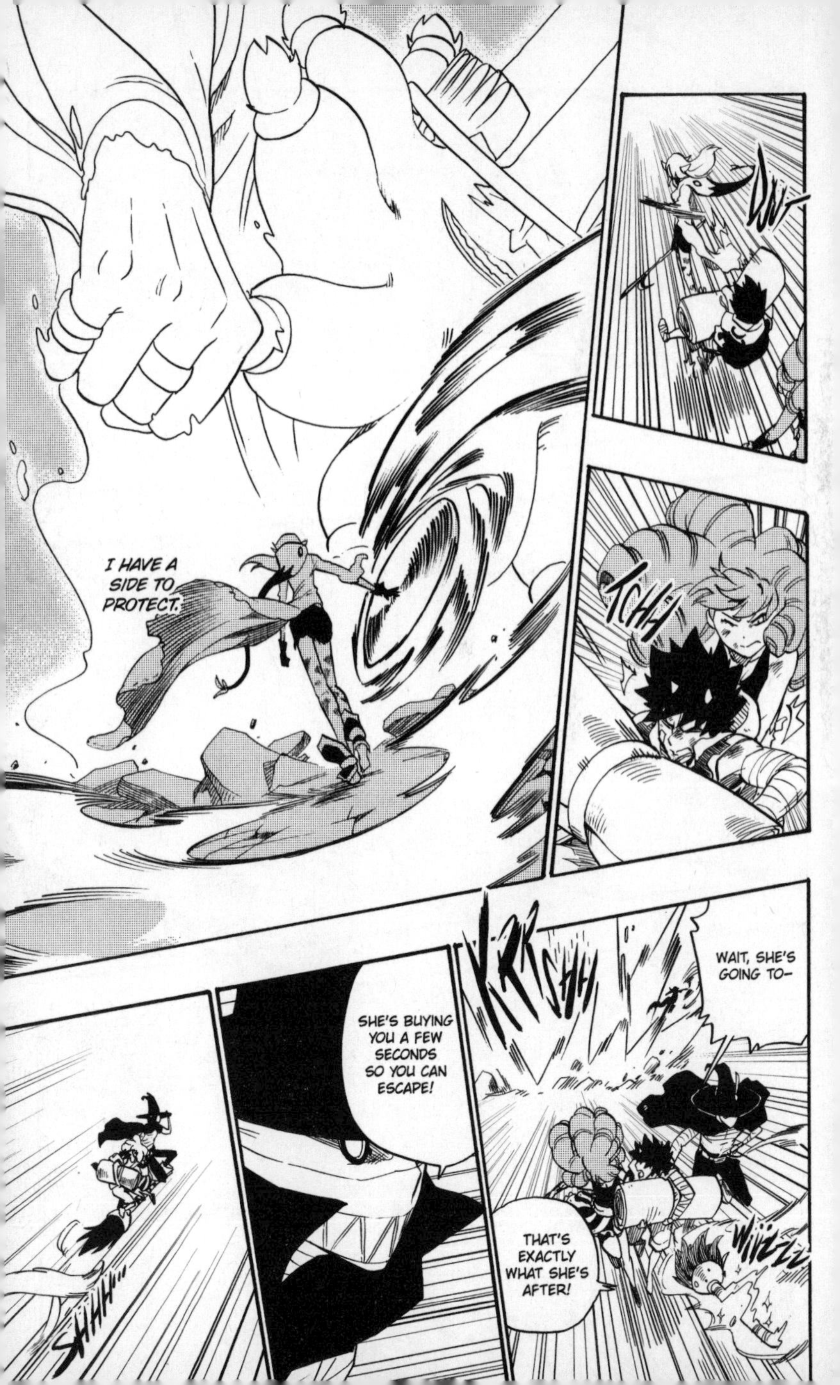
TCHH
I HAVE A SIDE TO PROTECT.
WAIT, SHE'S GOING TO–
KRRSHH
THAT'S EXACTLY WHAT SHE'S AFTER!
WHIZZZ
SHE'S BUYING YOU A FEW SECONDS SO YOU CAN ESCAPE!
SHHH...

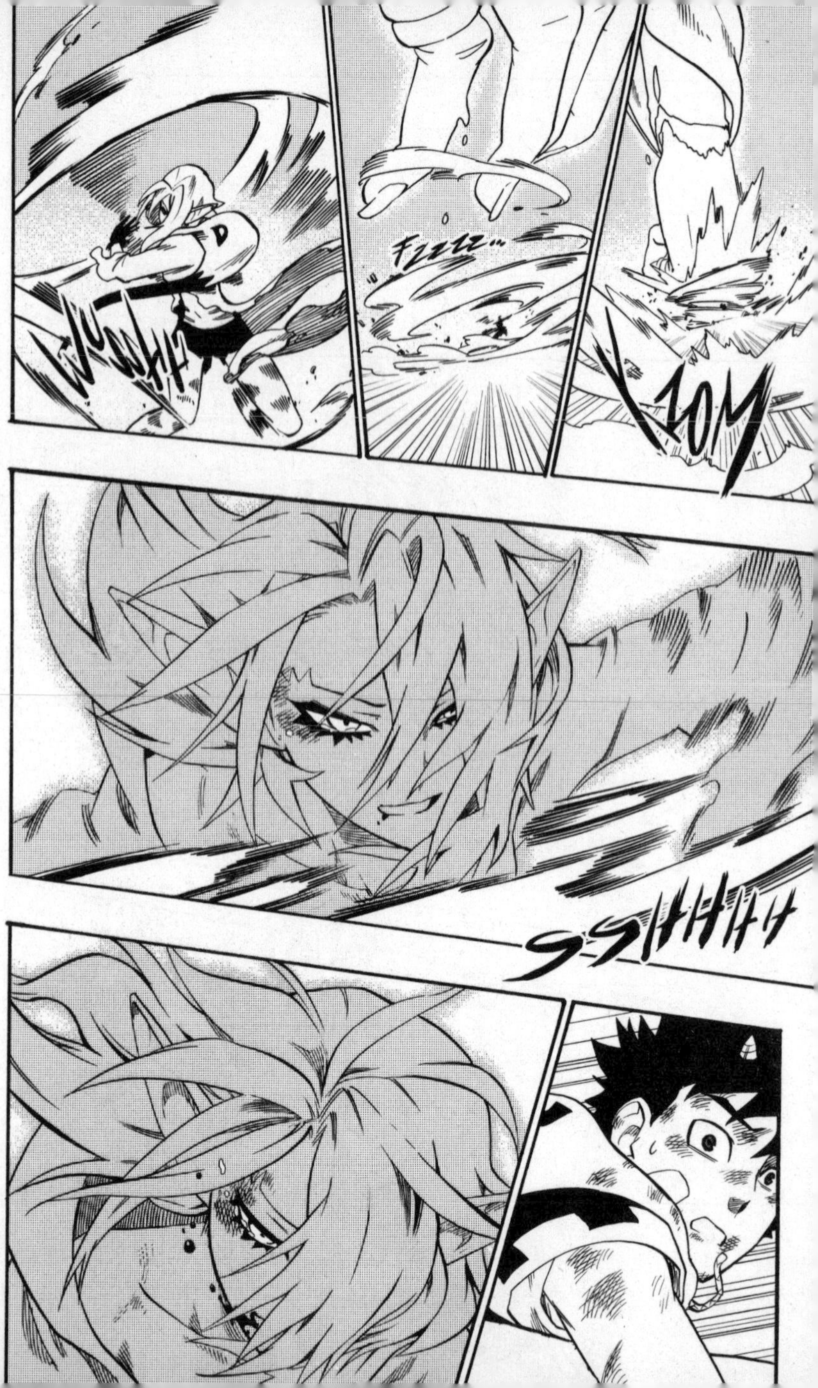
FZZZZ..
SSHHHH

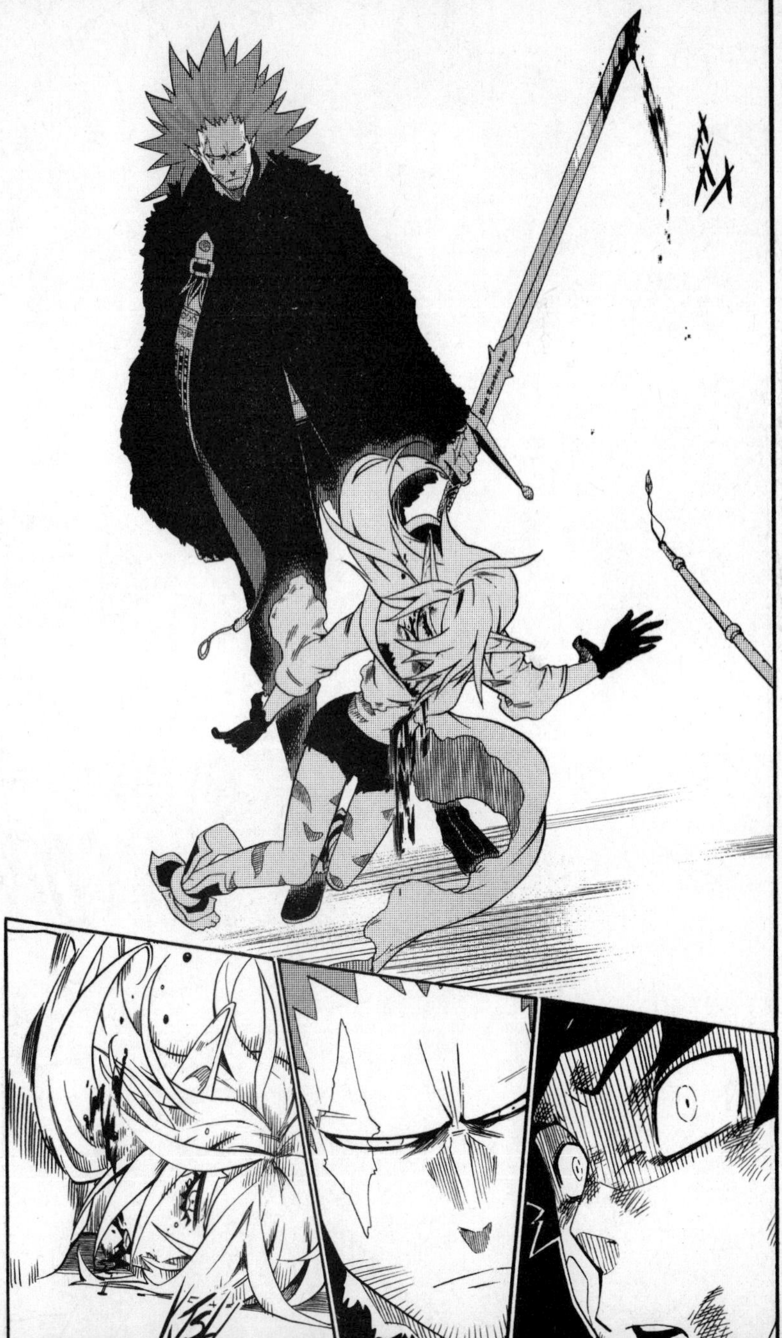

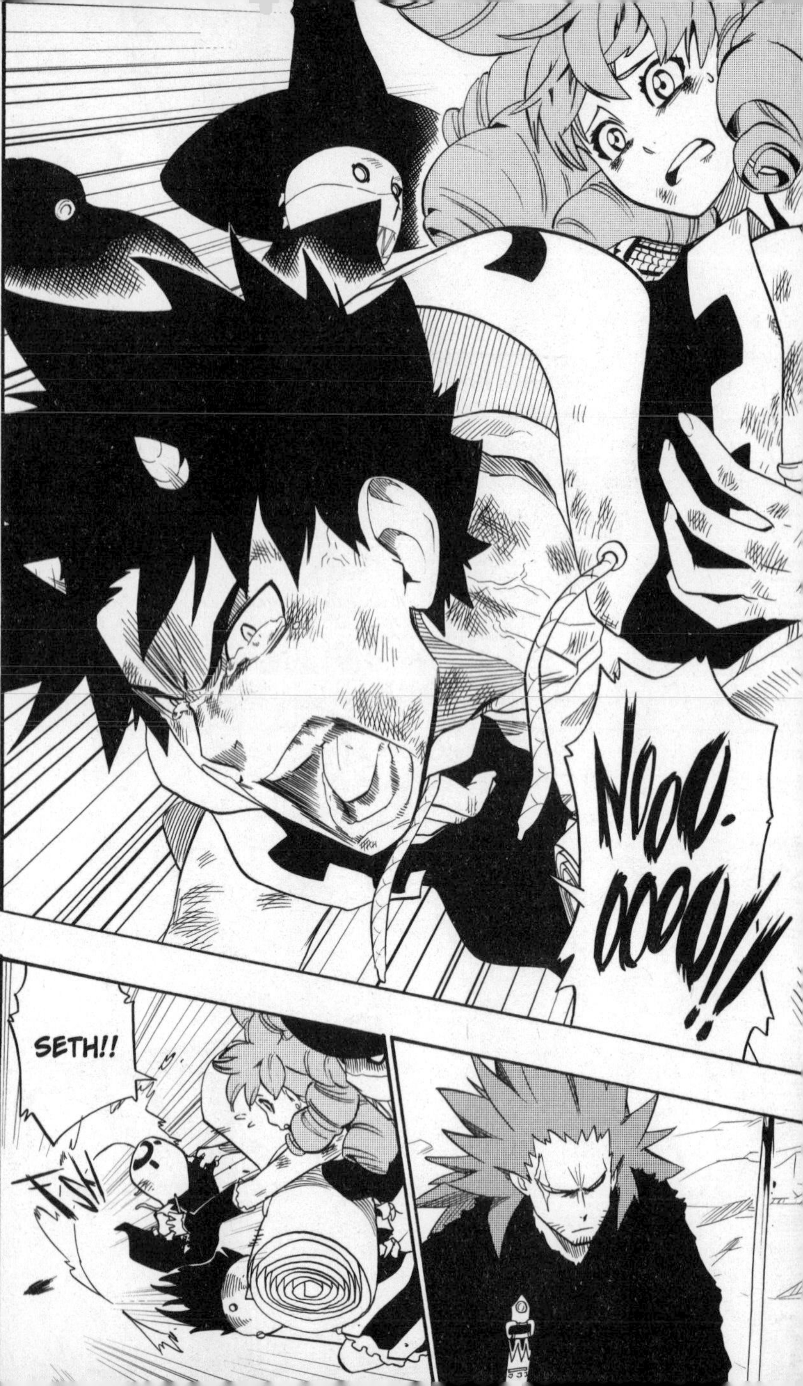
NOOO.
OOOO!!
SETH!!

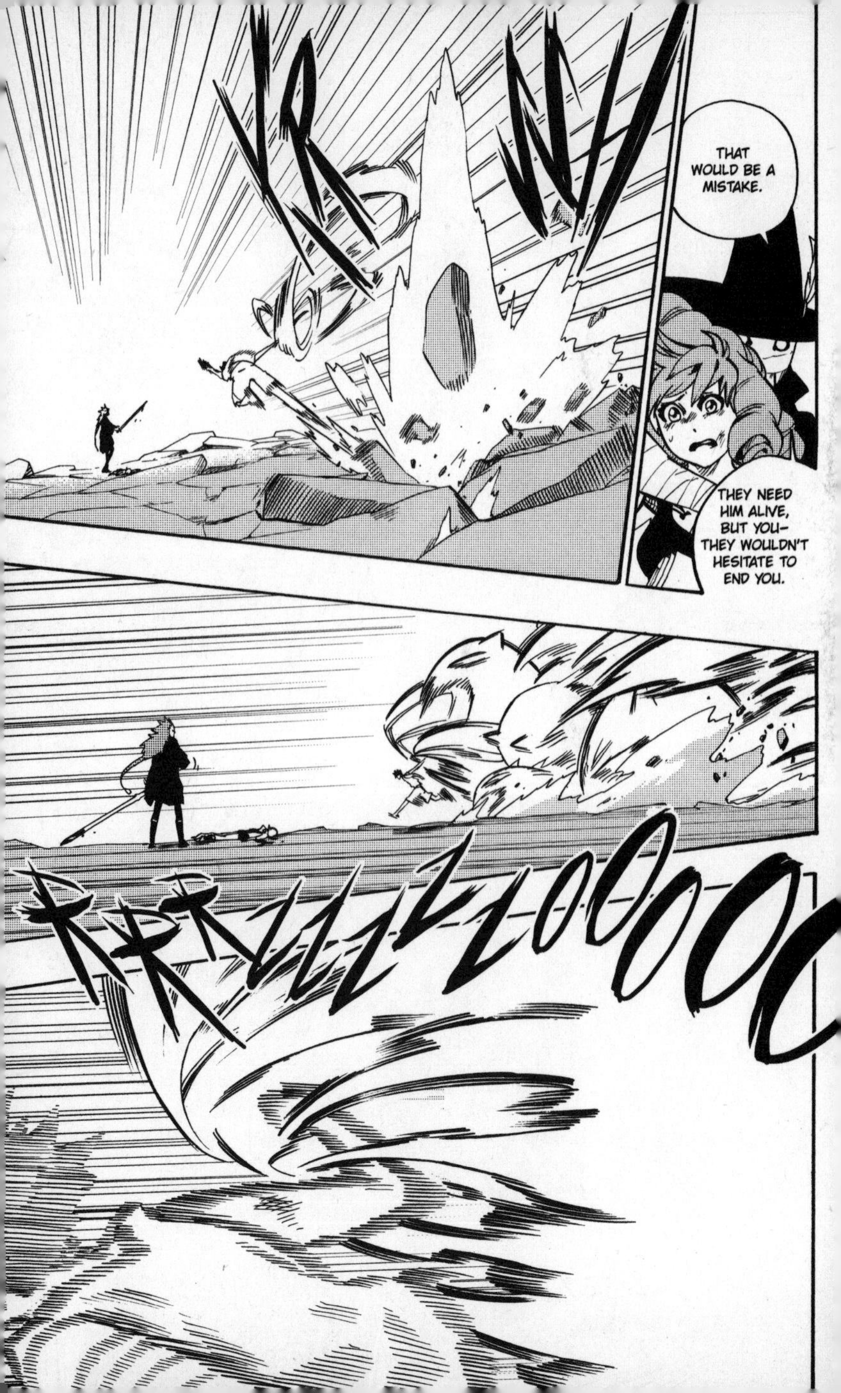
THAT WOULD BE A MISTAKE.
THEY NEED HIM ALIVE, BUT YOU— THEY WOULDN'T HESITATE TO END YOU.

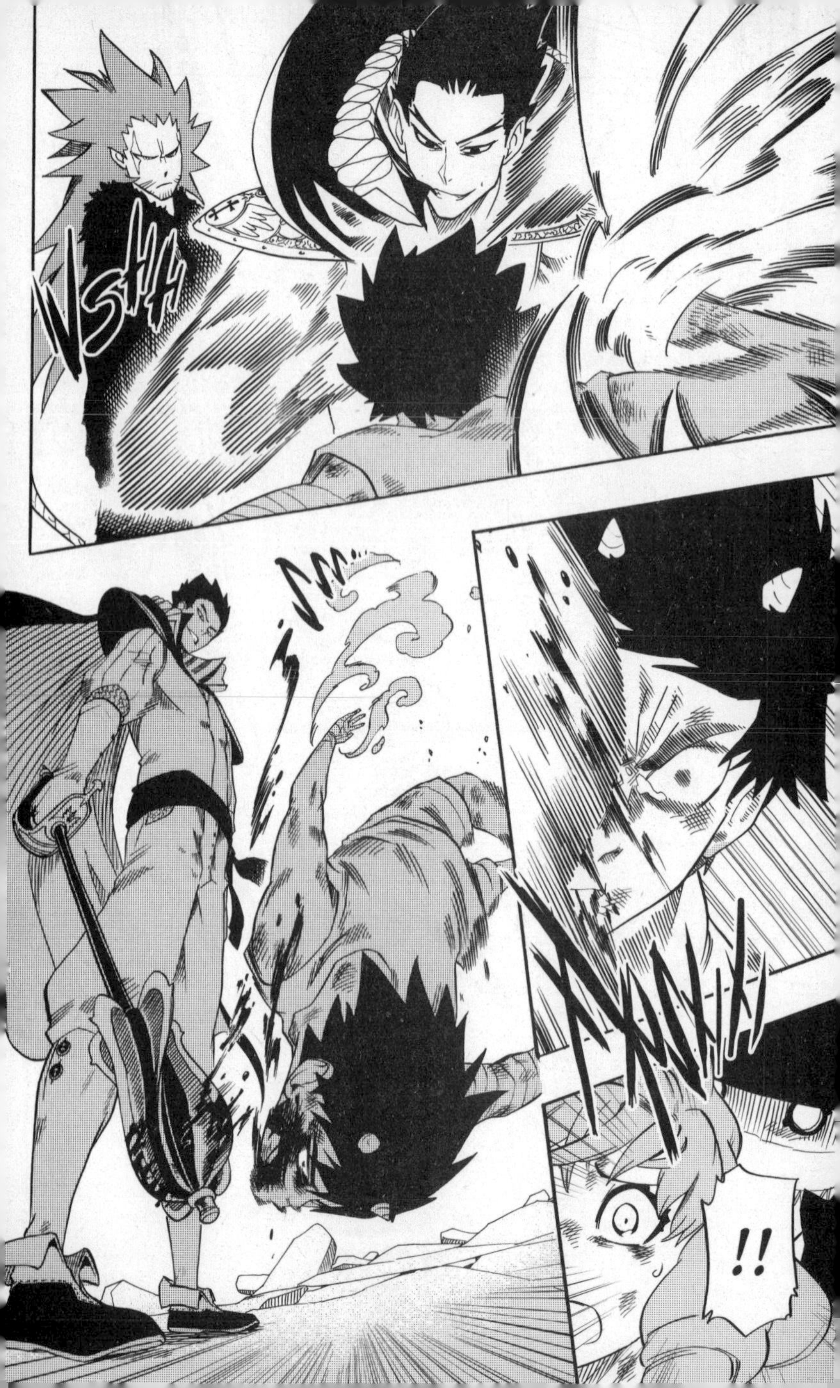

WSHH
!!

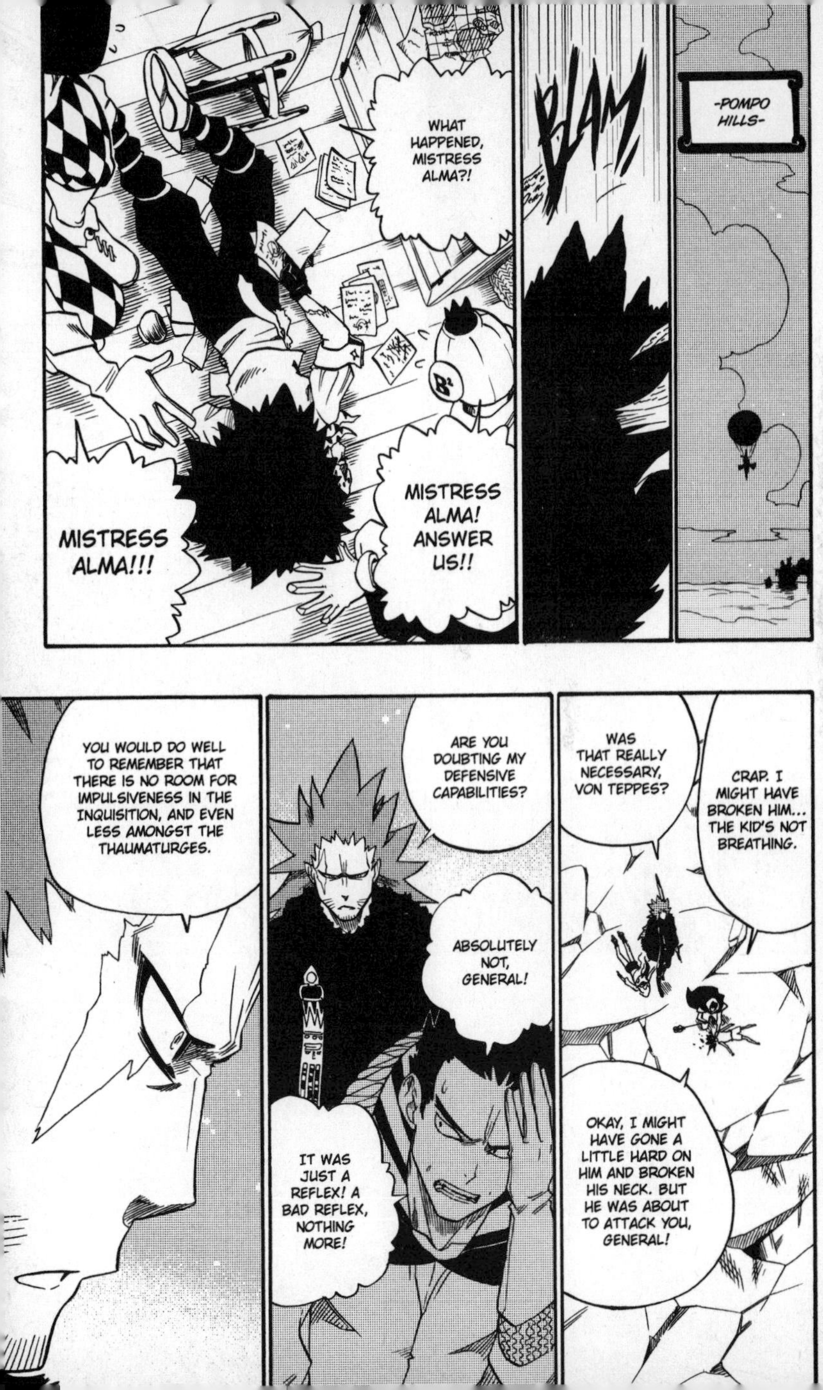
-POMPO HILLS-
BLAM
WHAT HAPPENED, MISTRESS ALMA?!
MISTRESS ALMA! ANSWER US!!
MISTRESS ALMA!!!
CRAP. I MIGHT HAVE BROKEN HIM... THE KID'S NOT BREATHING.
WAS THAT REALLY NECESSARY, VON TEPPES?
OKAY, I MIGHT HAVE GONE A LITTLE HARD ON HIM AND BROKEN HIS NECK. BUT HE WAS ABOUT TO ATTACK YOU, GENERAL!
ARE YOU DOUBTING MY DEFENSIVE CAPABILITIES?
ABSOLUTELY NOT, GENERAL!
IT WAS JUST A REFLEX! A BAD REFLEX, NOTHING MORE!
YOU WOULD DO WELL TO REMEMBER THAT THERE IS NO ROOM FOR IMPULSIVENESS IN THE INQUISITION, AND EVEN LESS AMONGST THE THAUMATURGES.

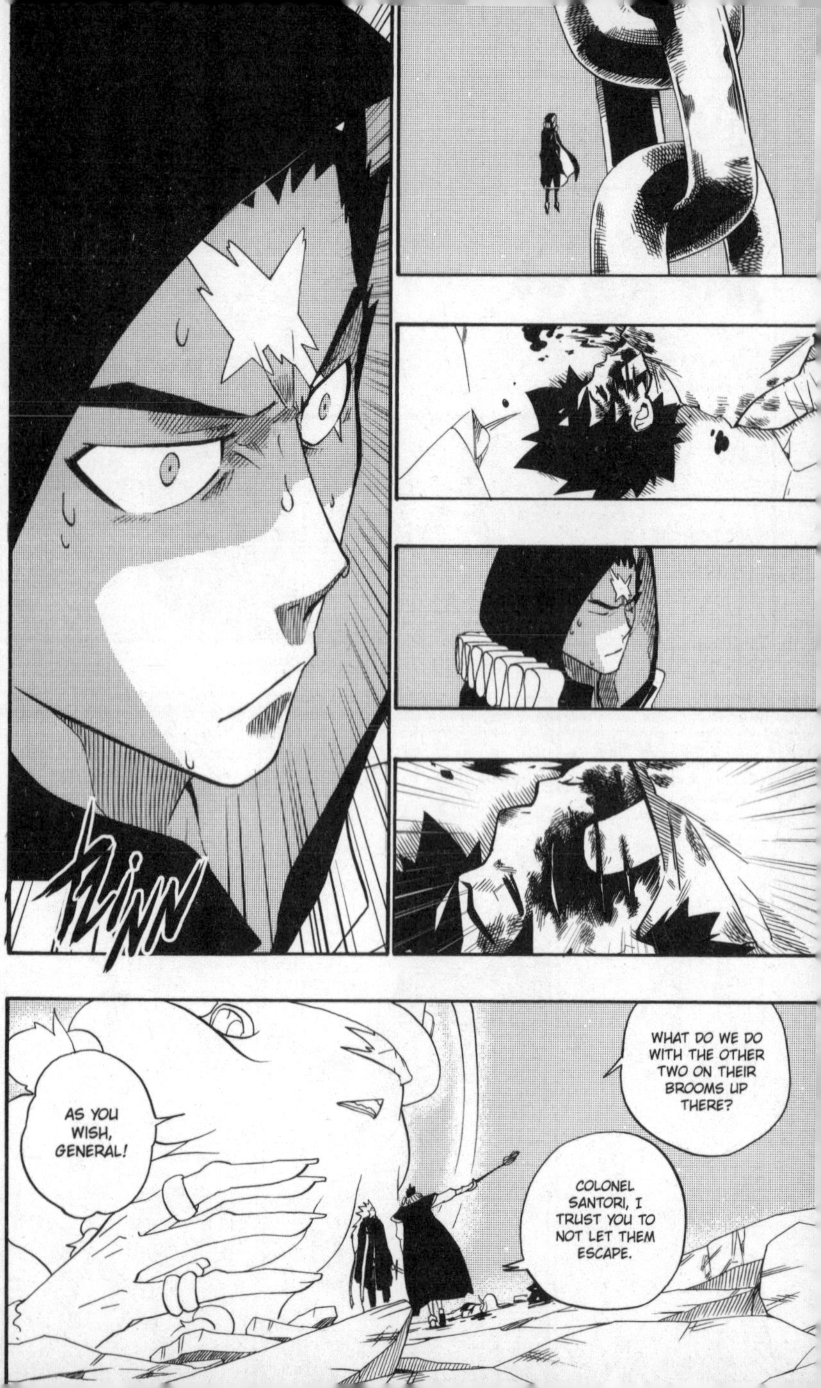
WHAT DO WE DO WITH THE OTHER TWO ON THEIR BROOMS UP THERE?
COLONEL SANTORI, I TRUST YOU TO NOT LET THEM ESCAPE.
AS YOU WISH, GENERAL!

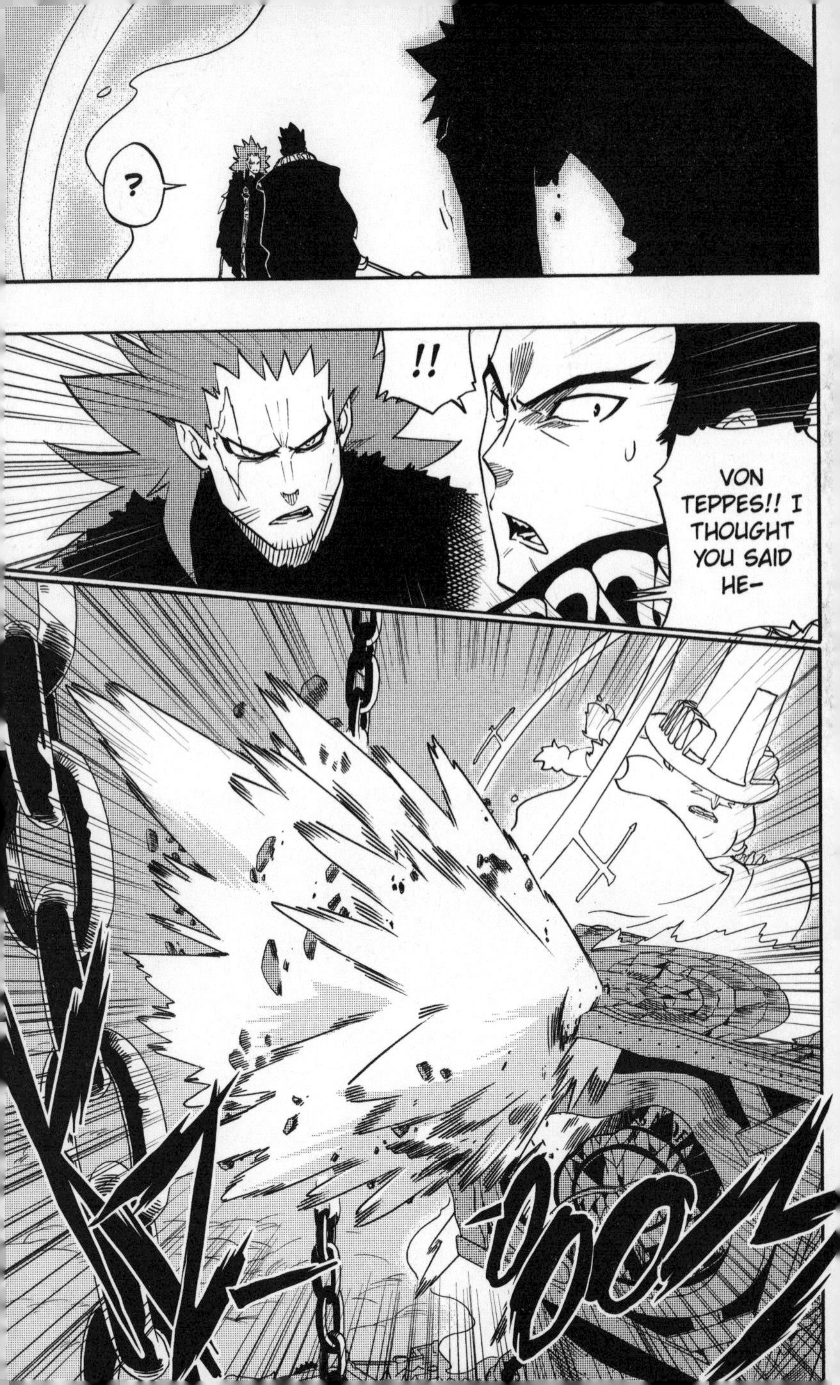
?
!!
VON TEPPES!! I THOUGHT YOU SAID HE-
KA-BOOM

# Chapter 27
# Post Tenebras Lux

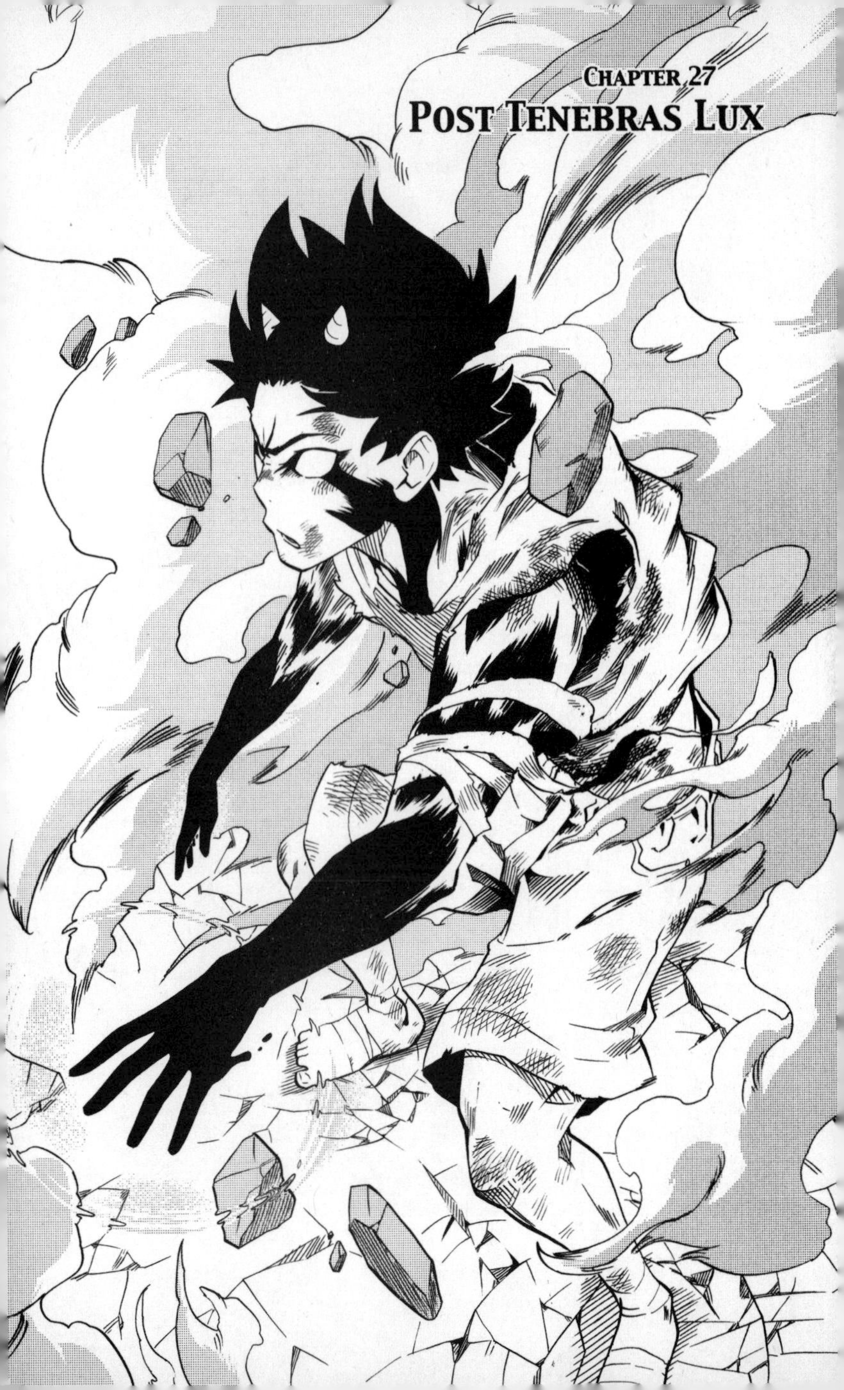

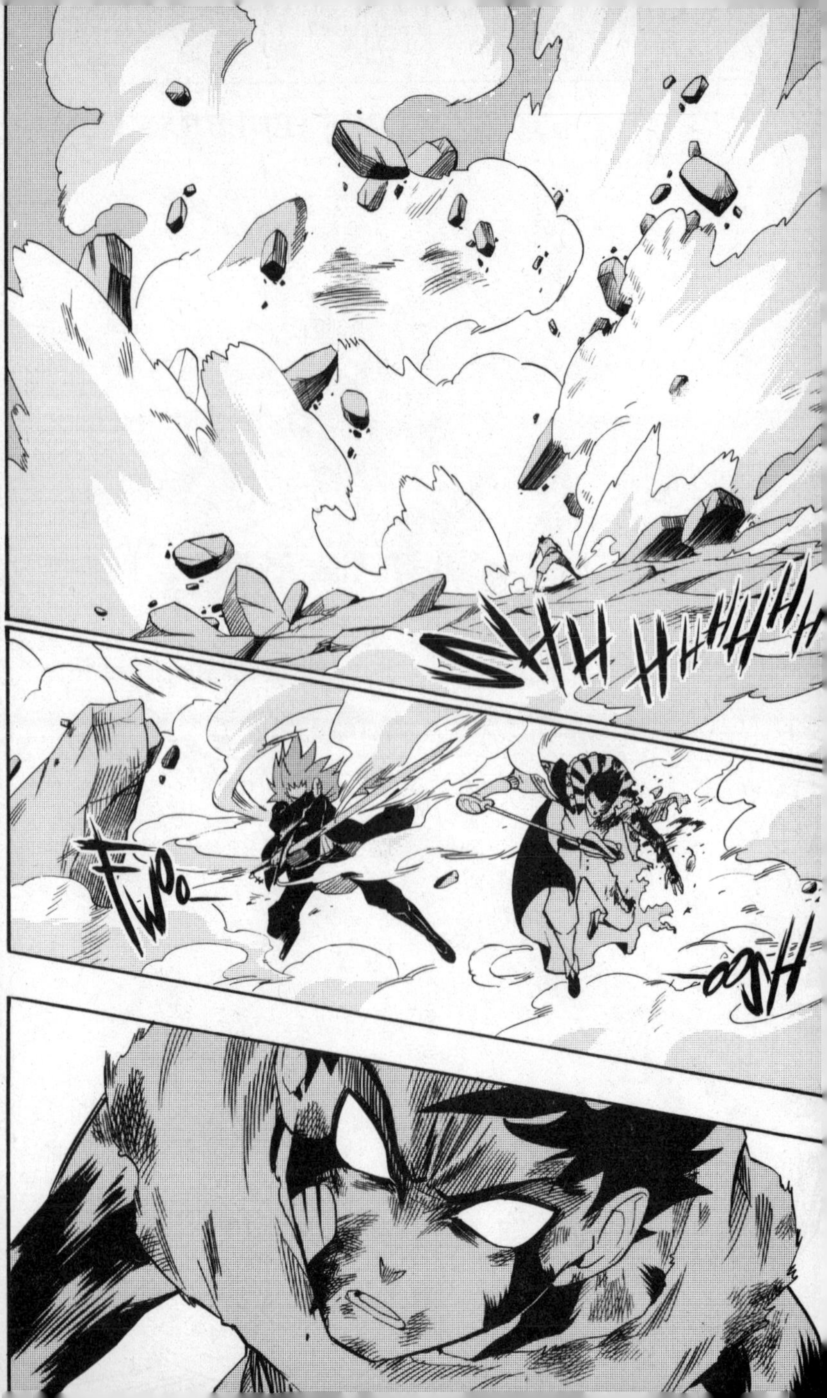
SHH HHHHHH
FWOO
OOSH

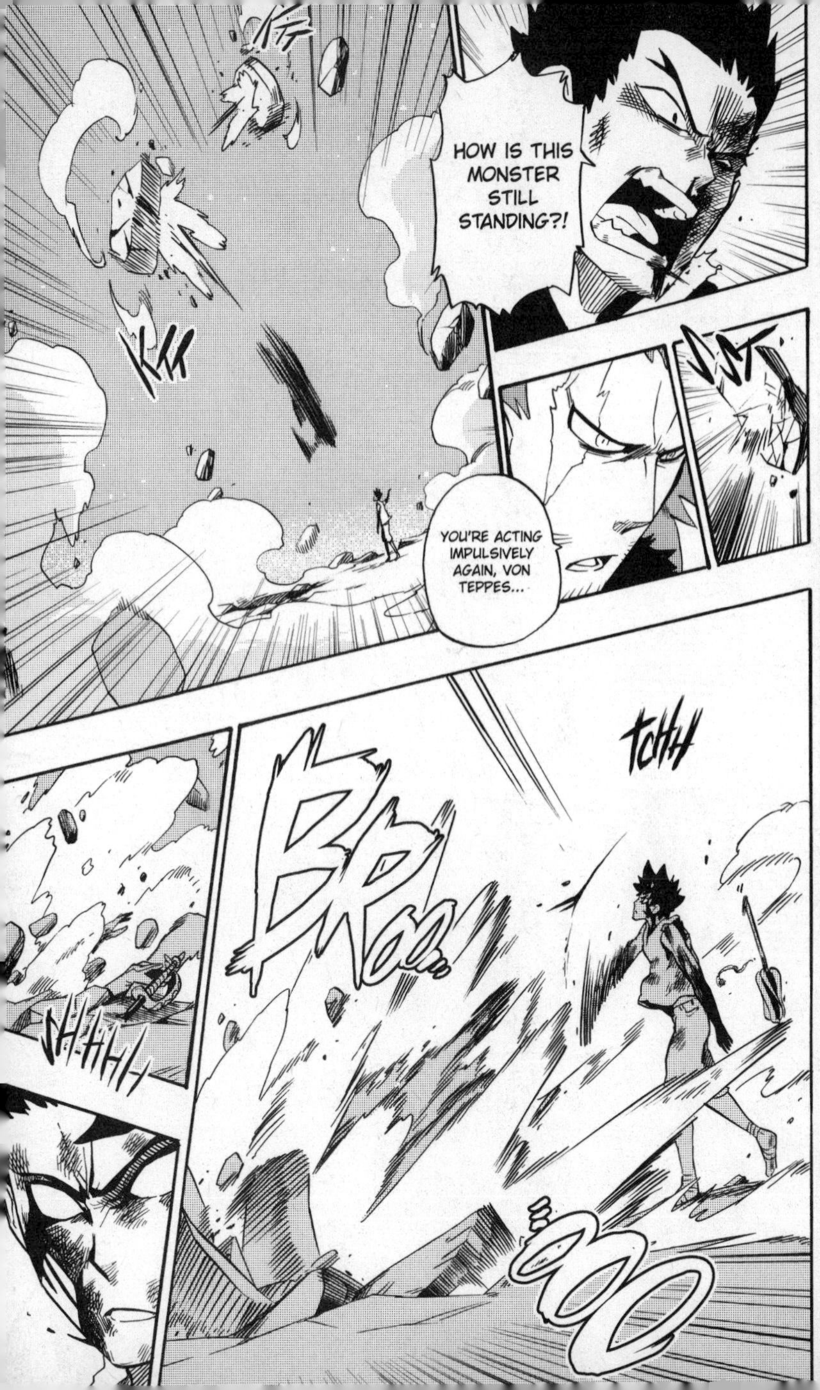
HOW IS THIS MONSTER STILL STANDING?!
YOU'RE ACTING IMPULSIVELY AGAIN, VON TEPPES...
TCHH

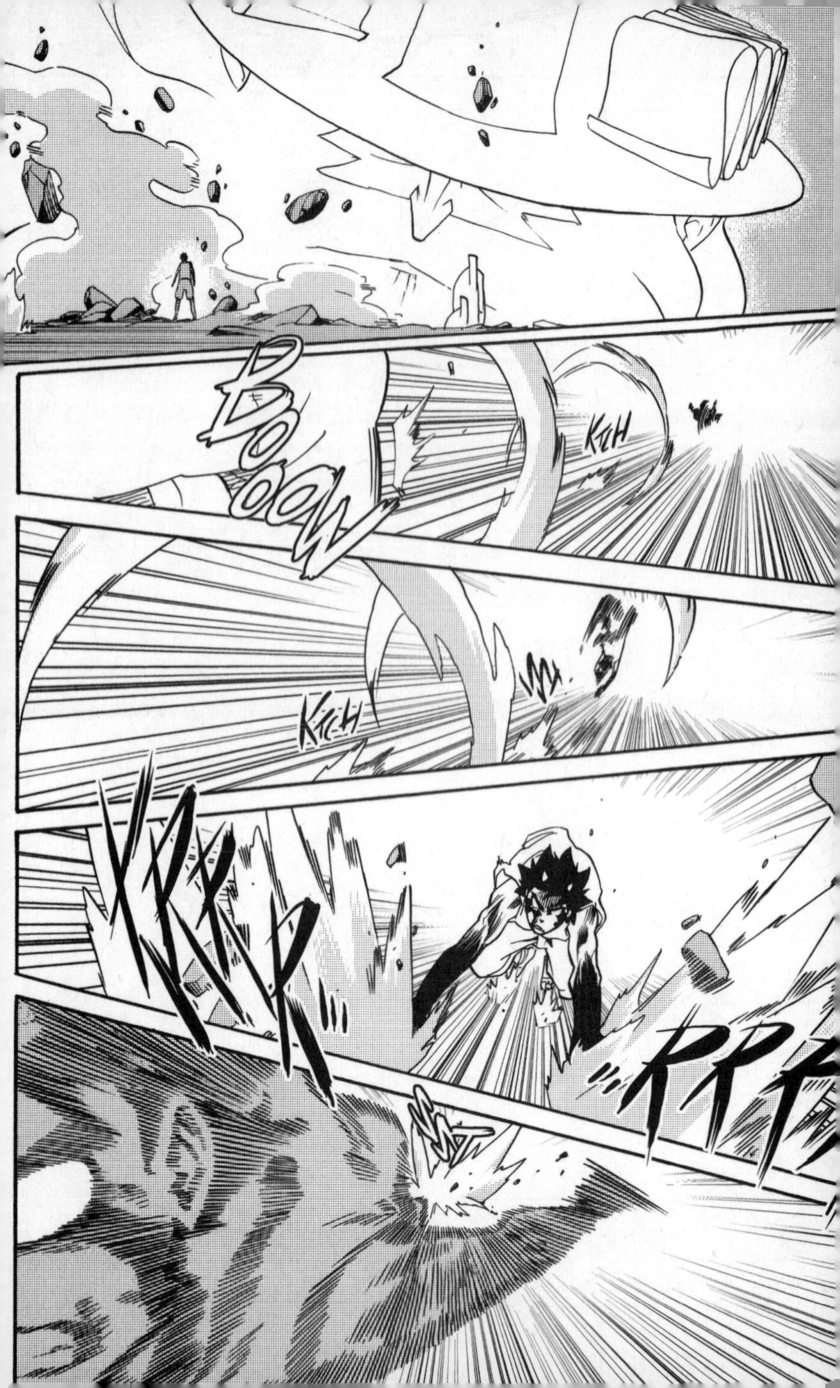
BOOOW
KTCH
KTCH
KRRR
RRR

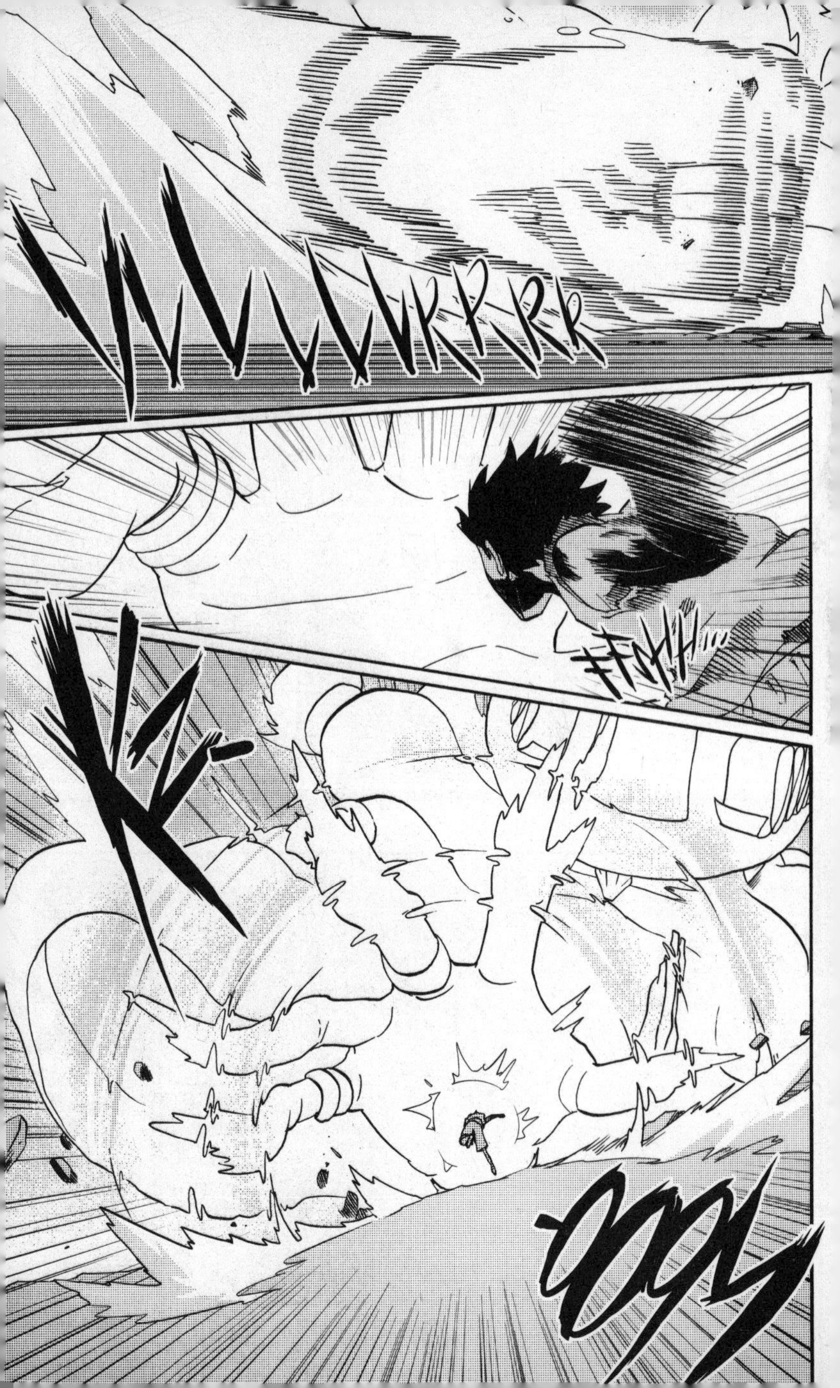
FFAH...

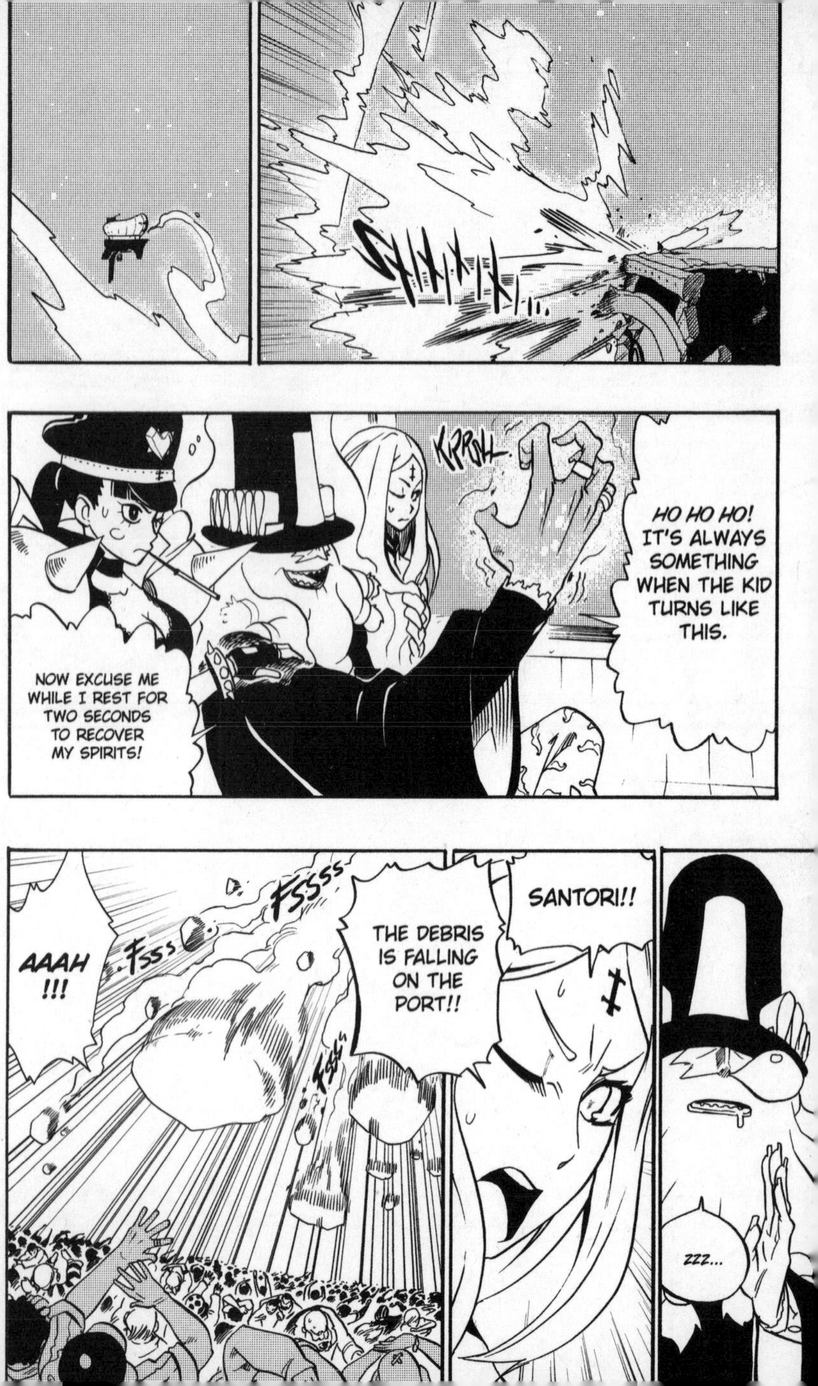
SHKKKKK
KIPROLL
HO HO HO! IT'S ALWAYS SOMETHING WHEN THE KID TURNS LIKE THIS.
NOW EXCUSE ME WHILE I REST FOR TWO SECONDS TO RECOVER MY SPIRITS!
ZZZ...
SANTORI!!
THE DEBRIS IS FALLING ON THE PORT!!
FSSSS
FSSS
FSSS
AAAH!!!

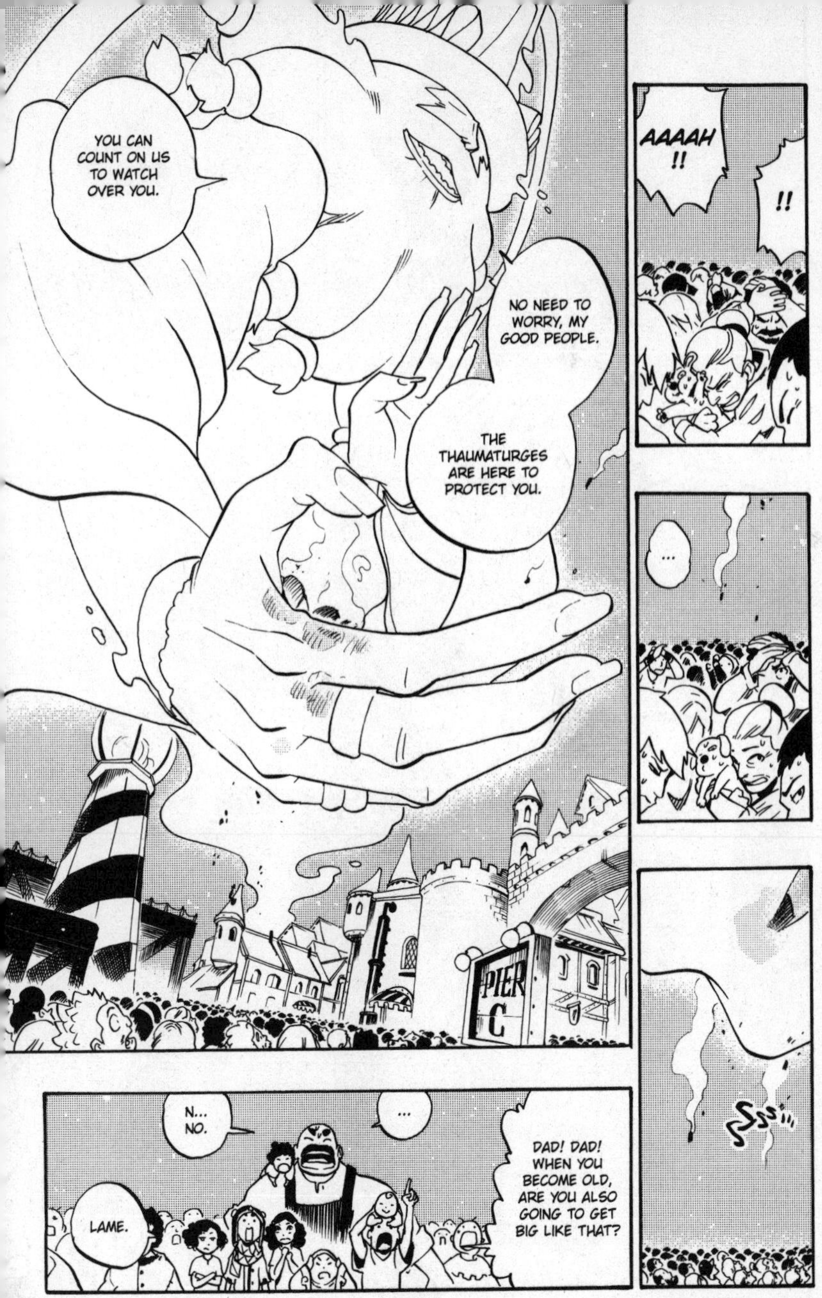
AAAAH!!
!!
...
Sss...
NO NEED TO WORRY, MY GOOD PEOPLE.
THE THAUMATURGES ARE HERE TO PROTECT YOU.
YOU CAN COUNT ON US TO WATCH OVER YOU.
PIER C
DAD! DAD! WHEN YOU BECOME OLD, ARE YOU ALSO GOING TO GET BIG LIKE THAT?
...
N... NO.
LAME.

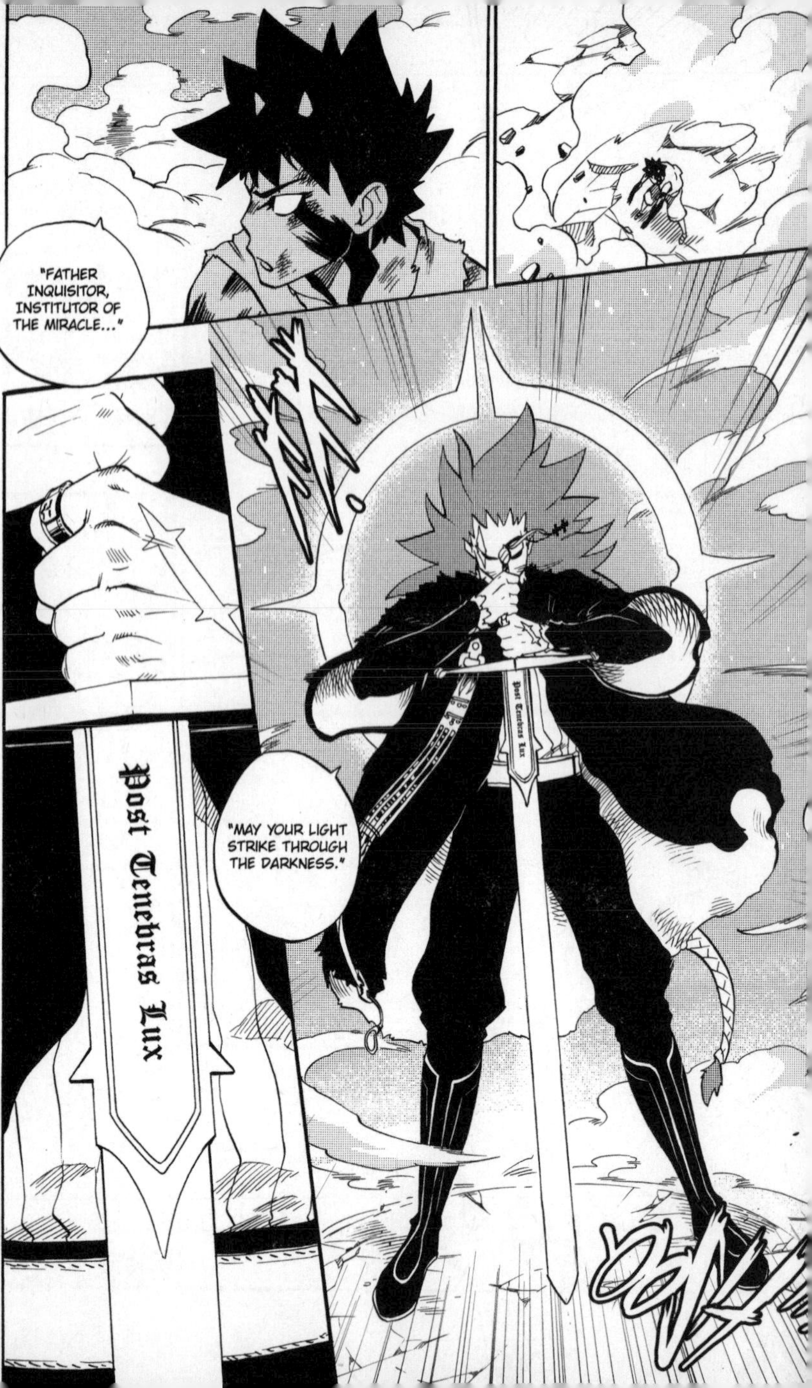
"FATHER INQUISITOR, INSTITUTOR OF THE MIRACLE..."
Post Tenebras Lux
"MAY YOUR LIGHT STRIKE THROUGH THE DARKNESS."
Post Tenebras Lux

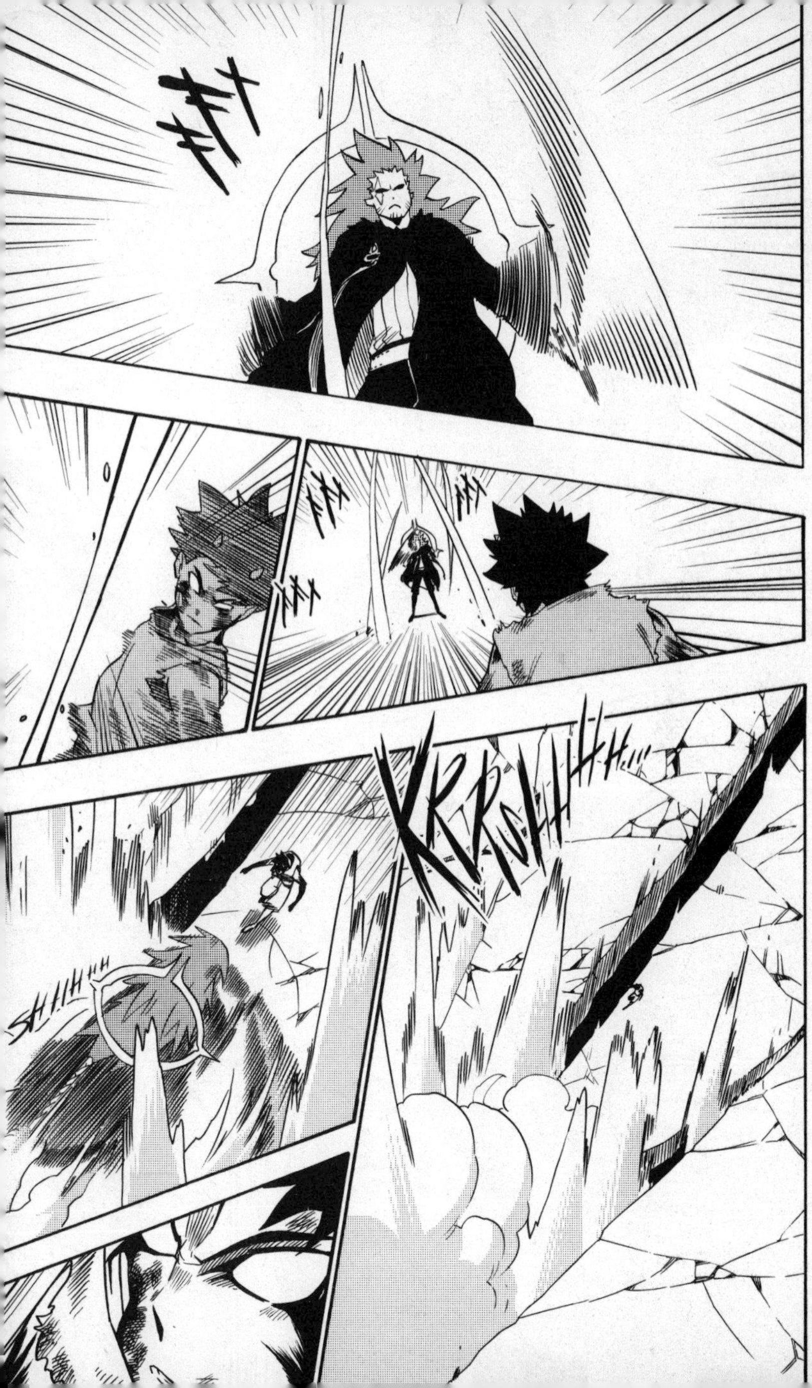
KRRSHHHH!!!
SHHHHH

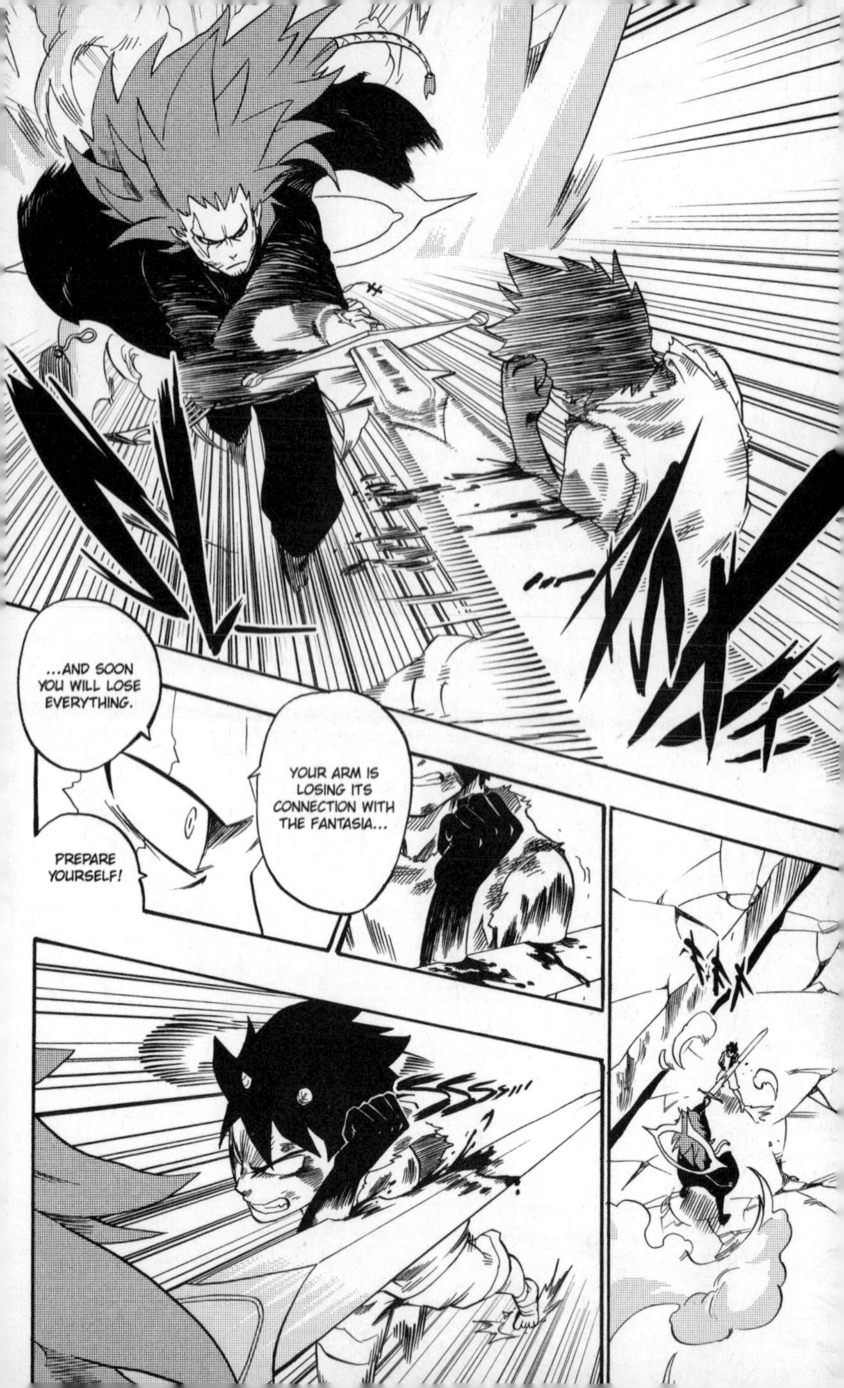
YOUR ARM IS LOSING ITS CONNECTION WITH THE FANTASIA...
...AND SOON YOU WILL LOSE EVERYTHING.
PREPARE YOURSELF!

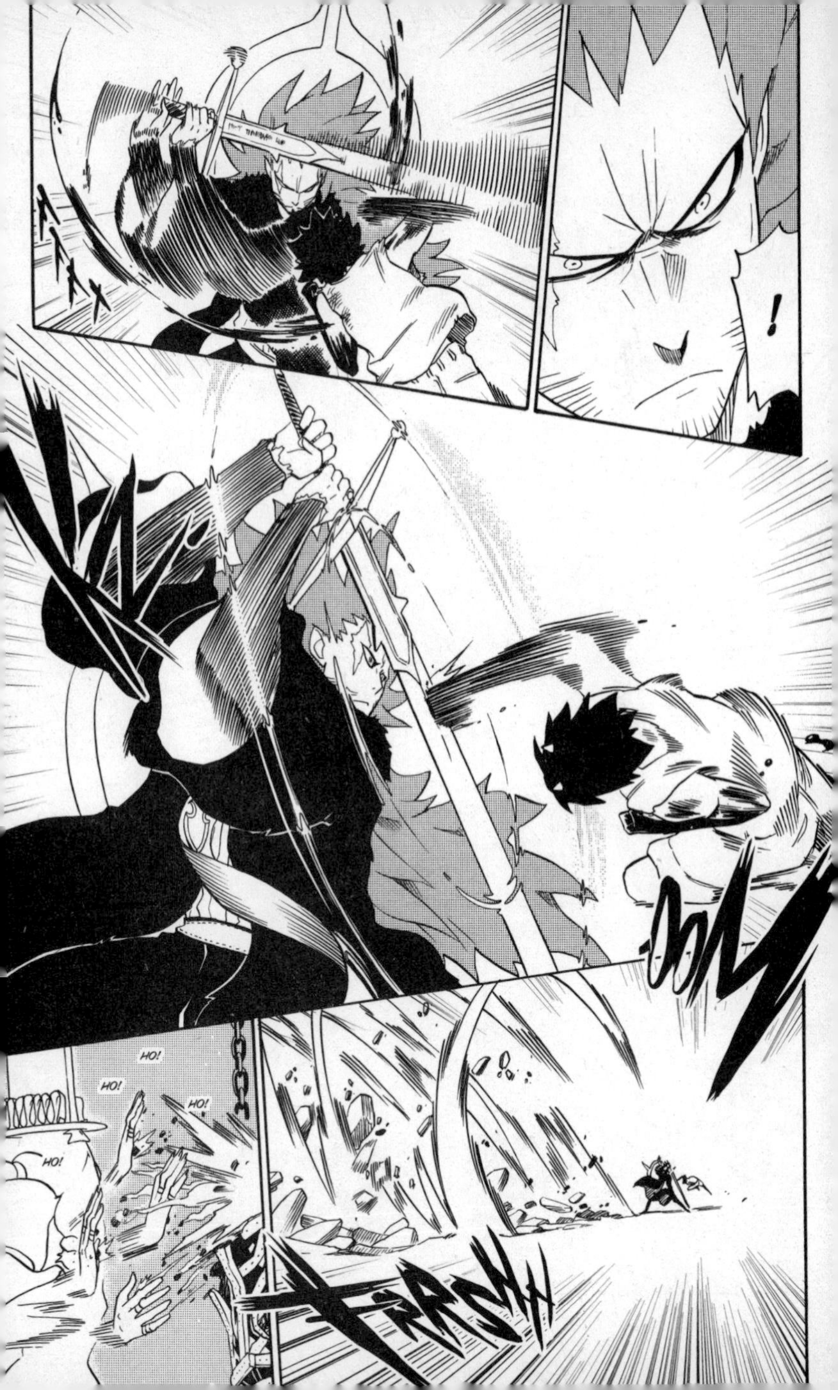
!
KRASH
HO!
HO!
HO!
HO!

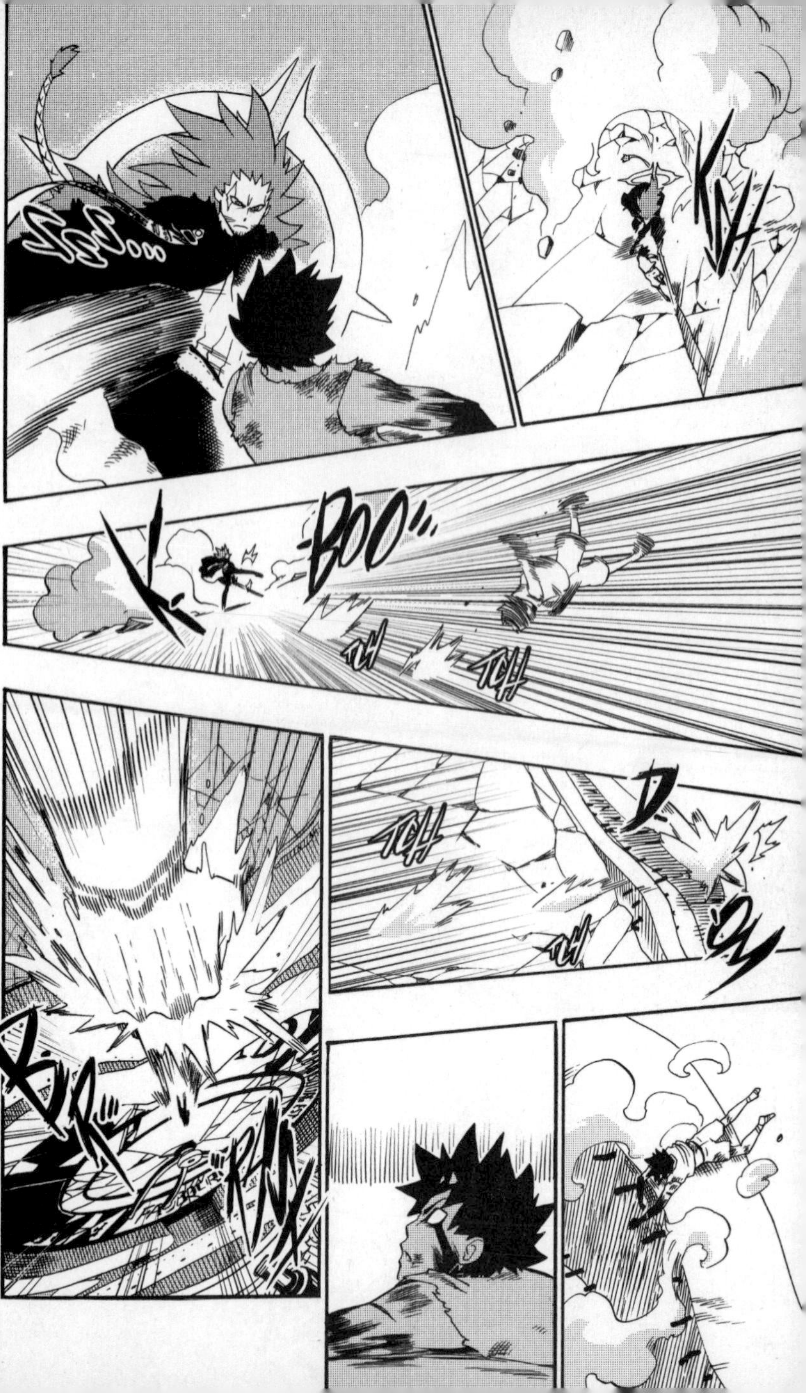
KSH
SSS...
-BOO
K-
TCH
TCH
D-
OM
TCH
TCH

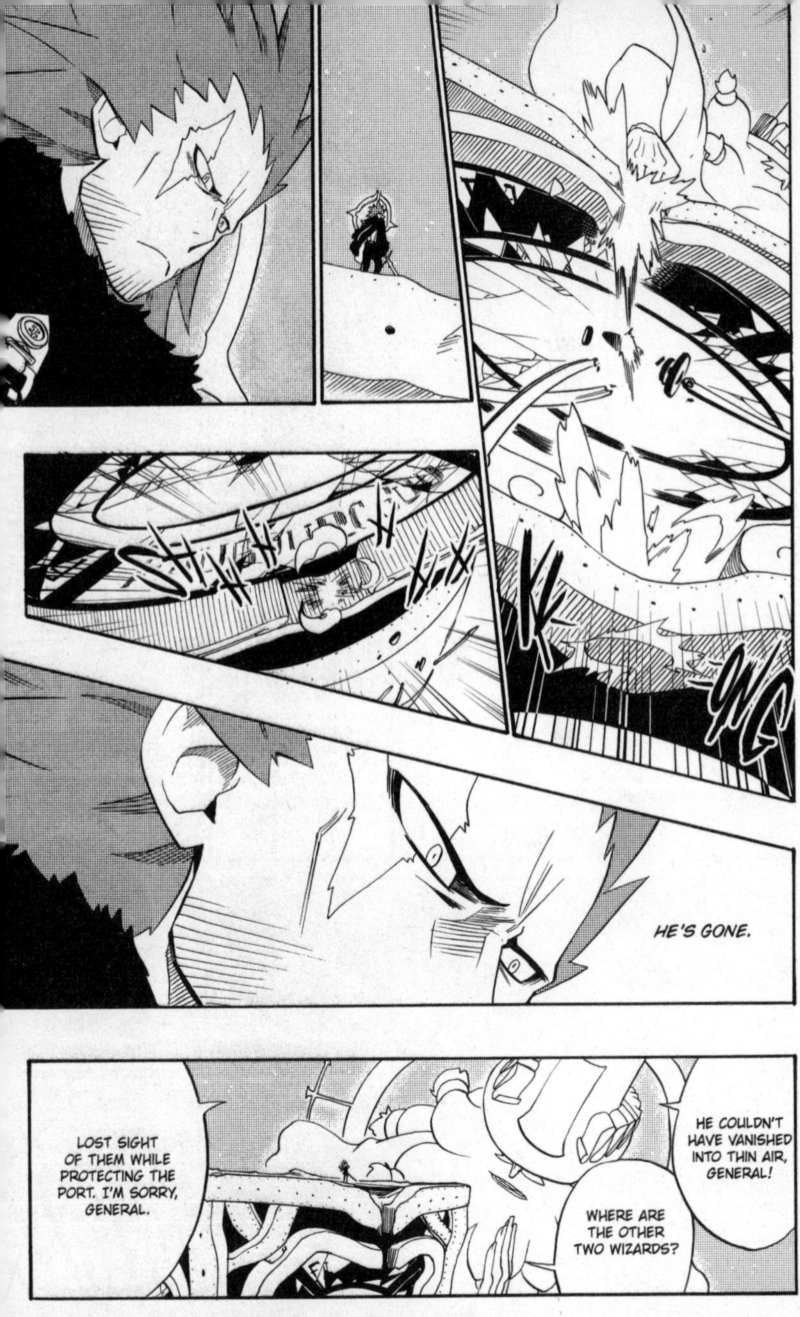
HE'S GONE.
HE COULDN'T HAVE VANISHED INTO THIN AIR, GENERAL!
WHERE ARE THE OTHER TWO WIZARDS?
LOST SIGHT OF THEM WHILE PROTECTING THE PORT. I'M SORRY, GENERAL.

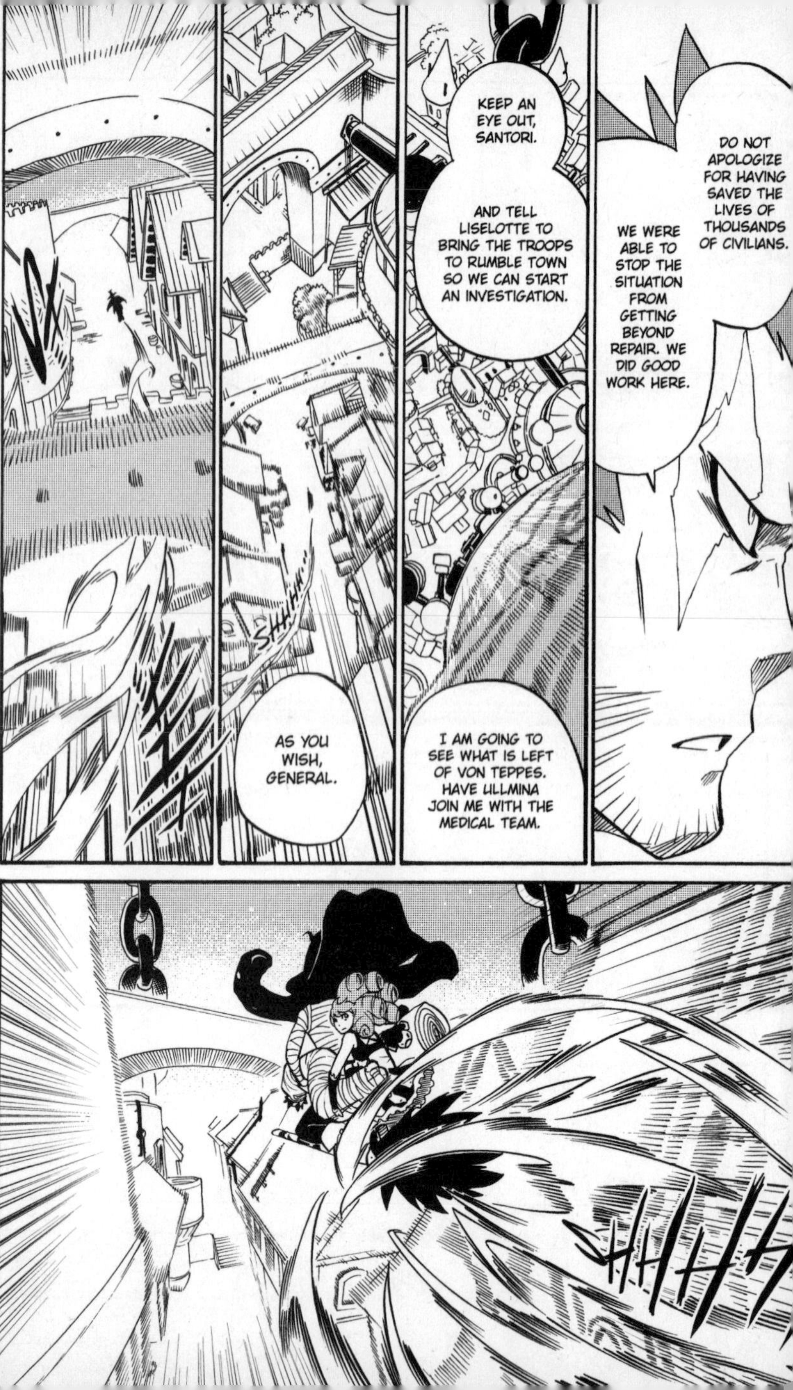
DO NOT APOLOGIZE FOR HAVING SAVED THE LIVES OF THOUSANDS OF CIVILIANS.
WE WERE ABLE TO STOP THE SITUATION FROM GETTING BEYOND REPAIR. WE DID GOOD WORK HERE.
KEEP AN EYE OUT, SANTORI.
AND TELL LISELOTTE TO BRING THE TROOPS TO RUMBLE TOWN SO WE CAN START AN INVESTIGATION.
I AM GOING TO SEE WHAT IS LEFT OF VON TEPPES. HAVE ULLMINA JOIN ME WITH THE MEDICAL TEAM.
SHHHH
AS YOU WISH, GENERAL.

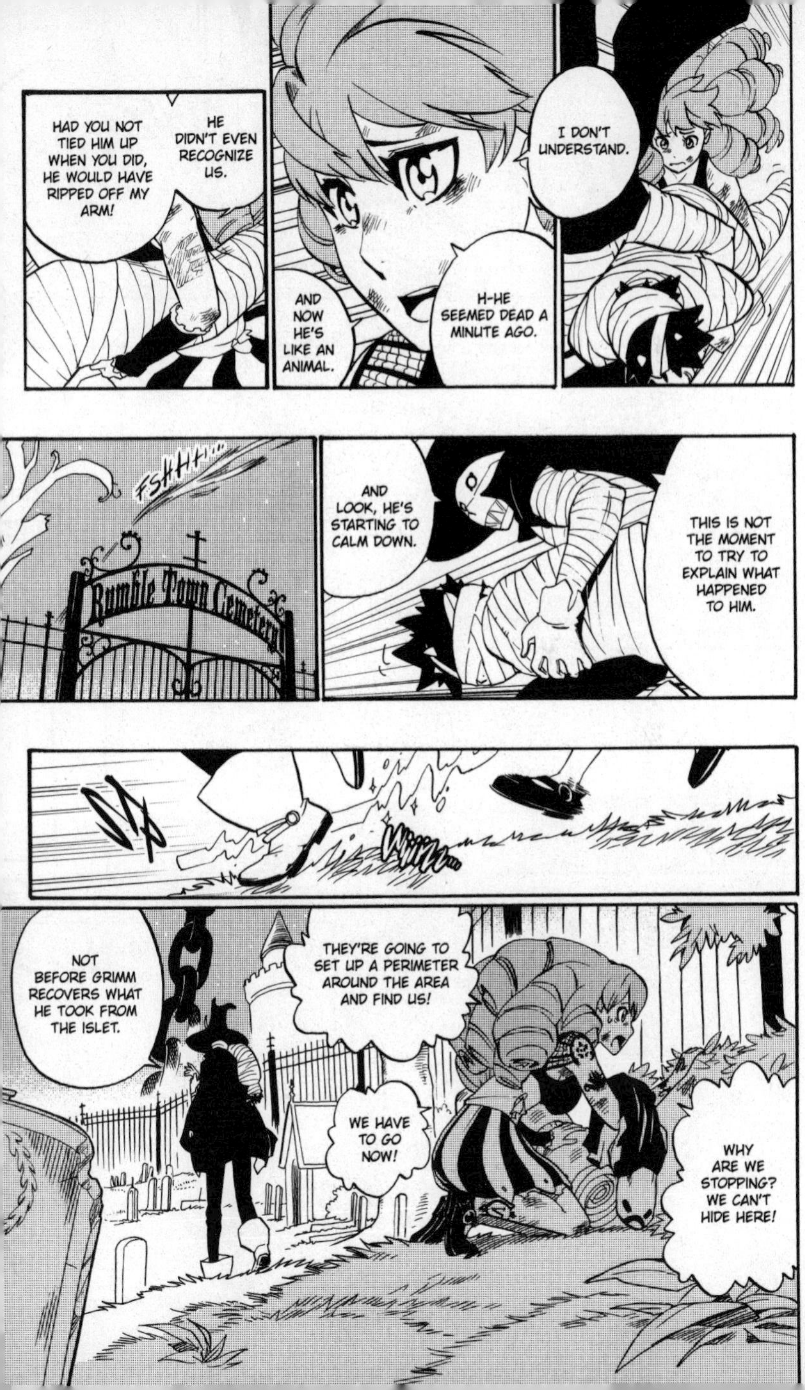
I DON'T UNDERSTAND.
H-HE SEEMED DEAD A MINUTE AGO.
AND NOW HE'S LIKE AN ANIMAL.
HE DIDN'T EVEN RECOGNIZE US.
HAD YOU NOT TIED HIM UP WHEN YOU DID, HE WOULD HAVE RIPPED OFF MY ARM!
THIS IS NOT THE MOMENT TO TRY TO EXPLAIN WHAT HAPPENED TO HIM.
AND LOOK, HE'S STARTING TO CALM DOWN.
FSHHH...
Rumble Town Cemetery
WHY ARE WE STOPPING? WE CAN'T HIDE HERE!
THEY'RE GOING TO SET UP A PERIMETER AROUND THE AREA AND FIND US!
WE HAVE TO GO NOW!
NOT BEFORE GRIMM RECOVERS WHAT HE TOOK FROM THE ISLET.

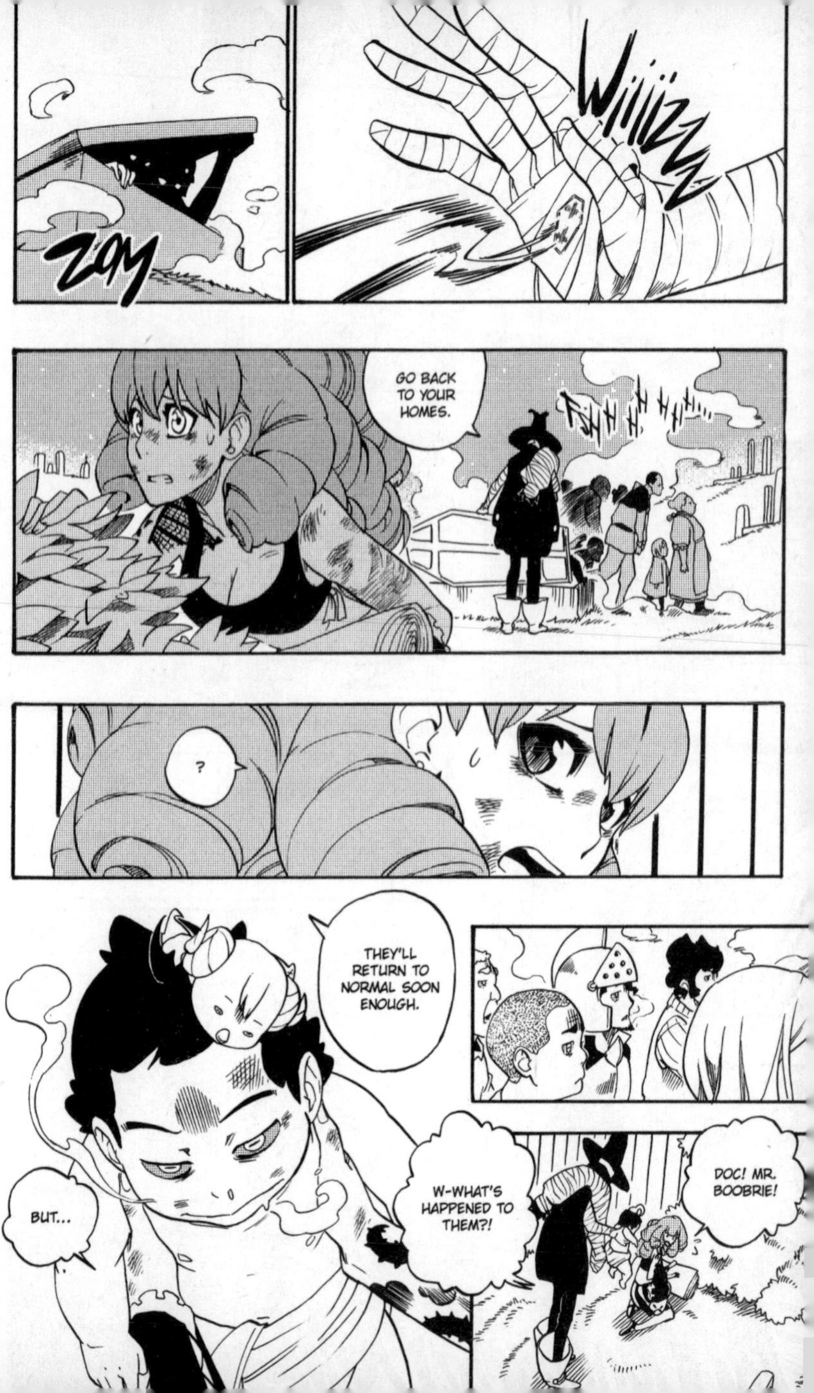
GO BACK TO YOUR HOMES.
?
DOC! MR. BOOBRIE!
W-WHAT'S HAPPENED TO THEM?!
THEY'LL RETURN TO NORMAL SOON ENOUGH.
BUT...

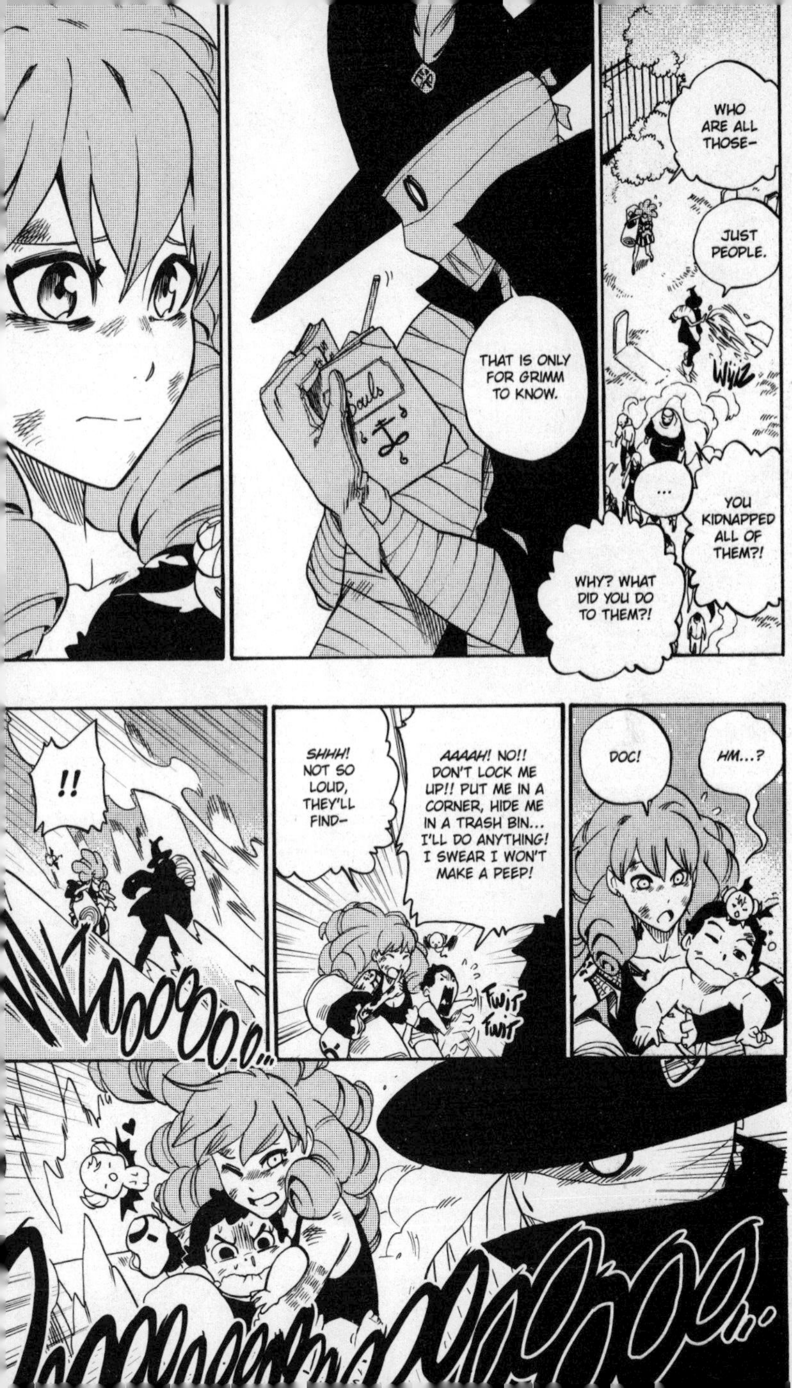
WHO ARE ALL THOSE-
JUST PEOPLE.
...
YOU KIDNAPPED ALL OF THEM?!
WHY? WHAT DID YOU DO TO THEM?!
THAT IS ONLY FOR GRIMM TO KNOW.
Souls
HM...?
DOC!
AAAAH! NO!! DON'T LOCK ME UP!! PUT ME IN A CORNER, HIDE ME IN A TRASH BIN... I'LL DO ANYTHING! I SWEAR I WON'T MAKE A PEEP!
SHHH! NOT SO LOUD, THEY'LL FIND-
FWIT FWIT
!!

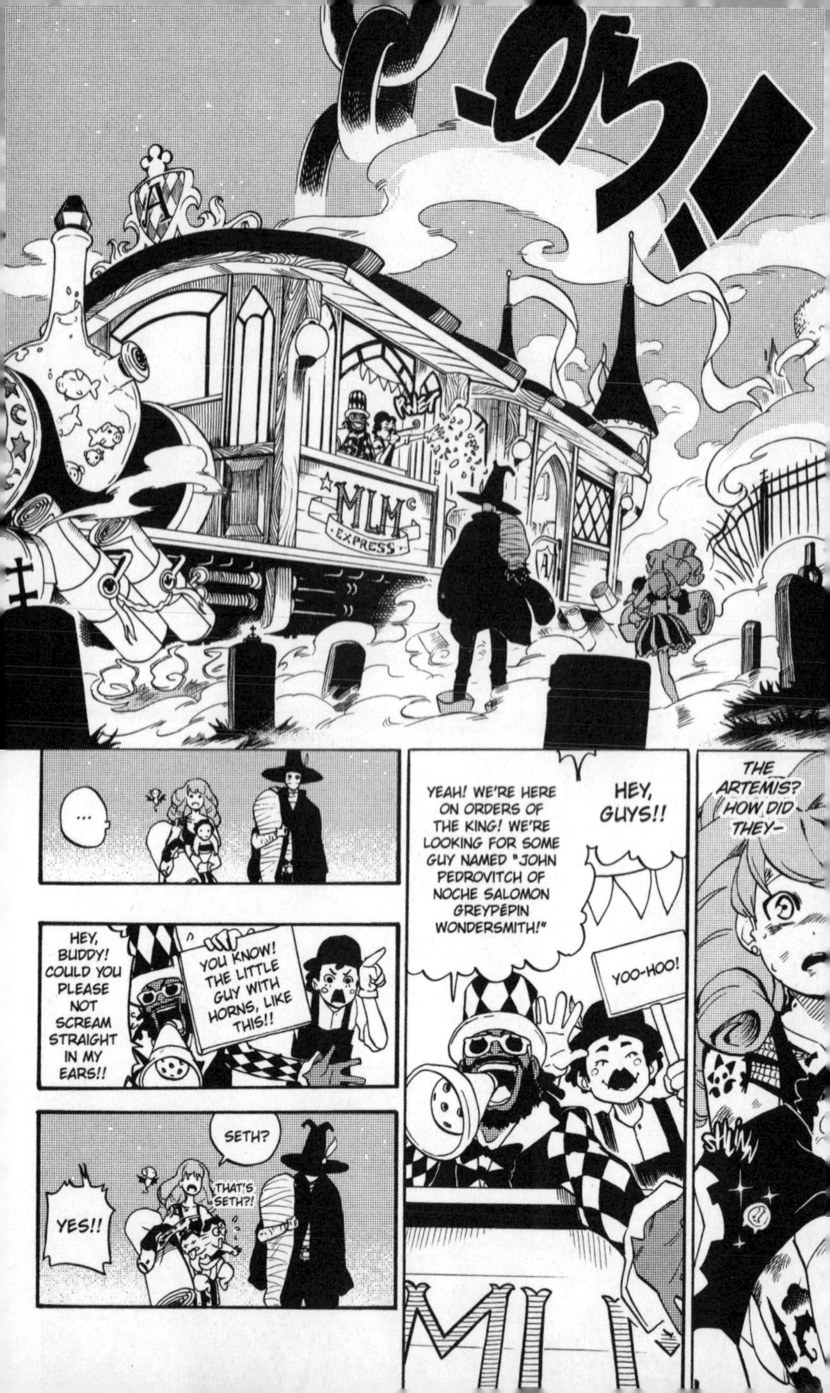

MLM EXPRESS
THE ARTEMIS? HOW DID THEY-
HEY, GUYS!!
YEAH! WE'RE HERE ON ORDERS OF THE KING! WE'RE LOOKING FOR SOME GUY NAMED "JOHN PEDROVITCH OF NOCHE SALOMON GREYPÉPIN WONDERSMITH!"
YOO-HOO!
...
YOU KNOW! THE LITTLE GUY WITH HORNS, LIKE THIS!!
HEY, BUDDY! COULD YOU PLEASE NOT SCREAM STRAIGHT IN MY EARS!!
SETH?
THAT'S SETH?!
YES!!

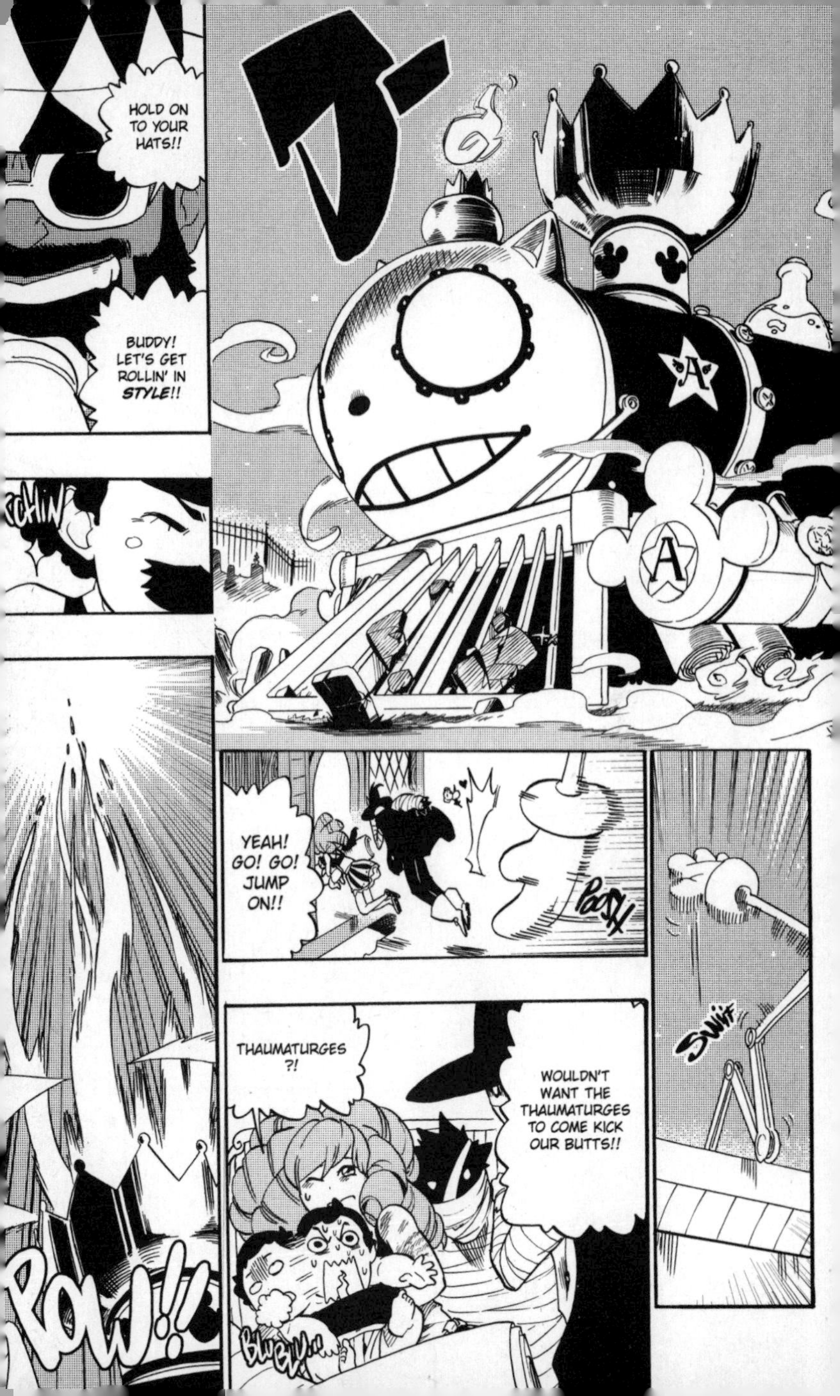
YEAH! GO! GO! JUMP ON!!
POOSH
THAUMATURGES ?!
WOULDN'T WANT THE THAUMATURGES TO COME KICK OUR BUTTS!!
HOLD ON TO YOUR HATS!!
BUDDY! LET'S GET ROLLIN' IN STYLE!!
KCHIN
POW!!

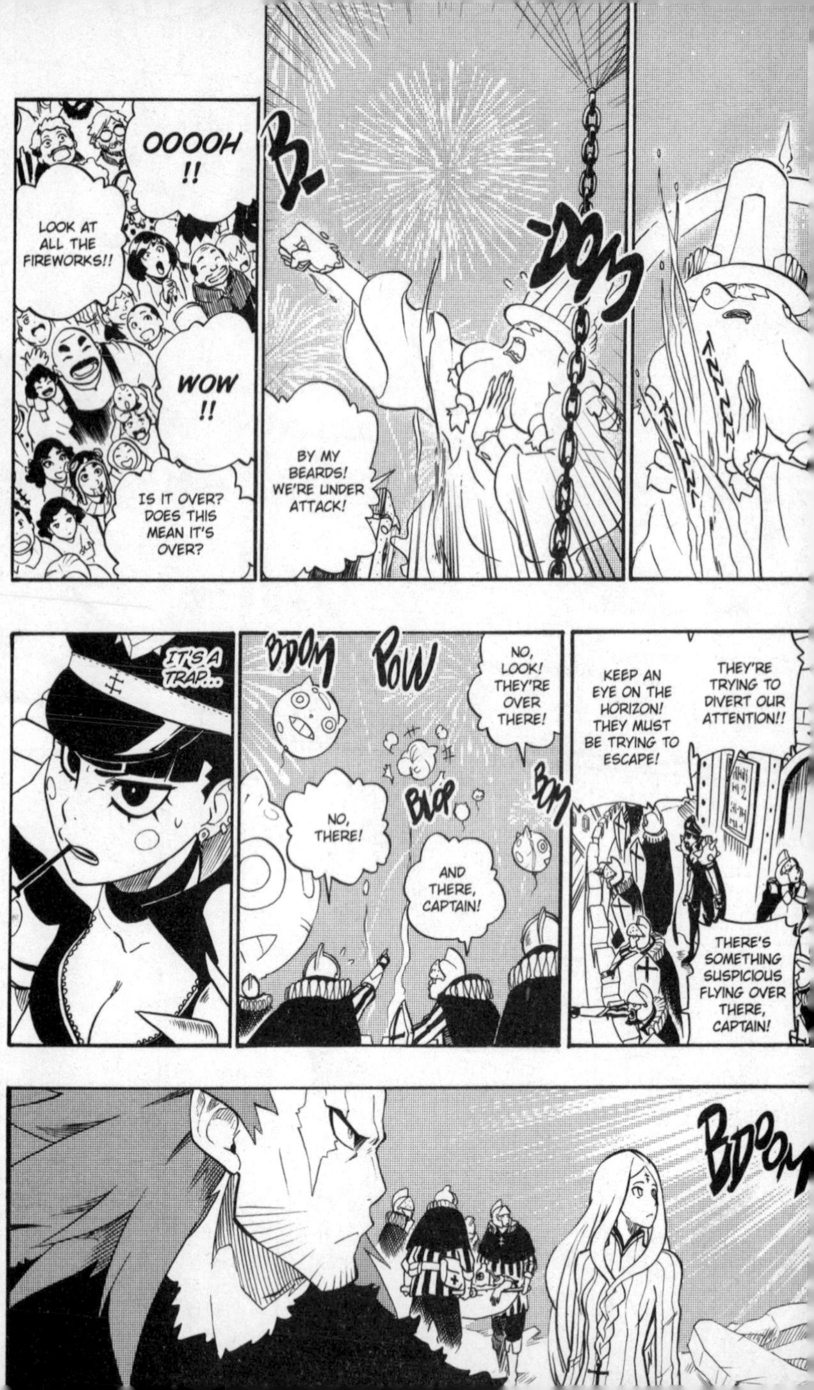
B-
-DOM
BY MY BEARDS! WE'RE UNDER ATTACK!
OOOOH !!
LOOK AT ALL THE FIREWORKS!!
WOW !!
IS IT OVER? DOES THIS MEAN IT'S OVER?
THEY'RE TRYING TO DIVERT OUR ATTENTION!!
KEEP AN EYE ON THE HORIZON! THEY MUST BE TRYING TO ESCAPE!
THERE'S SOMETHING SUSPICIOUS FLYING OVER THERE, CAPTAIN!
BOM
NO, LOOK! THEY'RE OVER THERE!
POW
BDOM
BLOP
NO, THERE!
AND THERE, CAPTAIN!
IT'S A TRAP...
BDOOM

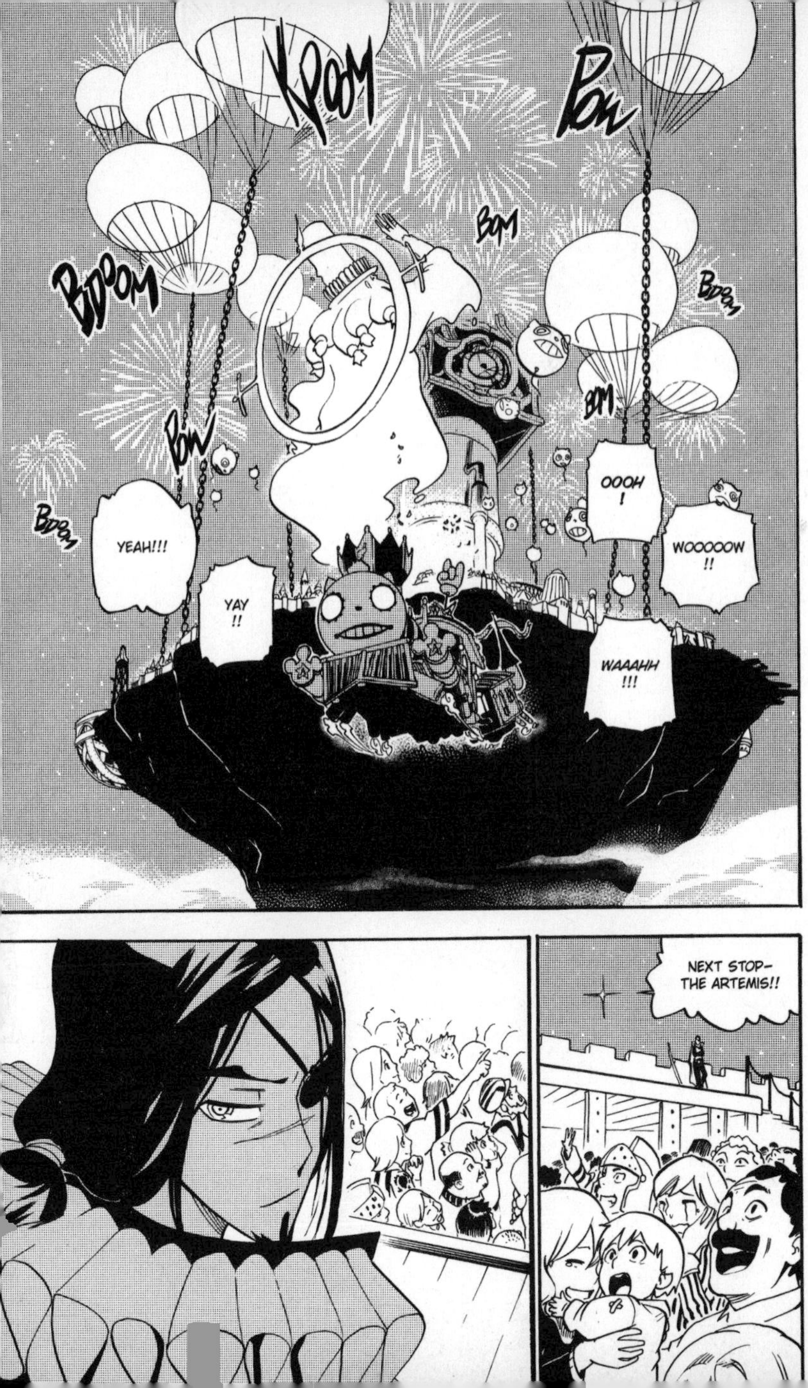
POW
KPOOM
BOM
BDOOM
BOM
OOOH!
WOOOOOW!!
BDOOM
POW
YEAH!!!
YAY!!
WAAAHH!!!
NEXT STOP— THE ARTEMIS!!

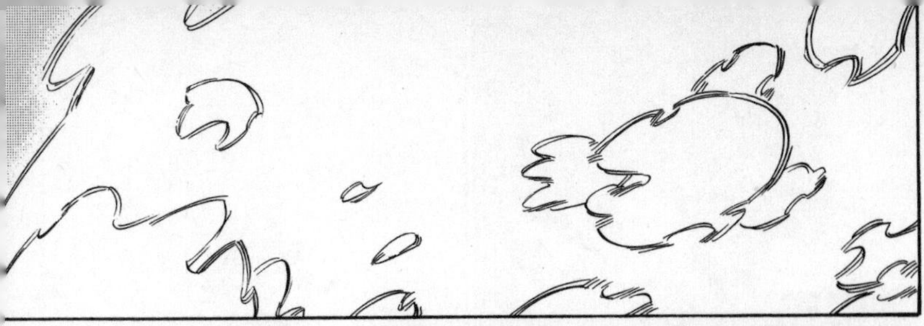

## Chapter 28 M.L.M. Show 2nd Edition

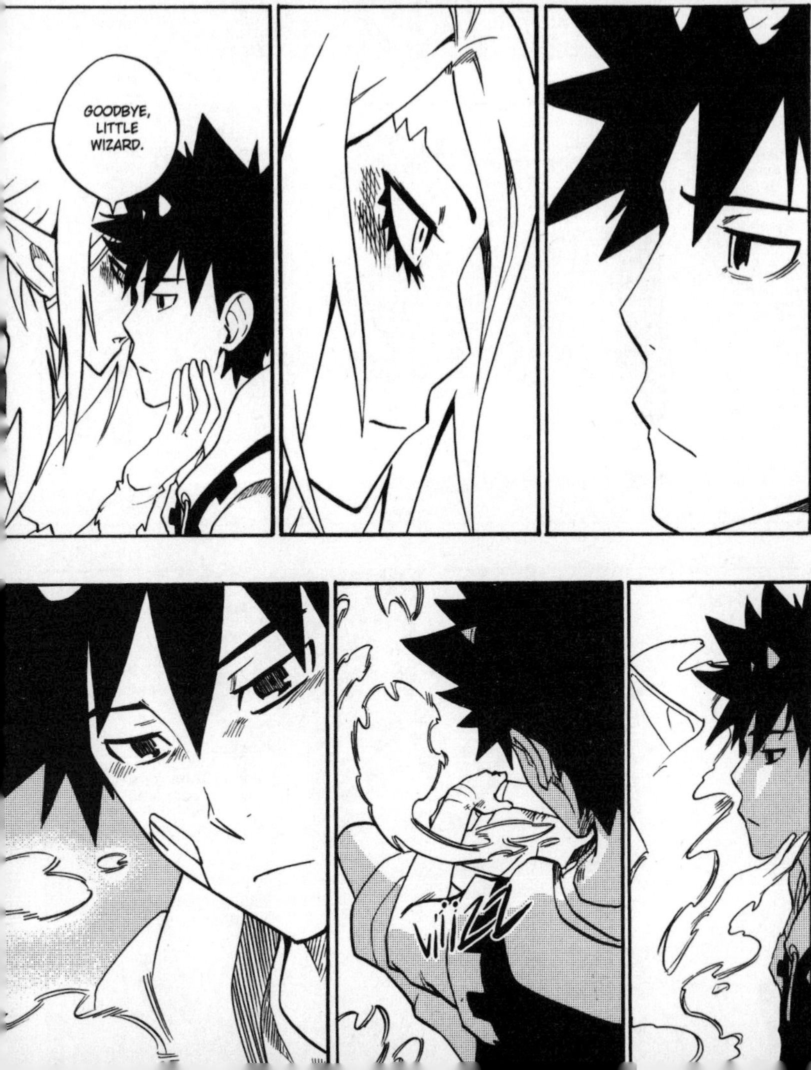
GOODBYE, LITTLE WIZARD.

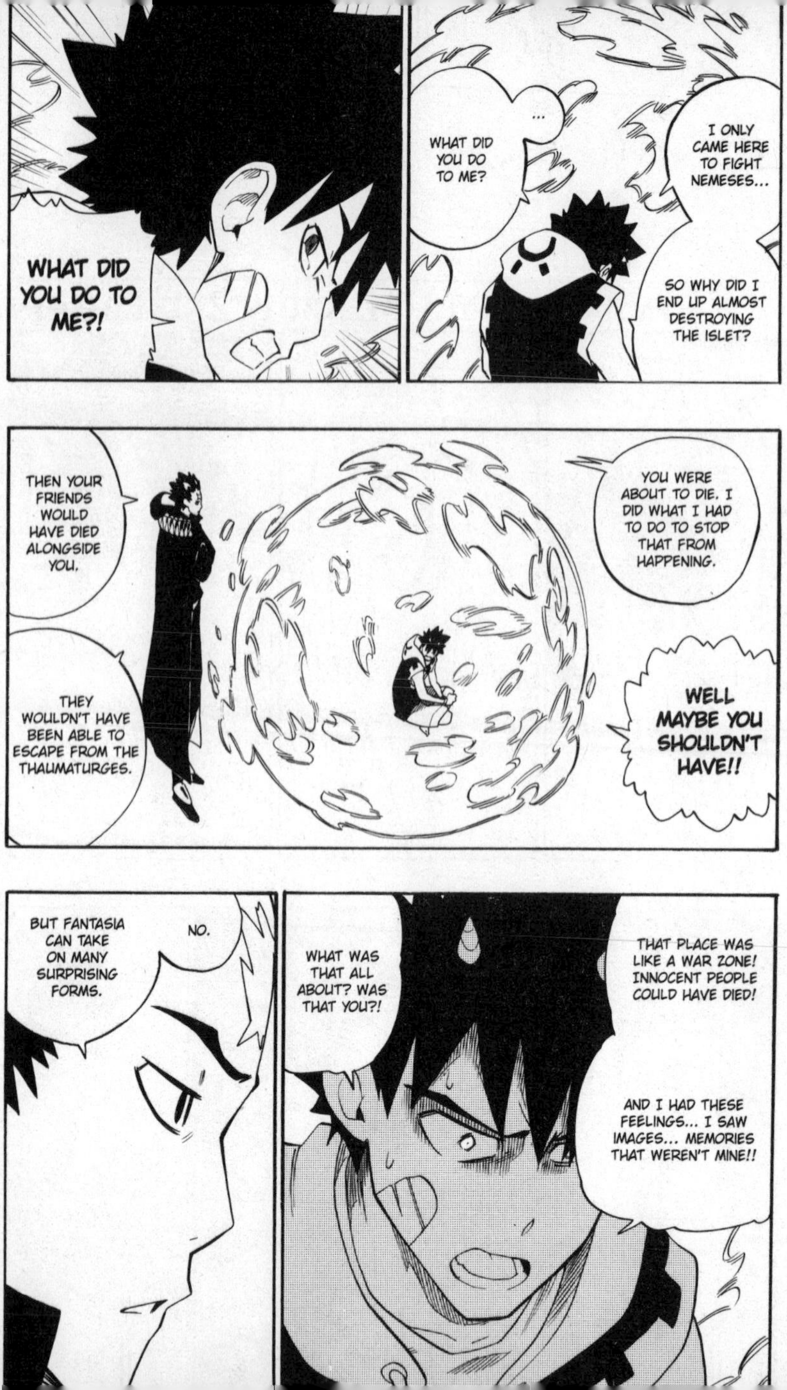
I ONLY CAME HERE TO FIGHT NEMESES...
SO WHY DID I END UP ALMOST DESTROYING THE ISLET?
...
WHAT DID YOU DO TO ME?
WHAT DID YOU DO TO ME?!
YOU WERE ABOUT TO DIE. I DID WHAT I HAD TO DO TO STOP THAT FROM HAPPENING.
WELL MAYBE YOU SHOULDN'T HAVE!!
THEN YOUR FRIENDS WOULD HAVE DIED ALONGSIDE YOU.
THEY WOULDN'T HAVE BEEN ABLE TO ESCAPE FROM THE THAUMATURGES.
THAT PLACE WAS LIKE A WAR ZONE! INNOCENT PEOPLE COULD HAVE DIED!
WHAT WAS THAT ALL ABOUT? WAS THAT YOU?!
AND I HAD THESE FEELINGS... I SAW IMAGES... MEMORIES THAT WEREN'T MINE!!
NO.
BUT FANTASIA CAN TAKE ON MANY SURPRISING FORMS.

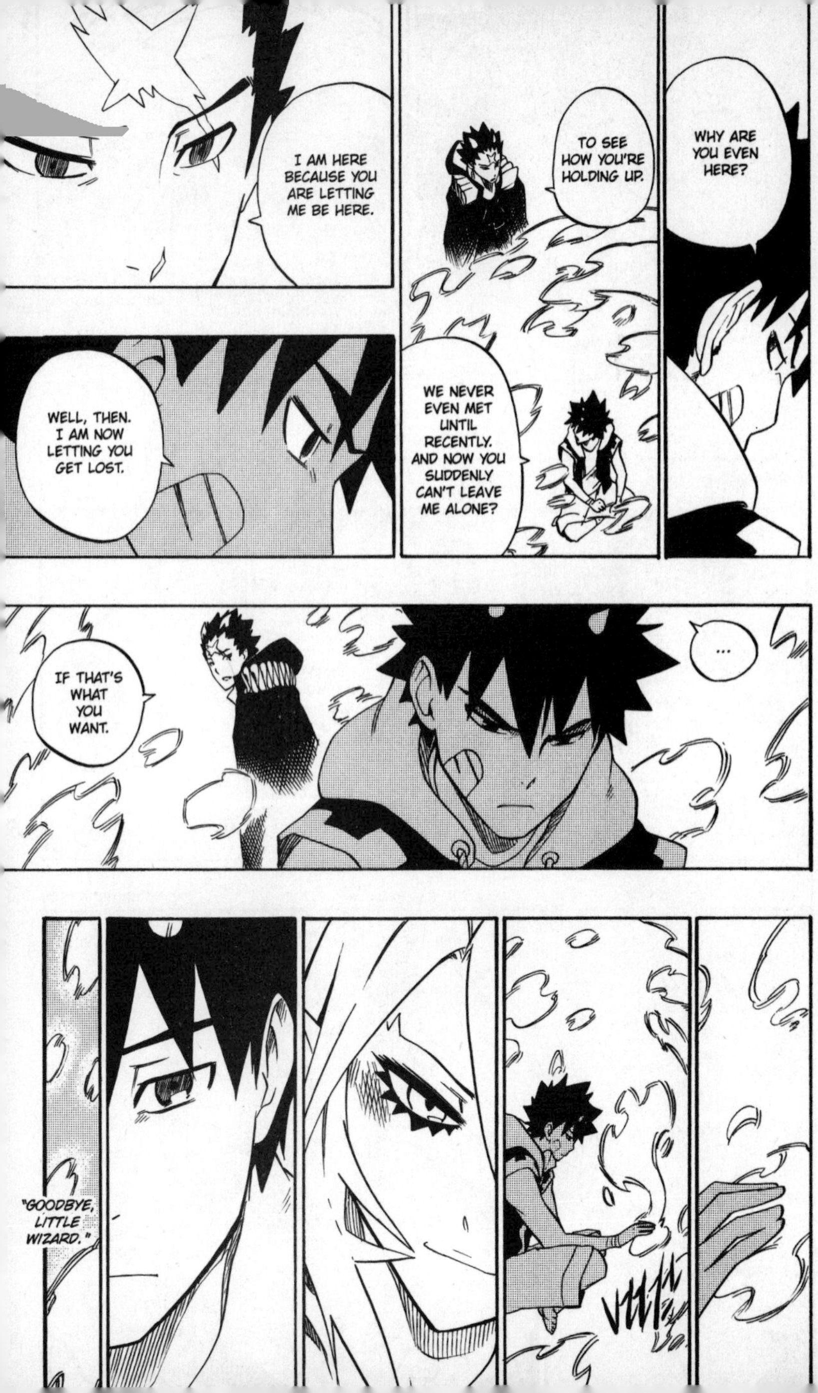
WHY ARE YOU EVEN HERE?
TO SEE HOW YOU'RE HOLDING UP.
WE NEVER EVEN MET UNTIL RECENTLY. AND NOW YOU SUDDENLY CAN'T LEAVE ME ALONE?
I AM HERE BECAUSE YOU ARE LETTING ME BE HERE.
WELL, THEN. I AM NOW LETTING YOU GET LOST.
...
IF THAT'S WHAT YOU WANT.
"GOODBYE, LITTLE WIZARD."

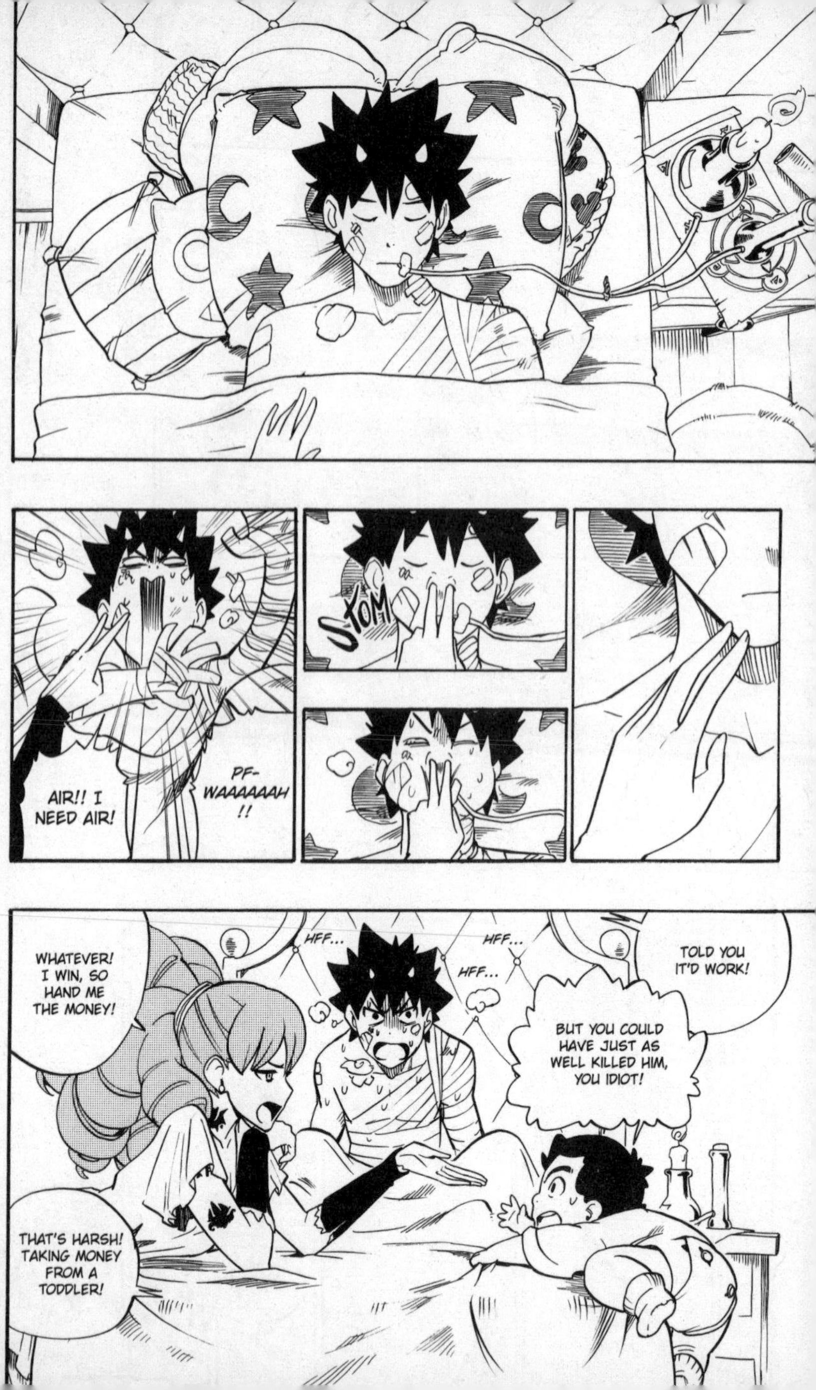
STOM
PF-WAAAAAAH!!
AIR!! I NEED AIR!
TOLD YOU IT'D WORK!
HFF...
HFF...
HFF...
BUT YOU COULD HAVE JUST AS WELL KILLED HIM, YOU IDIOT!
WHATEVER! I WIN, SO HAND ME THE MONEY!
THAT'S HARSH! TAKING MONEY FROM A TODDLER!

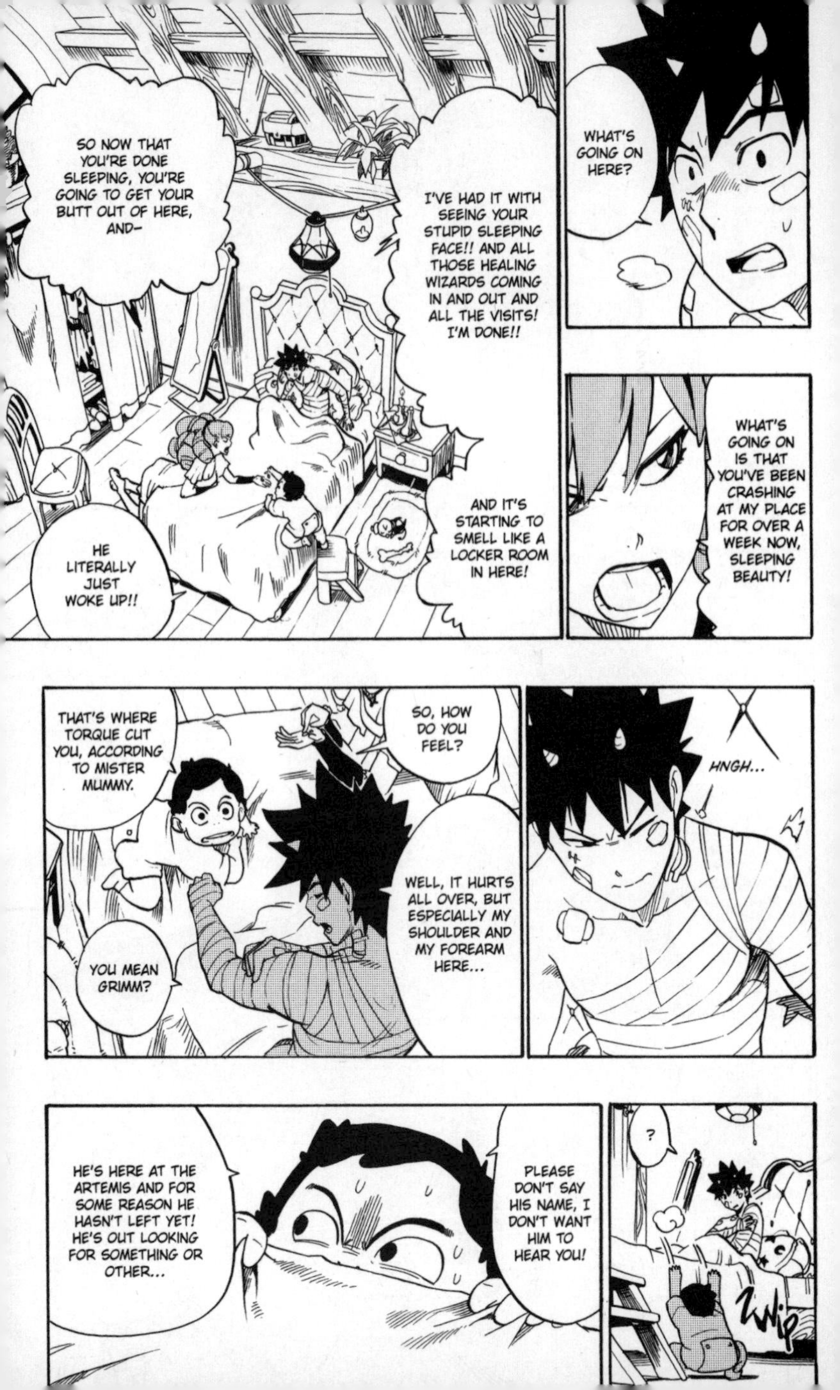
WHAT'S GOING ON HERE?
WHAT'S GOING ON IS THAT YOU'VE BEEN CRASHING AT MY PLACE FOR OVER A WEEK NOW, SLEEPING BEAUTY!
I'VE HAD IT WITH SEEING YOUR STUPID SLEEPING FACE!! AND ALL THOSE HEALING WIZARDS COMING IN AND OUT AND ALL THE VISITS! I'M DONE!!
SO NOW THAT YOU'RE DONE SLEEPING, YOU'RE GOING TO GET YOUR BUTT OUT OF HERE, AND–
AND IT'S STARTING TO SMELL LIKE A LOCKER ROOM IN HERE!
HE LITERALLY JUST WOKE UP!!
HNGH...
SO, HOW DO YOU FEEL?
WELL, IT HURTS ALL OVER, BUT ESPECIALLY MY SHOULDER AND MY FOREARM HERE...
THAT'S WHERE TORQUE CUT YOU, ACCORDING TO MISTER MUMMY.
YOU MEAN GRIMM?
?
ZWIP
PLEASE DON'T SAY HIS NAME, I DON'T WANT HIM TO HEAR YOU!
HE'S HERE AT THE ARTEMIS AND FOR SOME REASON HE HASN'T LEFT YET! HE'S OUT LOOKING FOR SOMETHING OR OTHER...

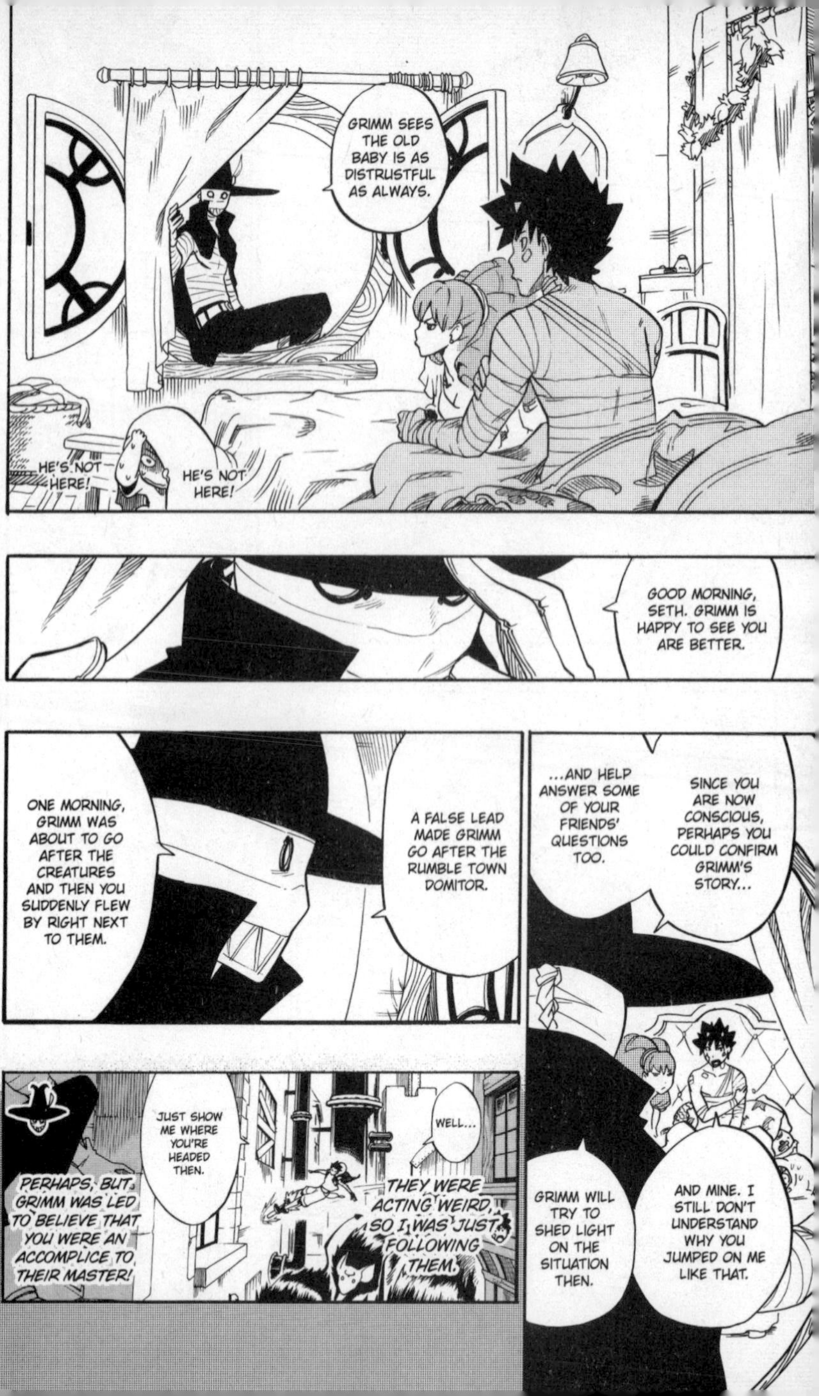

GRIMM SEES THE OLD BABY IS AS DISTRUSTFUL AS ALWAYS.
HE'S NOT HERE!
HE'S NOT HERE!
GOOD MORNING, SETH. GRIMM IS HAPPY TO SEE YOU ARE BETTER.
SINCE YOU ARE NOW CONSCIOUS, PERHAPS YOU COULD CONFIRM GRIMM'S STORY...
...AND HELP ANSWER SOME OF YOUR FRIENDS' QUESTIONS TOO.
AND MINE. I STILL DON'T UNDERSTAND WHY YOU JUMPED ON ME LIKE THAT.
GRIMM WILL TRY TO SHED LIGHT ON THE SITUATION THEN.
A FALSE LEAD MADE GRIMM GO AFTER THE RUMBLE TOWN DOMITOR.
ONE MORNING, GRIMM WAS ABOUT TO GO AFTER THE CREATURES AND THEN YOU SUDDENLY FLEW BY RIGHT NEXT TO THEM.
WELL...
THEY WERE ACTING WEIRD, SO I WAS JUST FOLLOWING THEM.
JUST SHOW ME WHERE YOU'RE HEADED THEN.
PERHAPS, BUT GRIMM WAS LED TO BELIEVE THAT YOU WERE AN ACCOMPLICE TO THEIR MASTER!

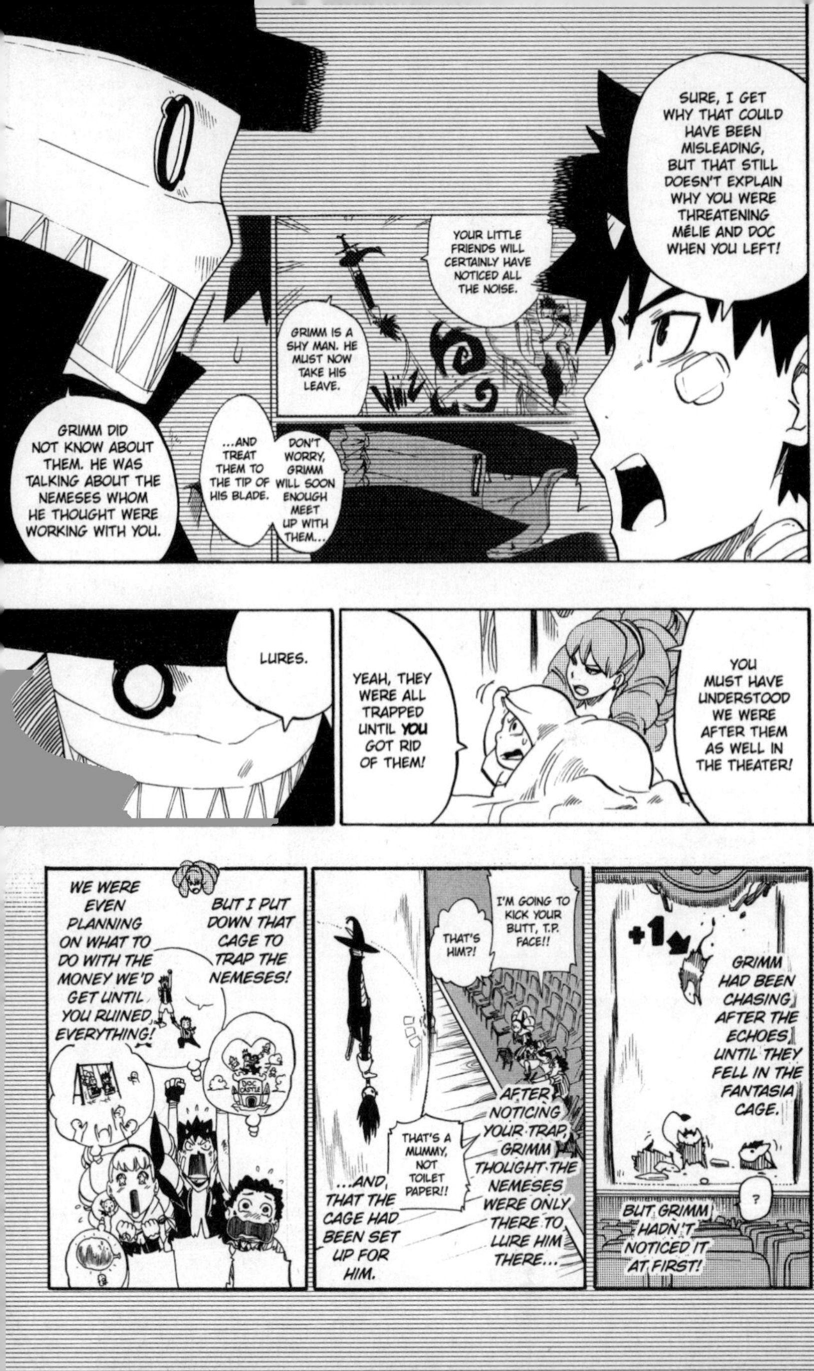
SURE, I GET WHY THAT COULD HAVE BEEN MISLEADING, BUT THAT STILL DOESN'T EXPLAIN WHY YOU WERE THREATENING MÉLIE AND DOC WHEN YOU LEFT!
YOUR LITTLE FRIENDS WILL CERTAINLY HAVE NOTICED ALL THE NOISE.
GRIMM IS A SHY MAN. HE MUST NOW TAKE HIS LEAVE.
DON'T WORRY, GRIMM WILL SOON ENOUGH MEET UP WITH THEM...
...AND TREAT THEM TO THE TIP OF HIS BLADE.
GRIMM DID NOT KNOW ABOUT THEM. HE WAS TALKING ABOUT THE NEMESES WHOM HE THOUGHT WERE WORKING WITH YOU.
YOU MUST HAVE UNDERSTOOD WE WERE AFTER THEM AS WELL IN THE THEATER!
YEAH, THEY WERE ALL TRAPPED UNTIL YOU GOT RID OF THEM!
LURES.
+1
GRIMM HAD BEEN CHASING AFTER THE ECHOES UNTIL THEY FELL IN THE FANTASIA CAGE.
?
BUT GRIMM HADN'T NOTICED IT AT FIRST!
I'M GOING TO KICK YOUR BUTT, T.P. FACE!!
THAT'S HIM?!
AFTER NOTICING YOUR TRAP, GRIMM THOUGHT THE NEMESES WERE ONLY THERE TO LURE HIM THERE...
THAT'S A MUMMY, NOT TOILET PAPER!!
...AND THAT THE CAGE HAD BEEN SET UP FOR HIM.
BUT I PUT DOWN THAT CAGE TO TRAP THE NEMESES!
WE WERE EVEN PLANNING ON WHAT TO DO WITH THE MONEY WE'D GET UNTIL YOU RUINED EVERYTHING!
DOC CASTLE

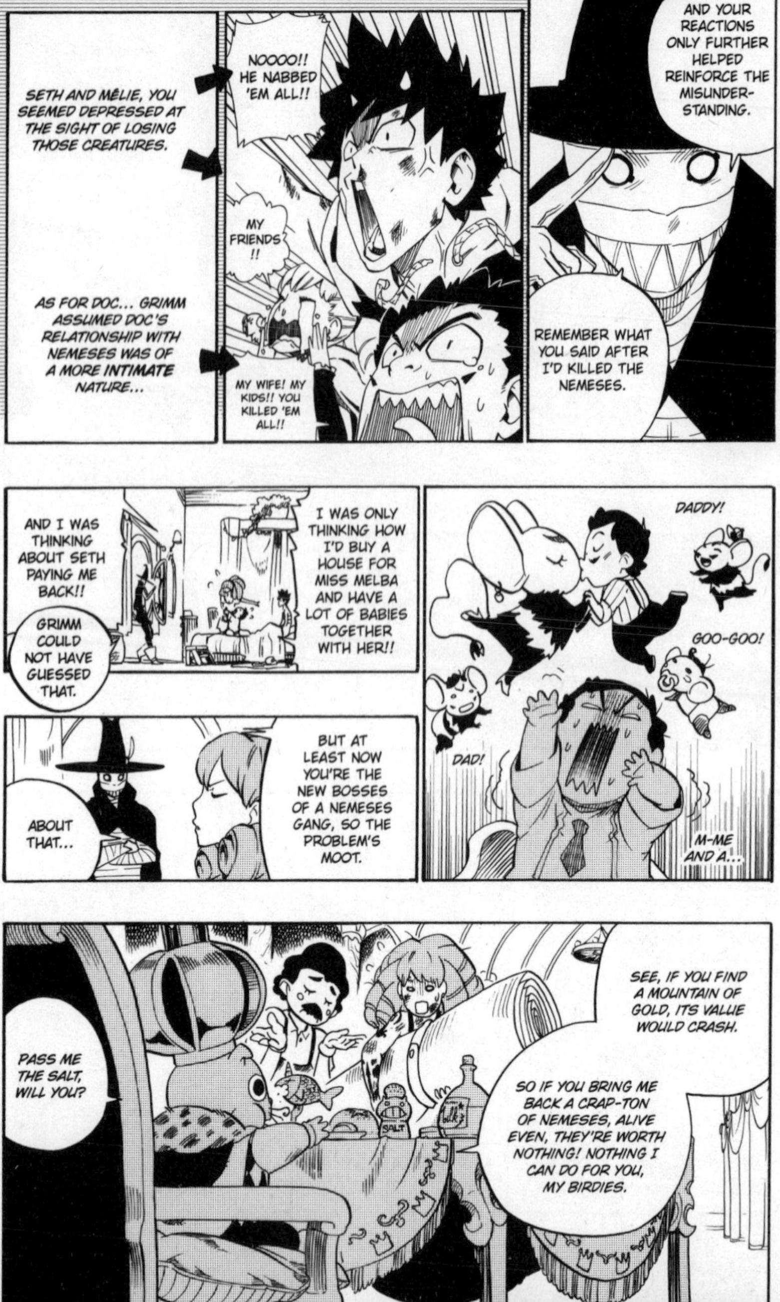
AND YOUR REACTIONS ONLY FURTHER HELPED REINFORCE THE MISUNDER-STANDING.
REMEMBER WHAT YOU SAID AFTER I'D KILLED THE NEMESES.
NOOOO!! HE NABBED 'EM ALL!!
MY FRIENDS!!
MY WIFE! MY KIDS!! YOU KILLED 'EM ALL!!
SETH AND MÊLIE, YOU SEEMED DEPRESSED AT THE SIGHT OF LOSING THOSE CREATURES.
AS FOR DOC... GRIMM ASSUMED DOC'S RELATIONSHIP WITH NEMESES WAS OF A MORE INTIMATE NATURE...
DADDY!
GOO-GOO!
DAD!
M-ME AND A...
I WAS ONLY THINKING HOW I'D BUY A HOUSE FOR MISS MELBA AND HAVE A LOT OF BABIES TOGETHER WITH HER!!
AND I WAS THINKING ABOUT SETH PAYING ME BACK!!
GRIMM COULD NOT HAVE GUESSED THAT.
BUT AT LEAST NOW YOU'RE THE NEW BOSSES OF A NEMESES GANG, SO THE PROBLEM'S MOOT.
ABOUT THAT...
SEE, IF YOU FIND A MOUNTAIN OF GOLD, ITS VALUE WOULD CRASH.
SO IF YOU BRING ME BACK A CRAP-TON OF NEMESES, ALIVE EVEN, THEY'RE WORTH NOTHING! NOTHING I CAN DO FOR YOU, MY BIRDIES.
PASS ME THE SALT, WILL YOU?
SALT

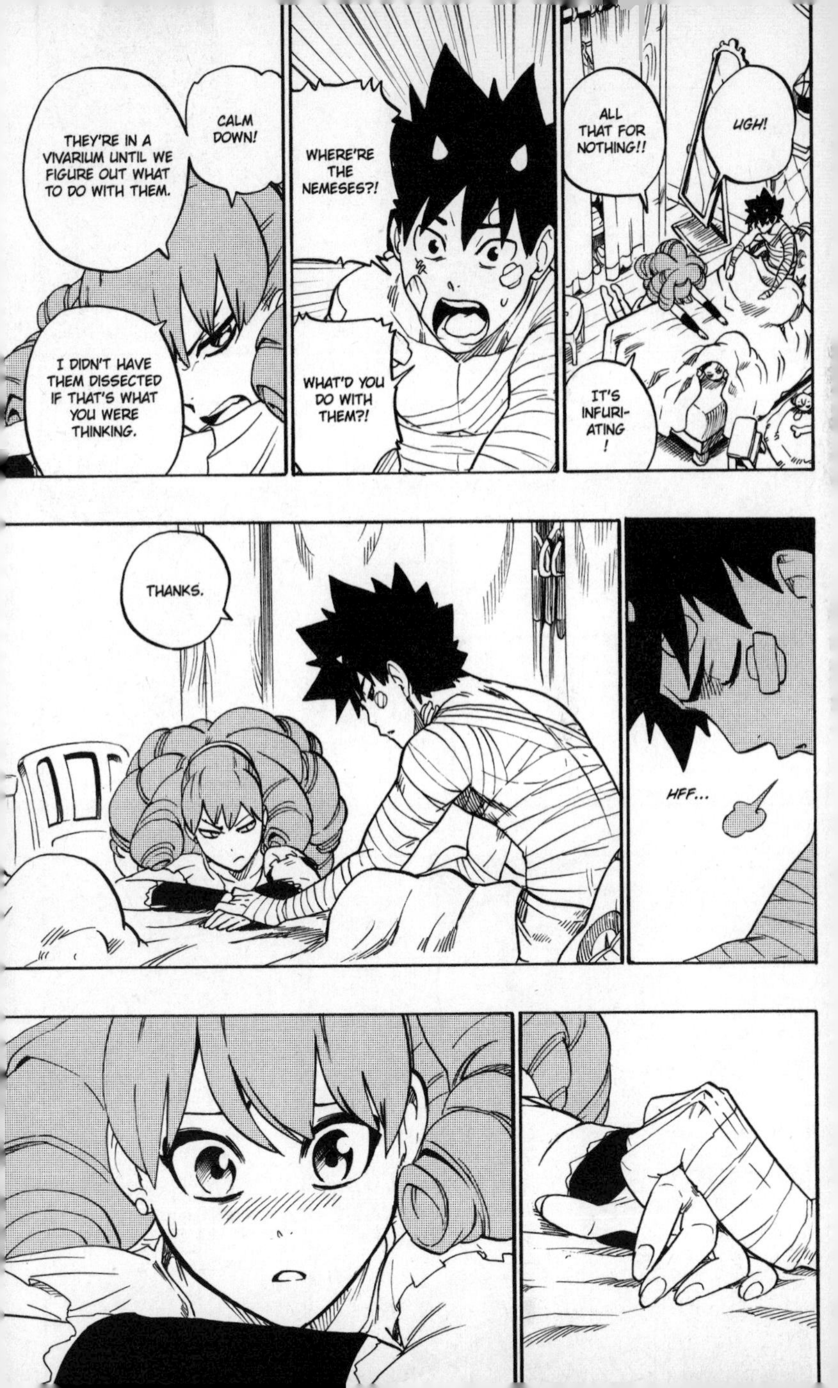
UGH!
ALL THAT FOR NOTHING!!
IT'S INFURIATING!
WHERE'RE THE NEMESES?!
WHAT'D YOU DO WITH THEM?!
CALM DOWN!
THEY'RE IN A VIVARIUM UNTIL WE FIGURE OUT WHAT TO DO WITH THEM.
I DIDN'T HAVE THEM DISSECTED IF THAT'S WHAT YOU WERE THINKING.
HFF...
THANKS.

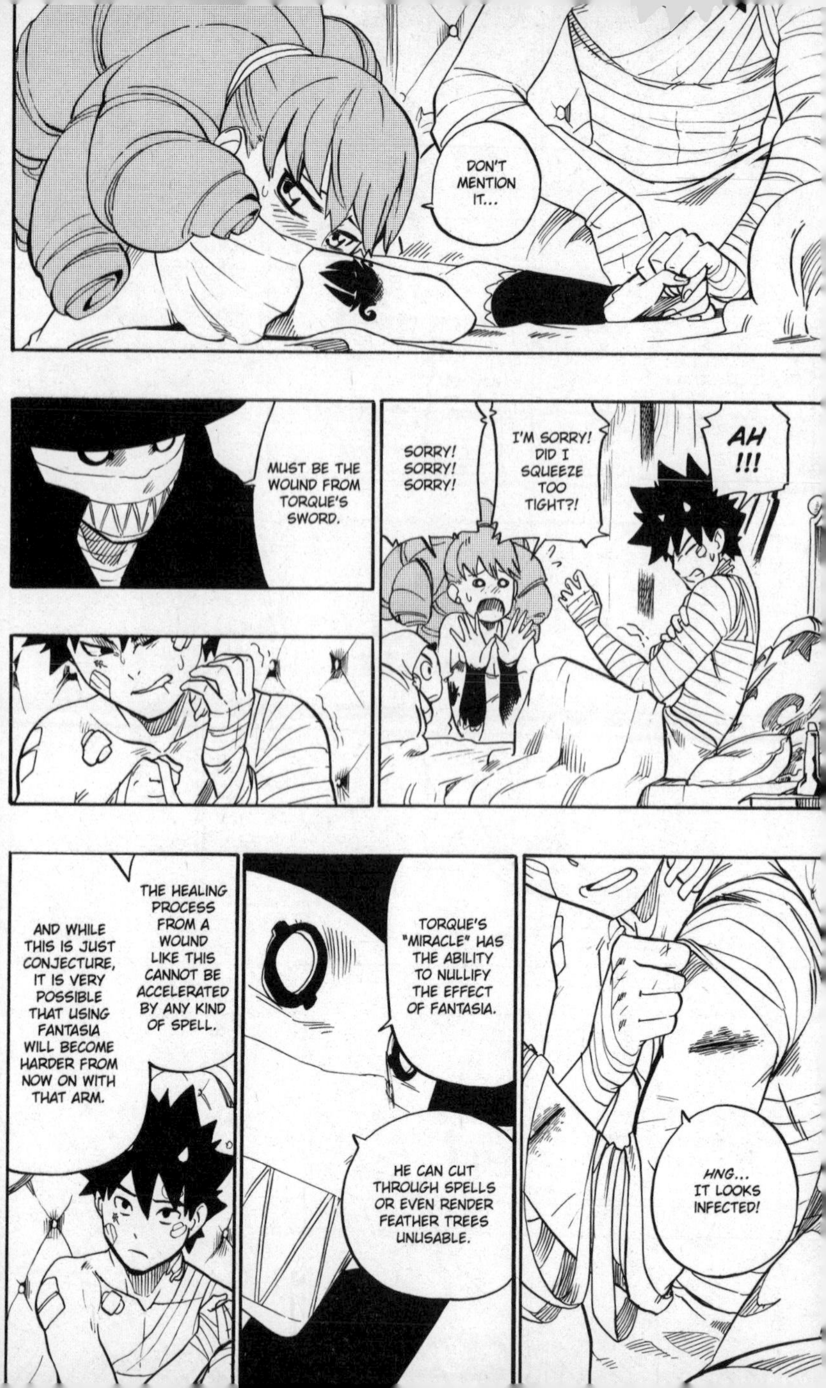
DON'T MENTION IT...
AH!!!
I'M SORRY! DID I SQUEEZE TOO TIGHT?!
SORRY! SORRY! SORRY!
MUST BE THE WOUND FROM TORQUE'S SWORD.
HNG... IT LOOKS INFECTED!
TORQUE'S "MIRACLE" HAS THE ABILITY TO NULLIFY THE EFFECT OF FANTASIA.
HE CAN CUT THROUGH SPELLS OR EVEN RENDER FEATHER TREES UNUSABLE.
THE HEALING PROCESS FROM A WOUND LIKE THIS CANNOT BE ACCELERATED BY ANY KIND OF SPELL.
AND WHILE THIS IS JUST CONJECTURE, IT IS VERY POSSIBLE THAT USING FANTASIA WILL BECOME HARDER FROM NOW ON WITH THAT ARM.

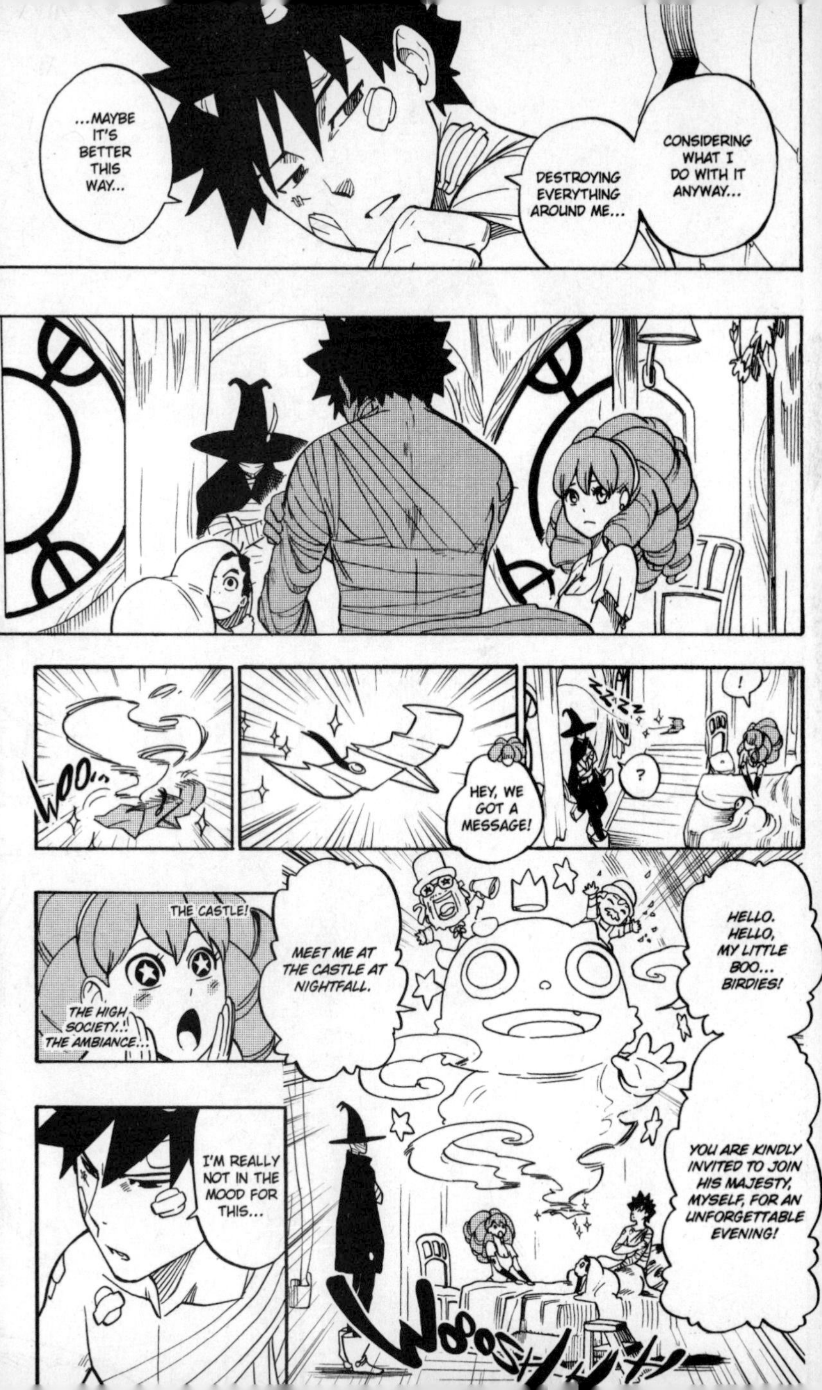
CONSIDERING WHAT I DO WITH IT ANYWAY...
DESTROYING EVERYTHING AROUND ME...
...MAYBE IT'S BETTER THIS WAY...
!
?
HEY, WE GOT A MESSAGE!
WOO...
HELLO. HELLO, MY LITTLE BOO... BIRDIES!
MEET ME AT THE CASTLE AT NIGHTFALL.
YOU ARE KINDLY INVITED TO JOIN HIS MAJESTY, MYSELF, FOR AN UNFORGETTABLE EVENING!
WOOOSH
THE CASTLE!
THE HIGH SOCIETY..! THE AMBIANCE...
I'M REALLY NOT IN THE MOOD FOR THIS...

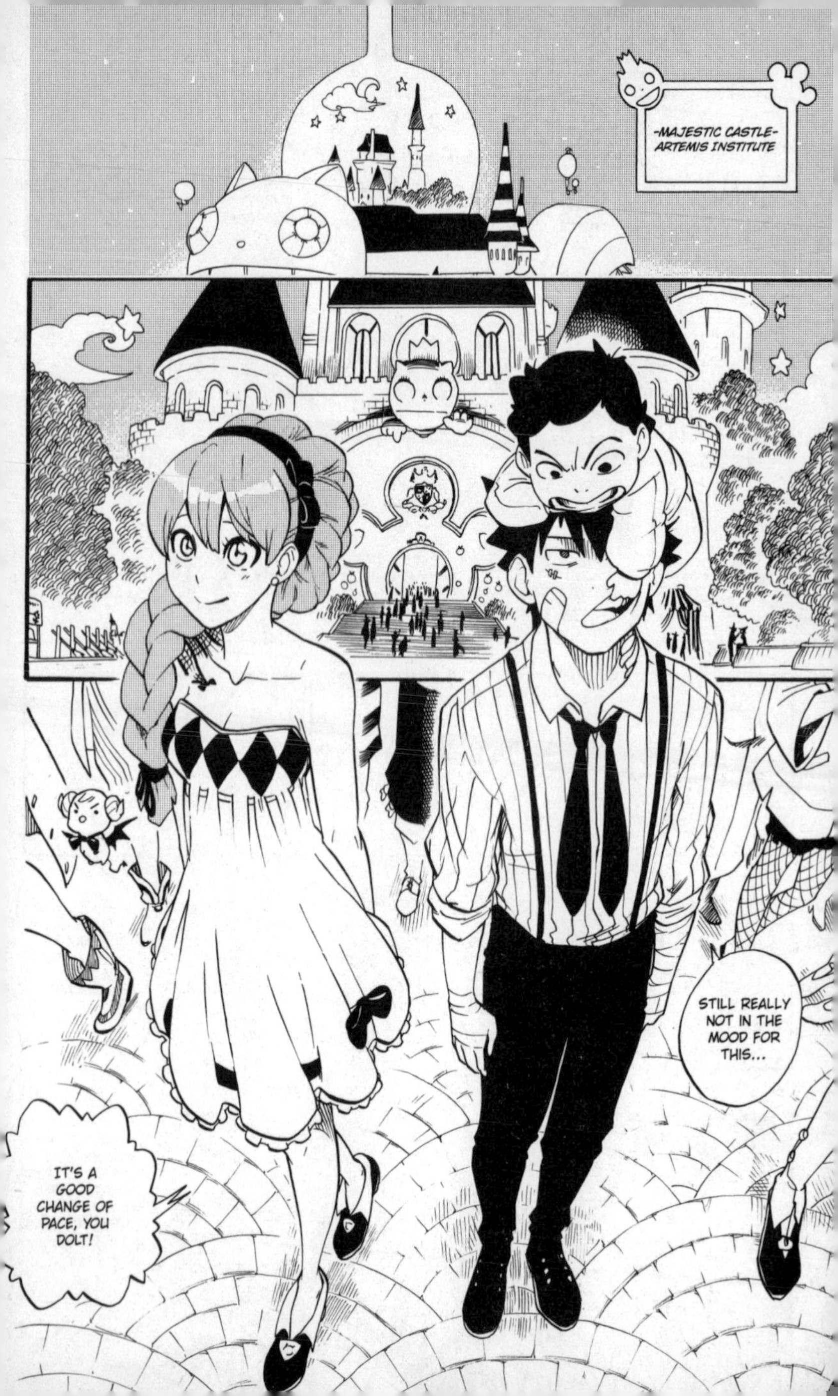
-MAJESTIC CASTLE-
ARTEMIS INSTITUTE
STILL REALLY NOT IN THE MOOD FOR THIS...
IT'S A GOOD CHANGE OF PACE, YOU DOLT!

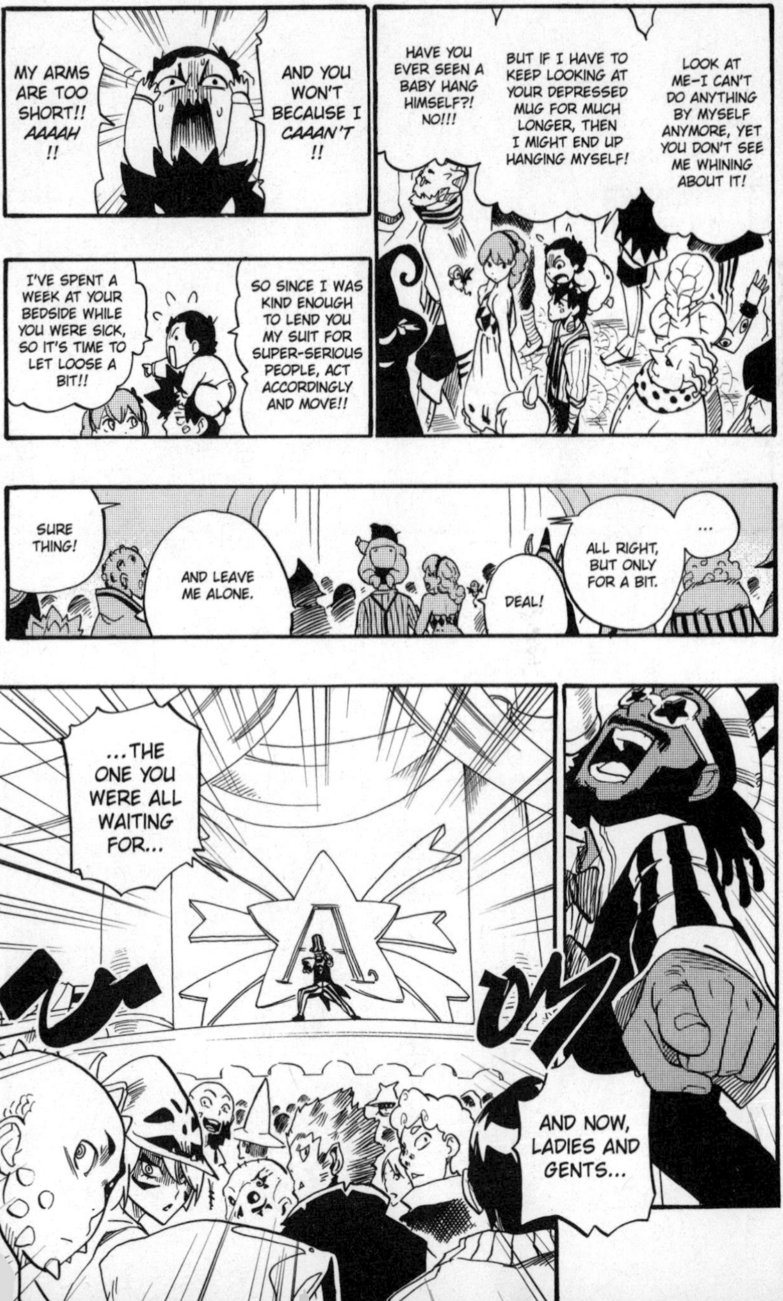
LOOK AT ME—I CAN'T DO ANYTHING BY MYSELF ANYMORE, YET YOU DON'T SEE ME WHINING ABOUT IT!
BUT IF I HAVE TO KEEP LOOKING AT YOUR DEPRESSED MUG FOR MUCH LONGER, THEN I MIGHT END UP HANGING MYSELF!
HAVE YOU EVER SEEN A BABY HANG HIMSELF?! NO!!!
AND YOU WON'T BECAUSE I *CAAAN'T* !!
MY ARMS ARE TOO SHORT!! *AAAAH* !!
SO SINCE I WAS KIND ENOUGH TO LEND YOU MY SUIT FOR SUPER-SERIOUS PEOPLE, ACT ACCORDINGLY AND MOVE!!
I'VE SPENT A WEEK AT YOUR BEDSIDE WHILE YOU WERE SICK, SO IT'S TIME TO LET LOOSE A BIT!!
...
ALL RIGHT, BUT ONLY FOR A BIT.
DEAL!
AND LEAVE ME ALONE.
SURE THING!
AND NOW, LADIES AND GENTS...
...THE ONE YOU WERE ALL WAITING FOR...

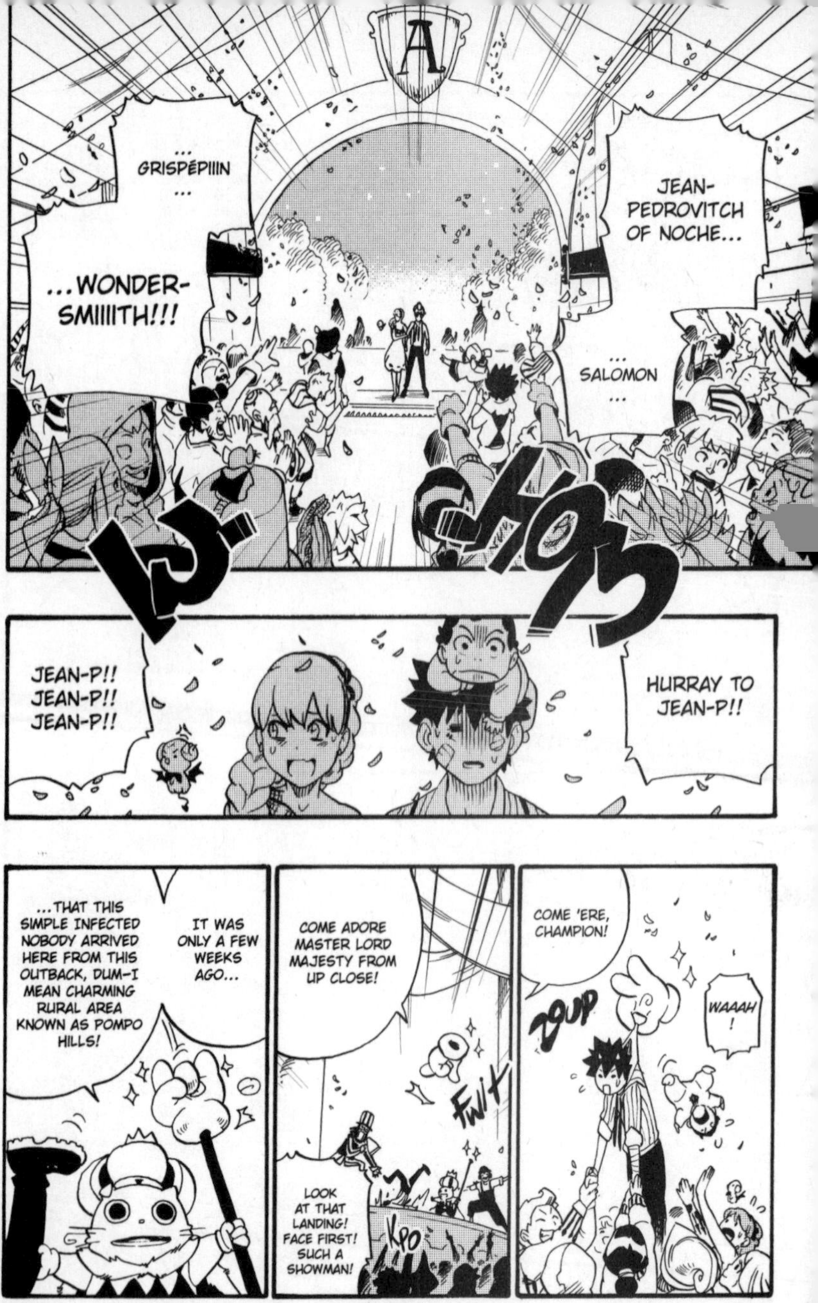
JEAN-PEDROVITCH OF NOCHE...
... SALOMON ...
... GRISPÉPIIIN ...
...WONDER-SMIIIITH!!!
HURRAY TO JEAN-P!!
JEAN-P!! JEAN-P!! JEAN-P!!
COME 'ERE, CHAMPION!
ZOUP
WAAAH!
COME ADORE MASTER LORD MAJESTY FROM UP CLOSE!
FWIT
LOOK AT THAT LANDING! FACE FIRST! SUCH A SHOWMAN!
KPO
IT WAS ONLY A FEW WEEKS AGO...
...THAT THIS SIMPLE INFECTED NOBODY ARRIVED HERE FROM THIS OUTBACK, DUM-I MEAN CHARMING RURAL AREA KNOWN AS POMPO HILLS!

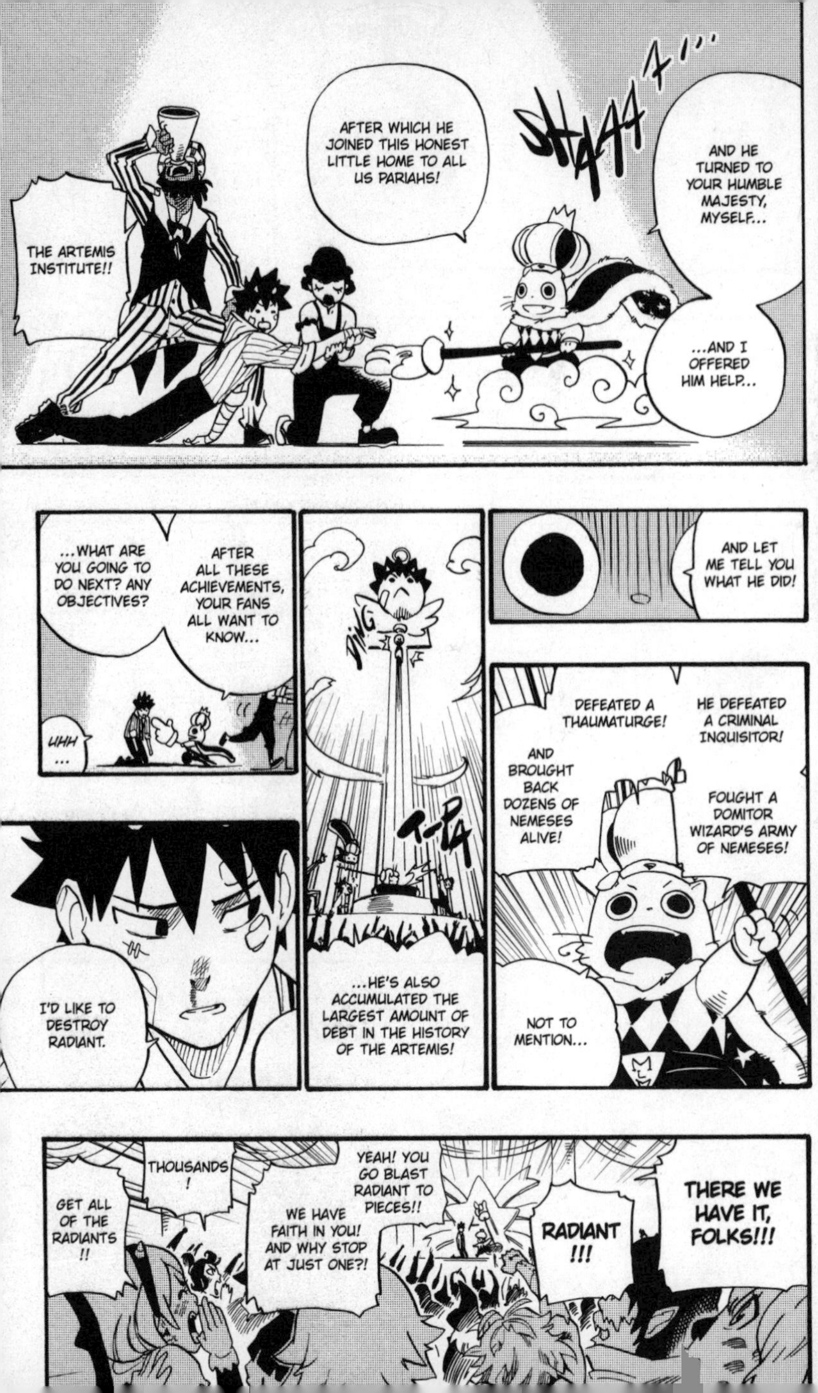
...AND HE TURNED TO YOUR HUMBLE MAJESTY, MYSELF...
...AND I OFFERED HIM HELP...
AFTER WHICH HE JOINED THIS HONEST LITTLE HOME TO ALL US PARIAHS!
THE ARTEMIS INSTITUTE!!
AND LET ME TELL YOU WHAT HE DID!
HE DEFEATED A CRIMINAL INQUISITOR!
DEFEATED A THAUMATURGE!
FOUGHT A DOMITOR WIZARD'S ARMY OF NEMESES!
AND BROUGHT BACK DOZENS OF NEMESES ALIVE!
NOT TO MENTION...
DING
...HE'S ALSO ACCUMULATED THE LARGEST AMOUNT OF DEBT IN THE HISTORY OF THE ARTEMIS!
AFTER ALL THESE ACHIEVEMENTS, YOUR FANS ALL WANT TO KNOW...
...WHAT ARE YOU GOING TO DO NEXT? ANY OBJECTIVES?
UHH ...
I'D LIKE TO DESTROY RADIANT.
THERE WE HAVE IT, FOLKS!!!
RADIANT !!!
YEAH! YOU GO BLAST RADIANT TO PIECES!!
WE HAVE FAITH IN YOU! AND WHY STOP AT JUST ONE?!
THOUSANDS !
GET ALL OF THE RADIANTS !!

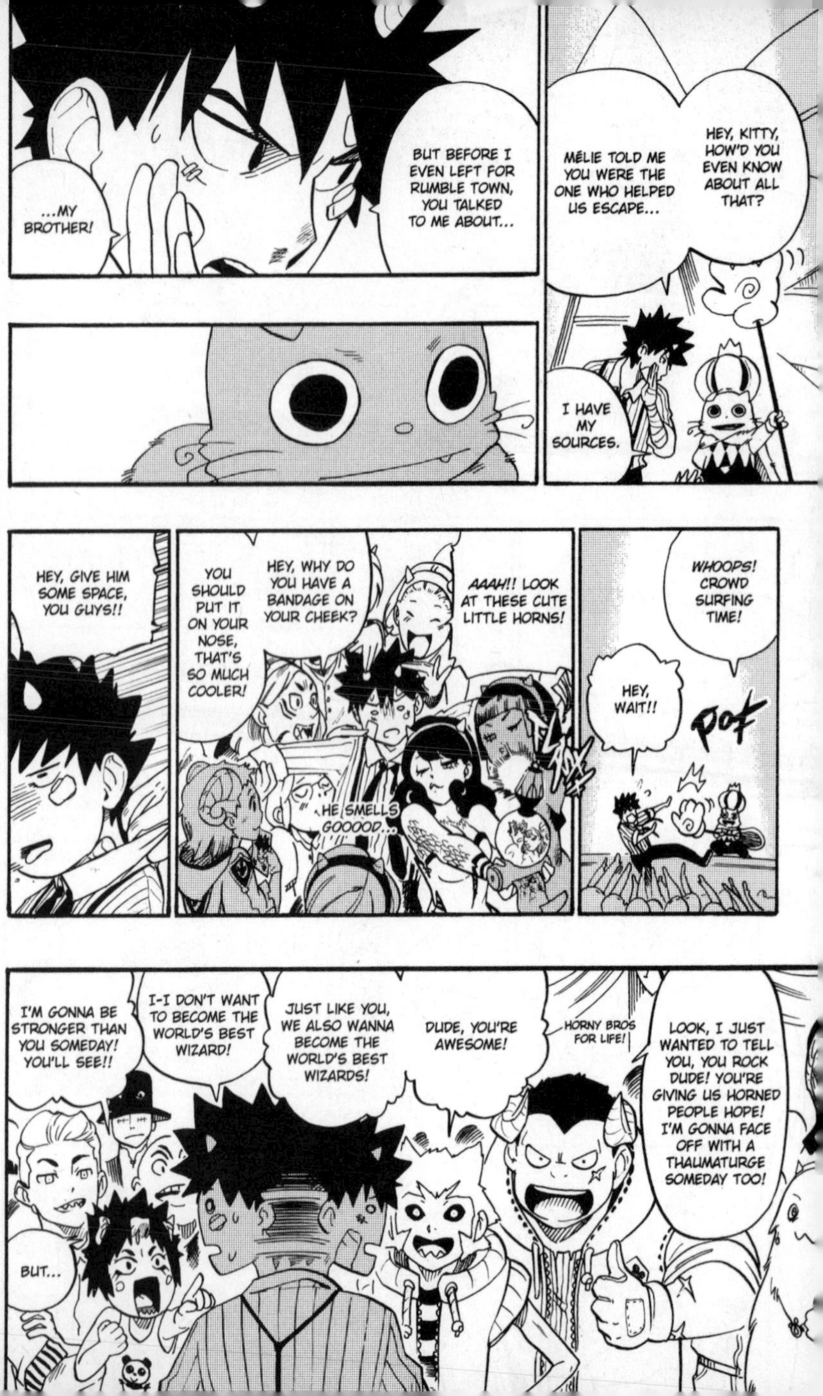
HEY, KITTY, HOW'D YOU EVEN KNOW ABOUT ALL THAT?
MÉLIE TOLD ME YOU WERE THE ONE WHO HELPED US ESCAPE...
I HAVE MY SOURCES.
BUT BEFORE I EVEN LEFT FOR RUMBLE TOWN, YOU TALKED TO ME ABOUT...
...MY BROTHER!
WHOOPS! CROWD SURFING TIME!
HEY, WAIT!!
POF
AAAH!! LOOK AT THESE CUTE LITTLE HORNS!
HEY, WHY DO YOU HAVE A BANDAGE ON YOUR CHEEK?
YOU SHOULD PUT IT ON YOUR NOSE, THAT'S SO MUCH COOLER!
HE SMELLS GOOOOD...
HEY, GIVE HIM SOME SPACE, YOU GUYS!!
LOOK, I JUST WANTED TO TELL YOU, YOU ROCK DUDE! YOU'RE GIVING US HORNED PEOPLE HOPE! I'M GONNA FACE OFF WITH A THAUMATURGE SOMEDAY TOO!
HORNY BROS FOR LIFE!
DUDE, YOU'RE AWESOME!
JUST LIKE YOU, WE ALSO WANNA BECOME THE WORLD'S BEST WIZARDS!
I-I DON'T WANT TO BECOME THE WORLD'S BEST WIZARD!
I'M GONNA BE STRONGER THAN YOU SOMEDAY! YOU'LL SEE!!
BUT...

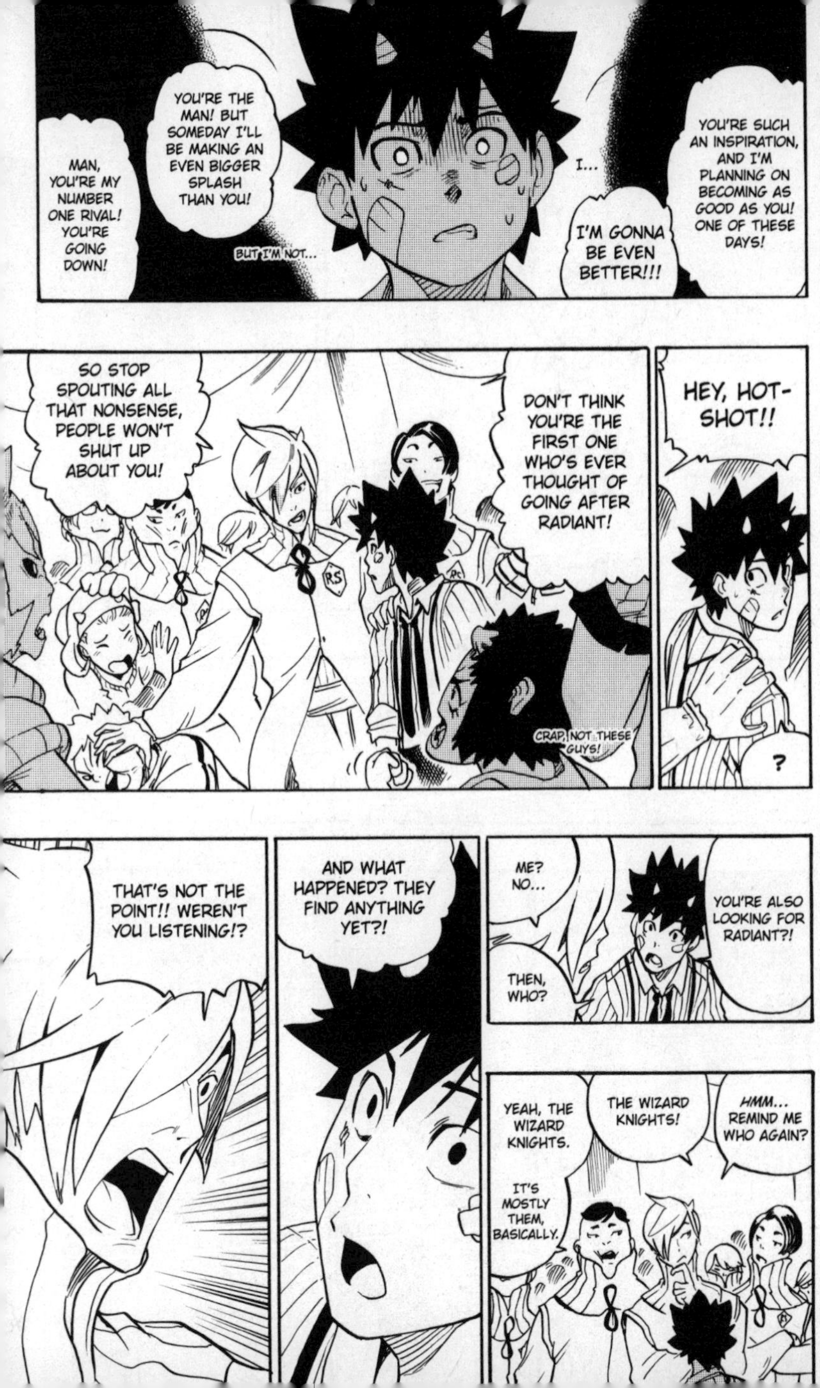
YOU'RE SUCH AN INSPIRATION, AND I'M PLANNING ON BECOMING AS GOOD AS YOU! ONE OF THESE DAYS!
I...
I'M GONNA BE EVEN BETTER!!!
YOU'RE THE MAN! BUT SOMEDAY I'LL BE MAKING AN EVEN BIGGER SPLASH THAN YOU!
MAN, YOU'RE MY NUMBER ONE RIVAL! YOU'RE GOING DOWN!
BUT I'M NOT...
HEY, HOT-SHOT!!
?
DON'T THINK YOU'RE THE FIRST ONE WHO'S EVER THOUGHT OF GOING AFTER RADIANT!
CRAP, NOT THESE GUYS!
SO STOP SPOUTING ALL THAT NONSENSE, PEOPLE WON'T SHUT UP ABOUT YOU!
YOU'RE ALSO LOOKING FOR RADIANT?!
ME? NO...
THEN, WHO?
HMM... REMIND ME WHO AGAIN?
THE WIZARD KNIGHTS!
YEAH, THE WIZARD KNIGHTS.
IT'S MOSTLY THEM, BASICALLY.
AND WHAT HAPPENED? THEY FIND ANYTHING YET?!
THAT'S NOT THE POINT!! WEREN'T YOU LISTENING!?

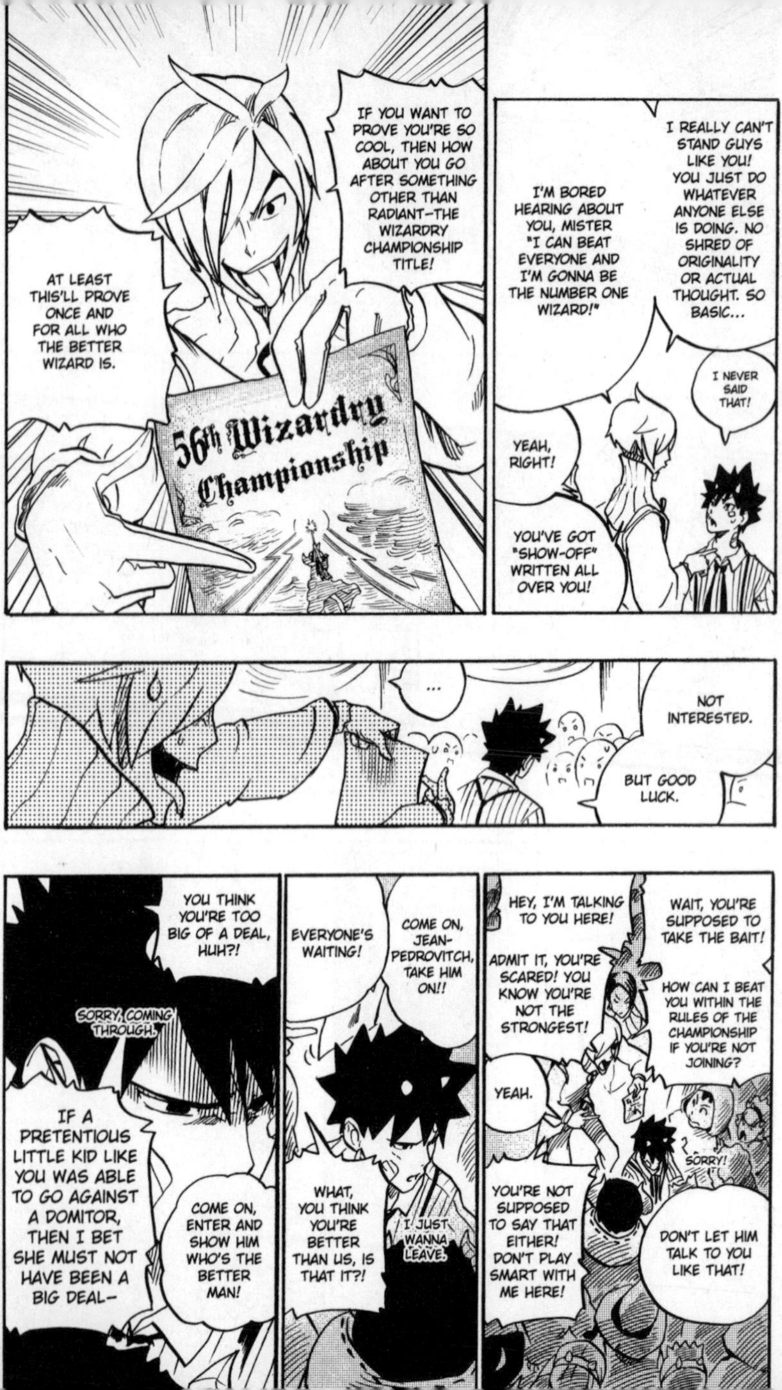

I REALLY CAN'T STAND GUYS LIKE YOU! YOU JUST DO WHATEVER ANYONE ELSE IS DOING. NO SHRED OF ORIGINALITY OR ACTUAL THOUGHT. SO BASIC...
I'M BORED HEARING ABOUT YOU, MISTER "I CAN BEAT EVERYONE AND I'M GONNA BE THE NUMBER ONE WIZARD!"
I NEVER SAID THAT!
YEAH, RIGHT!
YOU'VE GOT "SHOW-OFF" WRITTEN ALL OVER YOU!
IF YOU WANT TO PROVE YOU'RE SO COOL, THEN HOW ABOUT YOU GO AFTER SOMETHING OTHER THAN RADIANT—THE WIZARDRY CHAMPIONSHIP TITLE!
AT LEAST THIS'LL PROVE ONCE AND FOR ALL WHO THE BETTER WIZARD IS.
56th Wizardry Championship
NOT INTERESTED.
BUT GOOD LUCK.
...
WAIT, YOU'RE SUPPOSED TO TAKE THE BAIT!
HEY, I'M TALKING TO YOU HERE!
HOW CAN I BEAT YOU WITHIN THE RULES OF THE CHAMPIONSHIP IF YOU'RE NOT JOINING?
ADMIT IT, YOU'RE SCARED! YOU KNOW YOU'RE NOT THE STRONGEST!
YEAH.
SORRY!
DON'T LET HIM TALK TO YOU LIKE THAT!
YOU'RE NOT SUPPOSED TO SAY THAT EITHER! DON'T PLAY SMART WITH ME HERE!
COME ON, JEAN-PEDROVITCH, TAKE HIM ON!!
EVERYONE'S WAITING!
I JUST WANNA LEAVE.
WHAT, YOU THINK YOU'RE BETTER THAN US, IS THAT IT?!
YOU THINK YOU'RE TOO BIG OF A DEAL, HUH?!
SORRY, COMING THROUGH.
COME ON, ENTER AND SHOW HIM WHO'S THE BETTER MAN!
IF A PRETENTIOUS LITTLE KID LIKE YOU WAS ABLE TO GO AGAINST A DOMITOR, THEN I BET SHE MUST NOT HAVE BEEN A BIG DEAL—

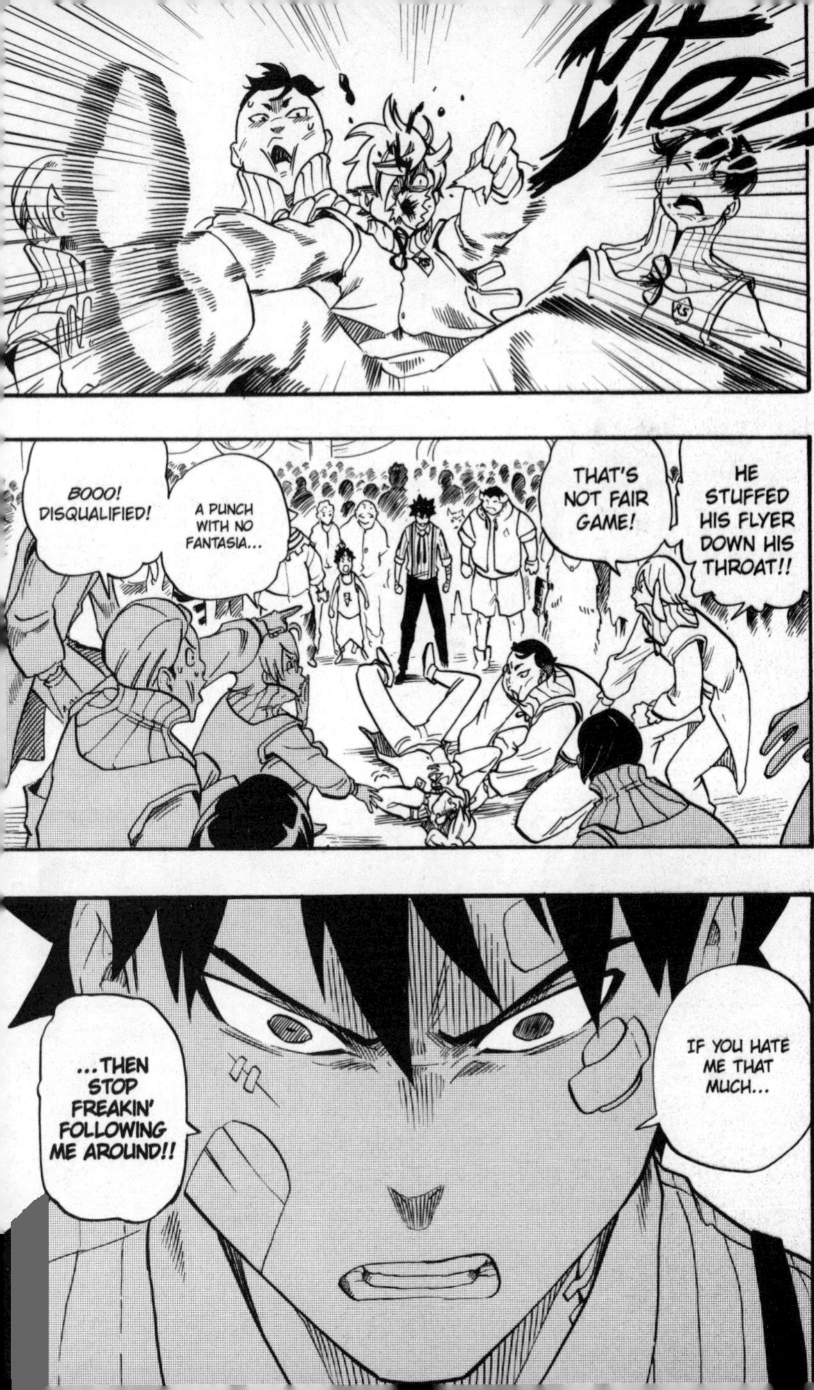
HE STUFFED HIS FLYER DOWN HIS THROAT!!
THAT'S NOT FAIR GAME!
A PUNCH WITH NO FANTASIA...
BOOO! DISQUALIFIED!
IF YOU HATE ME THAT MUCH...
...THEN STOP FREAKIN' FOLLOWING ME AROUND!!

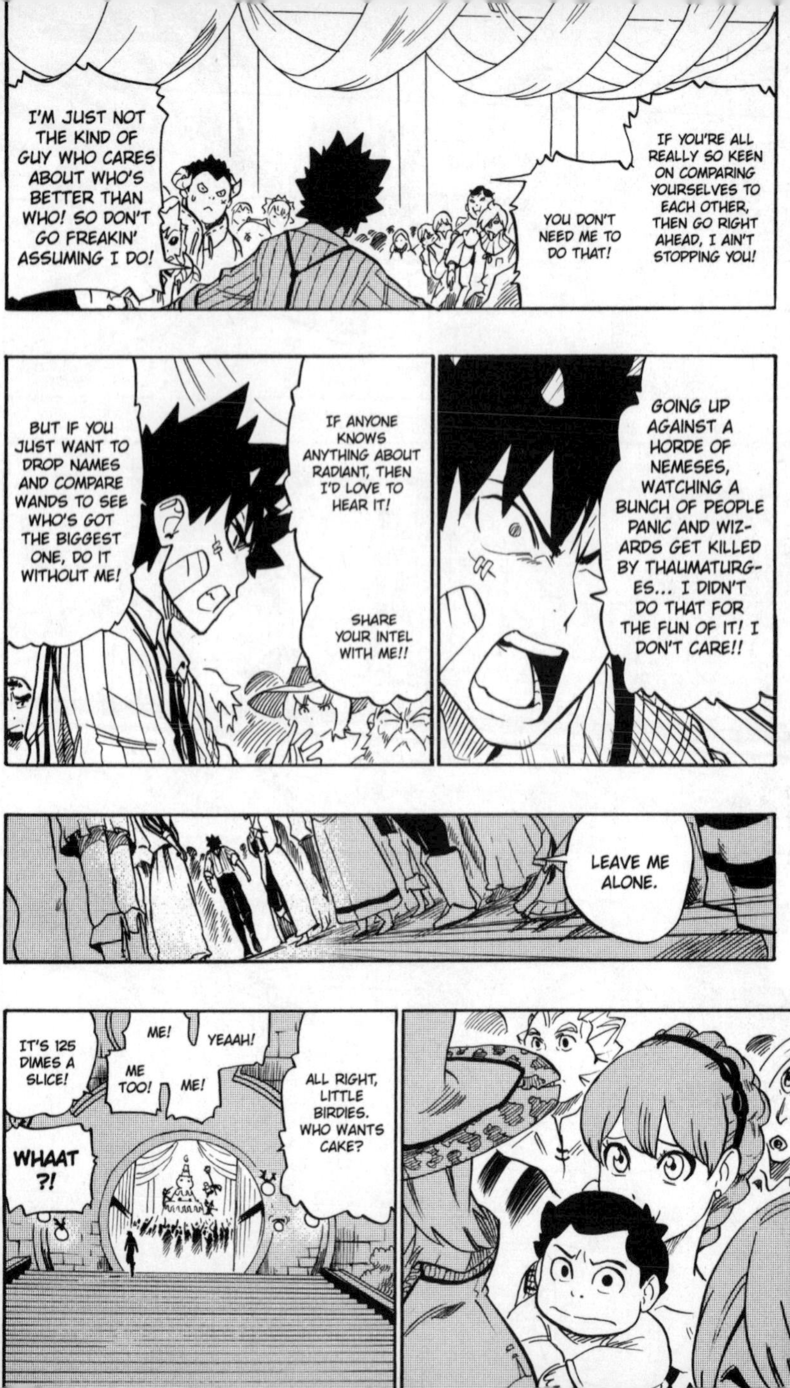

IF YOU'RE ALL REALLY SO KEEN ON COMPARING YOURSELVES TO EACH OTHER, THEN GO RIGHT AHEAD, I AIN'T STOPPING YOU!
YOU DON'T NEED ME TO DO THAT!
I'M JUST NOT THE KIND OF GUY WHO CARES ABOUT WHO'S BETTER THAN WHO! SO DON'T GO FREAKIN' ASSUMING I DO!
GOING UP AGAINST A HORDE OF NEMESES, WATCHING A BUNCH OF PEOPLE PANIC AND WIZARDS GET KILLED BY THAUMATURGES... I DIDN'T DO THAT FOR THE FUN OF IT! I DON'T CARE!!
IF ANYONE KNOWS ANYTHING ABOUT RADIANT, THEN I'D LOVE TO HEAR IT!
SHARE YOUR INTEL WITH ME!!
BUT IF YOU JUST WANT TO DROP NAMES AND COMPARE WANDS TO SEE WHO'S GOT THE BIGGEST ONE, DO IT WITHOUT ME!
LEAVE ME ALONE.
ALL RIGHT, LITTLE BIRDIES. WHO WANTS CAKE?
YEAAH!
ME!
ME!
ME TOO!
IT'S 125 DIMES A SLICE!
WHAAT ?!

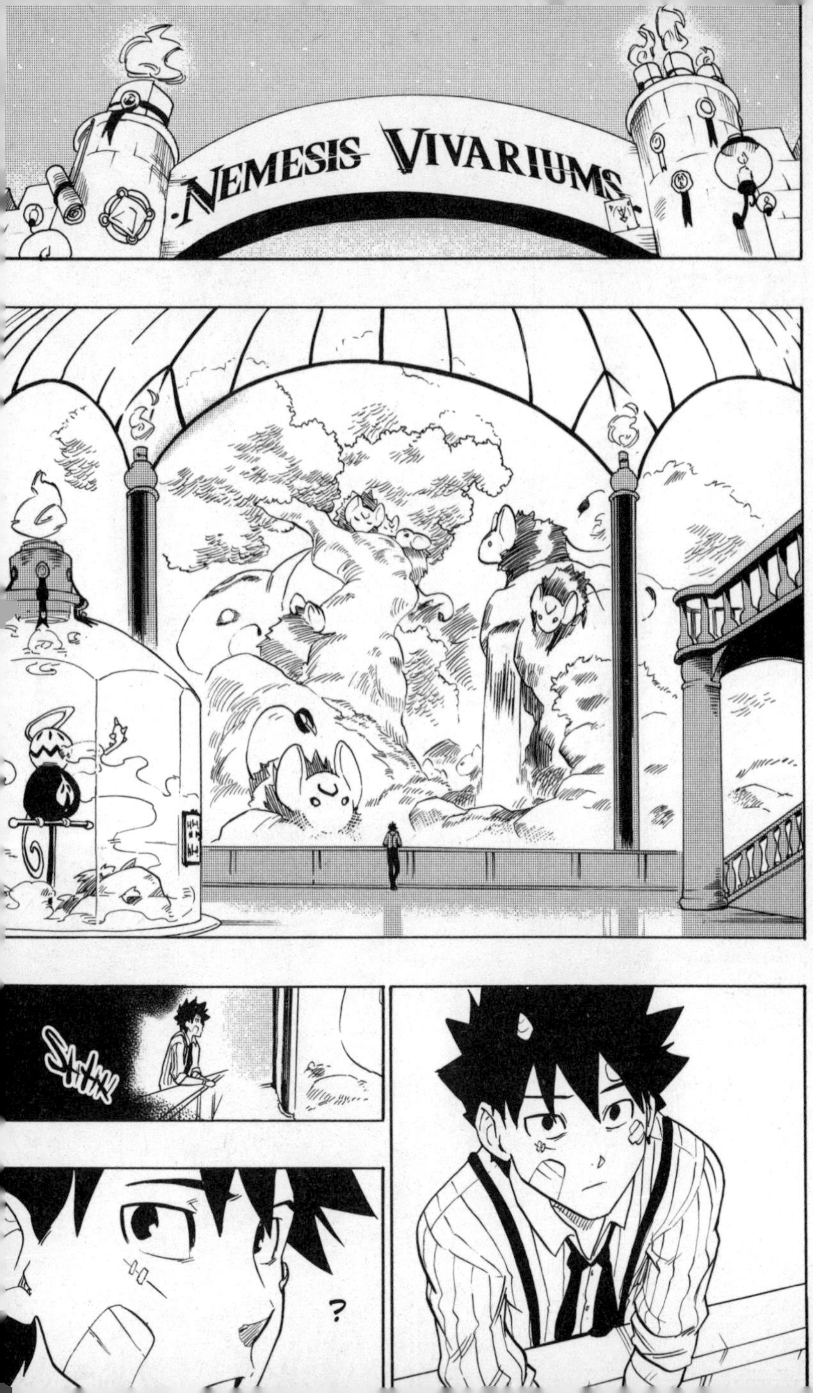
NEMESIS VIVARIUMS
?

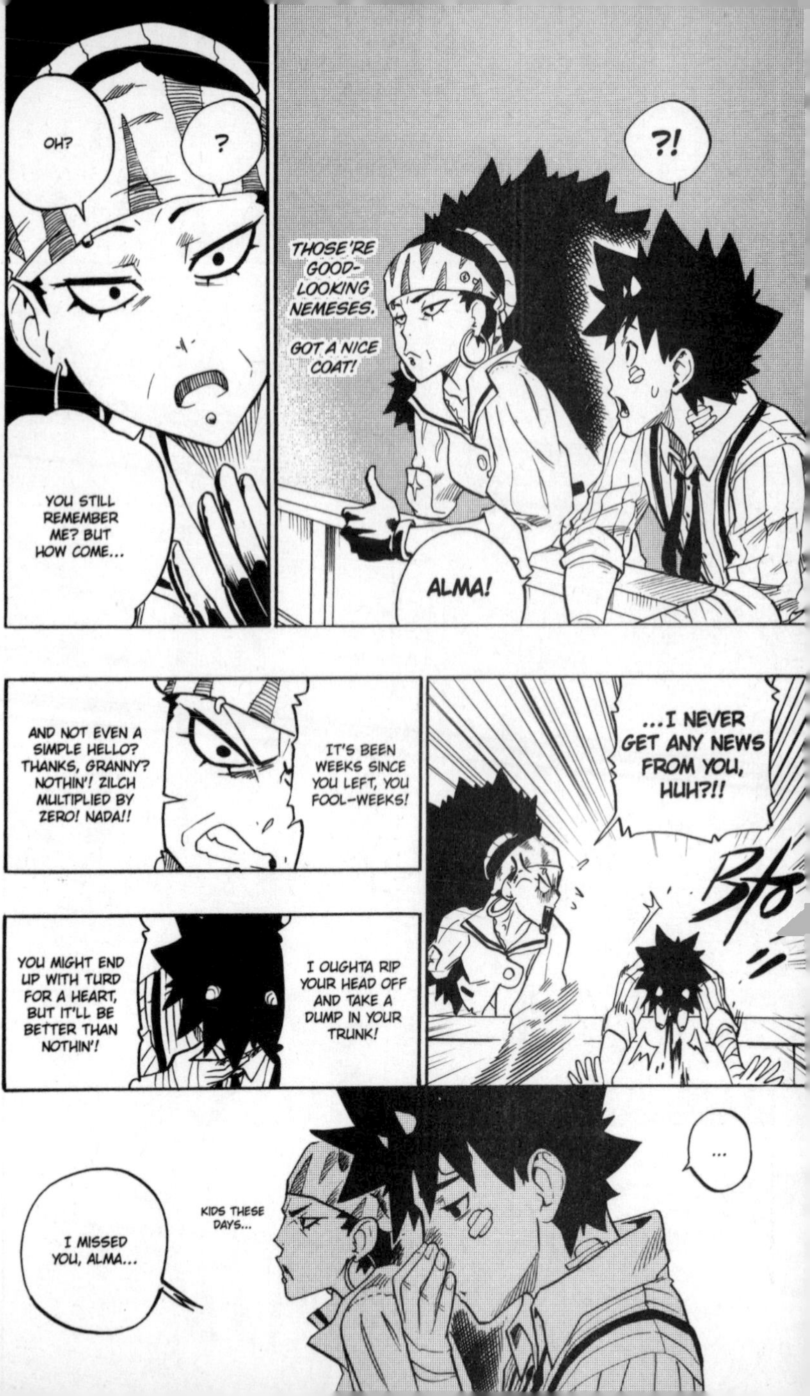
?!
THOSE'RE GOOD-LOOKING NEMESES.
GOT A NICE COAT!
ALMA!
?
OH?
YOU STILL REMEMBER ME? BUT HOW COME...
...I NEVER GET ANY NEWS FROM YOU, HUH?!!
IT'S BEEN WEEKS SINCE YOU LEFT, YOU FOOL-WEEKS!
AND NOT EVEN A SIMPLE HELLO? THANKS, GRANNY? NOTHIN'! ZILCH MULTIPLIED BY ZERO! NADA!!
I OUGHTA RIP YOUR HEAD OFF AND TAKE A DUMP IN YOUR TRUNK!
YOU MIGHT END UP WITH TURD FOR A HEART, BUT IT'LL BE BETTER THAN NOTHIN'!
...
KIDS THESE DAYS...
I MISSED YOU, ALMA...

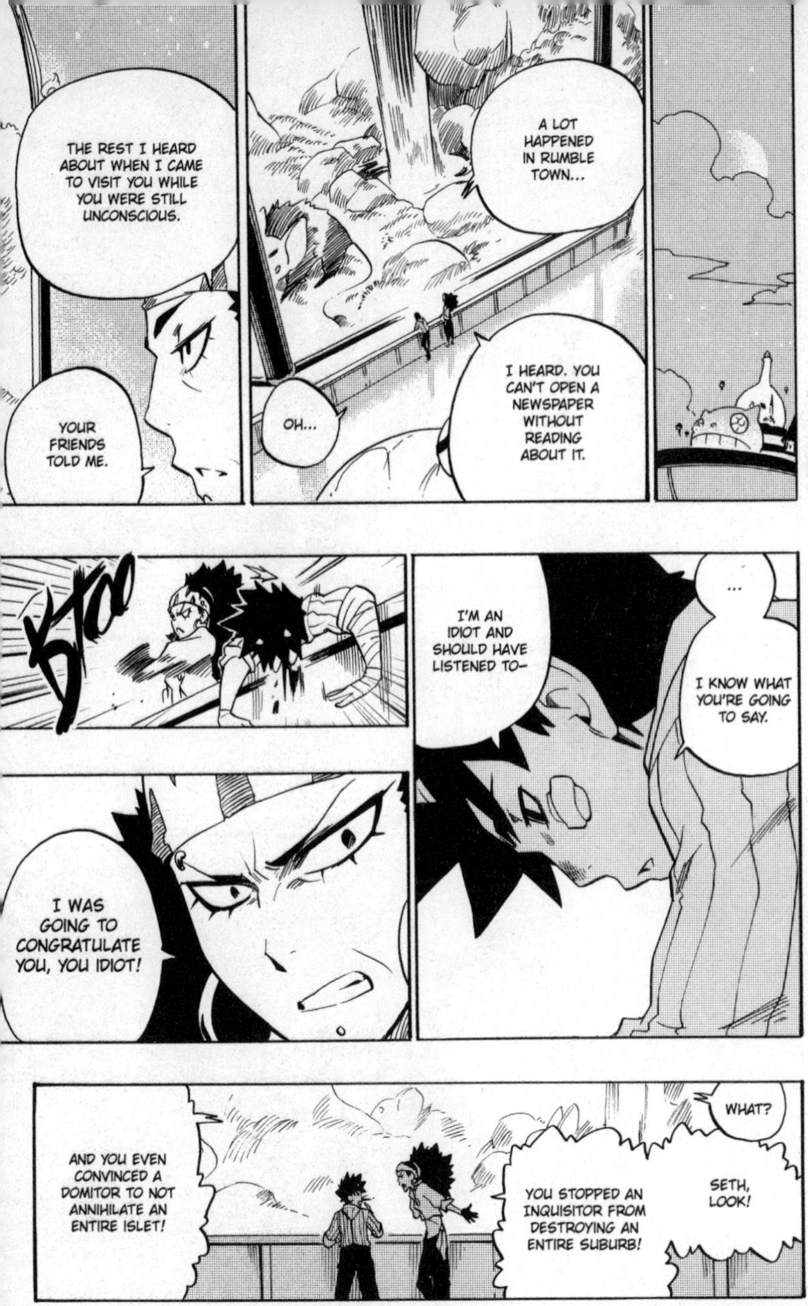
A LOT HAPPENED IN RUMBLE TOWN...
I HEARD. YOU CAN'T OPEN A NEWSPAPER WITHOUT READING ABOUT IT.
OH...
THE REST I HEARD ABOUT WHEN I CAME TO VISIT YOU WHILE YOU WERE STILL UNCONSCIOUS.
YOUR FRIENDS TOLD ME.
...
I KNOW WHAT YOU'RE GOING TO SAY.
I'M AN IDIOT AND SHOULD HAVE LISTENED TO-
I WAS GOING TO CONGRATULATE YOU, YOU IDIOT!
WHAT?
SETH, LOOK!
YOU STOPPED AN INQUISITOR FROM DESTROYING AN ENTIRE SUBURB!
AND YOU EVEN CONVINCED A DOMITOR TO NOT ANNIHILATE AN ENTIRE ISLET!

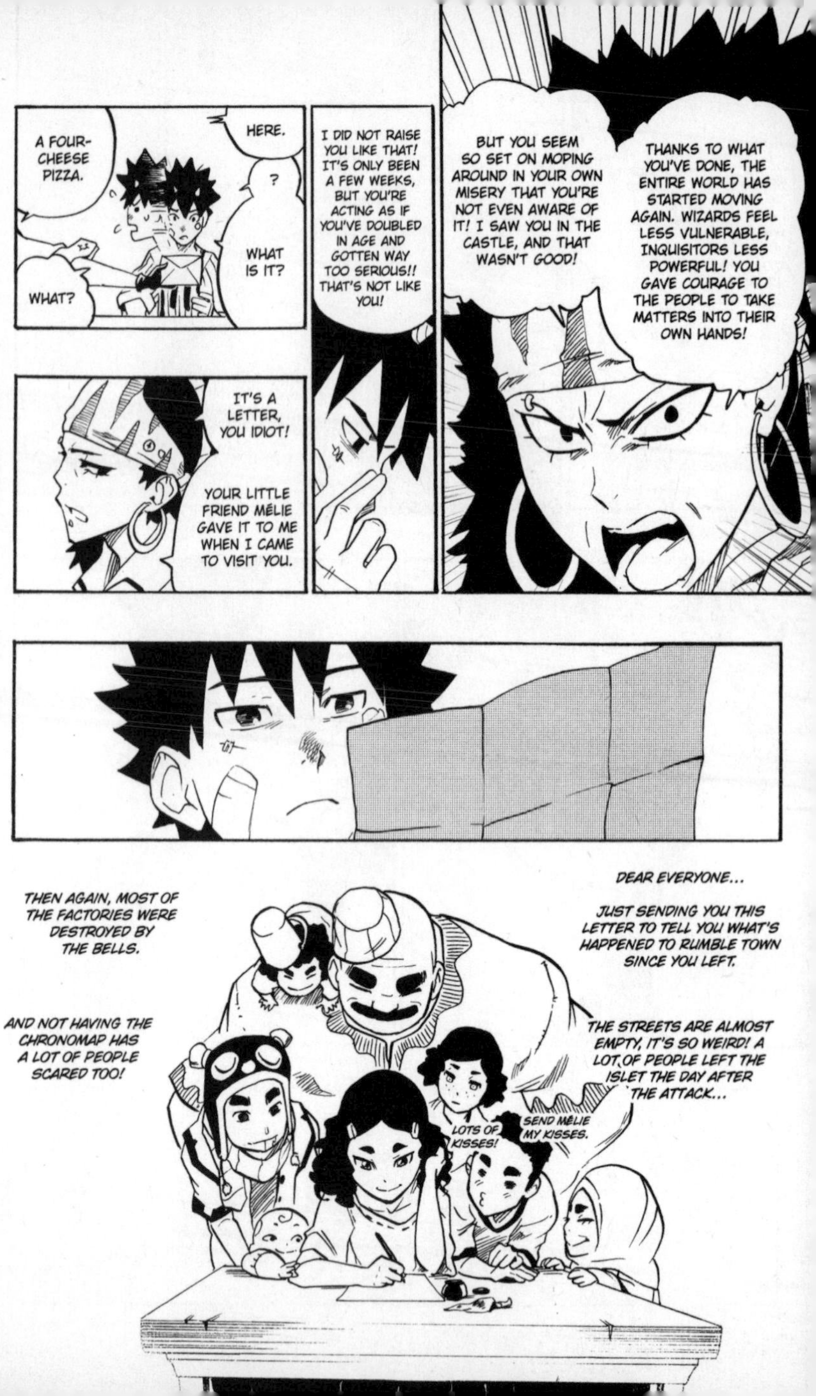
THANKS TO WHAT YOU'VE DONE, THE ENTIRE WORLD HAS STARTED MOVING AGAIN. WIZARDS FEEL LESS VULNERABLE, INQUISITORS LESS POWERFUL! YOU GAVE COURAGE TO THE PEOPLE TO TAKE MATTERS INTO THEIR OWN HANDS!
BUT YOU SEEM SO SET ON MOPING AROUND IN YOUR OWN MISERY THAT YOU'RE NOT EVEN AWARE OF IT! I SAW YOU IN THE CASTLE, AND THAT WASN'T GOOD!
I DID NOT RAISE YOU LIKE THAT! IT'S ONLY BEEN A FEW WEEKS, BUT YOU'RE ACTING AS IF YOU'VE DOUBLED IN AGE AND GOTTEN WAY TOO SERIOUS!! THAT'S NOT LIKE YOU!
HERE.
?
WHAT IS IT?
A FOUR-CHEESE PIZZA.
WHAT?
IT'S A LETTER, YOU IDIOT!
YOUR LITTLE FRIEND MÉLIE GAVE IT TO ME WHEN I CAME TO VISIT YOU.
DEAR EVERYONE...
JUST SENDING YOU THIS LETTER TO TELL YOU WHAT'S HAPPENED TO RUMBLE TOWN SINCE YOU LEFT.
THE STREETS ARE ALMOST EMPTY, IT'S SO WEIRD! A LOT OF PEOPLE LEFT THE ISLET THE DAY AFTER THE ATTACK...
SEND MÉLIE MY KISSES.
LOTS OF KISSES!
THEN AGAIN, MOST OF THE FACTORIES WERE DESTROYED BY THE BELLS.
AND NOT HAVING THE CHRONOMAP HAS A LOT OF PEOPLE SCARED TOO!

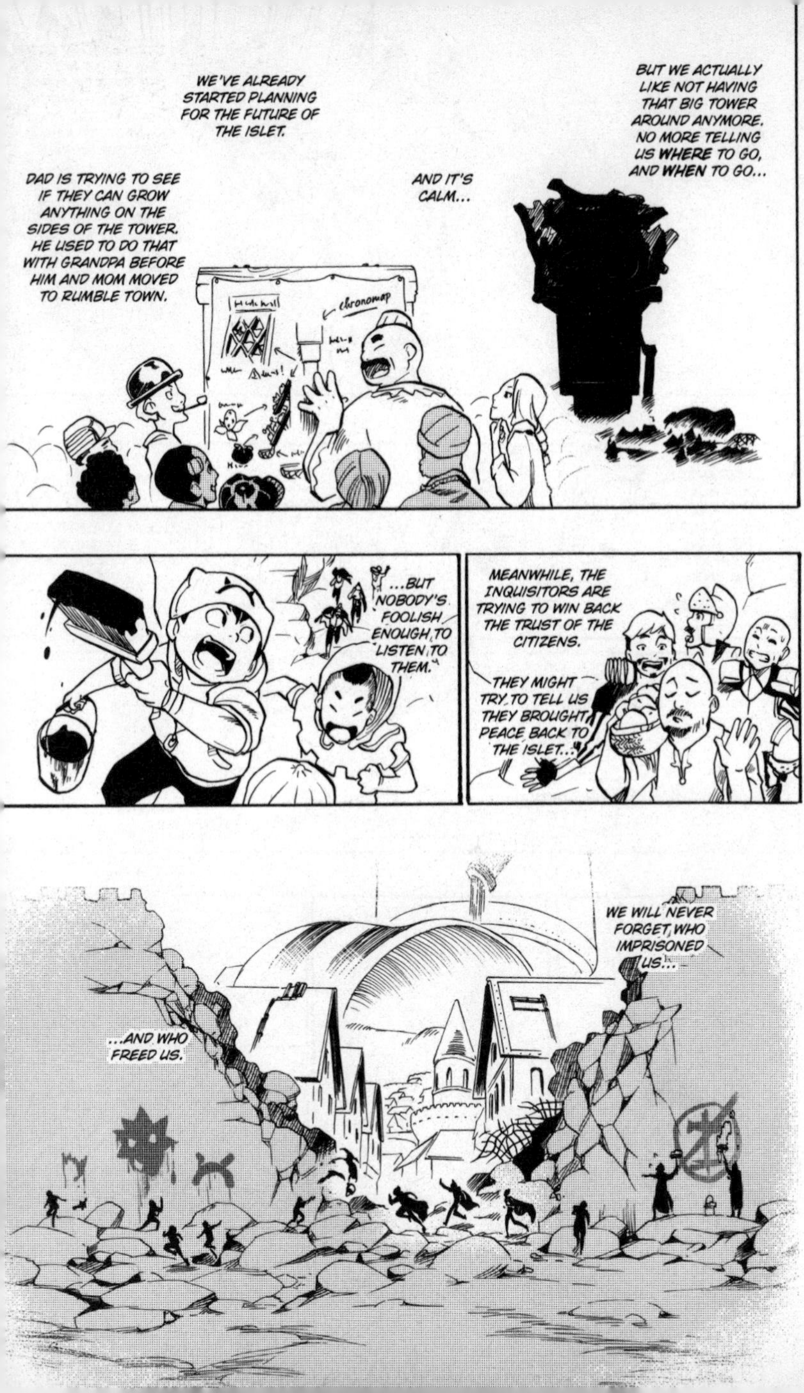
BUT WE ACTUALLY LIKE NOT HAVING THAT BIG TOWER AROUND ANYMORE. NO MORE TELLING US WHERE TO GO, AND WHEN TO GO...
AND IT'S CALM...
WE'VE ALREADY STARTED PLANNING FOR THE FUTURE OF THE ISLET.
DAD IS TRYING TO SEE IF THEY CAN GROW ANYTHING ON THE SIDES OF THE TOWER. HE USED TO DO THAT WITH GRANDPA BEFORE HIM AND MOM MOVED TO RUMBLE TOWN.
chronomap
MEANWHILE, THE INQUISITORS ARE TRYING TO WIN BACK THE TRUST OF THE CITIZENS.
THEY MIGHT TRY TO TELL US THEY BROUGHT PEACE BACK TO THE ISLET...
...BUT NOBODY'S FOOLISH ENOUGH TO LISTEN TO THEM.
WE WILL NEVER FORGET WHO IMPRISONED US...
...AND WHO FREED US.

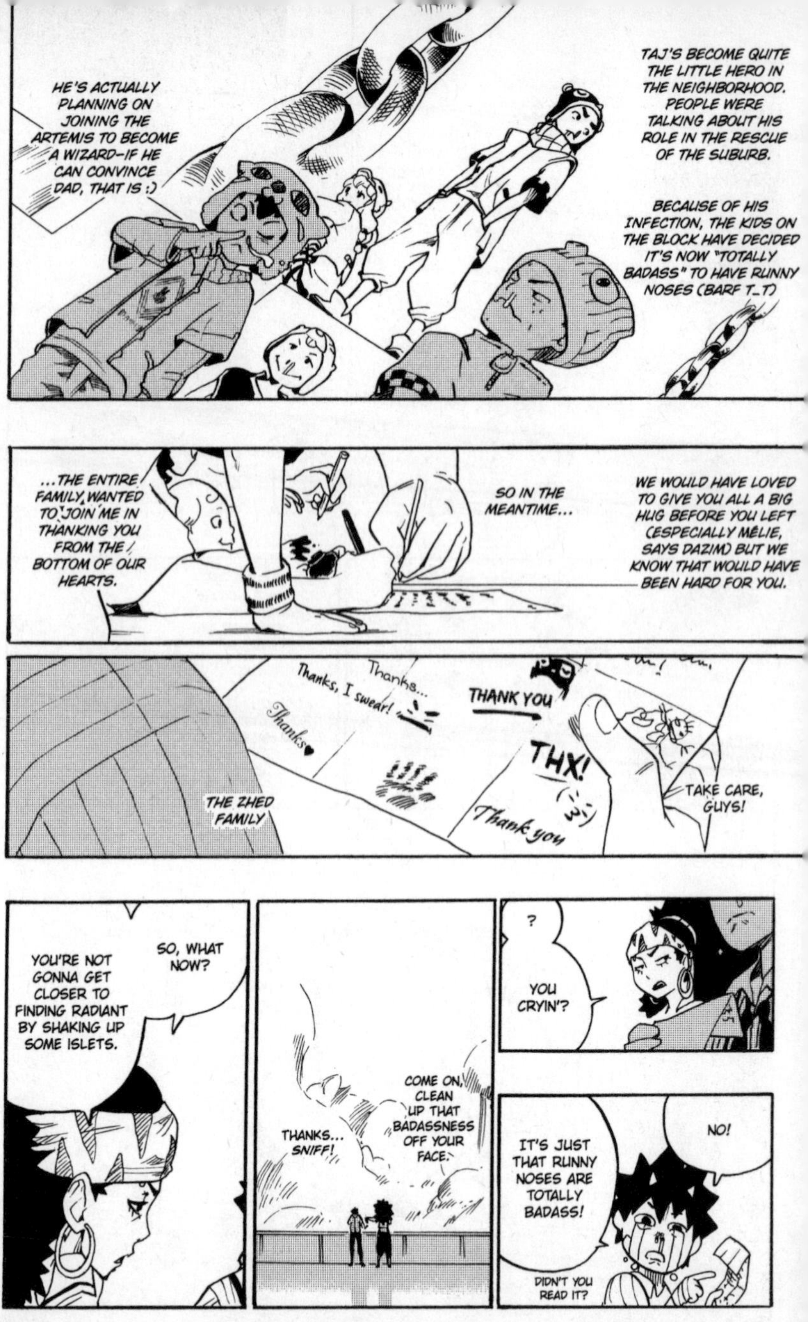
TAJ'S BECOME QUITE THE LITTLE HERO IN THE NEIGHBORHOOD. PEOPLE WERE TALKING ABOUT HIS ROLE IN THE RESCUE OF THE SUBURB.
BECAUSE OF HIS INFECTION, THE KIDS ON THE BLOCK HAVE DECIDED IT'S NOW "TOTALLY BADASS" TO HAVE RUNNY NOSES (BARF T_T)
HE'S ACTUALLY PLANNING ON JOINING THE ARTEMIS TO BECOME A WIZARD—IF HE CAN CONVINCE DAD, THAT IS :)
WE WOULD HAVE LOVED TO GIVE YOU ALL A BIG HUG BEFORE YOU LEFT (ESPECIALLY MÉLIE, SAYS DAZIM) BUT WE KNOW THAT WOULD HAVE BEEN HARD FOR YOU.
SO IN THE MEANTIME...
...THE ENTIRE FAMILY WANTED TO JOIN ME IN THANKING YOU FROM THE BOTTOM OF OUR HEARTS.
THANK YOU
THX!
TAKE CARE, GUYS!
Thank you
Thanks...
Thanks, I swear!
Thanks♥
THE ZHED FAMILY
?
YOU CRYIN'?
NO!
IT'S JUST THAT RUNNY NOSES ARE TOTALLY BADASS!
DIDN'T YOU READ IT?
COME ON, CLEAN UP THAT BADASSNESS OFF YOUR FACE.
THANKS... SNIFF!
SO, WHAT NOW?
YOU'RE NOT GONNA GET CLOSER TO FINDING RADIANT BY SHAKING UP SOME ISLETS.

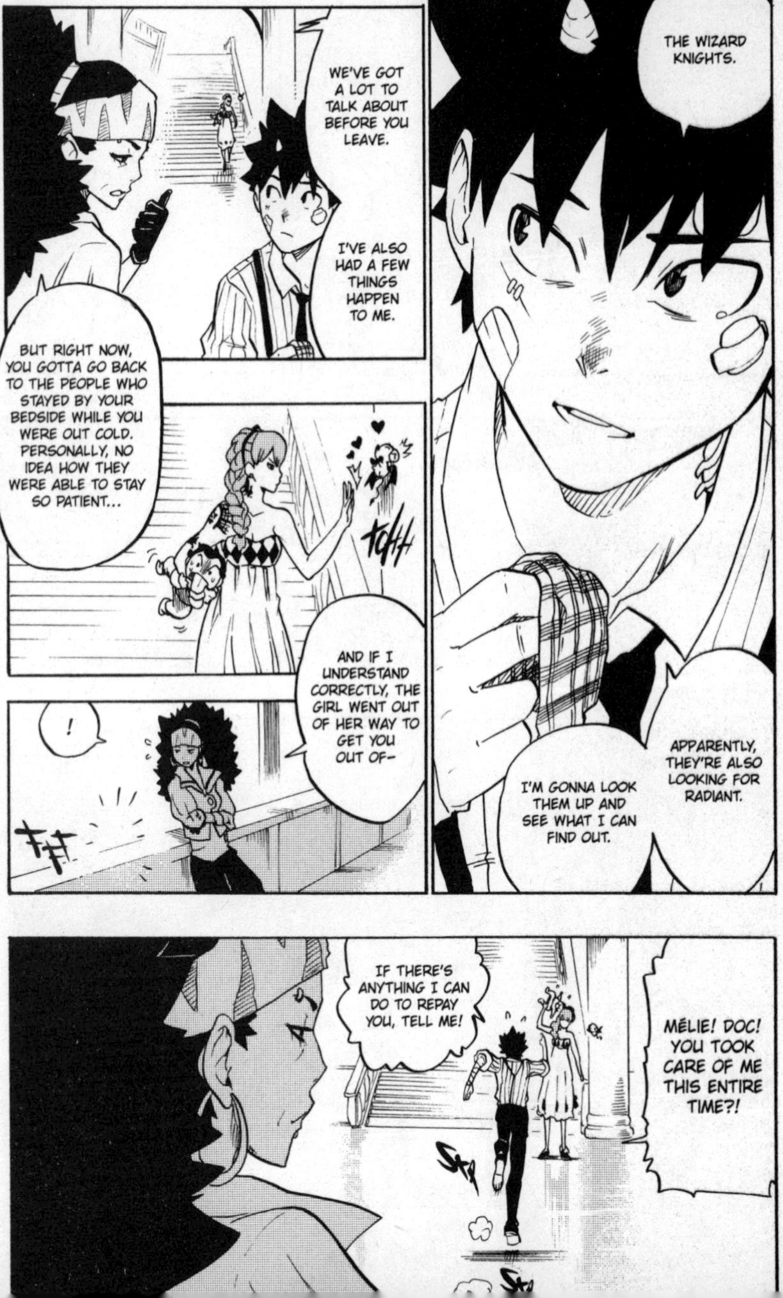
THE WIZARD KNIGHTS.
APPARENTLY, THEY'RE ALSO LOOKING FOR RADIANT.
I'M GONNA LOOK THEM UP AND SEE WHAT I CAN FIND OUT.
WE'VE GOT A LOT TO TALK ABOUT BEFORE YOU LEAVE.
I'VE ALSO HAD A FEW THINGS HAPPEN TO ME.
BUT RIGHT NOW, YOU GOTTA GO BACK TO THE PEOPLE WHO STAYED BY YOUR BEDSIDE WHILE YOU WERE OUT COLD. PERSONALLY, NO IDEA HOW THEY WERE ABLE TO STAY SO PATIENT...
TCHH
AND IF I UNDERSTAND CORRECTLY, THE GIRL WENT OUT OF HER WAY TO GET YOU OUT OF–
!
MÉLIE! DOC! YOU TOOK CARE OF ME THIS ENTIRE TIME?!
IF THERE'S ANYTHING I CAN DO TO REPAY YOU, TELL ME!

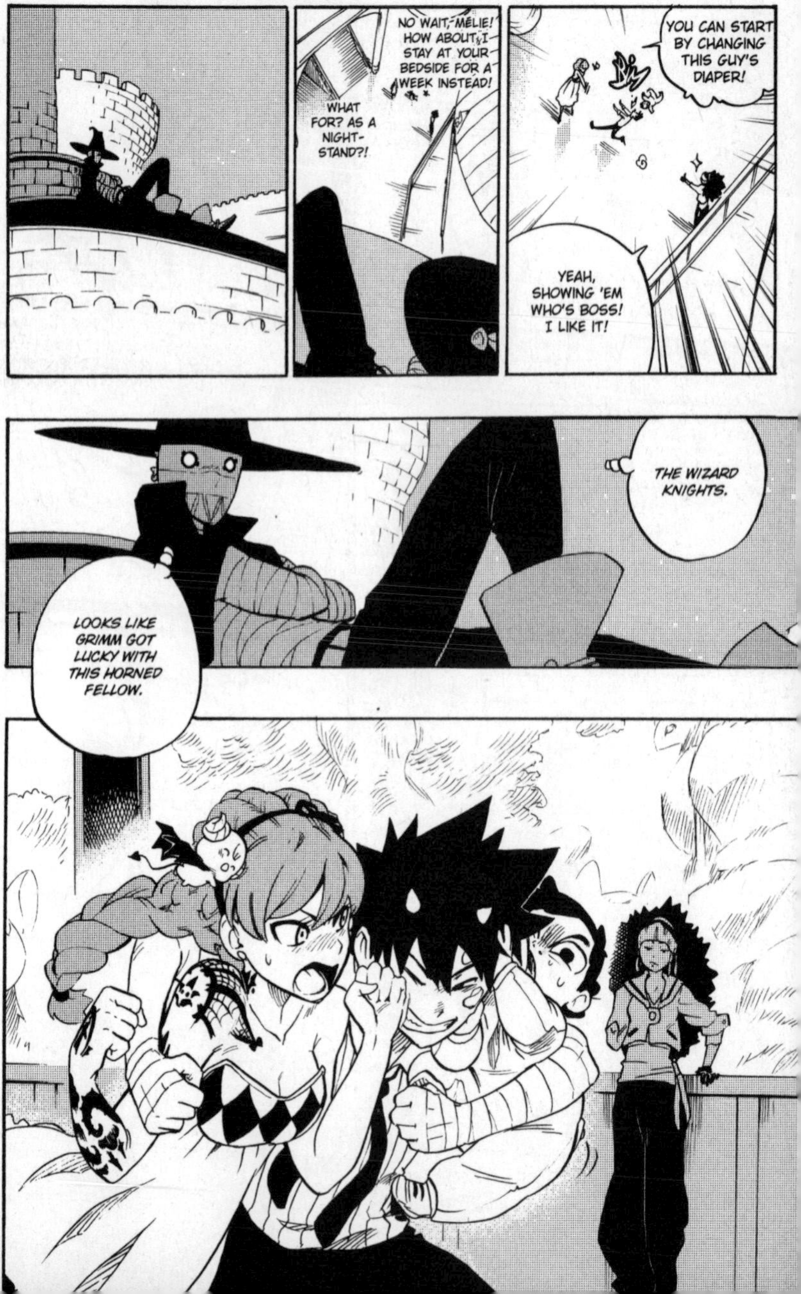
YOU CAN START BY CHANGING THIS GUY'S DIAPER!
YEAH, SHOWING 'EM WHO'S BOSS! I LIKE IT!
NO WAIT, MÉLIE! HOW ABOUT I STAY AT YOUR BEDSIDE FOR A WEEK INSTEAD!
WHAT FOR? AS A NIGHT-STAND?!
THE WIZARD KNIGHTS.
LOOKS LIKE GRIMM GOT LUCKY WITH THIS HORNED FELLOW.

**To be continued...**

# READERS' FAN ART

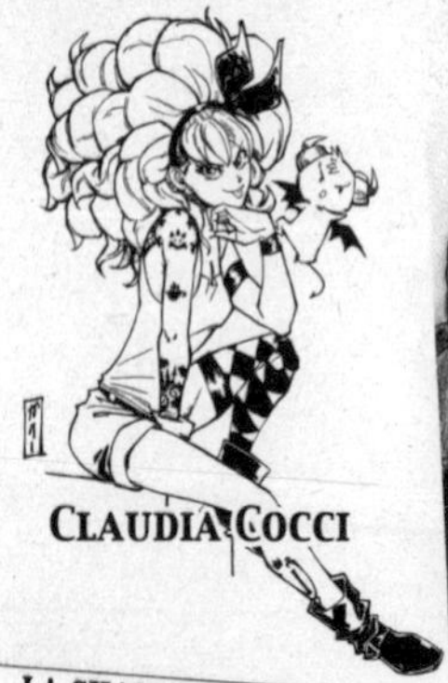
CLAUDIA COCCI

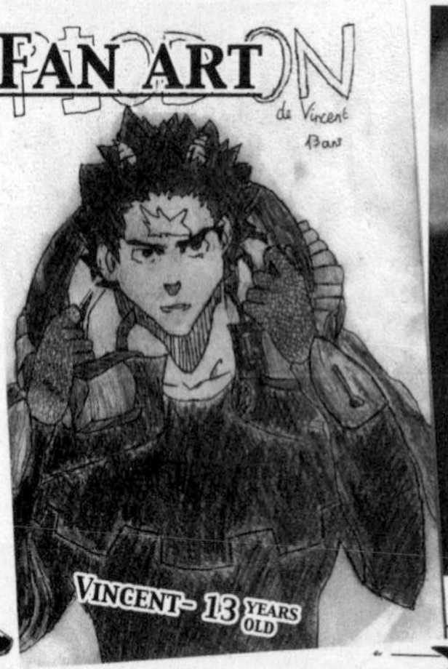
PHODON
de Vincent Bars
VINCENT- 13 YEARS OLD

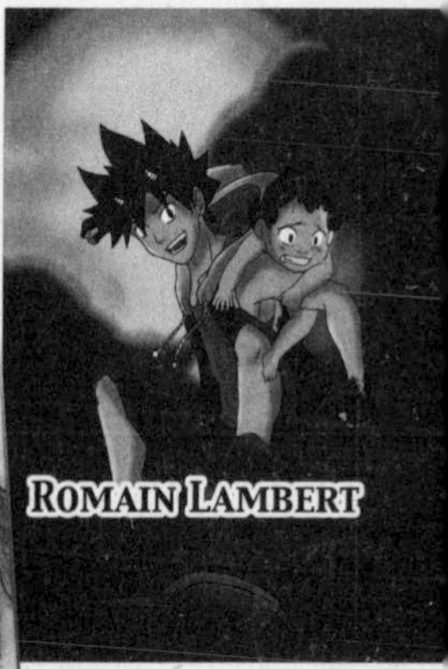
ROMAIN LAMBERT

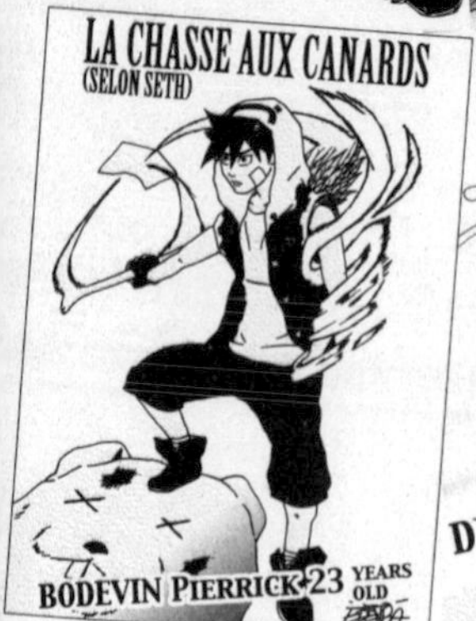
LA CHASSE AUX CANARDS
(SELON SETH)
BODEVIN PIERRICK 23 YEARS OLD

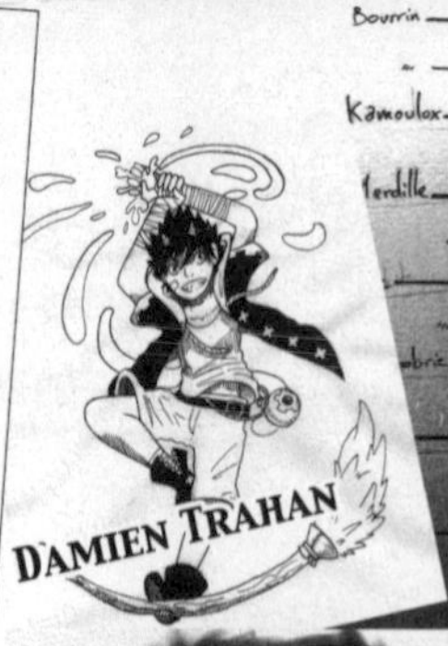
DAMIEN TRAHAN

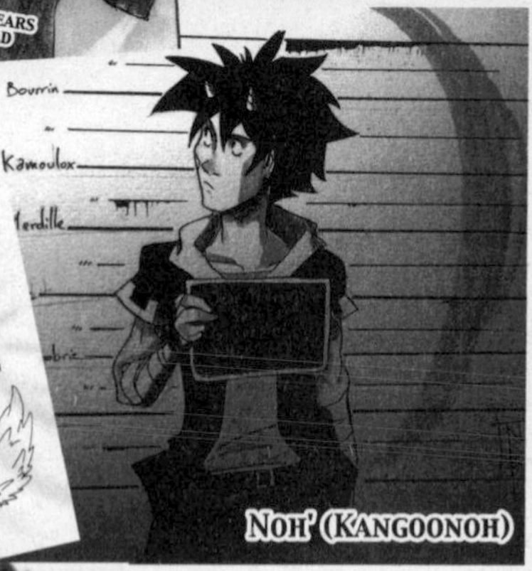
Bourrin
Kamoulox
Merdille
NOH' (KANGOONOH)

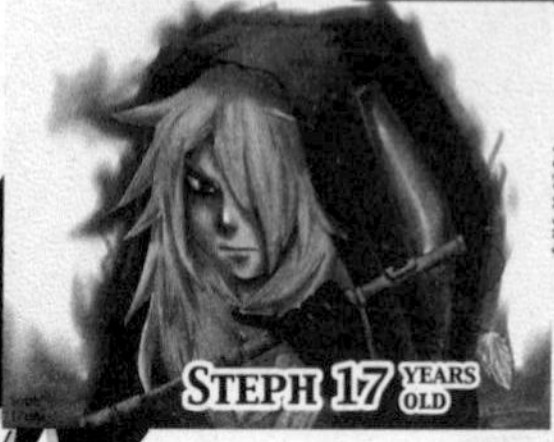
STEPH 17 YEARS OLD

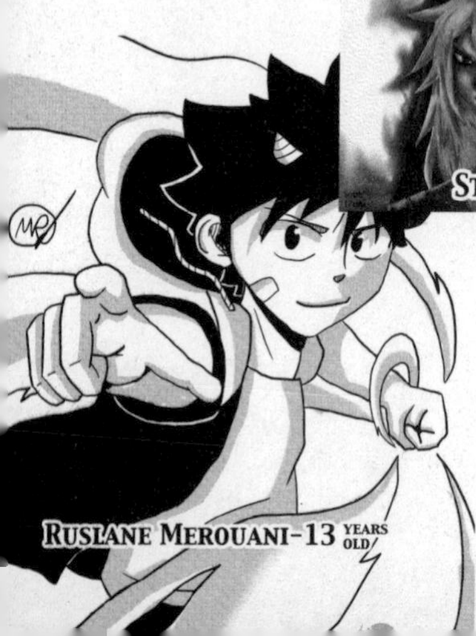
RUSLANE MEROUANI-13 YEARS OLD

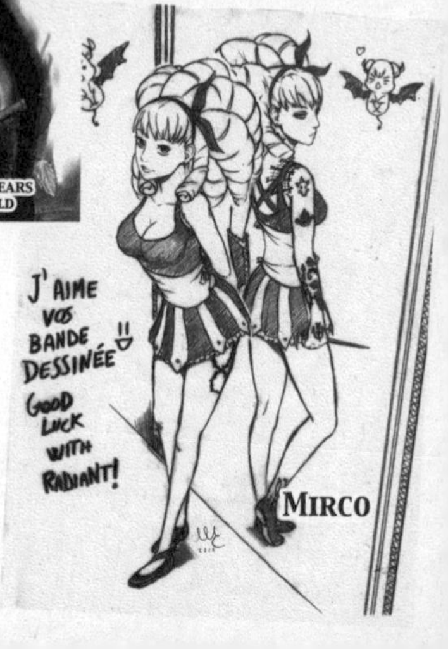
J'AIME VOS BANDE DESSINÉE !!
GOOD LUCK WITH RADIANT!
MIRCO

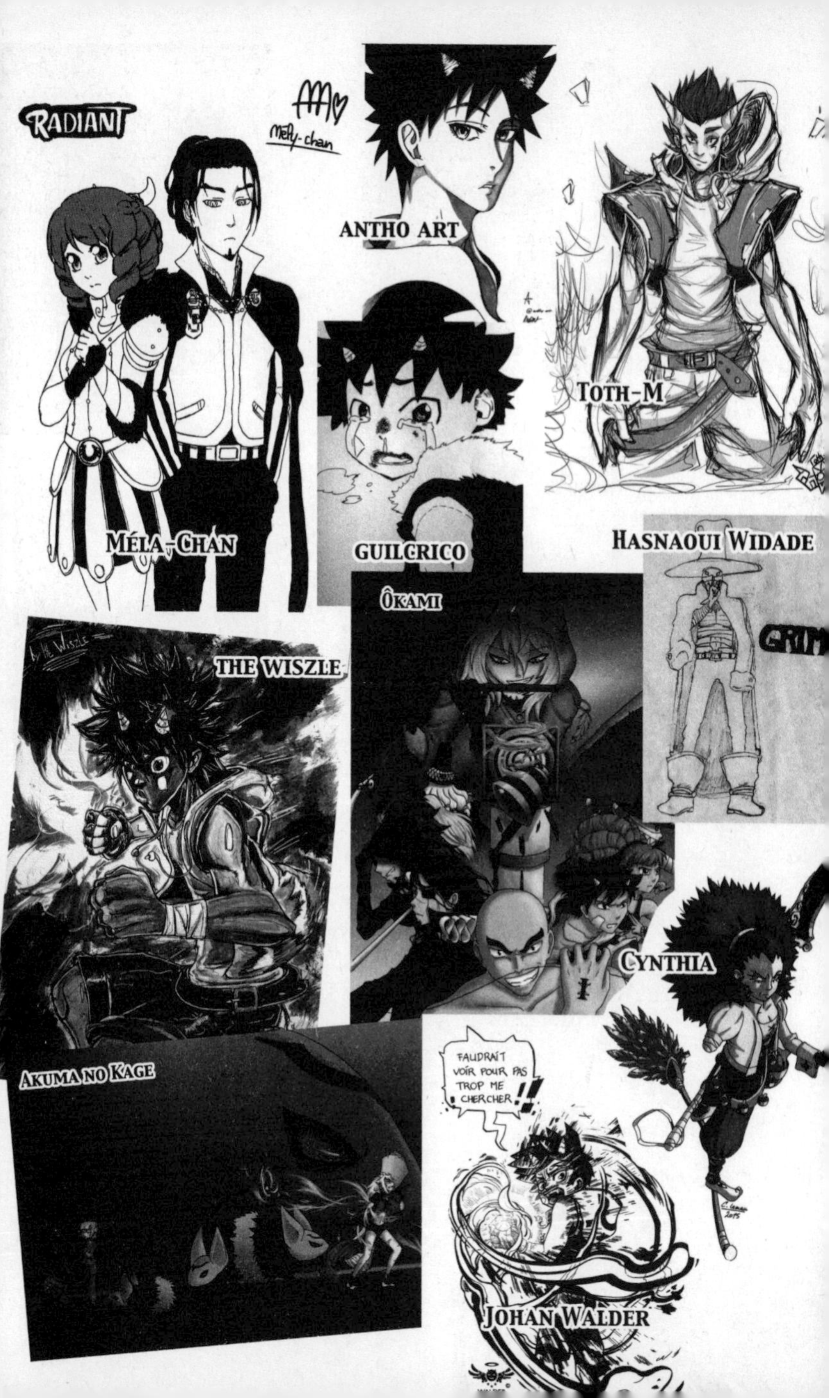
RADIANT
ANTHO ART
TOTH-M
MÉLA-CHAN
GUILCRICO
HASNAOUI WIDADE
ÔKAMI
THE WISZLE
CYNTHIA
AKUMA NO KAGE
FAUDRAIT VOIR POUR PAS TROP ME CHERCHER !!
JOHAN WALDER

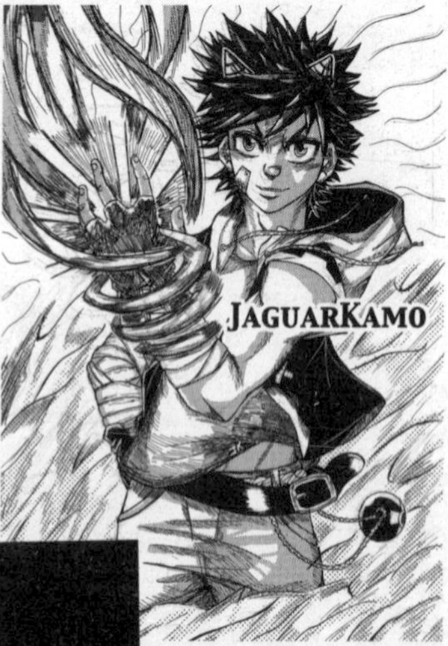
JaguarKamo
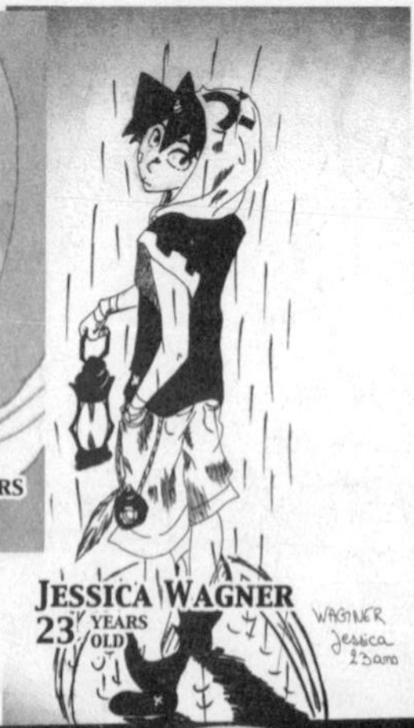
Jessica Wagner
23 years old
WAGNER
Jessica
23ans
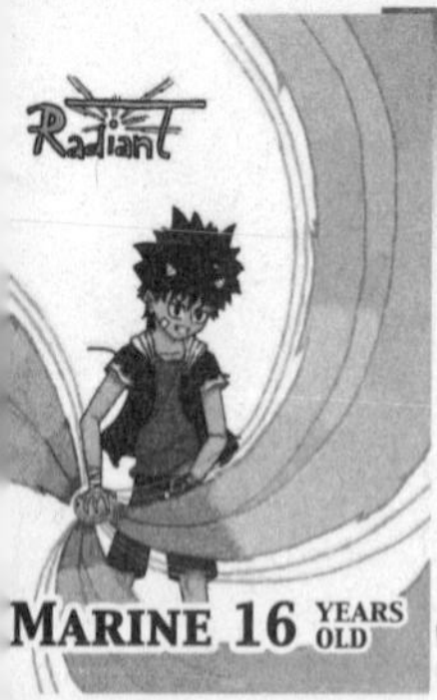
Radiant
Marine 16 years old
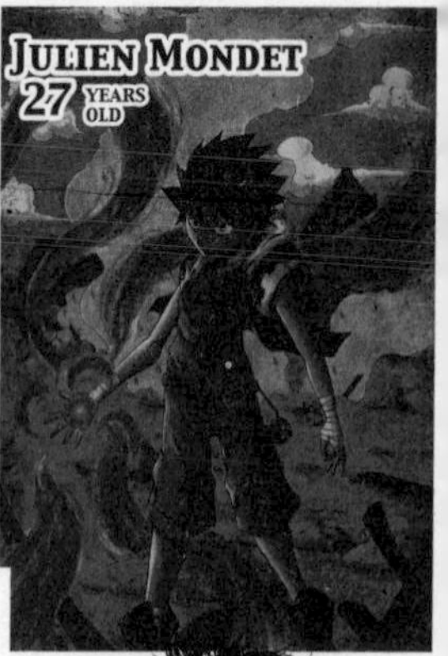
Julien Mondet
27 years old
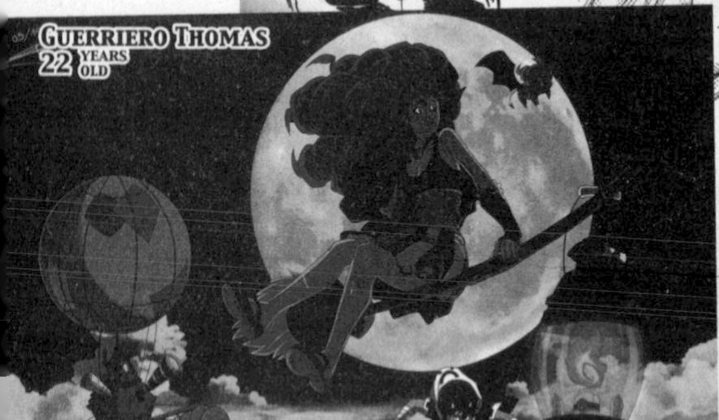
Guerriero Thomas
22 years old
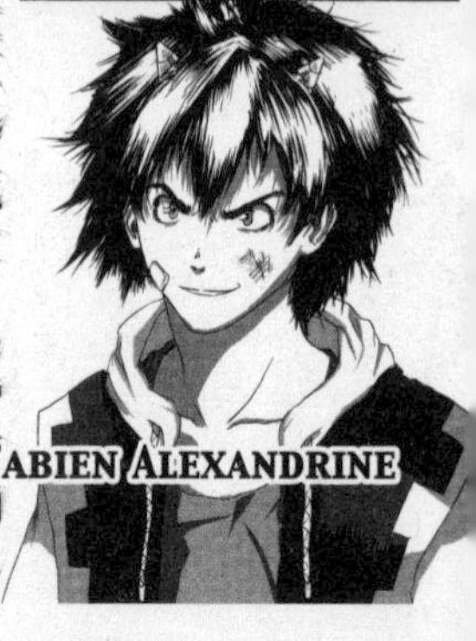
Fabien Alexandrine
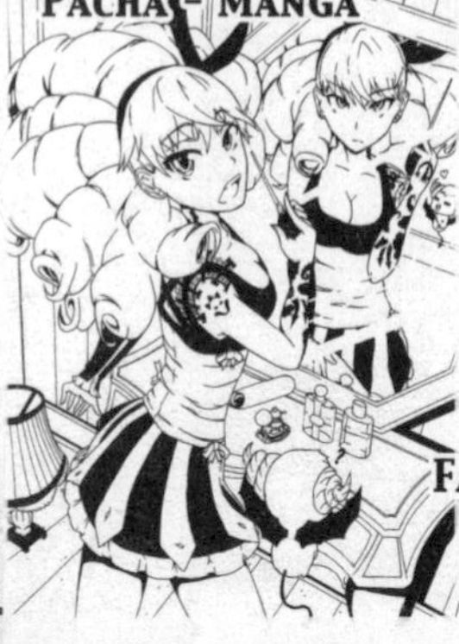
Pacha-manga
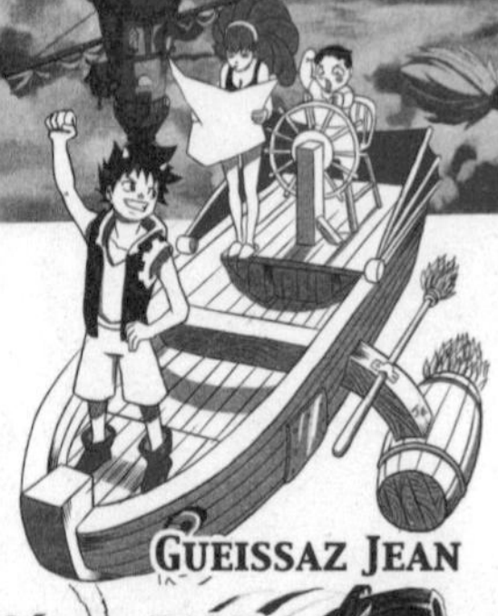
Gueissaz Jean
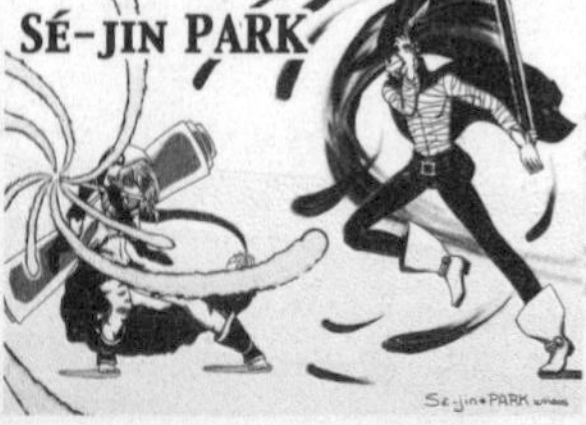
Sé-jin PARK

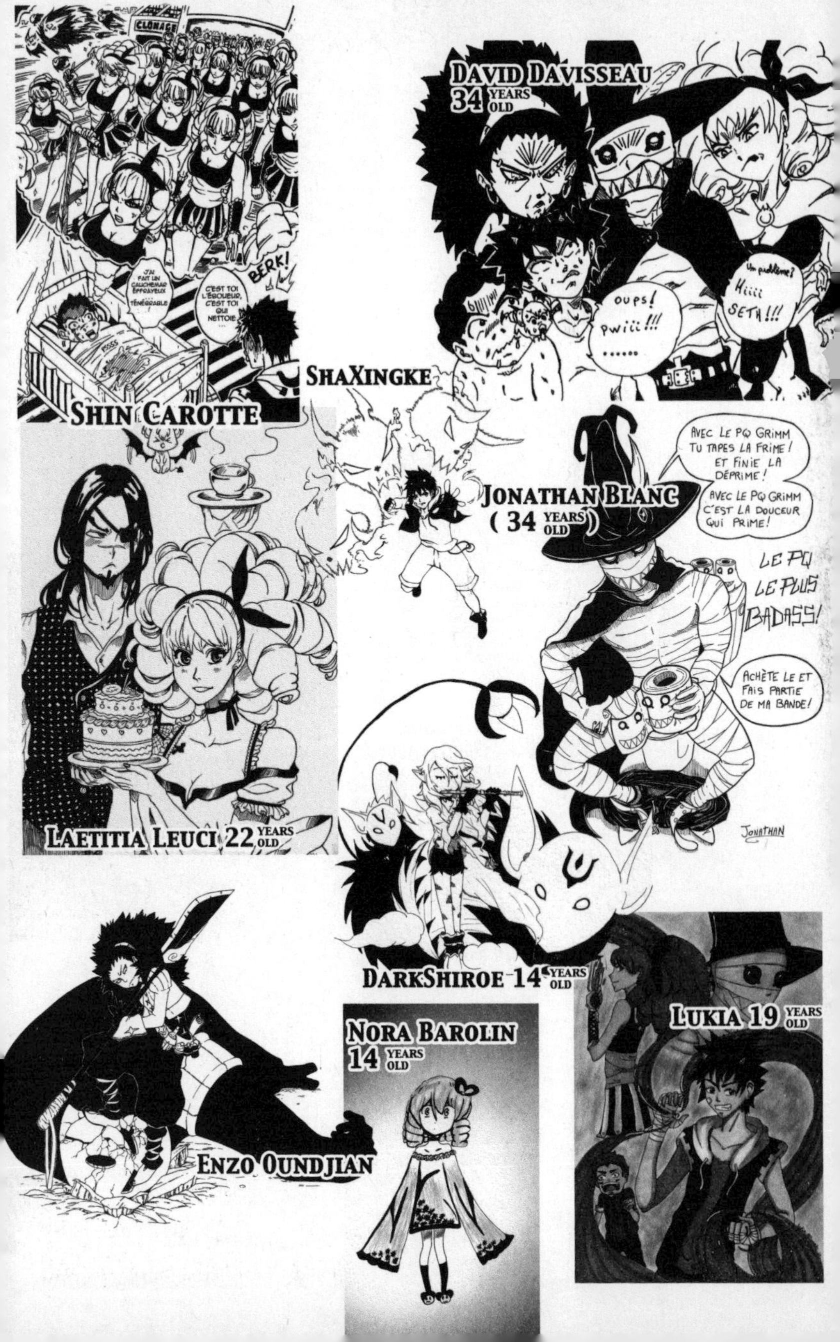
DAVID DAVISSEAU
34 YEARS OLD
Un problème? Hiiii SETH!!!
OUPS! PWIII!!! ......
CLONAGE
BERK!
C'EST TOI L'ÉBOUEUR, C'EST TOI QUI NETTOIE ...
J'AI FAIT UN CAUCHEMAR EFFRAYEUX ... TÉNÉBRABLE !
PSSSS
SHIN CAROTTE
SHAXINGKE
AVEC LE PQ GRIMM TU TAPES LA FRIME! ET FINIE LA DÉPRIME!
AVEC LE PQ GRIMM C'EST LA DOUCEUR QUI PRIME!
LE PQ LE PLUS BADASS!
ACHÈTE LE ET FAIS PARTIE DE MA BANDE!
JONATHAN BLANC
( 34 YEARS OLD )
JONATHAN
LAETITIA LEUCI 22 YEARS OLD
DARKSHIROE 14 YEARS OLD
LUKIA 19 YEARS OLD
NORA BAROLIN
14 YEARS OLD
ENZO OUNDJIAN

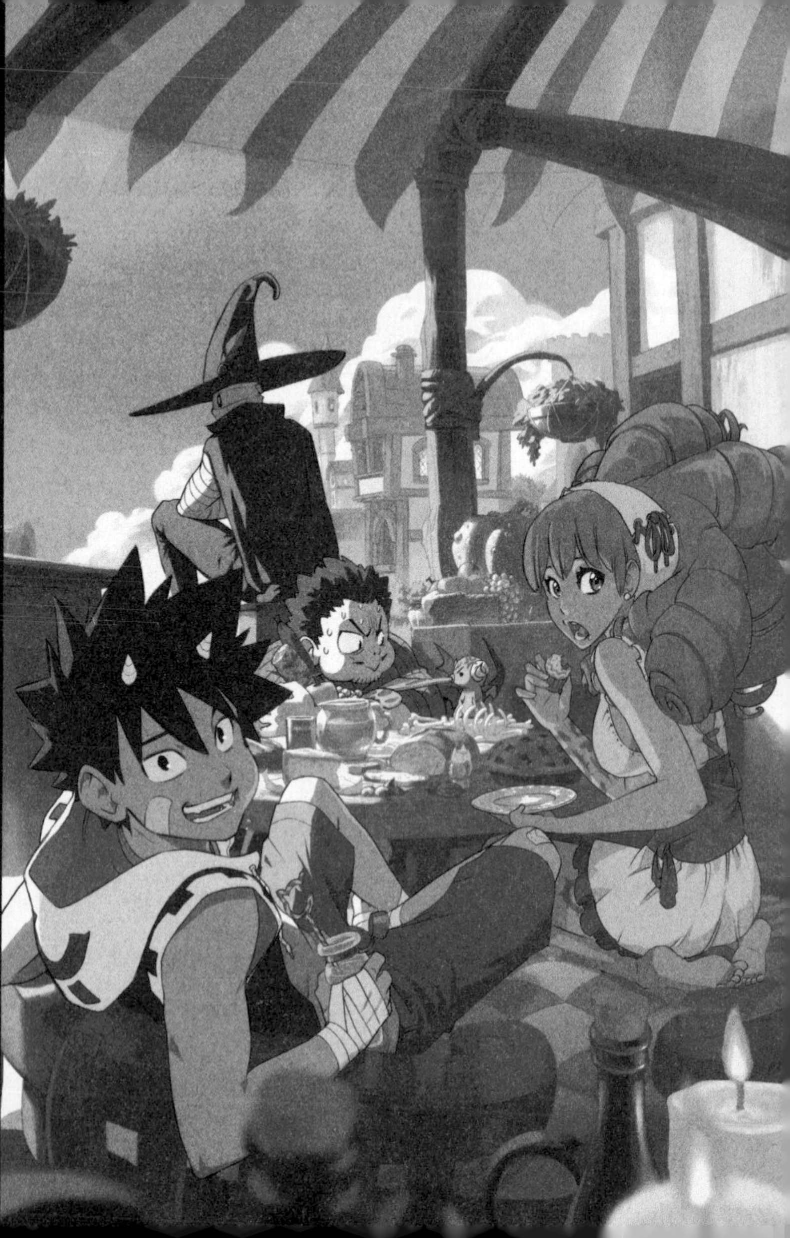

# RADIANT

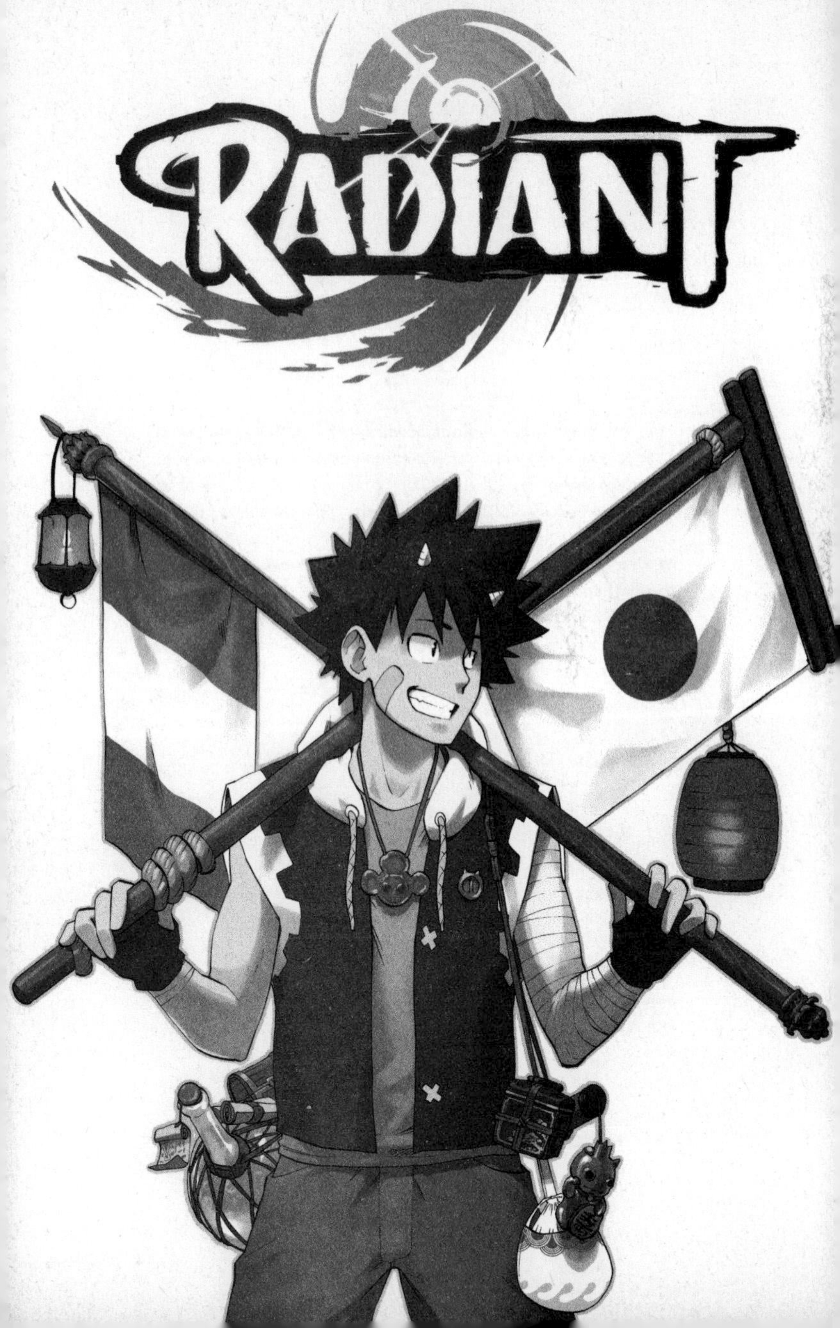

NOW YOU TOO
CAN TEXT
GRIMM TO YOUR
FRIENDS!!

```
      A
    / |
   | |
   (°ww°)
   __M M__
  /    V    !
```

"Oh, no. There's no way *Radiant* will ever be published in Japan!"
That's what I said when someone once asked me that question...
But bing! Bang! Boom! It actually came out in the Land of the
Rising Sun in August 2015! I'm so happy, I'm speechless *u*!!

Wait a second...did I just discover how to make wishes come
true?! Then let's do this, "Oh, no. There's no way someone will
make Seth and Mélie figurines! Oh, no. There's no way it will ever
be adapted into an anime and a video game! Oh, no. There's no
way I will ever sleep again..."

—Tony Valente

**Tony Valente** began working as a comic artist with the series *The Four
Princes of Ganahan*, written by Raphael Drommelschlager. He then launched
a new three-volume project, *Hana Attori*, after which he produced *S.P.E.E.D.
Angels*, a series written by Didier Tarquin and colored by Pop.

In preparation for *Radiant*, he relocated to Canada. Through confronting
caribou and grizzlies, he gained the wherewithal to train in obscure manga
techniques. Since then, his eating habits have changed, his lifestyle became
completely different and even his singing voice has changed a bit!

# RADIANT

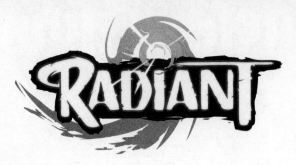

**RADIANT VOL. 4**
**VIZ MEDIA Manga Edition**

STORY AND ART BY **TONY VALENTE**

Translation/**(´･∀･`)ｻｧ?**
Touch-Up Art & Lettering/**Erika Terriquez**
Design/**Julian [JR] Robinson**
Editor/**Marlene First**

Published by arrangement with MEDIATOON LICENSING/Ankama.
RADIANT T04


Printed in the U.S.A.

Published by VIZ Media, LLC
P.O. Box 77010
San Francisco, CA 94107

10 9 8 7 6 5 4 3 2 1
First printing, March 2019

VIZ MEDIA
viz.com

ratings.viz.com
RATED T TEEN

**PARENTAL ADVISORY**
RADIANT is rated T for Teen and is recommended for ages 13 and up. This volume contains fantasy violence.

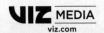

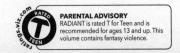

# Black ✦ Clover

## STORY & ART BY YUKI TABATA

Asta is a young boy who dreams of becoming the greatest mage in the kingdom. Only one problem—he can't use any magic! Luckily for Asta, he receives the incredibly rare five-leaf clover grimoire that gives him the power of anti-magic. Can someone who can't use magic really become the Wizard King? One thing's for sure—Asta will never give up!

SHONEN JUMP

VIZ media

www.viz.com

# DEMON SLAYER
## KIMETSU NO YAIBA

*Story and Art by*
**KOYOHARU GOTOUGE**

In Taisho-era Japan, kindhearted Tanjiro Kamado makes a living selling charcoal. But his peaceful life is shattered when a demon slaughters his entire family. His little sister Nezuko is the only survivor, but she has been transformed into a demon herself! Tanjiro sets out on a dangerous journey to find a way to return his sister to normal and destroy the demon who ruined his life.

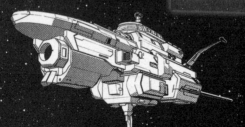

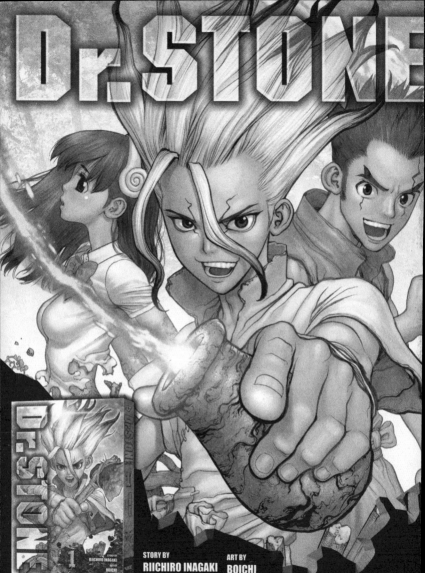

# Dr. STONE

STORY BY
**RIICHIRO INAGAKI**

ART BY
**BOICHI**

One fateful day, all of humanity turned to stone. Many millenni
later, Taiju frees himself from petrification and finds himse
surrounded by statues. The situation looks grim—until he rur
into his science-loving friend Senku! Together they plan to resta
civilization with the power of science!

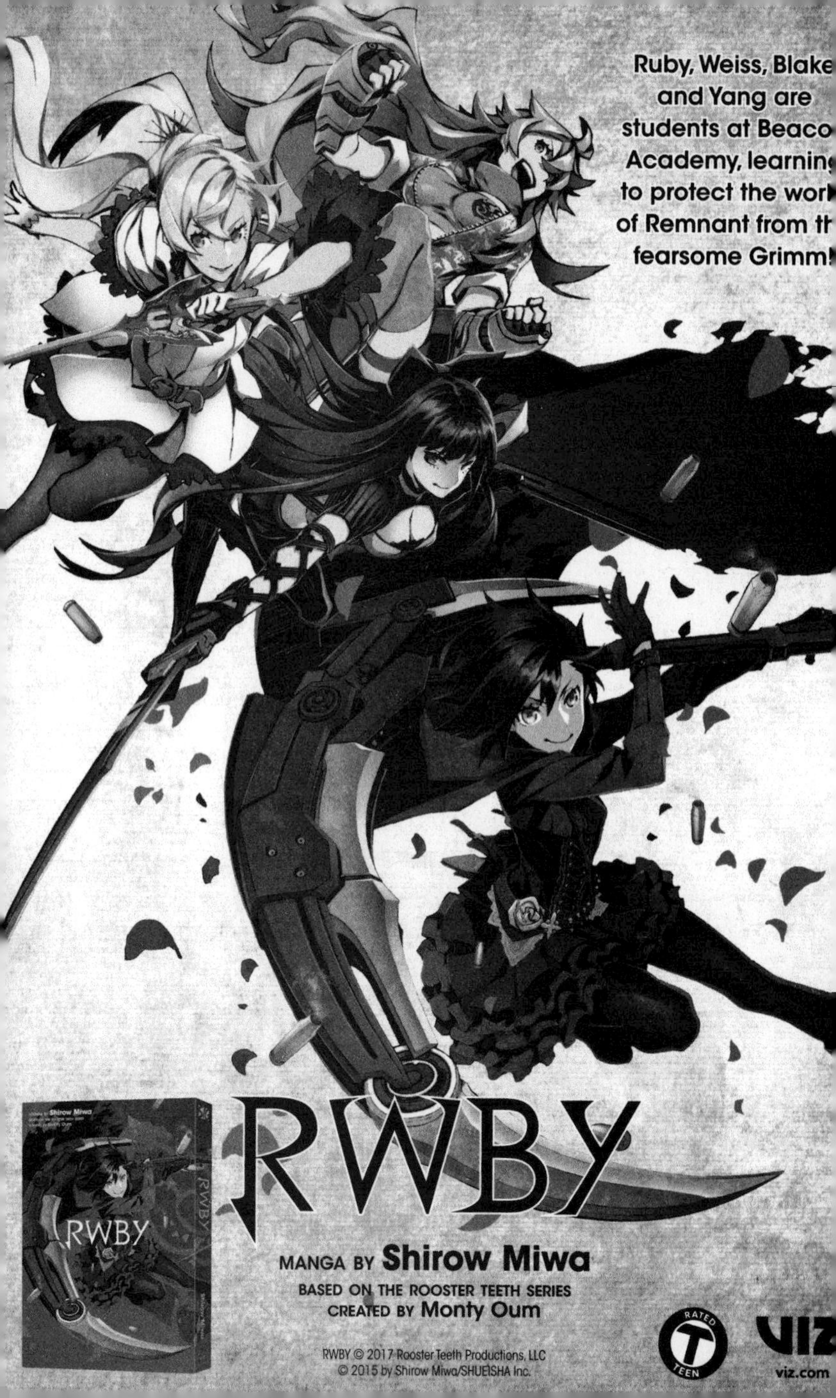
Ruby, Weiss, Blake
and Yang are
students at Beaco
Academy, learnin
to protect the wor
of Remnant from th
fearsome Grimm
RWBY
MANGA BY Shirow Miwa
BASED ON THE ROOSTER TEETH SERIES
CREATED BY Monty Oum
RWBY © 2017 Rooster Teeth Productions, LLC
© 2015 by Shirow Miwa/SHUEISHA Inc.
RATED T TEEN
VIZ
viz.com

# YOU'RE READIN
# THE WRONG W



RADIANT reads from right to left, starting in the upper-right corner, meaning that action, sound effects, and word-balloon order are completely reversed from English order.

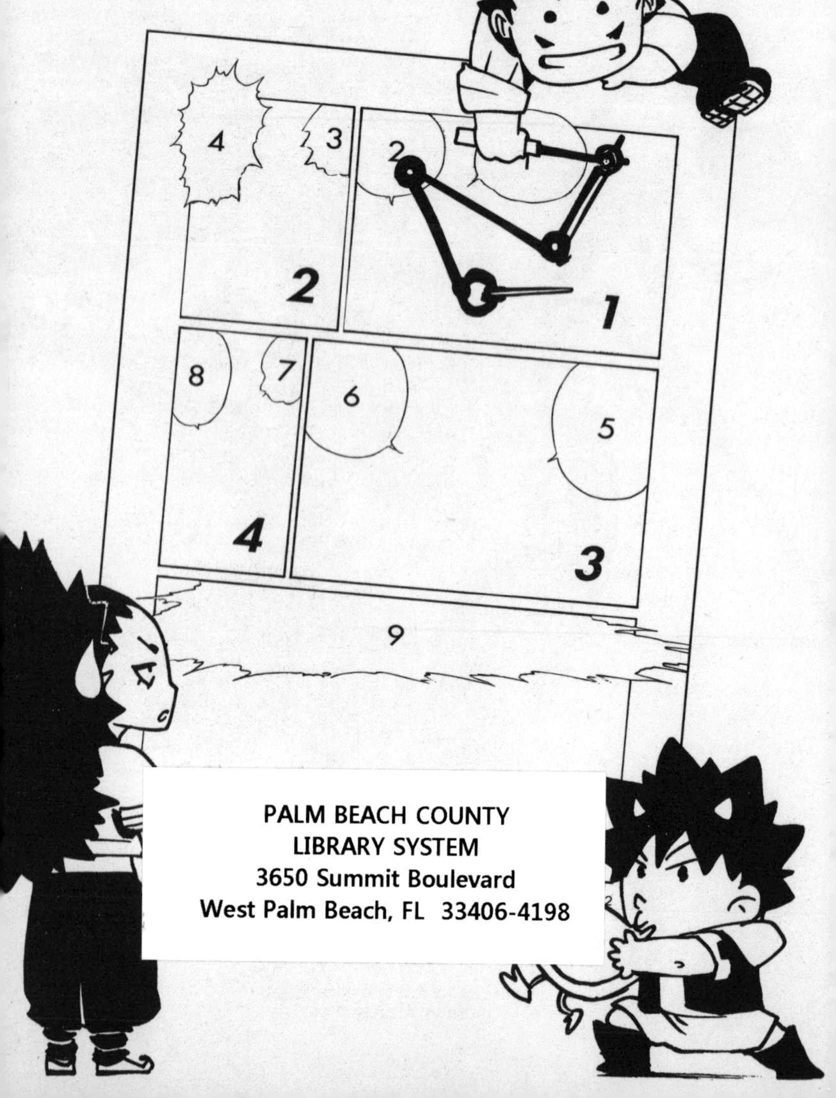
1
2
3
4
2
5
6
7
8
3
4
9